Commercial Culture

Commercial Culture

The Media System and the Public Interest

LEO BOGART

New York   Oxford
OXFORD UNIVERSITY PRESS
1995

Oxford University Press

Oxford   New York   Toronto
Delhi   Bombay   Calcutta   Madras   Karachi
Kuala Lumpur   Singapore   Hong Kong   Tokyo
Nairobi   Dar es Salaam   Cape Town
Melbourne   Auckland   Madrid

and associated companies in
Berlin   Ibadan

Copyright © 1995 by Oxford University Press, Inc.

Published by Oxford University Press, Inc.
200 Madison Avenue, New York, New York 10016

Oxford is a registered trademark of Oxford University Press

Library of Congress Cataloging-in-Publication Data
Bogart, Leo.
Commercial culture :
the media system and the public interest /
Leo Bogart.
p.   cm.
Includes bibliographical references and index.
ISBN 0-19-509098-5
1. Mass media – Economic aspects – United States.
2. Mass media policy – United States.
I. Title.
P96.E252U627   1995   338.4′730223 – dc20   94-6149

2 4 6 8 9 7 5 3 1
Printed in the United States of America
on acid-free paper

For Agnes

Acknowledgments

This book has been gestating for many years, but I first had the opportunity to organize its contents while I was a Senior Fellow at the Gannett Center for Media Studies (now the Freedom Forum Media Studies Center) at Columbia University. I owe a great deal to the Center's remarkable director, Everette E. Dennis, who has continued to provide invaluable help and counsel. Naomi Diamant, a scholar of distinction, was my conscientious and efficient research assistant. Among the Center's dedicated staff, Lisa De Lisle, Paul Eisenberg, Deborah Rogers and Mark Thalhimer were most helpful. Useful comments on the manuscript, or on sections of it, have been offered by Agnes Bogart, Joseph Spigelman, Melvin A. Goldberg, Eli Noam and Sidney W. Dean, Jr. Ann Brady provided documentation. Marie Thornton helped as I was getting started. I am very grateful to them and to all the others from whom I have learned along the way.

Contents

IV. Dynamics of Commercial Culture

V. Is There a Better Way?

Commercial Culture

Introduction

American mass media are the world's most diverse, rich and free. But their dazzling resources, variety, and influence cannot be rated by the envy they arouse in other countries. They must be judged by how they live up to their potential. This book focusses not on the glories of media—vividly displayed to us everywhere, all the time—but on what is wrong with them and why, and on how they may be made better.

New books on the media appear almost every day. There are already tens of thousands, ranging from popular biographies of long-dead film stars to scholarly research on the economics of teletext. What seems like a fresh insight to an unwary novice may strike the specialist as an empty cliché, evidence that everything that can be said on the subject has already been written. Not so. The media scene keeps changing; its vast scope and complexity make it hard to grasp as a whole—which is my effort in this book.

Media are a compelling presence in our lives and a powerful force that shapes our future. I shall look at how they relate to each other and argue that we cannot afford to take them exactly as they are. In taking this perspective, I shall try to combine what I have learned as a student of media and as a practitioner in the field. This experience makes me keenly conscious of the media's failings but affectionate toward the talented people who bring about their triumphs.

Whatever is wrong with the media is commonly excused on the grounds that they are creatures of the market, that they give people what they want. This book takes issue with that premise. My basic thesis is that the future direction of the media should not be left to market forces alone. A world of new communications technology requires a coherent national policy, respectful of the American tradition of free expression and subject to constant public scrutiny and debate.

American media and the commercial culture they carry are undergoing a critical transformation, which has several aspects: The individual means of mass communication—from the book to the compact disk—have been submerged into an interlocked system dominated by a disturbingly small number of powerful organizations. The traditional distinction between individual and mass communication is disappearing. Economic support for the entertainment media is shifting from advertisers directly to consumers, without any corresponding change in the philosophy underlying media content. Entertainment increasingly overshadows information, blurring the difference between what is real and what is not, and thus weakening the public's will and capacity to confront the world and its problems.

This profound and rapid change is commonly masked as a series of unrelated and concurrent events and circumstances. Consider the following items, which were topical as I was writing. They will quickly be forgotten, but they reflect trends of long-lasting consequence:

• The Clinton administration announced plans to create a "national information infrastructure," offering "universal service" and "open access." Vice President Al Gore called for a "public right of way" on the "information superhighway." A federal court decision gave the regional Bell operating telephone companies the right to carry video entertainment over their lines. Anticipating the breakdown of past restrictions on their activities, the companies moved into the cable television business. They were spurred by technological developments that speeded and amplified electronic communications.[1]

• The Federal Communications Commission placed new limits on cable subscription rates. As a result, a huge telephone company, Bell Atlantic, and Tele-Communications, Inc. (TCI), the nation's top cable television firm, broke off their planned $33 million corporate merger, which would have been the largest in history.[2] The FCC ruling was also blamed for the collapse of another proposed $4.9 billion joint venture of Southwestern Bell and Cox Enterprises, a multimedia conglomerate.[3]

• Two other telephone companies were major players in an intense bidding war over Paramount Communications, itself a creature of a series of corporate mergers and acquisitions. Nynex put $1.2 billion behind the winning bid by Viacom, a large media conglomerate; BellSouth had $1.5 billion behind a rival hostile offer by QVC (a cable television direct sales operation), and proposed to take over its 22% share of TCI's clone, Liberty Media.[4] The price of Paramount stock was driven up to over 40 times earnings, reducing the share value of the two bidding corporations. Viacom's major stockholder, Sumner Redstone, (who had $348 million to gain under a prior agreement if Paramount took QVC's offer) said, "If I were offered $1 billion, I would not walk away from the dream. This is not about money. It is about what we can do by bringing the two companies together."[5]

• In the midst of this mad scramble, all the participants were engaged in side deals of their own. Viacom sought to merge with one of its backers, Blockbuster Entertainment (an empire that began with a single garbage truck). Paramount added Macmillan to its Simon and Schuster, Prentice-Hall, and Pocket Books imprints in the world's biggest book publishing enterprise.[6] QVC made a failed bid for its competitor, the Home Shopping Network, which was controlled by Liberty Media. John Malone, the principal owner of Liberty and TCI—while his deal with Bell

Atlantic was gestating – was reportedly negotiating with the Japanese electronic giant, Matsushita, for purchase of a 50% interest in its American film and publishing subsidiary, MCA. QVC's Barry Diller, who earlier had built the Fox TV network, tried unsuccessfully to merge QVC with CBS.

• Congress prepared to authorize the first auction sale of a part of the energy frequency spectrum. Although this was to be limited to personal communications services using advanced technology, it was the first time that communications franchises ("licenses to coin money") had not simply been given away.

• Congress passed a Cable Television Consumer Protection and Competition Act that altered the balance of power between cable system operators and the television networks, and the Supreme Court was set to rule on its constitutionality. The key issue to be decided was whether the First Amendment protected cable, like newspapers, from any controls over content, or whether it had only the more limited protection accorded to on-air broadcasters.

• The District of Columbia Court of Appeals temporarily stopped the FCC from enforcing rules restricting indecency in public access cable programming, thus highlighting the fact that different rules over content applied on cable and on the air.

• Billionaire businessman H. Ross Perot became a wild card in the game of national politics, having first announced his 1992 presidential candidacy on a television talk show. Spending nearly $60 million of his own money, he bought half-hour stretches of network time to talk about himself, was treated as a full contender in televised debates with the two major party candidates, won 19% of the popular vote and continued to be an unpredictable political force long after the election. During the campaign, the successful contender, Bill Clinton, donned dark glasses to play the saxophone and romp with country music performers on television entertainment shows. (He avoided the tough Sunday interview programs, according to one of his campaign advisors, because "that's not where the people we wanted to reach were."[7]) After he won, his inaugural committee covered its $28 million costs by selling exclusive television rights to the celebrations.

• Televangelist Pat Robertson was a prominent speaker at the 1992 Republican National convention. Soon afterwards, his entertainment company, owners of the highly profitable cable Family Channel, paid $68.5 million for the British parent company of MTM Productions, a leading supplier of mainstream U.S. television programming.

• Echoing his infamous predecessor, Spiro T. Agnew, Vice President Dan Quayle (himself an heir to a newspaper publishing fortune) launched an attack on something he called "the cultural elite," and blamed it for the breakdown of the traditional nuclear family. To illustrate his charge of a conspiracy to legitimize illegitimacy, he cited the imaginary divorced heroine of a popular prime-time television soap opera, "Murphy Brown," who had had a child by her former husband. The show's producers flailed back in an episode that showed the heroine watching film clips of Quayle's address and then delivering her own impassioned rebuttal. To make peace, Quayle sent a stuffed toy elephant to the "baby," further compounding the blur between the fantasy of the show and the reality of the election campaign. President George Bush joined Quayle in charging the media with a "liberal" bias. A survey showed that 89% of the public could correctly identify "Murphy Brown," while only 19% could place former Defense

Secretary Casper Weinberger, who had just been indicted in connection with the illegal exchange of Middle Eastern hostages for arms to Iran.

• Los Angeles erupted in riots that were televised live, with ample reminders, to would-be looters, that the police had largely withdrawn from the scene. Subsequently, the talk-show host Phil Donahue flew two gang leaders, Bone of the Athens Park Bloods and L'il Monster of the Eight-Tray Gangster Crips, to New York for guest appearances.

• There was a run on music stores after Warner Brothers Records (a division of the huge media conglomerate Time Warner), under great pressure from police groups and their supporters, stopped distribution of an album by the Rap performer Ice-T. It included a song called "Cop Killer," with the refrain, "Die, pig, die!" Time Warner's Atlantic Group distributed rapper Akinyele's recording, "Vagina Diner," advertised with a cartoon that showed an unclad woman served on a spoon dripping liquid. Warner Books published a photo album imaginatively titled, "Sex," featuring the entertainer Madonna. It was accompanied in the same heavy plastic wrapping by an audio recording. Gerald Levin, president of Time Warner, appeared at the book party wearing a black leather jacket emblazoned with the portrait of another company property, Bugs Bunny.

• *Better Homes & Gardens* offered advertisers a "Green Thumbs Database" that would provide "tip sheet" components bound selectively into the magazine to reach only specific kinds of readers, with narrowly defined characteristics and interests.

• The *Pittsburgh Press* ceased publication after a bitter strike, though Pittsburgh was one of those cities in which, under the Newspaper Preservation Act of 1970, antitrust rules had been set aside to permit failing dailies to survive by joining in cooperative publishing arrangements. Within a year, from Anchorage to San Antonio, eight large cities lost their surviving second newspapers, leaving three-fifths of the American population with no more than a single local monopoly daily to report the news.

• Xerox announced the development of a flat television display panel no thicker than a pad of paper. Like similar Japanese products using liquid crystal technology, the device, accommodating both pictures and text, could be the key to developing a constantly updated paperless newspaper customized to the interests of the individual reader. (The Knight-Ridder newspaper chain already had a program under way to develop this device; its *San Jose Mercury News* offered an electronic news service accessible on a home computer).

• Saatchi and Saatchi, one of the handful of giant holding companies that handle the lion's share of the world's product advertising, formed a third international network of its own advertising agencies; this move made it easier to acquire and manage the accounts of client companies in direct competition with each other.

• The Federal Communications Commission announced a fifteen-year plan to phase in high definition television. All 150 million existing receivers in the country would be usable but obsolete; new ones would have an interactive capacity, making them instruments of personal as well as mass communication.

• The FCC, with backing from the courts, set aside the Financial Interest and Syndication Rule, which had restricted the television networks' ownership and sale of rerun rights to more than three weekly hours of their prime time shows. As a result of the rule, Hollywood's big studios had taken over the production of 70% of network programming.[8] In 1995, the networks would be free to acquire a financial interest in programs produced outside, to compete in the $5 billion worldwide market for programming, and eventually to merge with studios. This made network ownership more attractive; it prompted Paramount and Chris-Craft to announce plans for a fifth network, and Time Warner and the Tribune Company for a sixth (WB).[9]

The Administration, the courts, and the Congress were all embroiled in the battles over who should own and control the public's main source of entertainment. As these items make clear, the state of the mass media urgently requires reassessment. A number of themes that echo repeatedly throughout this book deserve to be underlined at the outset.

Technological progress has bound the individual mass media together into an interpenetrating system. Print and broadcasting have long been regarded as channels through which people tap into widely shared forms of information and amusement, while the mail and telephone are instruments used for exchanging messages one on one. That distinction no longer holds in the era of computers, videotex, facsimile transmissions, ink-jet printing and multimedia CD-ROM discs. On that most personal instrument, the telephone, prerecorded messages confront batteries of answering machines; 800 and 900 numbers, advertised in broadcast and print, interact with programs and periodicals. Is direct mail a mass medium, when recipients get individualized mailings that address them by name? How should we classify videotex, through which subscribers can select information from large databases? Individually addressable forms of communication cannot really be classed as mass media, even though they may replace or cut into mass media functions. ("Customized" publications that substitute, eliminate, or add modular elements of content do not belong under the heading of individual communication, because their components are created for more than one recipient at a time.)

As we phase into new forms of communication, the old precepts and rules no longer apply. A new structure will arise not as the result of consumer decisions in the marketplace, but as the outcome of political struggles already being waged, and for very high stakes. Communication in all its aspects—mass and private—was a $400 billion industry in 1994.

Just as a clean line can no longer be drawn between individual and mass communication, the distinction has blurred between advertising-supported and consumer-supported media. In 1992, $206 billion was spent on mass communications— those produced and distributed in identical form to people in different locations. Of this amount, $36 billion (or 25%) went to media like billboards and direct mail made up exclusively of advertising. (While these advertising-only media are an important part of the mass communications system and influence the others, they are discussed only incidentally in this book, which focusses on media that the public consumes directly and by choice.) $49 billion (24% of all spending on mass media) was spent on books, newsletters, films, videos and musical recordings that contained little or no advertising. The largest share, $120 billion (46%), was accounted for by media that include advertising along with other forms of content and that advertisers support either wholly or in part.

Media have the premier place in American leisure as they compete for both money and time with many alternative forms of recreation. Since the advent of television, people spend more time with the media than they do in family activity, at school, or in learning at work.

How do media manage to capture so much of the public's time, attention, and disposable income? They serve a variety of functions: to inform, to beguile, to amuse, to stimulate, to provide a bond to others, to distinguish ourselves from others, to recreate our own emotional experiences and those of others, to save time, to pass the time. The fascination that media hold for us is expressed in their own content by their preoccupation with themselves and with each other. Our interest in their personalities, politics and fortunes reflects an acknowledgment of the many hours that we spend with them, the influence they wield over our knowledge and imagination, and the power they exert over every aspect of our society and our values.

Sociability through conversation and play provides the original and fundamental means by which human beings everywhere spend time not devoted to the necessary tasks of living. Sociability allows them to recuperate from the stresses and energy drains those tasks impose. Media have steadily encroached upon the time once dedicated to direct personal contact.[2] The fantasies they bestir and the thoughts they set in motion often seem more vivid and meaningful than activities in which we actually take part. The media allow us to position ourselves in time and space in ways that our ancestors could not envision.

Channels of communication are important only because of what passes through them. Media touch us closely because they remain a relatively constant part of our life experience. Other institutions may have a more powerful impact, but not a more persistent and lasting one. Family affiliations and friendships change as an individual matures and ages. School occupies a limited span of years. Only a minority of the population are faithful churchgoers. In contrast, media are part of everyday life from early childhood until death, and thus establish a pervasive intimacy. Moreover, media have a universality that is absent from other institutions. They provide a common vocabulary of ideas and images that transcends barriers of social class and geography, eases casual contacts, and creates links among strangers. These common ideas and images, which make up the national culture we share, emanate largely from the media, which are run by the rules of the market that apply throughout our economy.

Does the market give the public what it wants and needs from the mass media? Wants and needs may be incompatible; the best ideas are not always the most successful. To a substantial degree, I shall contend in these pages, media tell us the wrong things. In the name of giving us what we want, they give us more and more of what we never needed in the first place. They have been run on the principle that filling the public's preferences always serves the public's interest, as it may with demand for shoes or cheese. But, as we enter the twenty-first century, this assumption does not hold up.

There is nothing reprehensible or ignoble in serving the market. The architect, the package designer, the engineer in a corporate laboratory, are all productively engaged in creating ideas for sale. The composer of radio advertising jingles also fulfills a socially useful function, by helping to promote the products that engineers and designers make. So does the composer of theme music for the soap opera that carries those commercials. But activities that are constructive when considered individually, case by case, may have an undesirable impact in the aggregate. This phenomenon is readily visible on the industrial scene, for instance, in the high social cost of cleaning up after individual companies that economize on waste management in the interest of business efficiency.

What the media say, how they present our world to us, is of a different order of importance than most other appetites the market is left to satisfy. Ideas and images are different from material possessions because they fill our minds and form our character. Media not only teach us about other people; they tell us who we are, shape our interests and tastes, and help us to create our selves.

Why is the market inadequate? All that we find stupid, sleazy or outrageous in mass media is there, after all, because there is a demand for it. The market encompasses the most bestial impulses of our nature as well as the most nearly divine. Suppose that much of the media products we collectively consume fail to meet their own producers' standards of honesty or excellence, that some is over the edge in exploiting violence, sadism, or prurience. These propositions can be bitterly argued, but if they are true (and I shall argue that they are), would they not merely reflect the inherent weaknesses of human character, the limitations of intelligence and curiosity, the irresistible need to conserve energy and to avoid effort?

It is true that media entrepreneurs—publishers and producers—flourish only when they serve the market, but they do not merely satisfy demand; they generate it. The messages that media feed the public are products of the institutions that transmit them. Those institutions are not immutable. They are wards—and, in some instances, creations—of the state and its laws. That means that they can be, must be, and actually are continually modified.

The media are not run through open-market choices by the public. To a large extent, the rules are politically determined. The wealth media generate gives rise to conflicts of interest that take the form of political battles. In turn, media, since the founding of the American Republic, have been an integral part of the national political process. Media make possible the free flow and clash of opinions essential to the functioning of democracy.

Why should we want the media to be different? They have been criticized since their beginnings, and for good reasons. This book explores four different aspects:

1. The media are saturated with excessive and obsessive commercialism.
2. The content and character of most media have been geared to serve advertisers' purposes rather than the public's. Consumers of communication judge it by its value and meaning; advertisers judge it by its efficiency in disseminating what they call "exposure opportunities." Unfortunately, advertisers are often misguided in their assumptions about the nature of communication. This means that their own purposes, as well as the public's, are served poorly.
3. The quest for audiences leads to the pursuit of sensation. The degrading effects of triviality, banality, and vulgarity are multiplied when more people are subjected to them for more hours.
4. Media sensationalism distorts our perceptions of the world by confusing illusion and reality; it deflects the public's attention from the problems that society must face.

To the degree that these shortcomings go uncorrected, the media system fails the society that pays its upkeep. To the four criticisms just mentioned, I must add a fundamental structural flaw:

Power over media and their content is concentrated in ever fewer hands, not necessarily ruled by wiser heads.

Culture itself is a form of power, and a source of power.[3] The ability to influence people's thoughts and emotions has attractions that far transcend money. For our remotest ancestors, art was a means of communing with the supernatural forces that determined human destiny. Rulers have always surrounded themselves with artists and have attained glory from their creations. In contemporary times, totalitarian societies have placed high priority on mobilizing the arts to support the system. In democracies, politicians cultivate the endorsements of rock stars and poets.

Some American media enterprises are great money-makers, but all of them also represent nonpecuniary powers—to motivate and change public opinion, to influence the course of history. With rare exceptions (public broadcasting, university presses, and a handful of subvened publications like *Harper's* magazine and *The Christian Science Monitor*), they are operated for profit rather than to advance public enlightenment, serve the political order or a religious cause, or glorify their owners. While noneconomic motives are always present in the operation of media, just as they are in other types of business enterprise, these can generally be tolerated only as long as they do not permanently interfere with the main objective—to maximize the return on the owner's investment. For this reason, an ancient and inevitable tension pervades the necessary partnership between creators and disseminators of ideas.

As power over media—like power in every other type of industry—is held by fewer people, it acquires politically dangerous possibilities. The organizations that manage the technological aspect of communications—like General Electric, Sony, Matsushita, and the regional telephone companies—have also increasingly claimed the right to provide its substance. The battle over this issue is waged on different fronts and by different armies. It is generally defined as a fight over money, when it is really about the control of ideas. The main weapon is the rhetoric of civil liberties.

Freedom of speech and freedom of choice surely protect offensive speech and foolish choice, and it is not easy to tell where protection of idiosyncratic expressions gives way to active encouragement and promotion of abhorrent conduct. Deviant opinions and tastes carry greater consequences when they are promoted for profit by giant multimedia conglomerates than when they are voiced as the honest expressions of eccentric minorities.

Do individual media choices serve the common benefit, as market doctrine would have it? Commercial culture devotes only a minor part of its content to the task of intellectual or spiritual enrichment. An inordinate share of its messages are dedicated to consumption rather than to productive endeavor. This emphasis acts as a great economic stimulus. However, since the whole weight of our communications system is placed on encouraging individual wants, the needs of society at large are neglected and undervalued.

Mass communication must be regarded as a public matter rather than as a private affair between two contracting parties. Media magnify our individual abilities to shun the consequences of what we do or what we supinely allow to be done around us.

If we can get away with it, we prefer not to pay for any of the costs of public goods directly, but we accept them if they are diffused, as a general burden.

Paying for what is ultimately in the common interest at the expense of one's immediate self-interest simply illustrates the more general human problem of how and when to defer gratification. We *do* attach value to expressions for which we individually do not want to pay. Whatever their view of specific controversial artists — and whether or not they have heard of them at all — Americans generally believe in the importance of the arts, including all those obscure arts to which they are personally unresponsive. A majority even believe that government should help support them.[4] Similarly, we believe in science and the pursuit of knowledge on all kinds of subjects in which we individually may not have the slightest interest. In short, it appears to be generally recognized that, in the realm of culture, the general good transcends the play of market forces. Yet except for a relatively minor expenditure on public broadcasting, this recognition is not reflected in the operation of the media system.

A great shift is now under way in the burden of economic support — from advertisers to consumers. New technology, most notably cable television and videorecording, has brought this about. The result is a continuing move from information to fictional entertainment. Hollywood dominates Americans' time far more than it ever did in its so-called Golden Age. Radio news survives only on relatively few stations. Local news shows — with their predictable chronicles of arson and assaults — account for the bulk of TV news-viewing, and network news ratings have dropped. The public at large once absorbed information inadvertently, serendipitously, by osmosis, through its almost universal reading of newspapers. Newspapers and news magazines continue to lose circulation and to intrude more fluff into their pages. The decline of daily newspaper competition has dramatically reduced the flow of detailed and complex information and the clash of considered opinion as an accepted part of everyone's daily routine.

Democracy depends on access to information, and a world of ever-growing complexity and specialization demands it in vastly increased quantities. However, new communications technology has done less to disseminate knowledge than to provide inexpensive, mindless diversion. The media are used less and less as a knowledge resource and progressively more as an anodyne that keep the public's mind off unpleasant facts. Commercial culture is increasingly irrelevant and evasive in relation to the urgent problems that confront society. It is deeply dedicated to an imaginary world crowded with formulaic thrills. It blurs the line between the real and the fictional, and thus weakens our grip on what is real.

We come to fiction as a pastime that diverts and relaxes us. But the symbolic content of fiction can only be useful if it is embedded in a context of fact. We must be able to differentiate the illusions it evokes from the reality of what occurs in specific places and times. This requires that information output be managed; it must be selected, packaged, measured, and labeled. As we move into the era of do-it-yourself media, the professional journalist has an added responsibility, but a diminished role. Thanks to mass media and to the Constitutional guarantee of press freedom, we know the world with an intimacy and depth unimaginable in past human history. Yet our knowledge remains incomplete, and our perceptions are often clouded.

Can media content be different and still remain acceptable? To answer no would deprive this book of its central point. Since tastes are formed, not predestined, and are to a very large extent the product of nurture, not nature, we should consider the possibility of inducing change—raising the level of mass communications content. The improvement need not wait upon a massive transformation of the whole society. It might be accomplished by modifying the media system.

The first part of this book describes the information and entertainment functions of media. It sets forth a central proposition: that the media must be regarded as a single interlocking system in which no element stands apart.

Part II discusses the dependence of the media system upon advertising, shows how advertising affects its substance and form, and points to some of the fallacies that underlie its preoccupation with audience size.

Part III reviews and appraises the discouraging consequences of this obsession, in its injection of banality and sensation into media content and its tendency to erode the distinction between the reality of journalism and the fictions of pastime entertainment.

Part IV discusses the ambivalence of media as outlets of creative expression and as phenomena of marketing entrepreneurship. It traces the transformation of media support from advertising to consumers and the growing preeminence of entertainment over information.

Part V considers the possibilities of change, strategies for inducing change, and the reasons for caution in attempting change in a system that, with all its faults, provides enormous pleasures and fosters political and personal freedom.

I

FUNDAMENTALS

1

What are "The Media?"

"Media." The very notion is of recent origin. The word now accurately describes a phenomenon rather than an abstract category covering a number of unrelated institutions. It combines dissimilar forms of communication under a common heading. How did the term creep into everyday language? What do media encompass, what do they do, what accounts for their hold over us? This chapter begins by considering the idea of the media and their roots in advertising and journalism. These are the principal points I shall make:

- Media are a reality, not just an abstraction.
- They deal both in information and entertainment, but often disguise information as entertainment.
- Media attract audiences because they fill time predictably; the character of those audiences is shaped by differences in the way people use time.
- As free time expands, so do audiences, changing the relationship between them and those who address them.
- Media facilitate the passage of time by organizing their output into standardized formats.

The Notion of "Media"

The term, "the media" is now applied collectively to the newsgathering organizations, but the media encompass all the other forms of mass communications apart from those that package the news—including entertainment television and magazines.

Books and periodicals, television, radio, film and recordings—lumping together all these diverse forms of communication as "the media" is a relatively recent practice. It appears, appropriately, to have originated with advertising. "It is hardly credible what wonderful advertising mediums children are," said an expert in Victorian England, ecstatic about the use of cheap labor to carry sandwich boards or hand out leaflets.[1]

The 1909 edition of Webster's *Dictionary* included among its definitions of the word "medium," "instrumentality, as in advertising medium." At about this time, the closely linked term "marketing" also came into use. In the context of the advertising business, media simply represented different methods by which advertisements could be delivered and products "marketed." Advertising agencies, beginning at the time of the first World War, set up media departments, to marshal facts and compare the channels — newspaper, magazine, billboard and car card space — through which their clients' messages could be disseminated. The Audit Bureau of Circulations was set up in 1915 to provide information that would facilitate the comparison and selection of publications.

The task of the agency's media specialists was to weigh alternative cost efficiencies, reader characteristics, and editorial environments, and to match them to the advertiser's objectives. Radio, and later television, complicated this task and encouraged specialization. But the use of the term "media" to describe all the forms of advertising caught on. People in every aspect of mass communication began to think of themselves as participants in "the media business."

Scholars of the subject, writing in arcane journals, began to refer to "media of mass communication." As a synonym for "means," their predecessors may have applied the term "medium" to the telegraph and telephone even before the invention of radio, but it was only in the radio era that distinctions began to be drawn between media of *mass* communication and those that connected individuals. Academic interest in mass media evolved in the years before World War II, largely as a byproduct of concern with propaganda and the Communist and Fascist techniques of mass persuasion. The *Public Opinion Quarterly*'s first article with the word in its title did not appear until 1951. The term "media" was not commonly used, or known, probably, by the general public, even though Marshall McLuhan's best-selling book, *Understanding Media*, gave it brief currency when it appeared in 1964.[2]

"The press," as a generic description of newspapers and working journalists, has been in use since the nineteenth century, and has been applied to news people in broadcasting since radio days. The idea of "media" as a common category rather than as a form of classification really seems to have acquired familiarity as a result of the spectacular growth of television news at the time of the Vietnam War, when journalists, seeking a comprehensive term to describe the enterprises for which they reported, found the words, "the press," imprecise and, perhaps, misleading.

In the Vietnam War years, the term "media" gained usage only after television news increased its air time and became a major journalistic force. The word "press" did not comfortably cover camera crews and others with no conceivable connection to periodical publishing or the printing arts. "The media" may also have become the preferred appellation applied to broadcast journalists by newspaper people, who thought of their television counterparts as part of show business and wanted to set themselves apart from them. For a time the phrases "print press" and "broadcast press" were used by way of establishing a distinction, but these awkward terms gave way to "the media," which often ended up as a synonym for television news.

The popularity of the term "the media" grew in proportion to the perceived political might of television, beginning with the struggles of the Johnson and Nixon administrations to sustain national policies that journalists increasingly questioned. Video reporting set powerful political forces in motion during the 1960s, both with respect to the Vietnam war and to civil rights. It also created powerful adversaries. Strong reactions came from a government that faced fierce campus opposition to the military draft and that saw its secret Pentagon papers spread over the front pages. The Nixon cabal saw "the media" as an implacable enemy—often, in fact, referred to as a singular noun, as though it were a unitary malevolent force.

The 1992 reelection campaign of George Bush harped insistently on the theme that Nixon and Agnew had raised two decades earlier. His main opponent, he reiterated, was "the media." There are still traces, somewhat softened, in the public's mind, of the Vietnam–Watergate era vision of journalists as a gang of negative-minded, possibly even subversive, leftists who have somehow managed to grab control of the public's main sources of information and who are bent on exercising a sinister power of their own in defiance of the elected government.

Public suspicion of journalists is periodically awakened by the visibility of the broadcasters during presidential campaigns and by the transformation of political campaign specialists and commercial producers into "media consultants"—themselves the subjects of films and TV specials. If the credibility of the press has become a major preoccupation of newspaper editors, as it did during the 1980s, it is in some degree due to the public's fairly recent perception of media power and to its uneasy recognition of its own dependence upon media sources of information. Media are important because they teach us so much and because we give them so much of our time.

Information and Entertainment

Media instruct; media divert. The two functions are inherently antagonistic, as we shall see throughout this book. Media convey the urgent messages of journalistic reportage. They also provide the easy alternatives that allow those messages to be shut out of mind. But information and entertainment cannot be unscrambled. All symbolic communication, including musical tones, fits under the heading of information. Conversely, acquiring information, even for purely utilitarian purposes, often has a recreational aspect.

The circus arts come close to being pure entertainment; the information they convey is totally subordinated to the pleasure they give. Noone can fail to be enchanted by animal trainers, tightrope walkers, or Chinese jugglers, or by sopranos hitting a perfect high C.

Overwhelmingly dedicated to entertainment, media also represent the principal form of acquiring knowledge. This dual function can be traced back to the earliest origins of theater, in the latter half of the sixth century BC. Drama was fundamentally didactic in aim, argues classical scholar Eric Havelock, in that it gave the Athenians a sense of identity as citizens of a city-state.

Its many composers—a more accurate title than authors—applied their skills to combining oral education with oral entertainment. . . . The plays were continual

reenactments of the civic scene, with which the audience was invited to identify. . . . Authors were recognized as poets rather than dramatists. The chorus
constituted the original and central element.[3]

The "nice balance between instruction and entertainment" tipped, says Havelock,
as written scripts came into use, allowing identical repetition of the same presentations.[4] Literacy enhanced and enriched the oral tradition immeasurably, not only by
reducing lapses of memory and the need for improvisation, but also by vastly
extending the array of information sources that could cross-fertilize each other.[5]
Writing made it possible to move from oral poetry to drama, where many participants
collaborated in a common civic enterprise.[6]

Potentially media can provide the means for people to manage their lives more
responsibly. The knowledge media convey is certainly not more vivid or meaningful
than what is acquired through direct personal experience, but it does cover a vastly
greater and more assorted range.

"Knowledge" is not identical with "information." It implies an element of
understanding, judgment and utility that is not inherent in the mere recording
of facts. The very term carries connotations of social uplift; it may be equated
with "truth," somehow distilled and separated from all the other content of human
communication. Yet its truth and significance are always matters of debate. We
might define knowledge pragmatically as the body of information and interpretation most widely accepted by experts who devote their lives to a subject. Humanity's lot could, in principle, be improved if such understanding were more broadly
shared. The problem is that it is easier to disseminate than to whet an appetite
for it.

Thomas Jefferson:

> The opinions and beliefs of men depend not on their own will, but follow involun-
> tarily the evidence proposed to their minds.[7]

The information we get from media shapes our ideas and values. In any society,
the beliefs held in common and the opinions under discussion at any given moment
both depend upon the information to which its members have access. Information
comes to us both as gradual incremental accruals of perceptions that shape our values
and our notions of what the world is like, and as specific facts we need to handle our
daily lives or to stimulate our creative thinking.

• General Minoru Genda, who planned the attack on Pearl Harbor, got his idea
for the Japanese air tactics a year earlier from newsreels showing American aircraft
carriers steaming in column formation. (He revealed this source of his inspiration in
1969, when he was invited to the U.S. Naval Academy under a "distinguished
visitors" program.)

Few people can claim to be innovators or originators of opinions; we tend to
express thoughts we have heard before. We apply to new situations a point of view we
acquired from previous exposure to the same or similar protagonists, institutions or
political labels. Our most fundamental *beliefs* are molded by our family upbringing,

our antecedents, our station in life, our occupation, and our schooling. But it is primarily the mass media through which we acquire our specific *opinions* on the many matters for which family, school, church, and job provide no automatic positions. The media play an essential but often invisible part in organizing our thoughts, both on distant and abstract matters and on those that are close to home.

• In a casual conversation, a friend begins to talk about the deterioration of the urban educational system, citing as evidence trends in teacher absenteeism, drug-related deaths among teenagers, and declines in grade-schoolers' reading achievement scores. I recognize all his source material from recent newspaper articles, and ask whether he would have recognized the signs of deterioration on his own. He readily acknowledges that he would not.

It took the initiative of an editor to assign a reporter to look into the relationships among small items that might in themselves seem trivial, to dig up data that, taken as a static phenomenon, might have little interest, and to organize and put everything together into a series of articles that make a point. Now a public issue is created, and a genuine public opinion is produced where previously there may have been none. If this journalistic initiative had not been exercised, the objective conditions would still have been the same. People would still have had thoughts about teenage drug addiction, teacher absenteeism, and pupils' reading ability. But these opinions would not have been held with the same conviction or discussed at the same level of concern as when they are perceived to be related to an urgent problem.

The greater the number of independent media voices, the greater the chances that such problems will be raised, talked about, investigated, clarified, and defined. Only the media can give us the sense that what goes on in the wider world is really our affair. Media are custodians of the public sense of responsibility for remote events; they constantly remind us of the linkages between our own destiny and those of people in distant places. Precisely as they seek to arouse our sense of responsibility, they become most passionate, and—becoming passionate—lend themselves to abuse and distortion in their view of the world.

The moral imperative has always been strong among the producers of mass communication, especially among those who are drawn to their profession by a creative impulse, by a sense of social or political mission, by a desire to find expression for their vision of the world. Yet the urge to express themselves, to pass on their private wisdom, is generally tempered by the need to find and maintain an audience. In the world of mass communication this has created the continuing dilemma of how to balance the public interest and the public's interests—a theme to which I shall return in Chapter 9. Establishing this balance between what must be said and what will be read and attended to has been a central concern of journalism since the first days of the periodical press. Even the most widely diffused and frequently repeated facts are generally ignored if there is no motivation to absorb them. That is why in most of the mass media, most of the time, knowledge is embedded within layers of amusement.

From the beginning, periodical publishing included a mixture of information and entertainment. A proper magazine, it was said in 1790, should be "very various and extensive" and should combine "utility with entertainment, . . . instruction with pleasure." The first American magazines had an avowedly instructional purpose. For example, the *New-York Magazine*'s objective was "to diffuse knowledge throughout a community, and to create in that community a taste for literature."[8]

Newspapers, in the eighteenth century, enlivened their content with nonfactual diversions—jokes, witticisms, wry or sarcastic comments, reports of real events that were humorous or curious rather than inherently newsworthy. Virtually every newspaper in the first half of the nineteenth century ran a poetry column.[9] Features and "human interest" stories leavened the diet of straightforward news reports. The prevailing editorial wisdom was that readers could sift what was important from what was not, and that a few drops of levity made the whole mixture more acceptable. Editors assumed that readers wanted changes of pace, and that confrontations with the strenuous and ugly facts of life that filled the news columns had to be punctuated with the second-hand pleasures of the imagination.

When information must be masked to be made palatable, the sugar coating tends to overwhelm its essence. Newspapers still provide a mix of news, opinion and entertainment, as they always have, but in the hunt for readers, news pages have become swollen with items and columns whose real purpose is amusement rather than enlightenment. The three newsmagazines followed a similar path, increasing the number of covers devoted to service topics and stressing the pronouns "you" and "we." *U.S. News* trademarked the slogan, "News You Can Use." *Time* magazine, squeezed by a decline in advertising revenues and relentless cost-cutting pressures from its corporate management, revealed plans in 1991 to cut back on its direct news reporting and to emphasize more utilitarian and "life-style" matter. It is not merely information and entertainment that media juggle, but various kinds of information that carry different levels of relevance, real and perceived.

Media as Pastime

Gardening hints are informative, as are the latest State Department reports on worldwide human rights abuses, but one is easier to take than the other. Why does the public want media to make the fewest possible intellectual demands? Certainly the media's great appeal lies in their ability to let us pass *time* agreeably. Entertainment must be savored within the time dimension; information exists largely outside of time. There is an aesthetic element involved in acquiring it, but information is mainly an end in itself rather than a tool for the pleasure of learning. Information is congruent with the world we experience directly. Entertainment takes us out of that world; it changes mood. To achieve this change, it does not have to induce fear and pity, purge our emotions, inspire our spirits or inflame our senses. It merely has to grab us long enough to take our minds away from the cares that would otherwise preoccupy them.

Pastimes generate large audiences because they require very little effort. Few intellectual demands are exacted by most media content, even by such utilitarian information as baseball batting averages, stock tables, and weather maps. But regardless of how much trivial, low-key subject matter they carry, most mass media also traffic in emotionally engaging (or, as psychologists would term it, "high-arousal") content. The exceptions might be publications dedicated to such matters as sewing patterns or home carpentry, or radio stations playing nothing but kitsch, or "beautiful music," with no potentially evocative vocal lyrics. Motion pictures are expected to bring us to a state of almost continual arousal; if they fail to do this, they put us to sleep.

Drama can facilitate the passage of time by keeping our attention occupied and turned away from unpleasant or mundane concerns, although it can also be irritating enough to inhibit the easy passage of time. (Something may be disturbing either because it is inherently repugnant or because it is difficult to comprehend without effort.) By contrast, a pastime evokes virtually no emotions, at least beyond the point of diverting attention from what is unpleasant or boring.

With media, we pass time differently from the way we do in life experiences, which are inseparable from our presence and participation and which occur in real time, in a setting that becomes a part of our memory of the events that make up the experience itself. Happy or traumatic, experiences are memorable for their singularity. We may remember a recurrent pattern of activities, like family meals, "hanging out" with friends at a favorite haunt, or working every day at a certain job, and say in retrospect, that we have "experienced" them. But they are not the unique occurrences that fix themselves in our psyches and that retain a permanent power to evoke reflection, nostalgia, or anxiety.

We also spend time in our media experience, but the experience itself exists apart from time, because we are always on the outside looking in. We can be captured and shaken by a poem, a film, a newspaper article, a book, even by something seen on television, but these impressions become fixed in time only to the degree that they become bridges to our own personal relationships: a poem recited to one's sweetheart, an article that occasions a passionate political argument, a film seen in the company of a departed friend.

Whether they take the form of imagery or of narration, media experiences cannot be as vivid, emotionally arousing and memorable as what actually happens to us. We can be touched either because what we see or read or hear produces a strong aesthetic response or because the intensity of what is being conveyed to us intrudes directly into our own personal experience. This may be done through art or through journalism that embroils us in current history.

The written language of print encapsulates and abstracts the meaning of events, permitting memory to focus upon their essence. While information in print must be sought out—and indeed will increasingly be sought out through computerized electronic means—knowledge conveyed in most films and broadcast programs is likely to be picked up incidentally in the pursuit of recreation. The diffusion of knowledge through this kind of incidental learning represents a communications process that is different from reading.

Messages conveyed through the audio–visual forms of communication occupy real time and, in that respect, resemble the flow of real life. They communicate at a fixed pace, while print can be regulated to suit the convenience of the reader. A well-prepared piece of text can pack enormous amounts of information into a limited amount of space, so that the readers rapidly absorb an extended dramatic experience. Broadcast and film offer to substitute mediated experience directly for the experience we might otherwise draw from life itself.

Why Media Unify and Differentiate

Because people use the media out of habit and conformity, and for the comfort of spending time agreeably, they often come to them for reasons that have very little to do with their specific content. Unless the breaking news is of great personal urgency, the morning paper is read in much the same fashion regardless of what is happening on a given day. The level of newspaper reading is about the same in cities whose newspapers run the gamut of quality. The car radio is tuned to a favorite station regardless of what tunes are being played. A great deal of movie-going merely provides young audiences with a pretext for leaving the house or for being together with someone in the dark. A couple checks to see what's at the movies because they want to go out that evening, or they might watch television at home because it is an effortless way of spending time.

Television audiences remain at approximately the same size regardless of the number of channels available or what they carry, regardless of the number of viewing choices, and regardless of whether programming is planned to maximize audience size, as it is in the United States, or devised to pursue ideological goals, as it is in China and was in the Soviet Union. Viewing is governed by the rhythms of daily routine rather than by the inherent attraction of its specific offerings.

It takes a national disaster or a political event of surpassing importance to attract more than the usual minority of housewives and retirees to the television tube at 11:00 in the morning. No matter how strong the attractions of programming may be at peak viewing hours of the evening, a certain proportion of people will always want to sleep, will hold evening jobs, or will prefer to entertain visitors, listen to music, read, go out for dinner or a show, play poker, or make love. Choices of specific programs or channels, like choices of specific reading matter, are made within the framework of the prior and more limiting decision to listen, watch, or read in the first place. The content is secondary to the activity.

Media audiences are shaped by the way time is spent at different social levels and in different periods of life. The variations in turn reflect how much discretion people have in determining how to spend time and also the value they put upon their time and upon potential media experiences. Those media that flow in time and that incur no visible additional cost through increased usage (electricity and maintenance are invisible) naturally generate disproportionately large audiences from people who have not yet entered the work force (radio) or who have left it (television).

That media habits are determined largely by the ebb and flow of disposable time is evident from their similarity in communities with widely varying media offerings. The United States encompasses a number of regional subcultures founded in differences in geography, history, economy, ethnic origin, and level of urbanization. These differences are to some degree reflected in media consumption patterns. Life on the freeways of Los Angeles leaves more time for radio and less for newspapers than it does in the subways of Boston. *The New Yorker* and *Vogue* are more widely read in New York City than in Manhattan, Kansas. But overall, the commonalities of media activity across the nation are more striking than the variations.

Pricing, as well as time, influences media habits. Poor people do not usually own expensive coffee-table art or travel books, partly because the imagery may be unwelcome or even disturbing to their self-esteem, but mostly because they cost too much. People with less money (who are also more likely to be young and dark-skinned) are less likely to be newspaper subscribers. They may rationalize their behavior by saying they are not all that interested, that they can get all the news they need from TV or radio. What they are really saying is that the paper lacks value; it is just not worth what they would have to pay for it. They will, however, read the advertising circulars that are dropped off at their doors and the free weeklies they can pick off a pile at the supermarket exit.

If people are attracted to media because they can spare the time or the money and because they possess the vocabulary required to comprehend their content, does this mean that audiences might be significantly different if everyone had infinite time, money, and comprehension? Probably not, because the choice of media is determined overwhelmingly by the substance and style of the ideas, images, and feelings that media communicate. Media exposure arises from habits that are formed fairly early in life, and media are attended to in a social context that resonates meanings over and above those carried by the sounds, words, and pictures they communicate through any particular vehicle at any given moment.

People get their knowledge from different media in different dimensions, and those who are more interested in information, like the news of the day, are precisely those who demand it of several sources. For many decades, each generation of Americans has been better educated than its predecessors. The market for trade books and the public demand for library books reflect the comparatively high reading predispositions of young people. The audiences for theatrical films and popular music have an even more youthful profile. (Two-thirds of musical recordings are bought by people under thirty.)

Media consumption reflects geography as well as gender, age and social class. Audiences for print are skewed upscale; for television, down. The larger economic base provided by metropolitan centers gives their residents access to more media choices.[10] Those in larger and wealthier communities have access to more retail outlets of all kinds; they have more opportunity and temptation to see a film or to browse for a book or record. (Media opportunities actually taper off more rapidly than family income as one moves from large communities to small ones.) The differences in people's media habits reflect much more than their conscious choices.

Mass media create widely shared common experiences, but they have become increasingly specialized in their appeal. Economies of scale in production have made it possible to reach large and ever larger audiences. It is commonplace to observe that a single radio broadcast of, say, a Bach cantata, reaches more people than heard it performed not merely in the composer's lifetime, but in all the centuries before the invention of broadcasting.

As the division of labor in society becomes more specialized and work life more segmented, the media have assumed greater importance as a source of common information, imagery, and interests. Even at elite levels of society, newspaper items are repeated conversationally without attribution, as though the teller had personally uncovered the story. When we ask, "Did you see the game on TV last night?" or, "Seen any good movies?" we are transcending the petty preoccupations of our own lives and finding a safe harbor of shared discourse.

Although huge audiences are generated for media's messages, they are also splintered by the proliferation of channels and vehicles. Thus, paradoxically, while media make possible a greater array of commonly shared experience, information, and symbolism than might once have been imagined, they also create the opportunity for ever greater individuation. No pair of identical twins reads the same books, goes to all the same movies, watches all the same television programs. Just as individuals' personalities and values are shaped by media exposure, the exercise of media preferences from an early age now represents one of the critical forms by which individuals manifest and shape their own identities.

Literacy, Leisure, and the Origins of the Media System

The American media system communicates through visual images, spoken words, and musical sounds. In spite of its strong audiovisual components, it started with reading matter, and it is still generally run on the premise that everyone can read.[11] However, literacy is not a prerequisite for the existence of a mass media audience, as is evident from the widespread diffusion of transistor radios and audiocassette players in impoverished countries where masses of people do not know the alphabet. The origins of media can be found in communications that existed before most people learned how to read.[12] Their evolution depended on the combination of literacy and leisure.

The very invention of printing reflected the growth of demand by a literate public; the availability of books, in turn, spurred literacy.[13] The growing dissemination of printed matter enhanced the status of reading as a skill that was not merely useful but universally accessible. And the spread of literacy was itself inseparable from the vast changes that were under way in society, in the relations of people to each other, and in the amount of time at their disposal.[14]

For centuries, the high cost of lamplighting fuel and of corrective eyeglasses inhibited widespread reading, especially since most books were printed in small type on poor-quality paper.[15] Relatively few people had both access to printed matter and the ability and the time to read it. Industrial technology, which created mass markets by lowering the cost of consumer goods, also made mass media affordable for ever larger numbers of people. The steam-driven press was invented in 1811, cylinder and rotary presses—essential for daily newspapers—arrived in 1815. The improvement of papermaking procedures brought further economies, thus permitting the production of inexpensive fictional drivel on a generous scale. Penny newspapers began the mass marketing of popular culture. In nineteenth-century America, universal literacy was fostered by an educational system that expressed the democratic ideology of the Founding Fathers and was challenged and stimulated by an endless stream of new immigrants eager to be assimilated into the dominant order.[16]

Free time, I have just said, defines the character of media audiences. Its growth also changed the relationship between the people who have something to say and those to whom they are saying it but who may only wish to be amused. As the sociologist Leo Lowenthal points out,

> with the beginning of bourgeois forms of life and thought, an ambiguous philosophy about the role of art also begins to develop—or perhaps one should say the role of

leisure, of which art seemed to be an essential part. . . . Montaigne suggests that man needs relaxation and distraction under the pressure of modern life, whereas Pascal says that if you seek distraction you lose your life's meaning.[17]

This debate poses an enduring dilemma that we shall encounter throughout this book: How can the urge for creative expression be reconciled with the demands of the market? Commercialization and professionalization, says Lowenthal, imply a separation of art for pleasure from art for art's sake. Wordsworth complains that the "beauty and dignity" of true art are threatened by "frantic novels, sickly and stupid German tragedies and the deluge of idle and extravagant stories in verse."[18] And in Germany Goethe writes Schiller:

> The strong affinity of the reading public to periodicals and novels arises out of the very reason that the former always and the latter usually bring distraction into distraction. . . . Everyone who fools the public by swimming with the current can count on his success.[19]

For most of the modern era, the bulk of rural and urban workmen toiled as long as there was daylight and devoted most of their few spare hours to the essential chores of housekeeping. The rise of industry and of routinized production methods heightened demand for diversions to counteract the strain and monotony of the workplace. Paradoxically, economic growth also gave people more time to enjoy both the individual entertainment of reading and the shared entertainment of public spectacles: theatrical and musical performances, sporting events.

On the American scene, Alexis de Tocqueville predicted that the pressure and boredom of work would lead to the need for exciting leisure-time diversions. "The object of authors will be to astonish rather than to please, and to stir the passions more than to charm the taste."[20] As the market for entertainment grew, entrepreneurial spirits rushed to fill the vacuum.

For the Victorians, as for their Puritan predecessors, the enjoyment of one's own free time required a convoluted justification:

> Rest is not idleness; in a very true sense it is a part, an integral part of work. . . . If we really work when we work, we need not be ashamed of periods of sheer inaction. . . . For nature is not idle with us at such times; she coils the uncoiled springs of action, screws up the wires which have been out of tune, tightens the rigging of our ship, sets the grass growing over the worn and bare places in the pastures of our minds, overhauls the lumber room of our memory, and puts the sap of life through a moral change.[21]

Leisure could be enjoyed without guilt—a comforting thought, since there was ever so much more of it and media were available to keep it occupied. The work week shortened.[22] New devices reduced the time required by household tasks and made it possible for many women to find employment outside the home. Washing machines and vacuum cleaners also created a substantial difference between the time budgets of the great majority of full-time housewives and their working husbands. (A large minority of women still enjoy more disposable time. Among men 18–64, 90% hold jobs; among women the proportion is 69%, and women's lives and media experiences go on for a longer time than men's.)

Reading novels and magazines became an overwhelmingly female preoccupation, while attending public entertainments remained a shared evening activity. (Magazines define gender-role functions much more sharply than other media. The heyday of the women's magazines began in an era when middle-class women stayed at home and servants were commonplace. The circulation of magazines directed primarily at women still far outweighs the circulation of those directed at men.)

Medical advances increased longevity. With the growth of private pension plans in the mid-twentieth century came a trend toward earlier retirement. This tendency was only partially offset by the advent of laws against age discrimination, a change in the legal age of mandatory retirement from 65 to 70, and by inflationary pressures that slowed the drift. People in their retirement years now account for a disproportionate and growing share of the total hours the public spends with media.

Until relatively recent times—and for that matter, still in many countries—leisure was the hallmark of a privileged aristocracy (a "leisure class," as Thorstein Veblen called it), who disdained disagreeable toil and disassociated gainful employment from the enjoyment of its fruits.[23] Since the possession of leisure was a strong indicator of social status, rentiers who did not have to work at all were at the very top of the ladder, spending their time as they wished.

Veblen's brilliant characterizations of the 1890s do not apply to America in the 1990s, when most people feel they have less free time than ever. Not too long ago, conventional wisdom expected an ever shorter work week and a life full of ever more leisure.[24] This expectation changed acutely with the move of women into employment. In the highest social stratum, there is a sharp generational difference between young women, with occupational skills, and their mothers, whose lives still center around home and friends. Men, however, obsessed by the goals and anxieties of achievement, work the longest hours of all. Their personal and business lives are intertwined to a degree that drastically limits the amount of personal time they can call their own. At the nether reaches of society, in the demoralized world of the urban slum, self-perpetuating patterns of dependency have produced an almost total absence of routine responsibilities, a life of aimless, dismal leisure in which television occupies an important place.

Leisure has not really defined the boundaries of media growth. In Japan, employers expect workers to read newspapers in the office, to be better-informed and thus more effective. In American offices, employers tolerate secretaries and receptionists who read paperback novels when there is nothing else for them to do. Salespeople have their cassette players on while they drive about on their calls, and radios are played in almost every machine shop.[25]

Media experiences have imploded upon each other, especially since the advent of broadcasting. It is not really possible to read two documents at the same time, though some executives pretend to do it. However, it is easy enough to read while listening to the radio, or even while monitoring television. (In this case, concentration can only be on one medium or another at any given moment, but exposure can be simultaneous.) It is certainly possible to listen to music on the radio while watching a TV talk show. Delegates at political party conventions watch the proceedings on portable TV sets, to get the big picture, and sports fans listen to the radio sportscast of a baseball game while seated in the stadium at a football match.

A not insubstantial part of television viewing (and probably almost all radio listening) in fact occurs at the same time as some other activity.[26] The decision to watch any particular program is often made by just one member of a viewing group, while the others go along to be companionable. People read, eat, play with children, and do housework while viewing. This reflects their relatively low level of involvement with the content of what is on the screen. If a program is truly absorbing to an individual, other activity comes to a halt. But this does not mean that viewers who are otherwise occupied are oblivious to the programming. They are still sensitive to the cues that tell them to stop and pay attention.

The electronic media have reduced loneliness for the growing number of solitary individuals in a society where young people marry later, where more of them stay unmarried, where divorce is more common, and widowhood lasts longer. Television is the great undemanding companion for anyone engaged in housework; an occasional glance at the screen picks up images that can be carried over by ongoing voices when visual attention is diverted elsewhere. Since the advent of the transistor, the cry of the portable radio is heard in every wilderness. Mass media are ubiquitous, not because they say what is compelling, but because they fill the hours.

Packaging Ongoing and One-Shot Media

To occupy time, mass media must be packaged or produced in advance for consumption. Whether they aim at limited audiences or at the general public, they differ from individual person-to-person communications because they represent the same duplicated messages delivered to many separated people.

The discipline imposed by packaging is exemplified in broadcast programming. In radio's early days, and for years afterwards in some countries, a cheerful anarchy prevailed, in which things took their natural course and programs ran on to their appropriate length. Today, there is standardized modularity almost everywhere and almost all the time. Viewers are conditioned to take their programs in standard chunks. The result is a fragmented communications experience quite distinct from that of the cinema, where one makes an excursion, dedicates oneself to what is offered, and sits still for the long haul.

Television programs often go beyond the half-hour norm, and television makes heavy use of special entertainment events, long sportscasts, and feature length films. But the half-hour time period remains the standard unit of measuring audience size, and this "slot" is therefore the yardstick by which programs are planned, compared, and evaluated.

The short, modular duration of television programs follows a format developed in radio. It was determined by a perception that the audience's attention would not hold very long for a communication limited to sound. (Indeed, some of radio's most memorable programs (like "Amos 'n' Andy" and "The Rise of the Goldbergs") were daily strips of 15-minute duration). Moreover, in the era of exclusive advertising sponsorship, most sponsors wanted to use their limited budgets on repeated messages at frequent intervals rather than on longer programs.

The serial drama in broadcasting (which I shall discuss further in Chapter 4) was based on well-established principles of how an audience could be lured back again and again by a story that was never resolved and that always developed new wrinkles. The *Scheherazade* recipe is surely more ancient than *The Arabian Nights*. In the nineteenth century, readers found serialized novels more enjoyable because of the suspense they generated. The motion picture serials of the thirties and forties brought the viewers back to the theater for each succeeding Saturday's episode. Much of the attraction of the daily newspaper rests on the fact that the developing news continually unfolds mysteries and creates new ones. Such contrived devices as the serialized feature story or the continuity comic strip were merely embellishments of the unresolved turns of the news itself.

Media that appear at regular intervals heighten the awareness of time. By predictably punctuating life's flow, they help bring order into the world. A medium that is produced on a continuing schedule must be accepted and expected as a matter of routine by the audience. One controllable aspect of this is in distribution; breakdowns and irregularities in delivery disturb the habitual reading pattern for daily newspapers more than dissatisfaction with the content. In both periodicals and broadcasts, content must astutely combine what the audience is already expecting or even looking for (the final sports results on the first page of Section III, the newscast every hour on the hour, the talk show host at 4 in the afternoon), with the totally unpredictable (who won the game, what happened on the news, who today's special guest turns out to be).

Media "packaging" — long taken for granted — is now challenged by the new forms of communication. (Among these must be numbered new channels of transmission — by cable, telephone line, optic fiber, or direct satellite-to-home broadcasting — and new forms of storing information: video cassettes, CD-ROMs, or videodiscs, with their freeze-frame capacity of moving from video motion to still picture to text.) The combination of these new forms enables televiewers equipped with a few gadgets to construct their own media environments; they can gain direct access to what will shortly be encyclopedic files of current news and advertising, back files of the same, texts of periodicals, and books and archives of films and television programming from around the world.

Past history suggests that these technological developments, now just beginning, will have profound effects on intellectual life. When books existed only in manuscript, scholars had to travel great distances to do collateral reading on a particular subject.[27] They were limited in their ability to compare texts directly and reflect on the incongruities. Once printed books stocked libraries, there was an enormous rise in the overall level of intellectual interchange and stimulation. With many more books assembled in one place, scholars could cross-reference a vastly greater number of ideas and pursue them simultaneously.

Computerized information systems may well represent a similar leap to a new level of potential inventiveness and productivity by making an even greater array of information almost instantly accessible on command. These systems increase the possibilities of uncovering unexpected connections among facts and ideas. (However, they also threaten to drown their users in overwhelming overloads of unmanageable data.) They will change and enhance the ordinary uses of information in daily life, and thus have a significant impact on mass culture as well as on science and scholarship.

We have moved closer to the vision of the free-flowing, freely accessible electronic data stream, where information and entertainment are customized to fit individual desires. This shift leaves less and less of a role for the professionals whose stock in trade is divining and creating mass appetites—packaging information and leavening it with the fun that brings in the customers.

Commercial culture is, by definition, produced for sale rather than to serve any higher spiritual purpose; it is in trouble when it can no longer be mass-produced. Computer-based technology can assemble, store, and retrieve mountains of facts. It provides a vast treasure house of easily and inexpensively accessible information—but only for the benefit of those with the means and motivation to seek it out. There is growing polarization, along social class lines, of entertainment consumers and knowledge consumers.

Does this mean the end of the familiar "packaged" media as we have known them in publications and broadcast programming? It is hard to see how it could. The public now devotes vastly more time to media whose content is preselected than to those that give the options of personal choice. People listen to radio music much more than to records or audiocassettes. They watch vastly more television than theater movies or videos. They read far fewer books than packaged periodicals.

Why? To some degree it is true, as editors and producers would claim, that they value the authoritative professional judgments that now control the planning and selection of media content. But there are two more important reasons.

The first is that packaged media require less effort and represent greater convenience than those that require an active search. That is why newspapers try to run their editorials, as well as Doonesbury and Ann Landers, in predictable positions every day. Anyone who has tried to retrieve teletext information from a computer terminal knows exactly how cumbersome the process is, compared with reading a periodical. Audiences resist exertion. Even with UHF television universally available, its audiences in noncable homes are much smaller than those of VHF stations, simply because UHF requires more fussing with the dial. Before remote controls were common, television networks vied especially for the early evening audience, since a large proportion of viewers stayed with a particular channel once they had tuned in, to avoid expending energy to change it.

The other important reason why the public values packaged media is that they are usually less expensive and thus appear to offer greater value. Partly this is because of production costs. Specialized media do not enjoy the economies of large size, and their charges to audiences and advertisers are correspondingly greater per unit than those of their counterparts who speak to "everyone." With individually "tailored" media the costs must go even higher. It is cheaper to produce 100,000 identical copies of a newspaper than the equivalent volume of content in 100,000 different assortments, as will be technically possible in the coming era of ink-jet printing (a process that permits changes in text from one copy of a publication to the next). Packaged media are cheaper for yet another reason, which is that advertising pays all or much of the cost.

Periodicals and broadcasts are produced on a regular predictable schedule to which the audience is accustomed; other media appear individually. The distinction is worth noting even though the dividing line between ongoing and one-shot media erodes in practice. A media vehicle of the ongoing type seeks to create patterns of habitual exposure. In the case of newspapers and magazines, incentive pricing is used to encourage subscriptions over purchases of individual copies. In both print and broadcasting, content is patterned to lure audiences back to what is familiar and comfortable or to satisfy their curiosity about the outcome of ongoing stories that are left unresolved.

Periodicals and broadcast programs must constantly change their substance, and, from time to time, modify their formats, to maintain the appearance of freshness and to sustain audience appeal. With books, films, videos, and musical recordings, each of which is unique, the audience must be attracted anew in every case. This necessity increases the uncertainties both for the producers and for the public and thus changes their relationship to each other.

Promotions of movies, television programs, and books focus on the content and its delights; those for magazines and newspapers commonly use special price offers or premiums as inducements. However, most of the advertising for musical recordings and videocassettes—also one-shot media—emphasizes price too. In this case, its promoters assume that the targeted public is already familiar, from broadcasts, with what is being offered, and that an incentive will activate an interest that already exists.

In the marketing of ordinary consumer goods, promotion can induce consumers to try a product and produce short-run sales; it cannot guarantee long-term growth in a brand's position. For repeated purchases the product itself must give satisfaction. A promotional announcement ("promo") for a television program may persuade us to tune in but not to stay with it if it fails to fulfill its promise. An ad may get us to buy a book or subscribe to a magazine, but once it is in our hands, we may not want to read beyond the first page. We can always cancel a magazine or newspaper subscription, but few people actually do so; booksellers are not always tolerant about returns.

One-shot media are unique in that—unlike other consumer goods and unlike continuing media, for that matter—there is no expectation of repeat sales. A film or book promotion can be moderately successful, up to a point, even if the promoted film or book disappoints the purchasers. (It is not apt to be a runaway triumph, of course.) Unlike the television executive whose advertising income depends on the ratings, the film-maker or publisher may feel that the promotion has done its job if the public has put its money down. Even though some additional sales will be lost because of bad word-of-mouth, people will tend to rationalize the wisdom of purchases they have already made. The book may remain on the shelf unread, but the buyer plans to get around to it some day. Few movie-goers walk out on even the most disappointing film, once they have paid to see it.

As financial stakes and risks increase, the willingness to venture dwindles. Because they must find their audiences afresh with every effort, one-shot media entail far greater risk to those who own them than those that are produced on a continuing basis. They require a different style of financing and management. In the Broadway theater, to which the movies have been closely linked, a couple of hit musicals can compensate for a considerable number of money-losing plays. The motion picture picture business has long had a similar feast or famine psychology.[28] The 5 % or so of musical recordings that really return a profit must compensate for the 95% that lose money or barely cover their costs. A handful of best-sellers allow a publisher to put out books of poetry at a loss.

Yet records, films, and books emerge as part of an ongoing flow of production from their respective establishments. Their producers constantly seek the continuity that comes with sequels and spin-offs—devices by which the success of a singular production can be extended by building on the public's familiarity with the original. The public is attracted to a new entry, in some measure—often overwhelmingly—because of its familiarity with the talented people associated with it. Star performers, directors, or writers can bring in audiences regardless of the merits of what they perform, direct, or write. The high-powered promotional apparatus that creates and sustains their reputations is intended to assure the public that their names are known quantities, even when the vehicle is itself an unknown.

Predictability and habit for the audience translate into security and predictability for the media producer, who can very well estimate how many people will be attracted and what kinds of people they will be. The more that content deviates from the established patterns, the more uncertain the estimates become. The audiences for specials, political and athletic events and other exceptions to the usual programming practices on television are difficult to guarantee in advance, much like the audiences for books and films, in which bigger budgets are often at stake.

Something changes when a unique cultural expression becomes the Book of the Month or the Thursday Night Movie. The need for a secure return on the producers' investment inevitably discourages experimentation. Instead of opening up other worlds, media lock their audiences more narrowly in the confines of what they already know. The tendency to deal in the formulaic is enhanced because of another complication, this one financial. The predictability of audience size has made the ongoing media the preferred vehicles for advertising, which cuts or eliminates their direct cost to the public. As media packaging takes new forms and the individual media consumer has wider choices, advertisers can no longer take audience size for granted. Their uncertainty wears down their confidence, which is essential to keep the whole economic support system running.

Packaging makes commercial culture possible because it organizes communications as items that can be mass-produced and marketed as commodities, substituted for each other to fill time. But packaging tends to develop a preoccupation with technique, to foster indifference to the substance of what is packaged.

Media in the future will change their character, assume new shapes, and be delivered via electronic devices that now can only be conjectured. I am not concerned here with trying to forecast how either the economic structure or the content of media will be altered as the revolution in communications technology runs its course. The changes will not affect media's basic functions of informing and entertaining, their ability to while away time, or the need for practitioners and institutions that can package them into marketable formats. That need remains regardless of how many choices open up for the audience. (An automated telephone answering system allows me to press one for sales and 2 for accounting, but someone must anticipate these options and provide the means for exercising them. The possibilities they offer are not the same as telling the phone operator whom I want to talk to and being told that she is out of the office today.) Packaging will always require packagers—the villains and heroes of this book.

This chapter has sounded themes that will be taken up as we move along: the pressures that the discipline of packaging imposes on the creative process; the difficulties of reconciling information and entertainment; the ability of media to reinforce individual identity as well as to establish common bonds; the crucial dimension of time that explains the power of media words and images. The rubric of "media," we have seen, covers a hetereogeneous array of communications with disparate and sometimes contradictory functions. They may or may not be vehicles of advertising; they may be continuing or one-shot, informational or entertaining, universal or specialized. Individually they are hard to classify. Taken together, they must be regarded as intermeshed institutions, producing the commercial culture that fills our hours and shapes our thoughts and moods.

2

The Media System

The individual mass media can no longer be considered apart from their relationships to the media system as a whole. The messages they disseminate have a cumulative impact that is greater than the sum of their individual effects.

Media—forms of human expression—have never functioned in isolation. Human beings exchange signals through many related modalities: words, tone, gesture, touch. Even the most primitive cultures communicate through combinations of percussive rhythm, dance, costume, adornment, makeup, music, and words. From the Egyptians' hieroglyphics to today's Conceptual Art, words and pictures have been combined to enrich meaning. The illuminated manuscripts of the Middle Ages and the woodblocks that accompanied the first books set in movable type combined two forms of communication, just like the phonograph records occasionally bound into magazines today.

Only a few years ago, it was not unreasonable to think of media one by one, as Marshall McLuhan did, when he considered the special properties of each and categorized them as "hot" or "cool." The various media remain distinct and identifiable in their characters, internal economics, and functions, and in the skills required to produce them—as befits their separate technologies and histories. But more and more they operate as parts of a system that must be regarded as an indivisible entity, with common elements of ownership, management, and content. This chapter examines the relationships among media and the growth of the organizations that link them. It considers the growing concentration of power and what it signifies for the goals and operating styles of media institutions as they expand. It makes these points:

- The people, content, and symbolic content of media are now largely interchangeable.
- Ownership is increasingly concentrated in large multi-media enterprises, many of international scope. Their rationale is "synergy"—the belief that activities in one medium can be profitably exploited in others.

- What happens in media that carry advertising affects the media that do not.
- The integrity of journalism is threatened when it is incorporated into media conglomerates whose main business is entertainment.
- Media that are operated as profit centers within corporate conglomerates are managed differently from the way they were as individual ventures, as book and newspaper publishing illustrate.
- Marxist criticism trenchantly analyzes the causes and failings of concentrated power over media but offers no attractive alternative.

How Media Interpenetrate

Media draw from common funds of capital and of creative and managerial talent. They feed upon each other's subject matter and personalities. The marketing of "spin-offs" begins with the first conception of a story, gig, or number.

The connections are not new. In American colonial times, printers published newspapers, books and other forms of reading matter; their creation, production, and distribution were completely intertwined. In the nineteenth-century, book and magazine publishing were occasionally combined in houses like Harper's and Scribner's. Journalists wrote books; newspaper editors took jobs at magazines. While switching formats, they remained essentially in the world of letters, no matter where they sat. Nineteenth-century authors extended their incomes by performing readings in public; the very structure and contortions of their plots reflected the need to meet the deadlines of the magazines where their works first appeared before they were published as books.

Telegraphy and photography, almost simultaneous inventions, were new forms of communication that could be applied to the publishing arts, but that were not mass media in themselves. By contrast, the phonograph brought a completely independent technology and also new techniques of mass reproduction. So did the cinema. Great industries stemmed from these distinctive modes of transmitting messages. Each was initially thought of as unique, since the forms by which they communicated had little in common with print. They did, however, derive their raw material from established print sources. Just as Elizabethan dramatists based their works on existing prose chronicles, Hollywood drew plots from magazines and novels. Emile Zola's novel *L'Assomoir* was made into a 5-minute film in 1902 – the first such adaptation on record.[1] In the 1930s a radio concert might be reincarnated as a phonograph record, a novel could be turned into a film script, a radio comedian might be born again in the movies. There was no particular reason to ponder the implications of such crossovers.

Musical recording, filmmaking, and radio derived their substance and their talent from the unbroken tradition of the performing arts. Radio employed actors, directors, and scriptwriters before it drew on the skills of journalists both to describe what was happening at political conventions, sports contests, and other live events and later to rewrite and comment upon the wire service news. But radio, like television – which emerged directly from it, using its people, organizations, and programming formats – could be looked upon as a world of experience unto itself.

Today, all news media make substantial use of the same great wire services. Feature and syndication services diffuse identical material to numerous publications and stations. Duplication of content is furthered by the widespread public relations practice of mailing press releases and unsolicited feature material directly to news organizations.

Media are sustained by the publicity and promotion they provide each other. Common symbols, images, and standards, common authority figures, a common cast of universally familiar characters are shared not only throughout a variety of media forms, but also among the various regions and social classes of American society. The effect is to homogenize national values.

Characters and themes, fictional and real, move freely among different media forms, between media and other forms of enterprise, and between advertising and entertainment. The distinctions have blurred between commercial and noncommercial messages. The production apparatus of television advertising is now inseparable from that of television programming, with the same technicians and talent operating in both domains. Michael Ovitz, a deal-maker whose Creative Artists talent agency has become a major force in shaping Hollywood's entertainment output, was also guiding Coca-Cola's advertising strategy in the 1990's.

Television commercials advise viewers to watch for a newspaper ad. Advertisements feature the testimonials of entertainment personalities; in reverse, beautiful advertising models are perceived by the public as part of the glamorous world of entertainment. Advertising slogans and campaigns are made (gently) the butt of televised humor. Advertising jingles are set to the musical themes of classical masterworks and popular songs. Tunes composed for advertising occasionally acquire second lives as popular songs themselves. Low-cost radio commercials use musical themes, sound effects, or the cadences of a familiar voice to evoke visual impressions that have already been created in their more expensive television equivalents.

The technology and substance of media have become an indissoluble blend. The entertainment media use identical recipes for suspense and laughter; the entertainers themselves are rarely identified with a single vehicle or outlet. Titles, plots, and fictional characters live separate lives in different formats. Hollywood gets more than two-thirds of its income from television and pay television rights and from video-cassette sales—not from theatrical showings.

A film exhibitor executive:

> Nobody goes to a video store and asks for a movie that was made for television. They have to have had a theatrical play. A movie is worth millions more because of its theatrical release. That establishes its quality. We want to see it a second time. It's the name recognition. The life of the video is longer than the theatrical life. A film has a short life span. There's not that urgency with a videocassette."[2]

In Hollywood, the same studios are used to produce television programs and feature films—not only routine half-hour serial dramas, but full-length "made for television" movies, which became increasingly costly productions.

The content of one medium feeds on others. A high proportion of magazine and newspaper content concerns the entertainment industry. Important novels (*After*

Many a Summer Dies the Swan, The Day of the Locust) have been written about Hollywood, and there have been bestselling books about the television networks. There are films and television shows about soap operas. From *A Star is Born* and *Sunset Boulevard* to *Barton Fink* and *The Player*, the film industry has been one of its own favorite subjects.

For those who want to recreate the familiar in a variant version, movie experiences can be evoked on a soundtrack recording. One film in three is based on a published book, but potboilers are also written to order, constructed from the plots of successful motion pictures to fulfill the exhortation, "You've seen the film; now read the book!" Yale professor Erich Segal, author of the sentimental bestseller *Love Story*, acknowledged that he had the eventual film version in mind as he concocted the plot of a new novel.[3] *M.A.S.H.* was a novel, then a film, then a TV series. Turner Broadcasting, not noted for originality, produced a series of books based on its television programs. Fox's television show, "America's Most Wanted," became the subject of a paperback published by HarperCollins, owned by the same company. Charles Addams' cartoon characters were transformed into a television show and then into films. Comic strip heroes (Superman, Batman, and Dick Tracy) have become the subjects of blockbuster movies.[4] Conversely, movies have produced three-dimensional characters (like "Ghostbusters" or the wizened "E.T.")[5]

At the very start of the Persian Gulf War, Warner New Media worked with its corporate partner, *Time*, to design compact discs (CDs), featuring the *Time* logo, that packaged the war as home entertainment. Correspondents were given 8-millimeter cameras to shoot video footage for sale to other news organizations while they covered stories for the magazine.[6] *Newsweek* introduced a CD edition.

Books, as originally written, are no longer trapped in the limits of print. By 1993, the market for audio books ("spoken word publishing") had reached $100 million, 40% of it fiction.

Media share common distribution systems. Nearly half of adult trade book sales are paperbacks; nearly four-fifths of these are of the mass market type.[7] With the growth of paperbacks, book marketing followed the lead of magazines and became linked to the grocery and drugstore business. In both industries, display racks and point-of-sale promotion became important retailing instruments. Packaging (in cover design), display, and promotional techniques were all derived from those of supermarket merchandise. By diversifying the array of retail outlets, paperbacks altered the economics of hardcover book distribution. Retail book chains also began to handle hardcover books as perishable goods, much like magazines. Slow-moving titles were quickly winnowed out, just as would be done for any weak brand of hairspray or ketchup.[8]

Media share talent. Show business figures who have achieved success in one medium or art form are able to transfer their reputations to become attractions in another. The stars are stars of stage, screen, and television. The same actors perform in films and television programs; they can be heard on records and cassettes and on the radio; their exploits are heralded in books, magazines, and newspapers.[9] (Not only do actors and singers move from the stage to film or radio but, in reverse, film actors of minor gifts but marvelous appearance, transformed into stars by skillful direction and heavy promotion, have developed ambitions and paraded their ineptitude in the legitimate theater.)

Neither are popular personalities and cultural icons restricted to a single medium. (Joyce Brothers, who gained celebrity as a contestant on a rigged TV quiz show, is, through her newspaper column, the most widely read and best-known psychologist in America.) Television makes entertainment stars out of working journalists. Walter Winchell and Ed Sullivan were among the first newspaper columnists to become stars of broadcasting. Their successors appear on television talk shows and publish books and magazine articles. Authors write film adaptations of their stories; these end up being played on television and sold on home videocassettes. (Sidney Sheldon was a successful film and TV script writer who took a large loss in income in order to begin his career as a bestselling novelist. He constructed the plots of his novels as though they were film scripts.)

Individuals pursue career paths that take them out of one medium into another. They go from Knight-Ridder newspapers to Playboy Enterprises (Derrick Daniels), from the London *Times* to Random House (Harold Evans), from the *Louisville Courier-Journal* to NBC News (Michael Gartner), from the *Los Angeles Times* to CNN (Tom Johnson), from NBC Television to Paramount Films (Brandon Tartikoff), from ABC to Disney (Michael Eisner).

Television writer-producers (Norman Lear and Mark Goodson), using the fortunes created by their programs to become major media entrepreneurs, entered the newspaper business. Lear's ACT III Communications became the owner of eight television stations, the country's ninth largest theater chain, and twelve trade magazines. On a lesser scale, TV personality Geraldo Rivera bought a New Jersey weekly.

There is also an interchange between the ranks of media producers and those who report on them as a news beat. Six of the *Los Angeles Times'* entertainment reporters got film industry jobs (presumably much better-paying) within a period of a few years. *The New Yorker's* film critic, Pauline Kael, followed a well-trodden path when she took a five-month leave to work for Paramount. Carl Spielvogel, the *New York Times's* advertising columnist, moved on to do public relations for Interpublic, and eventually helped to oust the agency's president, Marion Harper Jr., who had hired him. He then went on to start an agency of his own with one of Interpublic's big accounts, Miller Brewing. (He eventually sold out to the Saatchi brothers, but retained control of his shop, which, after mergers, was the giant Backer, Spielvogel Bates [later just Bates].)

This interpenetration of careers and symbols makes media content more inbred and homogeneous. It also shifts the balance of power from the lesser media to those with the largest masses of capital behind them: fiction books to film, cable to network television, recorded music to radio.

The recorded music industry is, in fact, inseparable from radio, which promotes the selections it plays just by identifying them. Mere exposure stimulates the desire for possession; extraneous urgings or inducements are not needed. Programming on the cable network MTV is actually an endless series of commercials promoting individual entertainers and recordings. The music-video format has had profound effects on the production style of television commercials and has spawned a whole genre of films: "Saturday Night Fever," "Flashdance," "Footloose." An MCA Records release in November 1985 promoted "Miami Vice":

Its riveting power flows in no small part from its producer's realization that mood and texture are as potent as plot and character to audiences whose lives are continually awash with non-verbal imagery. . . . The message of form is recognized as equal to the message of content.[10]

As one new sprout of expression emerges and establishes its viability (for example, in cable or specialty magazine publishing), it is likely to be snatched up by an established organization and planted into its corporate garden patch. This process gives American mass media a progressively greater evenness of tone, accentuated by their politically neuter character.

The concepts and vocabulary of consumer marketing have been taken over by the corporate world of media. As in the grocery business, any item can be regarded as part of a "product line." *Sports Illustrated for Kids* was a "line extension." ("Spaceballs," film-maker Mel Brooks' spoof of "Star Wars" and its ilk, showed toilet paper as one of the "line extensions.") Carrying this practice to a bold length, Robert Guccione's new *Spin* magazine, with a circulation of 300,000, included a condom with every copy of the November 1989 issue.

Business empires are created out of performers' reputations. Sony and the singer Michael Jackson announced a billion dollar arrangement to create films, shorts, TV programs, and a new record label. It was hailed by Sony Software president Michael P. Schulhof as "the forerunner of a new kind of entertainment deal."[11] Shortly afterwards, Time Warner announced a similar arrangement with the pop singer and all-purpose sex symbol Madonna, who was to receive up to $60 million for her own multimedia entertainment company. She explained that

"there's a group of writers, photographers, directors and editors that I've met along the way in my career who I want to take everywhere with me. I want to incorporate them into my little factory of ideas. I also come in contact with a lot of young talent [she herself was 33] that I feel entrepreneurial about.[12]

The artists were indistinguishable from their corporate entities. The individual components of their deals, as throughout the whole system, were inseparable from each other or from their social connections. The musician Quincy Jones was a partner of Time Warner's in a new company. Courtney Sale Ross, the wife of Time Warner's chairman, wrote Jones's biography, and Warner Brothers released a film based on it, that could only be purchased jointly with a compact disc or audiocassette. A videocassette was also separately available.[13]

The imaginary characters of the media have also become a significant force as products in the consumer market, where name recognition has a dollar value when it is translated into brand awareness.

• There was a natural connection between comics characters and the toy business, which Walt Disney himself was one of the first to exploit when he set up his character-licensing department in 1934. Disney turned the guileless Mickey Mouse into a large diversified corporation. The company's theme parks in the United States and Japan, (though not its troubled EuroDisney) provided a major source of income and made it a major hotel operator. Over forty products were part of the Disney

Babies line, starting with disposable diapers. McDonald's designed a children's meal around a Disney film character, "The Little Mermaid," and entered cross-promotional deals on Disney's "Dick Tracy" and "101 Dalmatians." Disney had similar arrangements with M&M Mars for the "Rocketeer" and with Mattel Toys for "Beauty and the Beast." A Disney Press was set up to exploit further publishing opportunities.

• Other film companies and the television networks have also entered into merchandising coventures with makers of products sold to children—CBS with Hasbro on "Wuzzles" and ABC with Lucasfilm in "Droids: The Adventures of R2D2 and C3PO."[14] A "Chester Cheetah" television program featured the totemic animal for Cheetos. Cereal companies introduced brands like Donkey Kong, E.T., Rainbow Brite, Gremlins, C-3PO, Mr. T, PacMan, and Smurfberries, all based on entertainment characters, and Nintendo, based on the computer game.

• The film "Batman" earned half a billion dollars from product licensing arrangements, more than twice its box-office revenues. Batman products were placed on sale even before the film opened, to heighten expectations. Apart from the cartoon figures, other film characters entered the game. "Back to the Future" sunglasses were being awarded as premiums by Pizza Hut. Pepsi-Cola built a $25 million advertising campaign around the wizened "E.T." featuring a rebate promotion on a videocassette.

• Mattel created "Masters of the Universe" as a set of toys (which did $500 million in volume in 1984) and then had Filmation Studios turn the characters into a syndicated cartoon television program. A fantasy film character named RoboCop became a successful toy; in reverse, General Mills' Kenner Products Division created animated shows based on its toys. CBS vice president George Schweitzer asks,

> "why should it be wrong if the toy inspired the program and not the other way around? We evaluate programming on entertainment value and not on its merchandising ability.[15]

Some shows based on toys that continued to sell successfully ("Transformers" and "Gobots") had poor ratings, while "Jem" was a popular Saturday morning program and a poorly selling toy. Tim Duncan, head of the Advertiser Syndicated Television Association, says

> "licensing out because a character is popular is very different from a marketing plan to support a toy by doing a show. . . . Disney did not put on "Davy Crockett" just to sell raccoon hats."[16]

This fine distinction is often lost in the world of synergistic marketing, in which real and imaginary characters alike are commercial symbols that carry make-believe into the tangible everyday world of toys and games and into the emotional realm of relationships between children and parents. The interpenetration of media extends beyond personal careers and corporate revenues; it affects the texture of everyday life.

Competition and the Media System

The interdependence of media is apparent even as they battle each other for income. Historically, in a steadily expanding market, media enterprises have not necessarily seen their competitors as a threat to their own survival, as they generally do today. From the invention of printing right through to the end of the nineteenth century, a publisher's ability to generate an audience was limited only by the extent of literacy (which was continually growing) and by the public's ability to pay (which generally continued to improve as industrialization raised standards of living and technical improvements reduced publishing costs). The success of any individual publisher did not automatically mean failure for his contemporaries. This is still true today for nonadvertising media. A best-selling book or record or a hit movie is in no way a threat to the chances for other books, records, or movies. By whetting public appetites, it may actually be an asset.

The situation prevailed as long as the audience remained the primary economic support of publications. When media became more and more dependent on advertising, competition was intensified because the financial base was much more restricted. (The price of newspaper and magazine subscriptions must be set in relation to advertising revenues. *Business Week* and *Forbes* compete for readers with newsletters and publishers of business books.)

A newspaper, magazine, or television station that expands its advertising generally increases its share of a more or less fixed volume of expenditures that has already been allocated to its particular type of medium in its market. However, the demand for advertising in a given medium is not totally inelastic. Media forms (billboards and radio, for example) compete with each other, and advertising competes with other forms of promotion and selling.

The advent of a new medium can rapidly enlarge the total volume of advertising investments. Television did this in the 1950s as cable did in the 1980s. Television captured audiences directly from other media as well as advertising revenues from some of them. It destroyed the giant mass magazines. Its advertising surge allowed it to attract talent and thus reinforced its audience growth. Television cut radio listening hours in half and turned radio into a quite different form of communication in format and spirit. Television's preeminence reduced yearly per capita film attendance (among individuals of 10 and over) from 34.7 after World War II to 4.5 in 1992 and brought major shifts in the content, style, and promotional methods of film-making. The consequences of advertisers' strategies are ultimately felt in all media, not just in those that actually carry advertising. This interaction is, in fact, the salient attribute of today's media system.

The Growth of Multimedia Enterprise

It is now common in the United States for the same company to own different media, even competing ones. Independent local newspapers as well as newspaper chains were among the first to acquire radio franchises in the 1920s. Those who missed this opportunity were often prompt to apply for television station licenses when the time came and to start up cable systems later. Newspapers owned or controlled 31% of all the radio stations in 1940 and 79% of all the television stations in 1953. The great growth in the number of stations reduced these proportions to small minorities. (The pattern was modified by FCC rules that restrict common ownership of stations and newspapers in the same market, except where "grandfathered" in before the rules were adopted.)

The early dispersion of newspaper interests into broadcasting provided the prototype for today's multimedia conglomerates. The first of these—years before broadcasting—may have been the newspaper empire of William Randolph Hearst, who went multimedia when he started *Motor* magazine in 1903. Hearst had more than merely sentimental links to Hollywood. His Cosmopolitan Films made theatrical movies. Beginning in 1911, the company produced newsreels, in association with Pathé, Warner, and other distributors. *Time's* Henry Luce also became involved with newsreels and film documentaries. Magazine publishers (like Time Inc. and Meredith) were early entrants into television, and cable attracted every type of existing media entrepreneur.

When Japanese electronics firms entered the American entertainment business to assure a supply of products for the output of their manufacturing plants, they were not the first to go this route. From its very origins, film production was linked to theatrical real estate. One Hollywood pioneer, William Fox, combined film and vaudeville turns in his theaters in 1908. He said, in a 1915 press release,

> "when I entered, actively, the producing field of motion pictures, I was actuated by a double motive. The so-called features that I had been selecting with all the care possible for my theaters did not fill my ideals of the highest standard possible in motion pictures. Therefore, I was fairly driven, in the interest of my patrons, and also as a secondary consideration in the belief that there was an immense demand for really good pictures, into the manufacturing end of the business.[17]

Multimedia enterprises continue to have different individual balances of media interest, but these undergo wide swings as they diversify their investments. Financial complementarity led magazine publishers like Time Inc., McGraw-Hill, Hearst, and Dell to become active in book publishing. (Books are a relatively slow-turnover business and require substantial investment, while periodicals have a rapid cash flow.)[18]

The merger of Time Inc. and Warner Communications in 1989 created a $12 billion corporation with vast holdings in film, television, cable, books, and magazines. It culminated a lengthy history of growing interdependence among what used to be entirely different communications formats.

The rationale behind the creation of these media empires, with their increasingly international character, lies in the assertion that the traditional dividing lines among individual forms of communication no longer apply in a world where computer technology has blurred the distinctions between broadcasting and print. CEO of a very large multimedia company:

> The delivery systems have changed in a major way and are going to continue to change because of technological breakthroughs. But the play is still the thing. The one thing that governs all of them is the content. By and large, when you talk about

programming choices—and they're more entertainment than information, though the two are mixed together—the biggest difference is in the way they're delivered. We have to be able to adapt to whatever are the delivery systems. That's why we have made the software of cable programming our highest priority. I don't mean to be pejorative about the people who manage the channels, the cable systems—but the content is the main thing.[19]

This philosophy lies behind the diversification of many large media companies. Paramount's 900-film library was one of the principal spoils in the battle that ultimately led to its acquisition by Viacom. Before the merger, Viacom already owned the MTV, Nickelodeon and Showtime cable networks. Paramount was in the film, book, and television businesses and owned theme parks, as well as Madison Square Garden, the New York Knicks basketball, and New York Knickerbockers hockey teams (which Viacom put up for sale).

Capital Cities/ABC moved beyond broadcasting to build an important newspaper chain and magazine group; Rupert Murdoch's News Corporation, originally a newspaper company, built a fourth U.S. television network (Fox) and satellite television systems in Europe and Asia. In the United States, Murdoch owned a magazine empire (part of which he relinquished to lighten his debt load) and had 55% of the market for preprinted newspaper grocery coupon supplements (FSIs, or free-standing inserts).[20] News Corporation's worldwide book publishing empire included such well-known imprints as Harper & Row, Collins (later merged again into HarperCollins), Scott, Foresman, Little Brown, and J.B. Lippincott. A press report announced that

> Harper's children's book authors may soon contribute to books for the Scott, Foresman & Co. division, which puts out textbooks; Collins marketing practices that doubled British sales of Agatha Christie mysteries are being applied to Harper paperbacks in America.[21]

In the wheeling and dealing financial markets of the 1980s, media properties were often "in play," and ownership turned over rapidly. The Marvel Entertainment Group, a leading comic book publisher, was purchased in 1986 by New World Pictures, (once described as "the Rent-a-Wreck of independent studios") for $50 million and resold to the Andrews Group three years later for $82 million.

The affairs of the corporate giants were themselves interwoven. Hearst teamed with Dow Jones to coproduce *Smart Money* magazine. Time Warner and Sony were joint participants in Digital Cable Radio, a system tied to pay cable television. Time Warner and Tele-Communications Inc. (TCI) (which between them provided service to 30% of cable households) collaborated on a new venture in interactive television. (TCI was a partner of Microsoft in an interactive cable test.) Time Warner also joined AT&T and Matsushita in another interactive TV company (3DO) and was a partner of Silicon Graphics in a third such enterprise. News Corporation's Fox and General Electric's NBC were linked in Sky Cable, a billion-dollar venture using satellite delivery of 108 channels via a small receiving dish developed by General Motors' Hughes Communications. (Sky Cable was also a British partner of Viacom's Nickelodeon.) Hughes, through its subsidiary DirecTV, also began satellite service in the

United States, with up to 150 channels (including 70 movie channels). TCI responded to this competitive threat by getting into the satellite broadcasting business itself.[22]

NBC's cable ventures already included CNBC (which swallowed the Financial News Network), an interest in the Arts and Entertainment network, and Sportchannel America. The company was heavily dependent upon the good will of cable systems operators like TCI's president, John Malone, who had earlier successfully kept CNBC out of New York and other markets.[23] Robert Wright, NBC's president, acknowledged in hearings before the Senate Communications Subcommittee that, because of pressure from TCI and other cable operators, his company had dropped its original plan to make CNBC a news network in competition with CNN.[24] In another indication of TCI's operating style, it dropped Lifetime (at that time partly owned by Viacom) from its systems when Viacom tried to buy the Learning Channel. The Channel was then bought by Discovery (partly owned by TCI) at a lower price than Lifetime had offered for it.

TCI had a 23% interest in Turner Broadcasting's CNN, of which Time Warner owned 25%. TCI was also a major stockholder in Black Entertainment Television, American Movie Classics, the Discovery Channel and the Fashion Channel. TCI owned United Artists Theaters, but sold them in 1992 to Merrill Lynch, from whom in turn it bought a half-interest in the Teleport Communications Group, which was developing new local telecommunications services to compete with the phone companies. Time Warner and Cox Enterprises each had a one-sixth share.

In the joint ventures, capital participations, and other uses of capital by media companies, traditional notions of competitiveness no longer seemed to apply, as ownership linkages became more and more convoluted. Universal and Paramount each owned half of the USA network; Viacom's Paramount owned the Madison Square Garden network.

These might be considered reasonable combinations, like the common ownership of movie theaters and studios that was ended by a court-ordered consent decree in 1949 and reestablished decades later. (Matsushita's MCA owned 49% of Cineplex Odeon, the country's second-largest theater chain.) But multimedia companies also combined bizarre and incongruent elements. Time Warner owned *Mad* magazine and DC Comics. It was linked to Polygram, owned by N.V. Philips and Siemens. Time Warner also had first refusal rights to buy management control of Turner Broadcasting, under certain circumstances. A Time Warner subsidiary, Media One, was engaged in in-store promotion. Time Inc. CEO Reg Brack boasted, "we're talking about being in the business of slicing cheese."[24]

MTV's owners, Viacom (which had originally been part of CBS), joined Robert Maxwell and British Telecom to start MTV Europe and eventually took over full ownership. The French publishers, Hachette, which had acquired a substantial group of American magazines (including *Woman's Day*), originally owned by CBS, merged with Matra, a maker of missiles.

The entry of the telephone companies into cable added to the tangle of interests. U.S. West, the Denver-based regional Bell operating company with a local telephone monopoly in fourteen Western states, entered into an agreement to purchase a $2.5 billion, 25.5% stake in Time Warner Entertainment. Two fifths of this amount was to be invested in upgrading Time Warner's cable systems to carry a variety of electronic information and entertainment services. U.S. West also joined the Digital Equipment Corporation in a test of video-on-demand technology, in which Bell Atlantic had already pioneered with a "Video Dial Tone."

BellSouth bought into a cable system in Las Vegas owned by Prime Cable, which also had a minority investment in a cable system in Atlanta, where Bell-South is located—thus raising the possibility of a regulatory problem. BellSouth and Cox Enterprises joined in an electronic classified advertising venture. The *Los Angeles Times* and Pacific Telesis jointly began a shopping information service that was to include both news and advertising. Pacific Telesis also announced that it would be investing $15 billion over five years to modernize its California distribution system to permit delivery of television and high speed data services, and brought legal action to challenge the restriction against telephone companies entering the cable business. Southwestern Bell bought two cable systems in the Washington area.

Other organizations rooted outside the media business have become important, including companies that are themselves big advertising clients. As this is written in 1994 (though the specific facts change almost daily), American Express owned *Travel and Leisure* magazine, which Time Warner contracted to publish. Xerox used to be a publisher; IBM still was (the New York Times Company produces two magazines for it under a management contract). IBM was engaged in joint ventures with NBC (Numedia, combining text and video for computer access) and with Blockbuster Entertainment (a scheme to permit films, music, and books to be produced in the store as compact discs for sale or rental from computerized files). IBM was also working with Bell South and six large newspaper chains to develop an electronic news service.

In 1990, the Hearst Corporation bought RJR Nabisco's 20% share of the cable sports network ESPN. The following year, Kohlberg, Kravis, Roberts, which controlled RJR Nabisco, also controlled a new media company, K-III, which purchased Murdoch's American magazine group, including such important titles as *Seventeen* and *New York* (but not *TV Guide*, which Murdoch retained). K-III controlled the nation's largest color magazine printing house and was planning a billion-dollar investment in cable systems. Lawrence Tisch's Loew's Corporation owned not only CBS but the Loew's hotel chain, Lorillard tobacco company, and Bulova Watch. Ronald Perelman controlled both Revlon and New World Communications, a large television station group in which Murdoch's Fox network requires a half-billion dollar interest. The Seagram Company (which also owned 24.3% of Du Pont) had bought 5.7% of Time Warner and was planning to increase its share to 15%.

The process of concentration was accelerated—in every media field, from motion pictures to daily newspapers—by ever-increasing capital requirements, which result from keener competition for scarce talent and from more complex technology. As economic risks rise, the advantage grows for organizations large and diversified enough to manage them comfortably.

The rising costs of production and distribution make it tough for newcomers to break in. Substantial investments are required to generate audiences, and audience levels must be sustained during an extensive trial period before the viability of an enterprise is assured. Escalating expenses put pressure on profit margins and demand huge resources—which is where giant outsiders like Sony or Matsushita enter the picture.

On the other side of the ledger, the growth of cable and the VCR introduced large sums of fresh capital and powerful new competitive forces into the programming market and vastly increased the value of talent of every kind. The result has been huge payments to film stars and directors, to university athletic departments and baseball players, to authors of what are forecast to be bestselling novels (destined ultimately to be filmed). The television entertainer Bill Cosby earned an estimated $115 million in the 1988–89 season. The comedian David Letterman was induced to shift from NBC to CBS by an offer of $270,000 a week.[25] High fees paid to stars escalate everyone else's wage demands, since the humblest technicians (and their unions) gauge their own expectations to what is obtained by performers they see at close range, and for whom they do not share the public's awe.

A typical hour of prime-time television programming in 1993 cost between $1 and $1.5 million to produce. Half of this amount represented "above the line" charges for talent and variable production expenses. The cost of making a typical film went from $9 million in 1980 to nearly $23 million in 1990, and the typical cost of advertising it went from $3 million to about $8 million. Disney's "Dick Tracy" cost $100 million to make and promote in 1990, with a budget split almost evenly between production costs and the expense of advertising and publicity. Still, it barely covered its costs, leading Jeffrey Katzenberg, the chairman of the company, in a widely circulated "internal memorandum," to question whether the day of the blockbuster film was over. (It was not.) As budgets expanded, the risk factor in film-making increased. Symptomatic of this risk, the individual studios' shares of the total theatrical film market have fluctuated wildly, reflecting the success or failure of individual movies.[26]

The corporate affairs of Hollywood leave their impression on the television audience. Even before the change in the financial and syndication rules, the networks were commissioning more and more of their own films, instead of relying on the studios' film libraries. (Their repertory had already been shown so often that the public had become bored.) While NBC showed thirty-five theatrical films in the 1979–80 season, it showed only thirteen in 1991–1992.

The nine major film studios still filled about 70% of the networks' prime-time schedule. Programming made by independent producers occupied only 14% in 1990, compared with 57% two years earlier. Since many of the same companies that own the big studios also own cable and satellite channels, these represent outlets for the old-formula output rather than for innovation. Package deals that the networks make for popular programs often include more uncertain new offerings from the same leading producers.[27] Thus the interactions of media organizations profoundly affect the assignments given to creative people as well as the messages that come through to the public.

The Concentration of Media Power

The concentration of power in fewer and fewer hands is part of a wider pattern that extends throughout American business, but it carries special dangers in the media's realms of culture and politics. Apart from the possibility of subverting media content to sinister and selfish forces, concentration encourages bureaucratic decision-making and discourages new ideas. Most media executives appeared to accept this condition philosophically, perhaps complacently.

A senior Hollywood executive:

> What's happening in this business is happening in all other businesses. Every business ultimately winds up concentrated.[28]

CEO of a large multimedia company:

> I would rush to have an economic way of having two or more economic survivors of every medium.[29]

Corporate giants in media, like others throughout American industry, are driven by the logic of the financial markets rather than by the philosophy that propels the individual media components of their businesses. This motivation creates particular problems in the case of activities that depend on creative talent, as media do.

Multimedia company CEO:

> Even though we all make the arguments that the products haven't suffered for it, they have. Look at newspapers. I know that they haven't improved as the competition has disappeared. While concentration adds to the ability to hire talent, it also carries a tendency of not developing as well or as quickly as you might like. . . . If we ever get to the point where medium-size or smaller innovators can't crack the market, you're going to see a lowering of quality. That's already happened in the field of videocassettes, because it's so dominated by the studios.[30]

Capital markets seek a high rate of financial growth that often can be obtained only through expansion and acquisition. Companies are considered to be financially healthy only as long as they get bigger year after year, and investors tend to judge them by their earnings, without particular regard to the quality of their products or services.

It is not necessarily efficiency that makes companies big. In the merger and acquisitions boom financed by junk bonds in the 1970s and 80s, smaller companies within every media field were swallowed by larger ones. The mergers and acquisitions frenzy of the 1980s was driven by arbitrageurs who bought and sold securities to take advantage of the swings that occurred from moment to moment, and by institutional investors who typically reviewed their holdings every quarter. The pension funds that dominate the financial markets are run by professional managers who think of the yield from investments in terms of the daily quotes and cannot be concerned with long-term payout. The merger process was fostered in the United States by tax regulations that set management's eyes on capital gains more than on earnings.

Between December 1986 and October 1988, twelve deals were made for over $11 billion of publishing properties. The manipulations involved in the transfers of media ownership sometimes were extremely convoluted, but ended in extraordinary gains for some resourceful or lucky parties. The Time Warner merger brought vast fortunes to the individuals who brought it about, but left the shareholders saddled with a debt of $11 billion.

Businesses have always been operated to earn money, but in the past this primary motive was often moderated by vestiges of the tradition of craftsmanship. Rightly or wrongly, most firms have been run on the theory of the better mousetrap: The world would beat a path to your door if you really had a product that was superior to the competition's. In the long run, profits would follow if you did very well what you set out to do and what you tried very hard to do better.

The world of deal-making for capital gains works on different principles. Artisanry and professionalism, the pride of doings things right and doing them well — these matter only insofar as they can be converted into bargaining chips. They have no independent utility or value. Deal-makers, to be successful, must be totally indifferent to the character of the businesses they buy or sell, except insofar as it determines risks and profits. Instant gratification on the bottom line takes precedence over the kind of orderly growth that requires a sustained investment in people, plants, and promotion. These are the elements that can easily be cut back, and the effects may not be felt until much later.

Of course, there is another point of view on what I have been saying. It can be argued that corporate raiding, merging, spin-offs, cutbacks and all the other accoutrements of short-run, bottom-line capital-gains thinking are a free market's way of maximizing efficiency and making economic resources more productive. This may be true in a society that sets no limits or rules of the game. But in a financial market that is both highly regulated and constrained by public policy, short-term success is often determined by the ability to maneuver to take advantage of the tax laws, not by the rules of efficiency or productivity.

Excellence and responsibility in mass communication require innovation, and innovation is born of competition. As power moves into fewer hands, it is harder for newcomers to break into the media world. Financial backing from the giant conglomerates has become indispensable to many new media ventures — like the Arts and Entertainment cable network (started by Capital Cities/ABC) and other cable operations. The publisher of *Sazz*, a new magazine aimed at high-income black women, sought venture capital, but could not get it until Fairchild Publishing (also owned by Capital Cities/ABC) came in as a partner. The corporation's knowhow then became a reassuring inducement to other investors. The ability of the giants to make risky investments has thus helped some fledgling media entrepreneurs; their dominance may also have inhibited others from trying their luck.

There are centrifugal forces at work that offset the tendencies toward concentration. In the past, new technology shattered and altered established forms of media power. Such developments as cable, video recording, desktop publishing and computerized information systems admit new people and new companies onto the scene — in spite of every preemptive effort by existing organizations that see their positions threatened. By opening up additional channels of communication, new media enhance diversity and force changes in the content and style of existing media.[31] But this process may not be taking place fast enough to offset the steady march of the giants.

Before the emergence of Murdoch's Fox network as a serious competitor, television had always been dominated by the three major networks that began in radio. As their market share slipped, network television offered an exception to the trend toward growing concentration. However, the broadcast networks have become significant forces in cable networking too, and concentration continues in the other important components of broadcasting. In 1972, the ten top multisystem operators represented 36% of cable households. By 1993 their share had risen to 54%.

The Hollywood studios (20th Century Fox, Warner, Disney, and King World) dominate the $3.4 billion television program syndication market (which sells to stations and cable networks). Their shows stay on the air longer, making it harder for smaller producers to get a footing. Block booking, which links new, untested programs to purchases of established ones, reinforces the hold of the larger companies. Roger Colloff, general manager of WCBS-TV, describes it as "a business of big boys, a business of haves and have nots."[32]

• The four leading book publishers account for about a fourth of the revenues in a $21 billion U.S. industry.[33] Six major record companies have 80% of the worldwide $30 billion market for recorded music (of which $9 billion is in the United States).[34] Much of the raw video news footage used by the American networks as well as by television broadcasters throughout the world came from two sources.[35]

Concentration has had overall effects on the media system, but it also brought individual companies to dominance in particular media. Time Warner had 21% of the $7 billion total of magazine advertising revenues.[36] Warner had 29% of the recorded music business and 18% of the motion picture business. Warner and Disney dominated children's TV. Through its Marvel and DC Comics, Time Warner had 85% of comic book newsstand sales and 67% of sales through specialty stores. Between them Time Warner and TCI owned cable systems that served a third of all cable households.

• Although three-fifths of the country's commercial radio stations lost money in 1991,[37] fifty accounted for half the industry's aggregate profits.
• In the music industry, half of the recordings were produced by affiliates of consumer electronics firms, and six companies had 96% of the sales on *Billboard*'s Top 200 list. The big record companies had acquired many of the smaller labels, and the top four firms had most of the hits. One industry observer commented, "It is cheaper to buy the entire company than individual artists and components."[38] This concentration had striking consequences for musical styles and tastes, since fewer producers tended toward greater similarity of output.[39]
• As the large media conglomerates entered the retail video business, chain management, with its computerized inventories and leveling tendencies, promised to homogenize the video sales and rental market, much as had happened in retail bookstores. (Blockbuster Entertainment, with 15% of the video rental market in its 3,500 stores, entered the film production business to create its own source of supply for predictably formulaic sellers.)

• The cinema advertising business was heavily concentrated. By 1993, Screenvision, a 6,600 screen theater network in 205 markets, accounted for 35% of the nation's 17,500 first-run movie screens.

In the case of almost every medium, a handful of companies dominate the market. More of them now do this on a worldwide scale.

Globalization

The worldwide influence of U.S. media keeps expanding, but they are increasingly parts of international empires.[40] The globalization of media existed long before their actual ownership crossed national boundaries. The Canadian Roy Thomson was the first notable press lord whose empire spanned the ocean, but long before him, British book publishers like Macmillan operated through subsidiaries in other English-speaking countries. Both the British *Daily Mail* and the *New York Herald* established Paris editions before the turn of the last century. Tauchnitz's paperback books, printed in Germany, were published in a variety of languages and distributed throughout Europe before the First World War.

Books have been translated for centuries, in pirated and authorized editions, but motion pictures were really the first mass medium to attract vast international audiences to creative expressions in their original form. Silent films spoke a universal language, and the idioms of Hollywood slapstick, romance, and Westerns were well established around the world long before the advent of sound made it necessary to add subtitling and dubbing to assure good communication. Charlie Chaplin's tramp and Mickey Mouse were familiar figures everywhere, years before the Beatles, Elvis Presley, or Batman.

The Associated Press, CNN, The New York Times News Service, the *Wall Street Journal*, and the *International Herald Tribune* are strong influences on the news received by elites everywhere. In recent years, television channels have multiplied in countries that were formerly limited to a few state-provided choices, thus increasing the dependence on American film and video libraries to fill air time. This very dependence has produced reactions, in the form of politically motivated restrictions, like those that Canada has long imposed on U.S. magazines and television programs and that the European Union now places on television programs. (Ratification of the General Agreement on Trade and Tariffs was jeopardized in 1993 by a dispute over a French tax on American films.)

Entertainment is the nation's second largest export. The heavy use of American films and programming in television around the world largely represents a one-way flow. (Foreign films have only a 2% share of the U.S. market—down from 7% two decades ago. By contrast, they represent over half the films shown in culturally nationalistic France.) By 1994, overseas distribution accounted for half of Hollywood's theatrical revenues, and the economics of production were increasingly international. According to Harvey Shepherd, president of Warner Brothers Television, "the foreign market is the difference between whether you make an hourlong show or no."[41] Although many British television programs have been part of the staple fare on American public television, they have never won the kind of mass audience in the United States that American TV shows command overseas, even without a language barrier.

Globalized media encompass not merely the simple export of films, television shows, and international editions of the *Reader's Digest*, *Time*, and *Elle*, but the planned creation of interlocking media production facilities designed to supply the growing worldwide appetite for entertainment and information.

* To illustrate the cross-national interdependencies of a global entertainment company—in England Murdoch took the *Sun*, which he acquired at a bargain price, from a circulation of 700,000 to 3.5 million, with the help of his bare-breasted page-3 girls. The *Sun* and the national Sunday *News of the World* earned about £20 million a year before Murdoch defied their entrenched trade unions and moved their production facilities to a modern plant. Annual profits rose to £155 million and made possible his purchase of the Metromedia stations and *TV Guide* in the United States. Murdoch took on American citizenship in order to meet the legal requirements to create a U.S. broadcasting empire. (There was no comparable barrier to foreign ownership of newspapers; he already owned the *New York Post*, which he was forced to sell in 1988—when he acquired a New York television station as part of a deal with Metromedia—but was permitted to reacquire in 1993.)

Murdoch's rival, the ill-fated Robert Maxwell, had established a strong American publishing presence and a satellite transmission service for newspaper advertising even before his dramatic takeover of Macmillan in 1988 and of the New York *Daily News* in 1991. European firms—Elsevier, Springer, Bertelsmann, as well as Hachette— were major forces on the book and magazine publishing scenes.

With the acquisition of 20th Century Fox by Murdoch's Australian-based News Corporation, of Columbia Pictures Entertainment by Sony, of MCA's Universal by Matsushita, and of MGM-Pathé by the French bank Crédit Lyonnais, Warner, Paramount, and Disney remained the only major Hollywood studios in American hands.

* Sony Pictures Entertainment owned two major film studios—Columbia and TriStar and CBS Records was renamed Sony Music. Sony was accused of "buying the soul of America"—verbiage that echoed the xenophobic protests in other countries against domination by American media. Sony spent an estimated $800 million to buy out producers Jon Peters and Peter Guber from their Warner Brothers contract.[42] "Far from taking over, the Japanese are being mugged," said *The Economist*[43] citing the extravagances of the film studios' American managements. Similarly, MGM added to the severe financial woes of its new French owner.
* The purchase of MCA by Japan's Matsushita Electric Industrial Company in 1990 meant that over a third of the three big networks' prime-time schedule was produced by foreign-owned companies. (MCA's president, Sidney Sheinberg, himself an attorney: "At MCA, litigation is a profit center."[44]) Matsushita's acquisition of MCA raised questions about the possible censorship of films and books in deference to the new owners' sensibilities. It was pointed out[45] that Japanese media routinely ignore such subjects as Japanese atrocities in World War II, the power of right-wing political groups, and the existence of an outcaste group (the *burakumin*). Matsushita's

president, Akio Tanii, "visibly agitated," refused to answer a question as to whether the company would permit MCA's Universal Studios to make films that might be interpreted as being critical of Japan. Subsequently, significant alterations were made in the script of a Universal film based on the travails of an American baseball player hired by a Japanese team. MCA also owned G.P. Putnam's, which had acquired Grosset & Dunlap, Berkely, and other publishers, and published some of the most popular current fiction. The United States was beginning to encounter some of the same anxieties that other countries had experienced for years in the face of what nationalists termed American "media imperialism."

Behind the expansion of all the global empires has been the assumption that public appetites for media information and entertainment, almost boundless, are fueled by growing economic power and by a universal and intense desire for greater choice. A parallel assumption is that advertising, the primary support of the media system, will continue to grow at a similar pace.

Synergy, Software, and Conflicts of Interest

The growth of the media conglomerates reflects a conviction that creative products can now have extended lives that see them cycle from one media form to another and on—as we have seen—into nonmedia forms like toys, novelties, and even food. Large expenditures on film talent can be justified by the secondary value of spin-off books and recordings. The underlying principle is that the transfer of symbolic messages across media boundaries permits a "synergy" that makes the whole larger and more profitable than the sum of its separate parts. However, media managements do not universally share an enthusiasm for the idea.
CEO of a large multimedia company:

> The part about synergy is baloney. I don't have to buy the company to do a deal. The things they think will happen mostly don't. Or they would happen anyway.[46]

CEO of a major media company:

> We haven't found any synergy, not between newspapers and cable systems, on the one hand, and magazines and books, on the other. Until someone actually affects the cross-usage of material, the whole process is either the use of the mechanics—like a distribution system—in common or creative material in common. In neither have you seen anything done yet by anyone, including those who own movie companies and studios. It's a grand concept, but none of us have seen it work yet.[47]

Regardless of such expressions of skepticism, the notion of synergy seemed firmly established as part of conventional media management wisdom. The central concept behind all this movement is "software" (described as "the key to growth," by a top manager of an expanding international media empire).
CEO of broadcast station group:

> Software is the name of the game. Hollywood's going to win no matter what.[48]

"Software," adopted from the realm of computers, is now universally used within the multimedia companies to describe the whole range of information and entertainment they produce. The analogy is an apt one. Computer software refers, not to the actual content—the data and words that the computer hardware manipulates—but rather to the instructions that activate the machinery and enable it to respond to the user's will. Software is, by definition, a matter of means rather than ends; it is impersonal, and it is fungible. It imposes a common order and system to serve a variety of purposes. Its only meaning resides in its ability to facilitate the management of meaning.

The common use of this neologism reflects disregard, perhaps even an unconscious contempt, for the content of communication. It reduces that content to a mere instrumentality for the achievement of corporate goals. It suggests an indifference to style and style's dependence on the modality of a particular media form. The great varieties of media content—mundane, stirring, evocative, or profound—are reduced to a common denominator of "input" to the "hardware"—the presses, transmitters, and studios that have traditionally been the objects of media investment. This has inevitable consequences both for the motivations of media producers and for the character of what they turn out.

CEO of a large multimedia company:

> I think we are failing to produce people who really love the business in the way they used to. The mobility of people plus the ability to stay with one company leads to a loss of quality and of the satisfaction that these people get out of the job, rather than just making a living at it. Living and dying with every line we write—that's not there. That's giving rise to the commoditization of advertising agencies and advertisers. The buyers see us merely as numbers. And our people don't respond. The unique editorial proposition is still what this business is all about. We haven't got that feeling for it any more. It's partly a function of the computer. In our training program, which is the best there is, they're talking about the statistics of the business rather than the feeling of the business. I would change that if I changed anything.[49]

Corporate ownership changes the traditional way in which publications and productions are regarded. They are no longer creative efforts; they are "products." In Hollywood, stars, directors, and scripts are "elements." The mere nomenclature arouses resentment from those who are responsible for producing ideas. Editors protested indignantly when one of their number, The New York Times Company's Seymour Topping, referred to newspapers as "properties."[50]

But media were indeed being treated interchangeably with other business properties. Twentieth Century Fox (with its profits from "Star Wars") and Universal (with profits from "Jaws") invested in Coca-Cola bottling plants.[51] Coca-Cola in turn bought Columbia Pictures and sold it to Sony, which already owned Columbia Records.

Not all attempts by multimedia companies to venture into other types of enterprises met with success. Playboy's clubs and casinos ended in disaster; its pay video channels had a high nonrenewal rate. Harcourt Brace Jovanovich at one point owned a chain of fish and chip restaurants as well as Sea World theme parks, which it sold to

Anheuser Busch in 1989. Overextended, HBJ gave up its publishing base in New York City and eventually was bought by General Cinema, which owned not only theaters but the Nieman Marcus department stores. (It changed the name back to Harcourt Brace, sharply cut back its trade publishing, and rechristened itself Harcourt General.)

Diversification raised questions of interest conflicts, as in the case of film studios and theaters.

A film distributor executive:

> If the studio that owns us tried to play only their pictures in our theaters, the Justice Department would object. It wouldn't be a prudent thing to do anyway. Suppose we had a string of bad product, we would be up the lake. Having more sources spreads the potential loss. These operations aren't going to be as integrated as they were in the past.[52]

Cost efficiencies are greater if media are able to seek out production facilities from any source, and profits are greater if production houses are not tied down to clients in the same corporate family. Time Warner's former CEO, Steven Ross, denied that any unit of his company would be forced to give preferential treatment to another: "It would be incredibly corrosive to tell [subsidiaries] what they should buy."

But the problem of balancing contradictory business interests is less acute than the congruity of business interests with professional ones. As conglomerates extended their operations beyond entertainment to encompass news media, the compatibility of corporate profit and independent journalistic judgments was inevitably called into question. This issue is raised when large regulated public utilities like the phone companies enter the news and information business. When an enormous consumer advertiser like General Electric is also a principal defense contractor, this should cause concern about its power to influence media content, even if it were not also the owner of NBC.

At the time of its merger with Warner, Time Inc.'s editor-in-chief, Jason McManus, addressed the charge that the company's publications would be used to promote its entertainment products:

> Such prostitution would destroy any news publication, any news organization. It reminds me of Jesse Helms's bizarre notion that if he took over CBS, he could shape its news in his own image. Perhaps he could, but the result would be a fresh definition of a Pyrrhic victory. Soon no one credible would be working for him and no one would be watching.[53]

To counteract concern that influence might be brought to bear on its editors, the PR director of *Time* came to the support of his new chairman: "Steve Ross doesn't even read *Time* magazine. It's a piddling part of the business." (Though allegedly beneath the boss's notice, *Time* carried more pages of advertising in 1990 than any other magazine.)

In spite of these impeccable utterances, Time Inc. managing editors, like other executives, were required to sign a pledge "not at any time [to] denigrate, ridicule or intentionally criticize the Company or any of its subsidiaries or affiliates, or any of their respective products."[54] McManus continued to maintain that this pledge did not inhibit the staff's freedom of expression.[55] *Time* magazine's critics were soon reportedly horrified by front-office pressure to be kind to products of the corporation's entertainment divisions; however, *Time*'s review of Warner Books' sequel to *Gone With the Wind* said, "frankly, it's not worth a damn."[56] This honest judgment could be tolerated within a large, complex company. It did not, after all, threaten any vital interest. Time Inc. editors were compensated on the basis of the magazine division's overall profitability, and thus had every incentive to temper their professional pride with awareness of profit and loss.

The Changed Goals of Media Management

Multimedia enterprises stifle innovation; they also stimulate it. Infusing similar or even identical value guidelines throughout all parts of the media system can discourage differentiation and unconventional ideas. To the contrary, the heightened rapidity of movement and exchange fosters cross-fertilization, adaptation of concepts, and shifts of perspective. The verdict as to effects must be a mixed one.

CEO of a large multimedia company, who formerly headed one of the media divisions:

> Neither people nor techniques travel as well as you would expect from medium to medium. We have done it successfully, but it's been more difficult than you would suspect.[57]

The same executive acknowledges the emotional strains faced by a manager who lacks familiarity with what specialists in his operating divisions know intimately:

> I simply cannot use my long career in one medium to understand the others. You can't get people to follow you or respond to your leadership unless you're sufficiently understanding of the business they're in. You have to know the complexities. You can, if you put the time into it, master all these businesses by reading and by visiting the installations, being a part of the operations. You have to make up your mind to do it, because it comes out of your own time, on Sundays and evenings. It comes out of your hide. Because of that, it inevitably shortens the tenure of people in top positions, if not their lives. The track you're on pulls you faster than if you were running a single-media company. There are two losses there. Undoubtedly there's a price paid in personal time. Also in the time you have to spend with people and to take a more deliberate approach in managing people. Everything has to be done at a more accelerated pace. There's an inefficiency that goes with that. Each business is managed independently. The kind of relationships that I once had with individual colleagues are hard to maintain in this kind of a life. In a creative business you have to be very careful about that.[58]

The ability to sense and respond to audience preferences is critical to the success of media enterprises so long as they face competition. In a monopoly situation, that sensitivity atrophies, if a medium (like a daily newspaper or a classical music radio station) is the only one in its market and nothing else represents an acceptable substitute.

The management of almost any kind of business can swathe its naked profit goals in a cocoon of pious public relations platitudes about its important social functions. In the media business such utterances are apt to reflect the actual beliefs, or illusions, of those who vent them.

ABC's founder, Leonard Goldensohn:

> I fear that one of the most insidious byproducts of the current merger mania may be the loss of a sense of stewardship, a value to which those of us in broadcasting have always been acutely sensitive. Because our business is more than a business. It is a public trust.[59]

Samuel Goldwyn may have been in the tradition of P. T. Barnum; and William Randolph Hearst, in that of Tom Paine—men in love with the words and visions they assembled and intoxicated by the power that came with control over words and visions that influenced large multitudes of people. It is hard to visualize Henry Luce or William Paley taking the same pleasure out of running garment factories or coal mines as they took from Time Inc. and CBS. Luce, whose will described Time, Inc. as "an enterprise operated in the public interest," lost $50 million in 11 years on *Sports Illustrated*. It seems unlikely that Time Warner, or even Time Inc. in the post-Luce era, would have been that patient or indulgent.

The managers who run today's giant media companies are less and less apt to be impresarios who rose from the professional ranks, and more likely to be business generalists who happened to drift into the media business. Their talent may lie in administration or in their shrewdness as financiers. (Like Time Warner's Steven Ross, who emerged from the shadowy world of funeral parlors, limousine rentals, and parking lots, Rupert Murdoch is an astute spotter of talent and trends and a bold investor. In contrast to Ross, he is also an accomplished journalist.)

In the age of the media corporation, long-range considerations and civic or sentimental interests are seldom tolerated. The top managements of large multimedia enterprises can hardly be expected to share the kind of deep personal involvement in the ethos of an individual medium that characterized the media moguls of another era—shrewd businessmen whose first love was the product of the companies they had built and who may have taken more pride in that product than in the profit (for which they also had a healthy respect).

It is easy to overromanticize such figures and to forget the degree to which the American media business has been beholden to outsiders throughout much of its history. Nineteenth century newspapers were owned by railroads and steel companies, for patently self-serving interests, if not for the money. (The Du Pont company did not sell its Wilmington papers to Gannett until 1978.) Bankers took over the ailing Hollywood studios when the Depression hit. (Producers presented their projects to distributors, who, if agreeable, become guarantors for the bank.[60]) Fleischmann Yeast money bankrolled *The New Yorker*; United Cigar money funded the Columbia Broadcasting System. NBC was originally set up by the electrical manufacturing industry to simulate the sale of radio sets, so that the wheel came full circle when it returned to the arms of General Electric in 1986. ABC, though it started as NBC's Red Network, moved into independent existence as a subsidiary of the Paramount Theater chain. The fact that there is ample historical precedent for the present state of corporate agglomeration in the media industry hardly moderates the need to examine the consequences for how the media are run.

Pressures for Profit: The Book Business

Media enterprises driven by the goal of financial expansion must operate differently from ventures that embody a personal vision—a point to which we shall return in Chapter 10. Media entrepreneurs, like their predecessors, the impresarios in the arts, once could take their chances and exercise their own predilections. The corporate media managements of the present prefer to concentrate on sure winners. Even with the best intentions, impeccable personal taste, and the highest intelligence, professional managers pursuing their rational profit goals must regard the actual content of their companies' output as merely instrumental to those goals.

In past times, media producers motivated by strong creative and professional urges and possessed of sufficient resources were always willing to bankroll ventures and talents in which they believed, confident that their good judgment would eventually triumph. Publisher Kurt Wolff:

> We try to win readers for works which appear to us to be original, of literary merit, and important for the future, no matter whether they are easily understood or not. . . . The effort is what counts; success is not the determining factor. Often it is an accident.[61]

Wolff published Kafka's first book in an edition of 800, of which only half sold in more than 5 years. But he kept publishing more of Kafka's writings. This sort of thing would be almost impossible to bring off in today's American book industry, where takeovers have led to predictable demands for greater efficiency. A book publisher would rather sell more hard copies and fewer paperbacks. Some authors would concur, if the royalties were better; others would prefer to have more people read their books.

Book publishing presents a prime illustration of the disparity between the commercial demands of the market (which mandates the efficiency of concentrating on a small number of bestselling titles) and the public's long-range interest in maintaining diversity. *Books in Print* showed 12,000 U.S. book publishers in 1991, but this business shows the same growth in concentration that characterizes film, television, and periodical publishing. The major players are all familiar: Time Warner, News Corporation, Newhouse, Paramount, Times-Mirror, The New York Times Company, MCA, and Bertelsmann.

Large houses are able to enforce economies by practicing sound management. (Compressing a few letters in the typeface saved the *Encyclopedia Britannica* two lines per page, the equivalent of a whole volume in the complete set.) Business, production, and marketing functions can be shared by all parts of a group, like

Paramount's Simon and Schuster, which produces titles under a number of imprints.[62] As the screws are tightened on budgets, fewer new titles are issued and small imprints owned by large publishers (like Paramount's Atheneum) disappear. Cost-cutting brings personnel changes at the executive level. Inevitably, the growth or imposition of corporate bureaucracies affects the human relationships out of which media creativity is nurtured. Walter Powell writes:

> As publishing houses are integrated into complex corporate structures, communications lines grow longer and the organizational hierarchy becomes steeper. Publishers work at a distance from writers, spending more time maintaining their organization than working on manuscripts.[63]

The editor-in-chief of a small publishing house owned by a conglomerate:

> The main pressures we feel are not pressures for greater profits. They don't even look at the figures on individual titles. What we feel are pressures for growth—to expand and do more books. . . . We cannot sustain growth really, they don't understand that. . . . There may not be any more books of real merit that we can do justice to.[64]

Publisher Kurt Enoch:

> There has been a sort of law: the wider the audience, the less provocative or disturbing to established ideas and taboos the medium has to be. The fundamental problem . . . is thus to achieve a mass audience while preserving the special virtues of books.[65]

Donald Busch, then president of Pocket Books:

> Our job is to survive, so that in the end the printed word and the book will survive. If in order to maintain the book we've got to do certain things, I'm not suggesting we either apologize for or be proud of what we are doing, but we have to be responsive to that audience.[66]

This refrain will become very familiar to us as we proceed. It is not just the imposition of corporate discipline that has transformed the book industry. A 1980 Internal Revenue Service ruling in a 1980 case involving the Thor Power Tool Company significantly affected the nation's cultural and intellectual life. By ruling that the value of inventory can be considered deductible only if it is sold below cost or destroyed, the IRS forced commercial book publishers (though not academic presses) to cut their back lists and to pulp books instead of remaindering them profitably. The net effect was to reduce the number of titles kept in print and to encourage the trend toward distribution and promotion of a limited number of hot titles.

Three other changes in distribution encouraged the process of concentration: the growth of the school market, of book clubs, and of chain bookstores.

• Most of all, book publishing was altered by the growth of huge bookselling chains. Of 1,000 full-service booksellers in the 1950s, only a comparatively small number lasted into the 80s. The two dominant chains, which between them do 62% of the total retail volume, are creations of department store merchants, not bibliophiles. (Waldenbooks was set up by Carter-Hawley-Hale; B. Dalton by Dayton-Hudson.[67]) Concentrated in suburban shopping malls, these firms followed the same business and merchandising rules as other chain retailers, centralizing and standardizing their operations and relying on relatively unskilled sales help. The introduction of "hyper-stores" stocking up to 100,000 titles opened the possibility of broadening reader choice, but it reflected the universal tendency for fewer outlets to handle a large share of the volume.

Chains keep computer records of an author's previous sales and base their orders on these, thus discouraging writers without a track record of great success. They will not keep books on the shelf, in their typical mall stores, for more than three months. This encourages publishers to concentrate on a few bestsellers at a time and to compete avidly for the same famous authors or for the same public personalities to whom reliable ghostwriters can be assigned.[68] As bestseller sales went up into the millions, there was more incentive for large houses to acquire smaller ones in order to get their backlists.

• There was a rising demand for school texts in an era of growing population and heightened educational aspirations.[69] Needless to say, the growth of the school age population has nothing to do with the quality of the textbooks being produced.[70] As the balance has shifted toward text and technical publishing, many trade publishers have almost given up on serious nonfiction books, which usually earn low profits.[71]

• Book clubs were caught up in the trend toward media conglomeration. (Double-day book clubs, owned by Bertelsmann, had several million members in the early 1990s. Time Warner's Book of the Month Club had 1.5 million, plus another 900,000 in affiliate clubs.) Book clubs increasingly develop and publish their own titles, written either by freelancers or by staff writers in their own publishing houses. Book club adoptions, like paperback editions and film or television rights, now make the difference between profit and loss in trade book publishing. And profit and loss in the book business can no longer be calculated except in relation to serialization, adaptation rights, and sponsorship—the elements that make publishing an integral component of the wider media system.

Books, the original mass medium, are still the most influential, because they disseminate, at length, the ideas that change the social order. Corporate concentration in book publishing (in contrast to most media) has not inhibited the dissemination of new ideas, though it has profoundly influenced the way ideas reach the public. In the case of daily newspapers, concentration has more serious consequences, because it hits people, literally, where they live.

Newspaper Chains

The local press gives American communities their individual identity and represents a fundamental source of the public's knowledge and opinions. How have newspapers been victimized by financial maneuvering?

• In 1986 the newspaper publisher Ralph Ingersoll Jr. bought the New Haven newspapers, an old family business, for $185 million on behalf of Mark Goodson, the television producer, under an arrangement that gave Ingersoll a management contract. He folded the evening *Journal-Courier* soon after. Ingersoll bought the *Register* from Goodson for $275 million in 1989, financing the purchase with junk bonds in partnership with Warburg-Pincus, a venture-capital company. By that time the paper's revenues had risen from $55 to $70 million. The following year, after several other publishing ventures soured, Warburg-Pincus took over all of Ingersoll's American properties, including the *Register*. The editorial staff was reduced from 151 employees to 108.[72] Now a smaller staff was producing a weaker product, one paper rather than two. The scale of such operations is relatively new, but the practices themselves are not.

Large newspaper groups own a substantial proportion of American dailies. The biggest 25% of the newspaper publishing companies have had about 80% of the circulation since 1923. Overall, concentration actually fell between 1947 and 1977, though the number of independent papers dropped sharply.[73] The Hearst chain's share of U.S. circulation declined from 10.4% in 1946 to 1.9% in 1992. Gannett, with eighty-one newspapers, had 9.5% of daily circulation.

One cannot generalize about the comparative editorial merits of chain and independent newspapers. (Great newspapers that are often thought of as independent, like *The New York Times*, *Los Angeles Times*, and *Chicago Tribune* have become chain flagships.) Chains have the capacity to attract ambitious individuals of great ability through the promise of ever-greater challenges and opportunities elsewhere. Chain newspapers are often more profitable than independents, in part because of tighter and tougher management methods. (Gannett's national ad rates at one point were 55% higher than those of a matched group of independent papers).[74]

The government has argued in antitrust suits that chains have been able to subsidize dailies that face competition in one market by virtue of their monopoly profits from others. In the case of *United States v. Lima News*, a consent decree enjoined the chain paper from lowering its rates to readers or advertisers, but left open the question of predatory pricing based on this kind of cross-subsidization.[75]

Cross-subsidization also has its positive aspects, as shown in Gannett's continuing support of its money-losing flagship, *USA Today*, which after eleven years, turned its first annual profit in 1993. If nothing else, this tenacity demonstrates that personal egos remain a mighty force in the media business. It also reflects management's appreciation of the paper's large cash flow and an appraisal that it would ultimately turn out to be a winner. In a number of other cases, failing newspapers have been sustained by the publishers' broadcast earnings, out of nostalgia, inertia, or a sense of public responsibility. Privately owned newspaper publishing companies like the Hearst Corporation have kept money-losing papers alive for years, while publicly held companies would have been forced to jettison them early on.

Still other papers have been maintained for political reasons by corporations and individuals in the United States, although not to the degree that is commonplace in the history of European journalism.[76] Backers of the notorious Sun Myung Moon started the *Washington Times* after the death of the conservative *Star*. Compared to the

Washington Post's 812,450 circulation, the *Times* had only 89,500 in 1993, and was losing money at the rate of $35 million a year.[77] Few funding sources exist for such large politically motivated subsidies, leaving second newspapers to sink or swim in the advertising marketplace, and increasing the pressure on them to perform profitably.

In the 1960s, Nick Williams, then the editor of the *Los Angeles Times*, was asked how many people were on his staff, and replied, "I don't have the foggiest idea." Few newspapers, even great ones like the *Times*, can today afford the luxury of operating in disregard of the most elementary economics.

When chains acquire independent newspapers, in case after case, the new ownership slashes the newsroom budget, with deplorable consequences for editorial excellence.[78] A newly appointed publisher in Tennessee was told by his chain owners that his assignment was to increase profits. Asking what the present profit level was, he was told he could not see the books until he took over his new job. When he did, he found that the profit level was already 40%.

Newspaper chain owner Dean Singleton once asserted, "We have debt to pay. Gannett has dividends to pay to stockholders. There's not much difference. We, as a newspaper industry, are making too much money. Our margins are too high, and we're taking too much money out, and we've got to put more money back in." Ralph Ingersoll II agreed. "If we continue to run the 35% to 40% margins that we can achieve, or the 55% margins that Thomson and Donrey can achieve, then we will be liquidating our papers, which is what Gannett has been doing to subsidize *USA Today*."[79] But a few years later, *USA Today* was still in the black and Ingersoll had been forced by his company's heavy debts to give up his American newspaper interests. What was absent, amidst all the commotion, was the voice of the journalist.

The Marxist Explanation

What are we to make of the apparently inexorable process of concentration that concerns us in much of this chapter? In classical Marxist criticism, power over media simply reflects the inevitable impulse of monopoly capitalism. Commercial culture — so goes this line of thought — perpetuates the existing social and economic structure, by making its principles the dominant and unquestioned ideology, suppressing any indications of its shortcomings and impermanence, and lulling the masses of the population into a mindless acceptance of the *status quo*. Thus the entire output of the mass media is being geared, consciously or unconsciously, to serve the ends of the corporate giants who are also the principal advertisers. This process occurs not so much because of the direct attention paid to the vested interests of individual corporations, but as a response to the prevailing interests of the system of which corporations are the principal powers and beneficiaries.

For 150 years, socialist movements, spurred by a revulsion against inequity and exploitation, have rejected capitalist consumer culture. It is ironic that Marxism, a doctrine that stresses the material basis of social behavior, finds the expression of materialistic, acquisitive instincts repellent.

Marxist theory designates as "false consciousness" the adoption of values and beliefs that do not coincide with an individual's "real" social class interests. It follows from this thesis that a media system tied to propertied power must inevitably reflect its dependence, by suppressing information and ideas that might be inimical to the status quo and by actively promulgating the values that would make the masses acquiescent, contented, and ignorant or contemptuous of alternatives to the established order of things.[80] The Marxist sociologist Antonio Gramsci preaches that the culture generally shared by members of a national society actually reflects the "hegemony" imposed by its ruling class, which the masses are induced to accept as natural and right.[81]

The social critics of the Frankfurt School (which flourished at the University of Frankfurt's Institute of Social Research during the Weimar Republic) feel it necessary to distinguish between mass culture and the technologies it uses, which presumably might be dedicated to more worthy ends.[82] Their premise is that the media system acts to debase true culture, whose essence is meaningful communication. Mass culture, they say, coopts and—by implication—corrupts genuine or high culture by making it familiar to everyone. Herbert Marcuse contrasts the "aesthetic dimension" to that of "One-Dimensional Man." Theodor Adorno equates commercial culture with the industrial techniques of mass production:

> The entire practice of the culture industry transfers the profit motive naked onto cultural forms. . . . The autonomy of works of art, which of course rarely ever predominated in an entirely pure form, and was always permeated by a constellation of effects, is tendentially eliminated by the culture industry, with or without the conscious will of those in control.[83]

Adorno once described his shock at hearing a young man whistling the opening bars of Beethoven's Fifth Symphony in a New York subway station. Taken out of its musical context, and reduced in its harmonic dimensions from orchestral volume to the thin, shrill piping of the tune, the theme became something entirely different from what the composer had intended it to be. Yet to the young whistler, the four-chord theme was itself the real thing, the quintessence of the symphony and the embodiment of the composer's creation. The distilled melody known from repeated exposure on radio or recordings represented the symphony for him—not the full and infinitely subtle live orchestral rendition that he had probably never heard. As Adorno's colleague, Leo Lowenthal, puts it,

> If Mozart and Beethoven are played over and over again for a listener who isn't able to appreciate the music, or if they're played as background music in cafes, department stores, restaurants, at the hairdresser's or dentist's, then I fail to see anything particularly valuable in it. . . . As a consequence of the capital structure within which . . . media are used, as a consequence of the political-economic *form*, the entire technological arsenal has been appropriated. The aesthetic and cognitive potential of film, radio and television hardly gets a chance.[84]

The very act of mechanical reproduction, says Walter Benjamin, distorts and destroys the artist's original creative act, and of course the only reason to mass-reproduce a work of art is for commercial profit.[85] One may accept the argument that a copy is not the same as the real thing and still reject the ensuing corollary. Surely the exposure of vast numbers of people to works of art reproduced by mechanical means (printing, film, audio, and video recording) encourages them to seek out the original — which is one reason for the growing attendance at art galleries and live concerts.[86] In any case, the march of technological progress cannot be arrested, and the aesthetic experiences of the future will overwhelmingly be second-hand.

To carry the Marxist argument to its conclusion requires us to put the whole social order in the defendant's box, along with the media system that is its voice. One need not go that far to acknowledge that the charges are so serious and so persistent that they cannot easily be dismissed. There is no rebuttal to the insight that media are part and parcel of whatever social system they serve, and that their content inevitably reflects the values of those in charge. Cultural institutions are necessarily embedded in their surrounding economic and political environment and can never break free of its influence and constraints. However, it is not easy to characterize with sweeping generalizations a society with fragmented and often antagonistic power centers, like the United States, endowed with an intricate media structure that supports channels of diverse expression. The supposition that media content reflects the selfish purposes of the ruling establishment was nowhere more clearly embodied than in the studied efforts at thought control in Communist countries where Marxist ideology was the state religion.

In this chapter, I have examined the concentration of media power as a consequence of the structural changes in the system that increasingly links every aspect of the media themselves. We have noted the ambiguous consequences of this change, as media enterprises mobilize greater resources but are increasingly deflected from the creative impulses of their progenitors. Though the Marxist critique of the media system is acute, it offers no viable alternative. We shall see this clearly as we turn our attention to the system's main source of support — its advertising.

II

ADVERTISING AS THE DRIVING FORCE

3

The Presence of Advertising

Advertising is a major component not only of the media, but of what we see and hear in everyday life. Is there too much of it? No, not from an economic standpoint. The answer might have to be different if we look at the media system in cultural and moral terms. If something is wrong, it is in the way advertising is allocated and managed rather than in the sheer amount of it.

This chapter examines what advertising has to say and how it is said in the assortment of channels that make up the media system. We shall look at advertising's effects on American manners and morals within the scheme of national values in which it is embedded and which it expresses. Key points:

- Advertising epitomizes the spirit of American commercial culture, which ranks material possessions high and assigns them a prominent place in everyday life. But what is advertised is not a mirror image of what is consumed.
- Advertising is a driving force in America's productive market economy; its history is closely linked to that of the mass media.
- It is a pervasive, intrusive element of media content, fragmenting communication and purveying messages that go beyond direct persuasion on behalf of whatever it sells.
- Advertising's hyperbole and distorted world view affect all social and political discourse.
- Advertising encourages us to focus attention on our individual wants and away from the needs we have in common.

Media and the Culture of Consumption

Thus far we have been reviewing the attributes of media, the ways in which they can be classified, and their interdependence. American mass media are *products* of the market for images and ideas and *instruments* of the market for consumer goods and services.

65

The commercial character of media has two different aspects. Commercial communication–advertising–is a component of mass media content and an influence on the character of other media content. In fact, it is to a large degree a prerequisite for media survival. But there are also important implications of the fact that media content is produced for sale, with creative expression subordinated to the demands of the market. The results may often be deplorable; if we consider them so, we must confront the perilous alternative–some form of official patronage–a point to which we shall return in Chapter 11.

The nonmaterial aspects of culture[1] can hardly be differentiated from its physical aspects–the layout of cities and landscapes, architecture, the design of clothing, furniture, and artifacts. All these shapes we impose upon our surroundings convey symbolic meanings and represent information of a kind. They refract the current state of values and beliefs about the purpose of life, the value of human beings, the structure of our relations with one another. Media are designed to do all this more purposefully than the bridges we build and the clothes we wear.

Our culture is commercial because of the central place in it of material goods and their symbols. But the term "commercial culture" can be used in another sense, as well, when applied to the flow of ideas and expression that shapes national character and outlook. By this narrower definition, contemporary American culture is commercial because, overwhelmingly, it is produced for sale to meet marketing requirements. In this respect it differs from the cultures of other places and times, in which expression has been valued either as an end in itself or because of its ability to please a patron. Commercial culture assigns no value or meaning to communications apart from their market value–that is, the price that someone is willing to pay for them.

We ingest ideas, impressions, and tastes through the mass media just as we buy goods and experiences. We embody our personal aspirations in the goods we consume, which save us time and provide personal comforts or aesthetic satisfactions. These benefits are enhanced by the goods' social meanings, by the sense of community they provide with others who own and value similar objects. Commercial culture is inconceivable without an abundance of goods.

The modern advertising-supported media system prompts the display–even the flaunting–of personal belongings as the expression of social and economic power. As Karl Marx noted in *Das Kapital*, material possessions have a "mystical character" both as signals of social status and as expressions of individuality. Paradoxically, the pressure to consume fosters both conformity and its opposite, idiosyncrasy– "keeping up with the Joneses" but also "being first on the block." Early capitalism's Protestant ethic (as Max Weber described it) stressed saving (and therefore investing for the future) over expenditure (and the enjoyment of life's immediate pleasures).[2] Fourteenth-century sumptuary laws in Italy and England restricted innovation; it was considered a sign of conspicuous consumption, and therefore unacceptable. Even the redoubtable Jonathan Swift wanted to "enact and enforce" such laws to prevent "all Excesses in Cloathing, Furniture and the like."[3]

But innovation is the engine of today's economy. As the market expanded toward its modern dimensions, Europeans began to increase the exchange value of objects by designing them to fit broad patterns of taste. This impulse sparked a system of commodity design that increased trade, heightened consumer appetites, and added to the demand for new kinds of merchandise.[4] An increasingly productive economy was able to move beyond the manufacture of raw necessities to the creation of luxuries and intangibles. Mass production and mass retailing meant the democratization of consumer products. Luxury became less mysterious as it became more accessible.[5]

New goods satisfied psychological impulses rather than immediate material needs.[6] It was important to be up to date; novelty and fashion remain a preeminent advertising appeal. The challenge to produce what is new, different, and improved is today a stimulus to technicians in the corporate research laboratory, but the perception of what is new may result from sheer artifice. In the domain of style, familiar ingredients are constantly reassembled.[7]

Commercial culture is a global phenomenon, highly visible even in places where capitalism has been rejected, manifested as a veneer on even the most backward societies. Poor countries have multilevel cultures in which an elitist superstructure of media content that follows familiar Western formats may coexist with an indigenous popular style. Kiosks that sell European high-fashion magazines also carry comic-strip romances on pulp paper. Radio stations interlard Brahms sonatas with recordings by local folk musicians. While this kind of incongruity fascinates the cultural analyst, no one else considers it bizarre.

Almost everywhere, American television programs, films, and popular music enjoy widespread popularity, and American news wire services are extensively used by the press. In Western Europe, the public's demand for expanded choice in television programming has strengthened the importance of commercial channels and diminished the audiences of stations run by government broadcasting authorities. Of 16,500 hours of televised fiction broadcast in Europe in 1988, only 11% was produced on that continent; most of the remainder came from the United States. The attractions of rock and roll, Western shootouts, automobile chases, blue jeans, and police dramas transcend national barriers. But commercial culture is so firmly rooted in the American experience that it can best be examined in its principal native habitat.

Life in today's America is dominated by financial transactions—anticipating them, engaging in them, and consuming what is acquired from them. This way of living requires a highly developed and productive economy, a universal and dense network of communications, and a high degree of literacy.

Have human beings always striven to accumulate more possessions? The lessons of comparative ethnology provide innumerable examples to prove the opposite, when this is not the custom of the tribe.[8] People exchange and consume goods and services in every society, but ours seems uniquely dedicated to that purpose. There are cultures in which sheer existence is so precarious that human beings find it hard to transcend the immediate tasks of obtaining food and shelter to survive. There are cultures whose members are primarily concerned with the integration of their individual existences into the pattern of nature and tradition. They are preoccupied with spirits, deities, or ancestors. There are cultures that value time, indolence, the warmth of personal relationships, the cultivation, for mere pleasure, of skills that cannot be sold.

We are not immune to the appeal of nonmaterial values in our own society. We practice the forms of religious worship and find places in our lives for affection, friendship, sport, and the arts. But the satisfactions we obtain from these activities are embedded in the tissue of our lives as consumers. The practices of religion, sport, and art acquire overtones of meaning from the social status of those with whom we engage in them and from the objects associated with them. Love is pursued in an automobile, at restaurants, in the movies. The zest for an active life requires running shoes, or perhaps, in some circles, even a private tennis court.

American society is suffused by commercial culture in two very familiar respects: Everyday life is saturated with commercial reminders, appeals, and exhortations; the vicarious experiences that people absorb through the mass media are organized and shaped to the commercial requirements of the marketplace. When a town in New Mexico renamed itself Truth Or Consequences after a radio quiz show, it was merely providing one more bit of bizarre testimony to the pervasive influence of the commercial culture. Day after day there is fresh evidence that life imitates art, if the artifices of commercial culture can be described as art.

Although the products of the American mass media system are widely adopted and adapted throughout the world, they never cease to arouse distaste, disparagement, and disgust from foreign observers. (A former French defense minister, Jean Pierre de Chevenement, accuses the United States of the "organized cretinization of our people.") American civilization has long attracted fierce attacks, not merely for its shortcomings, but for the self-righteous militancy with which it has exported them to the rest of the world. From the earliest days of the Republic, European travelers complained of "American materialism" and "vile cupidity." The *Edinburgh Review* asked in 1820, "In the four quarters of the globe, who reads an American book? or goes to an American play? or looks at an American picture or statue?"[9] Mrs. Frances Trollope wrote of America in 1832: "The immense exhalation of periodical trash, which penetrates into every cot and corner of the country, and which is greedily sucked in by all ranks, is unquestionably one great cause of its inferiority." From his more distant vantage point, Fyodor Dostoyevsky, in *The Possessed*, presented his vision of this boisterous, boastful, materially obsessed nation:

> I read in the paper the biography of an American. He left all his vast fortune to factories and to the exact sciences, and his skeleton to the students of the academy there, and his skin to be made into a drum, so that the American national hymn might be beaten upon it day and night. Alas! We are pygmies in mind compared with the soaring thought of the States of North America.[10]

What truth, if any, underlies this savage irony?

Advertising as a Component of Commercial Culture

American media are run on the premise that the market provides the public with the kind of messages it wants. But this argument does not apply, directly or indirectly, to all the advertising that represents a significant element of media content. Some ads are generally welcome (in print, the public tells pollsters); some are not (in broadcasting and billboards). It cannot be otherwise, because most advertising is consumed not for its own sake, but as an accompaniment to whatever has been selected as the main course. The advertiser's will prevails, not the public's. The structure of the media system is intertwined with that of advertising.

Secretary of Commerce Herbert Hoover, speaking of radio, 1922:

> It is inconceivable that we should allow so great a possibility for service, for news, for entertainment, for vital commercial purposes, to be drowned in advertising chatter.

It is mainly "advertising chatter" that funds the media—themselves part of a marketing structure in which the production of goods is governed by manufacturers' perceptions of consumer demand. For advertisers, media are vehicles for diffusing their messages, not avenues of public enlightenment or cultural enhancement. This is to be noted, not to be deplored. Advertising appears to be a necessary element of a competitive business economy. Much of it represents valuable consumer information. There is overwhelming evidence that the productive forces it generates far outstrip its incidental wastes and frivolities.[11] The competitive spirit it exemplifies promotes product innovation and manufacturing efficiency that keeps prices down.

If it is legitimate and socially useful to make a product, it is surely just as legitimate and useful to promote and sell it. The advertising money spent by individual business firms reflects its utility for them. Limiting the amount of money they could spend on it would restrict their ability to sell what they make; it would represent an unwarranted and politically dangerous interference with free expression. But we can accept the economic benefits of advertising without at the same time taking all its present forms and practices to be immutable.

When asked what American business does best, most Americans name promotion and advertising. In the United States, expenditure on advertising as a percentage of gross national product is much higher (2.2%) than it is in Japan (.95%), Germany (.9%), or any other nation. The United States represents a fourth of the global economy, but has nearly half the world's advertising. This means that advertising represents a higher proportion of the cost of goods. In part this is because a large share of the American civilian economy is devoted to the production of standard consumer items whose similar competing brands can be differentiated from each other only by intensive promotion.

Is the unusually important place of advertising in American life a mere expression of the materialism that already pervaded it before advertising became such a power? The exhortations of advertisers resonated to a chord that had already been sounded. The solid response to their messages, which prompted further increases in the budgets dedicated to them, may have been strengthened by the receptiveness of a public that already placed high value on information related to consumption. More likely, however, the growth of advertising resulted directly from the same forces that gave rise to the acquisitive spirit. Merchants and manufacturers actively promoted what they had to sell out of the same expansionary urge that possessed consumers, and in fact the whole nation. They hustled. Their philosophy was at the opposite pole from that of the traditional European businessman who waited for the customers to come into his shop or for orders to reach him. In a style that took the rest of the world a long time to catch up—and that much of it has still not attained—American business came to accept advertising as an essential operating cost, as essential as the cost of goods themselves.

Only in America?

Why did the commercial culture emerge in the United States and flourish to a degree that is approached only in highly similar countries like Canada and Australia? The answer must be sought first in the fact that for many years the United States has had the most productive and advanced economy in the world, with great resources to spend on entertainment and information as well as on mass marketing.

Another part of the explanation must be sought in America's democratic political institutions. A tradition of state support for the arts remains strong in Europe, a vestige of the absolutist era in which public monuments were constructed, landscapes embellished, and spectacles mounted to express the glory of the divinely appointed ruler. In the United States, which rejected such symbols and kept its public buildings and ceremonies on a modest scale, support for all the forms of creative expression tended from the very beginning to reflect the rules of the marketplace more than the tastes of government officials.

For most Americans, since early days, consumption has been linked to the work ethic. America has been castigated for its materialism since the beginnings of the Republic. Successive waves of immigrants have been preoccupied with the tasks of carving a livelihood from the raw resources of the continent. The frugality of colonial yeomen evolved into the canniness of Yankee traders. The New World meant material opportunity for millions of Europeans whose life course in their native lands seemed bleak and unpromising. The steadily expanding frontier promised greater material opportunity for native-born and immigrants alike. Cultural institutions deeply rooted in the aristocratic traditions of Europe had to be reinvented and evolved through independent effort. The fantasy of enrichment within the potential grasp of everyone set personal goals and defined national character. Achievement was expressed in terms of property, and the expansion of the nation's territories had its counterpart in the individual's pursuit of tangible wealth.

Americans take for granted, as essentials of existence, possessions that most of the world regards as exotic luxuries. Seven in ten consider aluminum foil and facial tissues to be absolute necessities of life. (But only 64% put the television set in that category.[12] Curiously, in spite of the American public's constant exposure to products that are newer and better than those they own, most express themselves as satisfied with their lot in life, presumably including their present assortment of possessions.[13])

The dynamism and optimism that pervade American society are strong positive offshoots of its materialistic orientation. So are the spirit of rationality and iconoclasm, the delight in problem-solving and the confidence that problems can be solved. But other less endearing traits and values have also been evident—avarice and the tolerance of avarice, a cynical view of human motivation, a skepticism of activities that cannot be justified in utilitarian terms. These negative attributes, so often associated with the insidious effects of advertising, have been identified with the darker side of American character long before advertising emerged as a visible force in the national economy and culture.

As the society grew larger, it could sustain the output of information and entertainment at different educational and social levels. Its culture became deeper, denser, with more forces at play that induced variety. The sheer size of the country's talent pool made possible a high technical level of professional performance in every cultural domain.

A nation whose independence was founded on the demand for freedom of trade quickly moved into a veneration of private business enterprise that was vigorously competitive, expansionary, and promotional in style. American industry was permeated by a philosophy of product and marketing innovation. Unconfined by the guild tradition, which inhibited the inventive spirit in Europe, commercial activity had an intensity that was reflected in the vigor of its advertising claims.

Advertising was from the outset perceived as the life blood of commerce. Its growth spurred the consumer economy and sharpened its competitive character. Advertising also must have had subtle effects on the ethos of business. Manufacturers and merchants inevitably identify with the slogans and claims that their copywriters invent for them and then model their own behavior to accord with this symbolic identity.

The great size of the advertising system has permitted the creation and support of an extraordinary number of media voices. Nine-tenths of the time the public spends with media goes to those that are advertising-supported, most notably television. Of American society's total annual $166 billion investment in the media system (and this sum does not include the media that are all advertising), 70% is represented by media that depend on advertising for a significant part of their revenue, and half is actually paid by advertisers. (The portion that advertisers pay is of course not the same as the proportion that their messages represent of total media output—measured in terms of the space and time dedicated to it, or in terms of public attention).

On-air commercial broadcasting is totally dependent upon advertising; it provides four-fifths of newspaper revenues and half of magazines'. This means that the people who manage most media enterprises regard advertisers rather than the public as their primary clients. (A. C. Nielsen, the principal source of television audience data, does not even rate shows without paid advertising, except by special arrangement.)

Media organizations work hard to generate audiences. They do so not as an end in itself, but because audiences are the commodity they sell to their real customers. The structure and content of most of the major media are profoundly affected, if not actively controlled, by the judgments and practices of advertisers whose interest in media structure and content is entirely instrumental and pragmatic. Advertisers have no functional concern with the meaning or consequences of mass communication except insofar as it provides a mechanism for the delivery of their messages to prospective buyers of their wares. This has three important consequences: (1) it makes advertising a significant component of the public's communication experience; (2) it affects judgments that shape nonadvertising content; and (3) it controls the life and death of individual media.

Media have raised their advertising rates almost steadily, faster than general inflation, while their audiences have mostly failed to grow. One reason why magazines and newspapers do not grow is that they charge their remaining readers more as others drop by the wayside. As a result, the cost efficiency of advertising declines, and advertisers are tempted into other forms of sales promotion. Promotion is used both to influence consumer demand directly (for example, through in-store merchandising, price-off coupons, premiums, contests, special offers, and events) and to ensure that the channels of distribution are kept open (by offering price or other incentives to dealers and salespeople). However, there are limits to the inroads that these methods can make. Short-run incentives to consumers or the trade depend for their success upon the existing reputations of enterprises and their products. Those reputations are built by advertising. There is no way that this essential function will lose its economic value. That means more spending and more advertisements through more vehicles in the future.

The enormous volume of advertising messages received and retained (even if many of them escape notice) unquestionably makes a substantial impact upon the American psyche. They account for a substantial proportion of all the communications that people receive from nonpersonal sources. Advertising occupies about a fourth of the roughly 25 hours the average person spends weekly with television and nearly a fifth of the 20 hours spent with radio. And advertising fills three-fifths of the space in newspapers and over half of the pages in magazines.[14] Other forms of commercial intrusion include point-of-sale promotion and direct marketing by telephone or the mail. (Advertising mail volume more than tripled in a recent 15 year period.[15])

All of this torrent of advertising is intended, to one degree or another, to be persuasive, whether it is embodied in the direct and urgent exhortations of a television pitch, or the informative detail of a newspaper classified ad. What distinguishes all of these messages is their commercial purpose. Other communications that have no such deliberate intent (like the costumes worn by celebrities) may also have commercial implications. The opposite occurs too: Communications designed for commercial purposes also convey noncommercial meanings. The constant repetition of images that become familiar, and thus acceptable, selectively reinforces certain social attitudes, presents reference points for our own appearance and behavior, and imposes cultural norms.

Advertising has increasingly encroached into media for which the audience has already paid heavily, like films, records, videocassettes, newsletters, and books. Long ago, booksellers advertised books within the text of other books; publishers continue to do so to the present day (most commonly on the back of the dustjacket). Videocassettes continue the practice, but more aggressively, and to the annoyance of the audience.[16]

In the days of silent movies, lantern slides advertising local businesses were routinely flashed on the screen between changes of reel, and cinema advertising remains a major medium in many countries. Though it had long died out in the United States, it was revived in the late 1980s as theater owners struggled to boost their revenues. However, this form of advertising can only be used sparingly. No captive audience would tolerate, on a large screen and in a dark room, the endless series of commercial interruptions that are passively accepted on home television.

Not only have advertisements taken advantage of the captive film audience; "product placement" has corrupted film production. Film studios routinely receive up to

$250,000 for introducing branded products into films. Philip Morris reportedly paid $350,000 to get Lark cigarettes displayed in "License to Kill," a James Bond thriller.[17]

There is no unwritten covenant between producers of entertainment and their audiences comparable to the one that leads the public to expect journalists to present the news without fear or favor. At televised sports events, cameras pan the arenas, with their painted brand logos for companies that are not necessarily the broadcast sponsors. Product mentions also find their way into television shows, raising objections from advertisers who have paid to insert commercials into the same programs.

An average of eleven plugs per hour for specific products and brands appeared in 1993 on each of the three major network owned and operated stations in Chicago, over half of them on news shows.[18] Advertisers provide their products free, and they are displayed without charge. (Payment would be illegal, if the sponsorship were not disclosed.) A Coke machine was introduced into a school cafeteria as an unavoidable presence in a network program called "TV 101." In another instance, a CBS soap opera crew spent two weeks at the Hyatt Regency hotel in Maui, and in exchange for expenses showed 70 seconds of hotel facilities.[19] Network officials defend such intrusions as a note of "realism."

Similar practices are at work in the book publishing industry. Dell has published romantic novels that insert the brand name Bel Air before every reference to a cigarette.[20] Bantam Books publishes premium books, bought in large quantities by corporations. Some are created especially for a particular promotion, like cookbooks, books on wine, entertaining, energy, the stock market, or the preacher Robert Schuller's *Move Ahead with Possibility Thinking*. On another front, Time Warner's affiliate, Whittle Communications, engaged in a scheme to produce books sponsored by advertisers and send them to a list of 150,000 politicians and business leaders. (Whittle also introduced "Channel One" into thousands of schools—a brief newscast with several minutes of commercials for candy bars, cereals, soft drinks, and other nourishing products aimed at the juvenile market. By 1992, it was generating $115 million of advertising). Marketing ingenuity always finds new outlets, but advertising continues to exert its most powerful presence in the main-line media.

Even if the mass media did not exist, the world of the average American would be full of vastly more communications than a century ago. We live in an environment where everything is labeled: streets, buildings, stores, products of all kinds. Notices of goods and services for sale come to us throughout the day from the emblazoned products that we see about us at home, at work, and on the street. We get constant reminders of our potential for consumption, of goods and services that might otherwise be out of sight. They are only a part of the stimulation we get from sights and sounds with contrasting meanings and associations.

As we walk through a city street or a suburban shopping mall, we must sort out the significance of myriad signals sent to us by every face and figure in the crowd, by every object in our field of vision, by every note in the enveloping sound. Perhaps primitive folk faced no less complex a task in sorting out the sensations that make up their environment, since every leaf and every blade of grass held meanings that are obscured for us.

Quite apart from the ads, the mass media shape standards of behavior, powerfully and continuously. The real-life personalities who appear in magazine and newspaper illustrations and the actors in televised dramas are role models whose dress and adornment we emulate, to whose home furnishings we aspire.

It is impossible to dissociate the ubiquitous exhortations of advertising from the innumerable other cues and reminders of material objects and nonmaterial pleasures that confront Americans in their daily environment. If advertising messages somehow all disappeared and the national standard of living remained at its present level, we would all still be continually exposed to the sight of products we do not own and of purchasable pleasures we are not enjoying. We would hardly yearn for comforts and perquisites beyond the necessities of existence if we were unaware that they existed. We are constantly looking at, hearing about, or reading about objects or experiences that stimulate our own acquisitive urges. An article of clothing may be even more enticing if it is worn by a passerby on the street than it would be in a shop window or in an ad.

Advertisements tell us to consume, and to consume now, right away. They represent an enormous affirmation of the importance and value of the material comforts that are available in a wealthy industrial society. They teach us to take pride in our outer appearance, in the way we present ourselves to others. They reinforce traditional conventions and values, in contrast with the moral anarchy that suffuses the surrounding news and entertainment. They represent a continuing advocacy for hedonism, for making our lives easier, more enjoyable. They urge us on to accumulate more goods and new experiences, and reassure us that these are well within our reach. They tantalize us with visions of pleasures beyond our capacities to taste and often beyond our ability to afford. The effigies of shoes, pretzels, and scissors that adorned the shops of medieval cities showed the illiterate what was to be found inside. They were invitations to enter and buy. As such they were more than a cue to identification; they stimulated demand as well. It is hard to draw the line between such designations, which still hang over the shops of Salzburg and Berne, and the sales messages embodied in the signs, awnings, and store windows of the American urban landscape.

Along with their constant reassurances of how lucky we are, advertisements also offer constant reminders of the possessions that we do not have, of the envied privileges of those who do have them. By urging us on to acquire more things, advertisements spur us on to work harder, to achieve more so that we too can acquire them. On people who feel personally inadequate for such achievements, they may have the different effect of creating illegitimate notions of entitlement—fostering the idea that possessions are so important that they must be acquired by any means. The constant display of goods on television must surely affect the moral judgments of normally law-abiding poor people who loot—whether in Panama City or in Detroit. Commercials on West German television undoubtedly assisted in the political education of the East Germans before the country was unified, no less than newscasts of Corazon Aquino's "People Power" in Manila helped prompt the turnout in Beijing's Tienanmen Square. The ideas and images that enter people's lives are inevitably expressed in their actions.

Historical Origins

Advertising is an integral element of media's content and essential to their finances. Its indispensability for the general economy is attested to by its ancient history.

BBDO's founder, Bruce Barton, hailed Jesus Christ as "the first advertising man,"[21] but there are even earlier examples. Babylonian papyrii offered rewards for the return of slaves. Advertising inscriptions appeared on the walls of Greek tradesmen and later in Pompeii.

Printing made it possible to distance the advertising message from the advertised goods and services. The first printed ads for books appeared in Mainz shortly after Gutenberg began publishing. In 1477, William Caxton issued handbills offering one of his books (the *Sarum Ordinal*) for sale "good chepe." As more people learned how to read, advertising messages could be put in words as well as in symbols. By the middle of the 1700s, bill-posting was prevalent in London.[22] At about the same time, merchandise began to be displayed in shop windows, which grew larger as plate-glass technology improved.[23] Starting in the 1830s, large effigies of consumer goods were wheeled around the streets in carts.[24] Sandwich men and other sign carriers added to the liveliness of the scene (introducing an incongruity that continues to echo in photographs that juxtapose the smiling faces on billboards with the grim figures of hungry derelicts).

Signs, sandwich boards, outdoor posters, and handbills—all represent pure forms of advertising, to which the public is exposed involuntarily. The media with which we are concerned in this book are those that attract audiences for nonadvertising reasons; their history, in the United States, has paralleled that of advertising since the days of the colonial press. Newspapers were often named or subtitled "The Advertiser," because that is in fact what they were. Commercial announcements received a prominence equivalent to news items. In early American and European newspapers, commercial news was printed without charge to advertisers, simply as something that the readers would want to know about.

These original advertisements were informative items that looked no different from the other news that surrounded them. The arrival of a ship with a cargo of certain goods, the auctioning of a property—this was news, reported as such. Readers were no less interested in such items than they were in other occurrences that affected their lives, aroused their curiosity, or gave them cause for conversation. Even though advertisers have long since had to pay to put their words before the public, advertising in the press is still important news, as reader surveys repeatedly attest.

In the nineteenth century, the addition of illustrations to ads, and the consequent increase in their size, gave them a distinctive appearance that set them off from the surrounding editorial matter. Subtle typographical cues allowed readers to compartmentalize the information before them into hierarchies of acceptability or believability. With the development of lithography and poster art, visual style and colorful imagery gave advertisements a strong independent identity. While early newspaper ads had relied on copy that was lean and matter of fact, late nineteenth-century posters used narrative or allegorical pictures to convey impressions of the product's virtues.

Newspapers' growth was made possible by two midcentury improvements in intra-urban and interurban transportation that eventually gave rise, respectively, to national and retail advertising. (1) Branded merchandise (like patent medicines) could be shipped by rail to communities remote from the place of manufacture. (2) Shoppers could reach downtown department stores from a wide area by omnibus or street car; they no longer had to walk—or come by horse and buggy—to the neighborhood shops. Both of these developments required continuous and intensive promotion to potential customers.

A.T. Stewart's Marble Dry-Goods Palace in 1846 combined a dazzling variety of merchandise with an architectural distinction that invited traffic. Newspapers, still deriving most of their income from readers, were slow to grasp the importance of this pioneer venture. Editors resisted the encroachment of advertising matter into the precious space available to tell the public about the serious events of the day. James Gordon Bennett permitted no ornamental cuts or illustrations for ads in his *New York Herald*, though he accepted ads from prostitutes.[25] The first full-page newspaper retail ad was placed by John Wanamaker in 1879, but newspapers' "agate rule" restricted the size of type. In New York, Macy's got around it by assembling small type into the appearance of giant letters surrounded by white space.

Brand names for patent medicines, soap, and other household products had already appeared by the time of the Civil War.[26] When a reader objected to some of the extravagant claims, Horace Greeley suggested that he "should complain to our advertisers themselves, who are not responsible to us for the style or language (if decent) of the advertisements, nor have we any control over them."[27] This kind of buck-passing is not unfamiliar today.

Messages, Messages

Advertising has grown at a faster rate than the consumer economy, but the increase in the number of advertising *messages* has outpaced that of advertising *expenditures*. In 1982, the Federal Trade Commission forced the abandonment of the National Association of Broadcasters' code, which had placed voluntary limits on the time devoted to advertising. The deregulation of broadcasting coincided with the introduction of the 15-second commercial unit and brought about an explosion in the total number of ads broadcast by a typical station. In one year, the number of additional commercials per network increased by more than half an hour a day. With more advertising positions also available on independent stations and cable, there was new competition for other media.

The effusion of messages is not translated into conscious communication in exact ratio to the time or space it occupies, nor does the public's exposure to advertisements increase in proportion to their growing quantity. Readers, viewers, and listeners have a built-in capacity for selective inattention. We must be selective in the way we process communications of every kind, lest they disappear in a blur of overwhelming confusion. Reading a periodical—unlike reading a book—entails the extremely rapid screening of vast quantities of unwanted information in order to concentrate on whatever is meaningful. The screened-out messages have not been ignored; they have been glanced at, passed over, and forgotten, literally, in the blink of an eye.

Selectivity works easily with print, where readers control their own pace. It is more difficult to manage in broadcasting, where messages succeed each other in real time. With broadcast commercials, some members of the audience leave the room; others let their attention wander. By 1994, four out of five television households had remote control devices, which encourage viewers to sample alternatives. Viewers are selective, to some degree, when they flick from one station to another, or when they use the videocassette recorder and the fast-forward device in playback. But this is hardly as easy as it is to move their gaze across a page, away from whatever has no interest.

The ability of viewers to recall one of the last cluster of commercials they had just been watching (an average of 4 or 5 minutes earlier) fell from 18% in 1965 (when free-standing commercials were still common) to 4% in 1990.[28] Just between 1986 and 1990, the public's ability to name *any* television commercial seen in the previous 4 weeks fell from 64% to 48%.[29] The reduction of viewer attentiveness brought about a frenzy of innovation as advertising agencies sought to break through the barriers of indifference with humor and special effects. The creative execution of ads, particularly of commercials, became more and more directed at grabbing attention rather than at communicating a product's advantages. (For example, ads for the apparel manufacturer, Benetton, featured a dying AIDS patient, a bloody newborn baby with its umbilical cord attached, a row of condoms, an albino Zulu woman and a black woman breast-feeding a white child.) Commercials stressed bizarre scenarios and evocative moods. "Atmospheric advertising" relied on visuals and music, without any words about the product.

Computer-generated special effects, shown first to great advantage in the film "Star Wars," revolutionized production. Film was given a grainy quality by "pushing" or "blowing out." People and objects could be floated against any desired background through "matting." Such new techniques liberated new creative possibilities and made commercials more imaginative. But in making them more fanciful, their creators also removed their content farther from the realm of reality and of genuine product information. Audiences became more cynical.

The average production cost of a national commercial was almost $200,000 in 1991.[30] This is a lot of money, but it is still low compared to the cost of making programs. For that reason, makers of commercials tolerate avant-garde ideas and tastes in imagery or appearance more readily than program producers.

Costlier productions made it possible to change scenes more rapidly. In 1981, 14% of the 30-second commercials had fifteen or more cuts. Five years later, this proportion had grown to 31%.[31] A musical theme, used consistently, enhances video memorability,[32] but by the start of the 1990s, the MTV style of fast-cut commercials with rock-beat musical accompaniment was acknowledged to be counterproductive. Research found that audiences were confused by the music, which overrode the product message.

The interruption of communication, exemplified by shorter commercials, with their agitated fast-cuts, represents another important effect of advertising's mere presence. Our reading of a book is interrupted when we put it down between sessions, our reading of a magazine or newspaper, when we flip from the start of a story to its continuation on another page or when our gaze shifts from one story to an ad or a cartoon on the same spread. But we do not put down a novel for the night in the middle of a gripping episode, and we do not move to an ad from an article unless the ad holds greater interest. Interruptions in reading are qualitatively different from the sharp discontinuities that occur when a commercial pod interrupts a television program.

The public is indeed resigned to broadcast interruptions; they are generally regarded as the necessary price that must be paid to assure "free" programming. But another price is being paid, too. When communication is scattered and fragmented, its meaning changes; it is inherently less compelling; the experience is trivialized. Whether we deplore this development or say with a sigh that it is just the way things are, this fragmentation is a significant byproduct of advertising's pervasive presence in our daily lives.

Lies, Damned Lies, and Advertising Claims

Advertising has always relied on secondary appeals that go beyond the product itself and its direct uses and benefits for the consumer. Every element—headlines, copy, music, models, backgrounds, vocal expression—is routinely manipulated to evoke alluring, and sometimes clandestine, gratifications. Consumers are not merely promised that the product will permit them to overcome their own glaring personal defects. There is an unstated implication that larger prizes may be within their grasp: eternal youth, universal admiration, sexual conquests, entré into the most sophisticated circles, a happy home life.

An individual may respond to advertisements that appeal to a highly diverse range of motivations—from the crude to the subtle—just as that person may respond to fiction written or filmed at different periods and in different styles. In the 1950s, much was made of the hidden motives—often illicit—that could be ascribed to even the most common type of consumer purchases. The "Strategy of Desire,"[33] practiced by masters of the black advertising arts, was supposed to conjure up powerful unconscious forces to harness the lusts for sex or mastery or anal possessiveness on behalf of the purveyors of branded merchandise. It was even speculated that such messages are buried subliminally beneath much of the advertising that one sees. The fact is that communication is more effective when it is open than when it is concealed.

Harry Wayne McMahan, consultant on TV commercials:

> If you've got nothing to say, say it!

David Ogilvy put it differently:

> If you've got nothing to say, sing it!

Hyperbole has always figured large in the art of advertising. In England, *The Publick Advertiser*, made up entirely of ads, proclaimed in 1657 that

> the drink called Coffee, which is a very wholsome and physical drink, having many excellent virtues, closes the orifice of the Stomack, fortifies the heat within, helpeth Digestion, quickeneth the Spirits, maketh the heart lighter, is good against Eye-sores, Coughs or Colds, Rhumes, Consumption, Headach, Dropsie, Gout, Scurvie, Kings Evil, and many others.[34]

Daniel Defoe, in his *Journal of the Plague Year*, cites posters advertising "INFALLIBLE preventive pills against the Plague . . . SOVERAIGN Cordials against the Corruption of the Air . . . The only TRUE Plague-Water."[35] His contemporaries knew better than to take such grandiloquent claims at face value.

"Ruin! Ruin! Ruin! Wasteful and Impetuous Sale" read the advertising headline for a department store in one of Anthony Trollope's Victorian novels.[36] In today's television advertising, beaming faces and dulcet voices lure us more subtly and gently and convincingly. But the gap still exists between what we see and hear and what we are willing to accept as the truth. It is not surprising, therefore, that the occupation of advertising still does not enjoy high esteem. (While 66% of the public give a high or very high rating to druggists, and 23% to journalists, only 7% bestow it on advertising practitioners.[37])

The rivalries of the business world find their expression in the marketplace when advertisements make invidious comparisons with competitors or take countermeasures to offset competitors' promotions or market tests. According to one account, "religious conflicts are those in which an advertiser hates a competitor 'with a passion' while 'banana conflicts' are those in which he goes bananas at mention of the other's name."[38]

Competitive scrimmaging can lead to peccadillos, sometimes to serious dishonesties, as in the instance of Volvo commercials whose producers mechanically weakened rival cars and reinforced the client's to "demonstrate" the strength of its construction in a commercial. This kind of nonsense sometimes starts out innocently enough. BBDO put transparent marbles into bowls of Campbell's Chunky Soup so that the pieces of meat and vegetables would show up at the surface in photographs instead of sinking to the bottom: a trick used to demonstrate a genuine product advantage. What is to be defined as misleading? Former Ogilvy and Mather ad agency Chairman Kenneth Roman points to the unpredictable consequences of taking the law literally.

> In California, for example, Proposition 65 mandates that food labels disclose all potential and carcinogenic ingredients. Sounds correct, right? Now as it happens the water in California contains trace elements of toxins. Therefore if you are a pasta manufacturer in California, and use California water to make your pasta, you would have to include a package label that warns of these toxins. In other words, in California, Pasta Kills.[39]

Adults presumably can take exaggerated product claims in stride, but advertisements addressed to children (over $1 billion's worth in 1993) are another matter. Young children looking at commercials cannot separate primary from secondary meanings as adults do. In fact, they find it difficult to distinguish commercial messages from program content. A child is less able than an adult to discriminate among messages and to pay attention only to those that may be useful. Second-grade children do not understand disclaimers, like "partial assembly required."[40] (The commercial nature of television's programming for children was and is a matter of great interest to MCA, actor Ronald Reagan's talent agency. One of President Reagan's last official actions was to veto legislation to limit television commercials in children's programming. The restriction was finally passed in 1991.)

Advertising styles, like those in other media content, undergo continual changes in popularity and fashion. The advertisements of the past always look quaint or ridiculous by comparison with the sophisticated techniques of whatever era or place we happen to judge them from. In 1931, a Scott ad prepared by J. Walter Thompson warned that "more serious than most men realize" were "the troubles caused by harsh toilet tissue." "I've got to have a . . . minor operation," the model suffering from "toilet paper illness" told a colleague.[41]

Advertising styles are, in fact, inseparable from more general cultural trends. Sexual imagery in advertising was ubiquitous in the late 1970s and early 80s. It appeared to be on the wane by the end of the decade, but then had a renewed burst of interest as creative people tried harder to break through the barrier of indifference caused by commercial clutter. Nudes became more common, shown individually and in mixed- and same-sex couples, with intimate relationships implied or even explicitly portrayed.[42] Thus advertisements conferred added social legitimacy to changes in mores that had already been celebrated in other kinds of media content.

The Varieties of Advertising

What we are being persuaded to buy is very different from what we consume, largely because expenditures on housing, utilities, medical care, and miscellaneous items account for 36% of the consumer's budget but for only 19% of total advertising.[43] Although nearly every type of enterprise in the consumer sector of the American economy does some advertising, expenditures in each category are not proportional to its economic importance. Some industries spend vastly more to advertise than others do. Advertising-to-sales ratios vary greatly, depending on the nature of both the product and the market. They are much higher for packaged goods, which are used and bought repeatedly, than for big-ticket items.

The emphasis and texture of advertising communications necessarily have a different cultural effect than the objects and transactions themselves. It is a mistake to think of advertising as monolithic in its impact on noncommercial values and attitudes. The media context determines how advertising messages are perceived. Since the mix of products and services advertised is different in each medium, the advertising in each appears in a distinctive communications environment and has different cumulative social consequences. For this reason, generalizations about the cultural effects of advertising may be misleading.

National advertising, intended to build awareness of a brand and to give it a distinctive reputation, features a different assortment of products and services than the local advertising run by stores.[44] Its advertisers are a limited and unrepresentative part of American industry. A Martian visitor who saw only newspaper classified ads or heard only radio commercials would have a very distorted notion of what American advertising is all about. A great deal—perhaps most of it, if we include packaging labels and store signs—is utilitarian and informative. It appeals to the most fundamental consumer desire, which is to find something that one already is looking for in a convenient location at the most reasonable possible price. Classified newspaper advertising is the best possible example, with its highly concentrated informational listings of houses, cars, jobs, and merchandise offerings.

The array of advertising is highly different in each medium because of the distinctive format through which it communicates, the characteristics of its audience—

including its breadth or degree of specialization—and its ability to meet particular types of communications objectives. Since television advertising is so omnipresent and time-consuming, it is easily, and mistakenly, identified with advertising in general, which is mostly quite different in function and technique. Newspapers and radio, which carry mostly local advertising for stores, services, and individuals, deploy a different spectrum of images than television and magazines, which primarily carry national ads for branded goods.

- For example, if we consider only *national* ads, food represents 22% of television advertising, 9% of magazine advertising, 3% of outdoor, and 4% of newspaper ads. Transportation, mainly airlines, represents 17% of national newspaper ads and only 2% of television.[45] More than one out of every five billboards is for a cigarette. (Tobacco advertising on television encountered mounting criticism before it was taken off the air in 1970.)
- In broadcasting, moreover, specific types of programs attract their own assortments of advertisers. (Of the advertising on Saturday morning children's programs, 30% is for cereal, 28% for toys and games, 20% for candy and snacks, and 7% for fast food.)
- Local accounts represent 88% of newspaper advertising and only 1% or 2% of magazine advertising. Thus the nature of commercial communication is very different in these two print media. Similarly, in broadcasting, local ads represent 78% of the total on radio and 29% of television.

Advertisers use human beings as instruments of mediation and persuasion differently in print and television. In print, the reader's eye confronts the merchandise directly. Advertising is the "good news" so generally absent from the surrounding columns of text. Newspaper ads, which are overwhelmingly retail and classified, tend to be nuts-and-bolts, price-oriented, descriptive, factual.[46] They are short on depicting human faces and figures, and relatively devoid of emotional overtones. National-brand advertising in magazines shows people more often, but emphasizes products.

By contrast, television puts the presenter or protagonist at the center of attention; it seems to require an intermediary—to capture and retain attention and to intrude a message that might otherwise be ignored. Nine out of ten television commercials show one or more people on camera. However, they are not necessarily the ones who tell the advertiser's story. In fact, the spokesman (male in four out of five cases) is not normally the principal protagonist. He may be simply a disembodied audio voice or may start that way and then appear in the flesh. Women are more likely to appear as product users; they play a more significant role in commercials than they do in drama, simply because such a large share of the messages are addressed to them. The protagonist is the consumer, the viewer's surrogate, while the spokesman is like a Greek chorus, emphasizing and reemphasizing the sales message. That is why the two roles are so commonly separated. Protagonists are usually dressed informally (in two out of three instances), spokesmen, however, wear business clothes (jackets and ties for three-fifths of the men who appear on the screen). Whether commercials tell a story, make a demonstration, present a testimonial, or offer a kaleidoscopic montage of brief snippets of imagery, they almost always rely on the protagonists—not the merchandise itself—to make the point.

The Content of Television Commercials

Television advertising is especially voluminous, intrusive, and compelling. It warrants an especially close look because it accounts for a large chunk of the total time that people spend exposed to advertising. Commercials have a common purpose and time dimension, but they come in a great range and diversity of styles and formats. I analyzed 100 of them in 1988. (They are not necessarily exactly like those on the air today, as you read this book, because styles of production are constantly changing, but they provide a sense of what is being conveyed with the cascade of TV messages that inundates us day and night).

Advertisements cast life in a happy glow. They are not part of the world of violence, anger, depression, and offbeat sex that fills the columns of the press and television's prime-time hours. Theirs is a world of pure romance and warm fellow-feeling, of strongly knit, secure family relationships, of individuals untroubled except by the fleeting, easily curable distress of bad breath, high cholesterol, or clogged drains.

The latent messages of television commercials are highly subordinate to the primary message of persuading viewers to buy a particular brand of merchandise, but this purpose does not lessen their impact; they are a continuing affirmation of mainstream, middle-class values. They preach the merits of physical beauty, health, and well-being.

The most significant incidental learning experiences for the audience derive from the identity and behavior of the characters in television commercials rather than from their settings. The characters represent idealized role models akin to those familiar in television and film drama. Their behavioral style, however, has a special intensity imposed by the short message length and the hard task of capturing attention at the time of the commercial break. Commercials move at a much more rapid pace than programs do, because there is so little time to say what has to be said.

Most commercials, like most print ads, focus rather narrowly on the products and keep the background settings to a minimum. Nearly all spotlight the brand rather than the generic virtues of the product. They emphasize comparisons, establishing superiority in pricing, quality, performance, or service. Novelty is highly praised; to be new is to be improved. Inanimate objects are venerated, endowed with the ability to arouse levels of emotion that most human beings normally feel only toward each other.

Kitchens and bathrooms seem to provide the most common domestic settings, but even when they are shown, only a small area is generally visible. The kitchens and bathrooms that we see are spacious, modern, and immaculate—except, of course, when some horrible defacing spill is quickly obliterated by a miracle cleanser or wipe. The sanitized, spotless upper-middle-class glory of kitchens and bathrooms is reflected in the other settings, indoor and outdoor—but in this respect the living arrangements of people in television commercials closely resemble those of the characters in television dramas, and before them, in generations of Hollywood films.

A note of glamour and opulence occasionally appears, if the product seems to call for it. But the everyday life of ordinary people is portrayed as taking place in spacious, well-equipped, squeaky-clean surroundings unmarred by wear and tear, inadequate maintenance, or the intervention of domestic forces unrelated to the plot.

Television and film *dramas* may stray from this vision of the wealthier suburbs to portray scenes of the urban underworld. Television *commercials* never intrude distracting and unpleasant touches of reality—nor is there any objective reason why they should, either in the advertiser's interest or in the social interest. In their idealized representation of what the material world looks like, television commercials reenforce the idea that it is the best of all possible worlds.

This thesis is even more forcefully apparent in the way commercials present people and their relationships. Television and film drama feature wide assortments of human types and temperaments, who experience tension and trouble. Advertisements show human conflict only in the most playful form. The people in television commercials are almost uniformly happy, healthy, and vigorous. With rare exceptions, they live lives devoid of unpleasantness, grief, stress, or pain; their occasional miseries can be alleviated quickly by a miracle drug. They are loving, caring, friendly, and supportive of each other. Their world is upbeat and uplifting in its mood, oozing false sentiment and simpering pseudo-humor. It is a world dominated by the euphoria of youth, with its people in a kinetic state of perpetual motion.

Except for occasional plain-looking actors used to convey verisimilitude in "slice of life" commercials or comparative tests of fabric softeners, or for character actors assuming the role of lovable old codgers, the people in television commercials are an unusually handsome and well-groomed lot, with regular clean-cut features. In their good looks, the performers are no different from their predecessors who graced print advertising long before television came along. Models used in print ads have always been abstract idealizations. The women, like those who once illustrated magazine fiction, are always lithe and lovely, the men, trim and firm-jawed. Art directors and stage directors have long understood that attractive individuals get attention, though it is possible that those who are extraordinarily good-looking may distract attention away from what is advertised.

The men, women, and children who inhabit the world of television commercials are predominantly of European origin. Blacks tend to have light skin and Caucasian features. More than the actors who appear elsewhere in television, those shown in commercials are a glorified abstraction of what America looks like. They also are an atypically youthful bunch rather than a cross-section. (The occasional lovable old codgers just mentioned, grandmotherly or grandfatherly, present a disparate element.) Two out of three visible adult spokesmen appear to be in their twenties or thirties; so are three-fourths of the adult protagonists.

To the degree that social class is discernible, from the setting, dress, or appearance of the actors, it is upper middle class in nearly half the cases and actually aristocratic in another 10%. In a very high proportion of commercials, the question of social class identification is avoided altogether by showing actors in sports clothes or déshabille and in neutral or ambiguous settings.

By contrast with the static world of print advertising, the models or actors in television commercials are shown in time, thus giving us clues to their behavior and character. The viewing public inevitably borrows what it sees them do into its own expectations and norms of personal conduct. This means that the roles they play, inconsequential in any individual instance, are significant in the aggregate as they assume an oft-observed pattern.

The people of television commercials are not only unnaturally cheerful; they appear to be positively manic in a high percentage of cases. They are given to excessive displays of emotion, positive emotion, in situations where most people would not move an extra muscle. Their appetites are voracious, their thirsts voluminous, their sensuality unbridled, their joy unconfined. Above all, they indulge themselves, and with no apparent fear of consequences.

The protagonists lovingly caress their skins, silky smooth after the application of an advertised unction; they chortle with joy as they chew large mouthfuls of the advertised fast foods; they exclaim with amazement as they see how the advertised polish cleans their floors. And all these expressions of delight have an almost pathological intensity.

Perhaps the most striking aspect of many television commercials is the amount of energetic activity that goes on, often to the accompaniment of frenzied rock music. People walk with brisk strides, they engage heavily in outdoor sports, they are passionate exercisers.

Romance (which raises its head in about one out of seven commercials) and sex are recurrent themes, almost inevitably in commercials advertising beauty products and fragrances, but in others as well, for soft drinks, air travel, apparel. Television commercial characters spend an inordinate number of hours in the kitchen and the bathroom; a lot of them are discovered in a state of undress, lathering, anointing, and spraying themselves in narcissistic ecstasy.

If the commercial people are smiling a good deal of the time, it is because of both their exceptionally warm and outgoing personalities and their extraordinary risibility. Research on the recall of commercials finds them positively associated with humor, a relationship not unknown to producers. A fourth of the commercials I looked at display humor, but remarkably few of them are really funny. Instead, they abound in what can only be described as false humor, or "cutesy" humor, in which actors make plays on words, or put on sly expressions, or knock each other about a bit, and then break into hearty grins or even simulated laughter. This kind of unwarranted reaction is akin to their exaggerated emotional displays. Taken together, the implication seems to be that in the fantasy world of television commercials people behave like amiable phonies and in ways that would arouse revulsion, or perhaps sympathy or concern, in real life.

To what extent does such repeated, heavily exposed behavior evoke imitation; to what extent does it merely create tolerance? Very likely it is accepted on its own terms, as a particular style of statement that is not to be taken literally or seriously, but rather understood as a conventional metaphor for meanings that both the advertiser and the audience expect to be translated. The very need for such translation seems to foster the idea that human communication is a devious matter, in which one must plunge below the surface to find out what one's interlocutor really means. In this sense, commercial communication undermines the face validity of communication generally, because it undermines trust.

The visual and auditory claims made within the same commercial may contradict each other or be inconsistent. Commercials use non-sequiturs and convey inferences that might be unacceptable in written form. Examples of confusion abound: (1) A long introduction voices over the video of a woman writhing lustfully on a bed; eventually and in all probability much too late, this is revealed as an ad for Ted Lapidus perfume. (2) A demonstration of baking soda put into a refrigerator actually was intended to represent an analogy to the principle behind a product called "Carpet Fresh." (3) A scene of wealthy customers being unctuously wined and dined in a bank's luxurious private dining room turned out to be a satiric depiction of affairs at a rival bank.

Commercials for competing brands of the same product are often so similar to each other that it is hard to tell them apart. The total impact of a given commercial is transformed when it is broadcast again and again, so that what at first exposure may be a positive response is transformed to indifference or hostility by excessive repetition.

The question of how well advertising performs is not central to my purpose, but it is worth noting that there is no winning formula, from the advertiser's perspective. The success or failure of a particular commercial, at least as measured by its memorability, is determined by its unique creative execution rather than by how well it conforms to any general ground rules. "Day after" aided recall levels (that is, the ability of viewers to remember a commercial, with some reminders, the day after it was on the air) are virtually independent of format and content criteria. In the aggregate, commercials that exhibit a particular characteristic get about the same recall scores as commercials that do not have it or that exhibit a contrasting characteristic. Commercials that are well-liked do not inevitably sell more of what they advertise.

Run-of-the-mill commercials seem to be somewhat different from the ones that win awards. Prize-winning commercials tend to be costly productions, with traceable story lines, memorable characterizations, and an above-average dollop of genuine humor. They meet the exacting criteria of the top professionals who participate in the judging, but there is no evidence that they are more persuasive than the average.

Innumerable commercials are devoid of product benefits, or carry tag lines or slogans unsupported by evidence, like "We make technology work for you." There is an abundance of gimmickry: a fake W.C. Fields, a talking apple, a talking cat, a pontificating 3-year-old, a woman garbed as a dog, a man pretending to be a flea, a man emerging from a suitcase placed on a hotel bed. Does such disturbing imagery serve or detract from the advertiser's message? What does it do to the credibility of the advertiser? What does it do, if anything, to the perception of television advertising in general, or perhaps even of all advertising?

I suggested earlier that, since advertising fuels the urge to consume, it also stimulates us to work harder, so we can earn and consume more. There is an anomaly here. Television advertising, with its continual hyped-up breathless euphoria, conveys the impression that life is easy, that good things are coming our way. Thus it *undermines* the work ethic, the old notions that life is a struggle, that good things must be earned through hard work, and that hard work requires preparation and the learning of skills. In the era of the hand-held calculator, no one needs to memorize the multiplication table.

The headline of Orson Welles's obituary in *Advertising Age* read, "Made Many Commercials." Although Welles had other claims to fame, he said: "I'd rather make an honest commercial than a dishonest film."[47] Adults of normal intelligence understand that the presenters and protagonists whom they see in television commercials are paid actors, and make appropriate allowances for their overenthusiastic and unnatural performances. What implications does this have for their expectations of other people and for their own interpersonal conduct? Children at play incant the words of TV advertising slogans and jingles. Do the rest of us also incorporate them into our styles of speaking, thinking, and dissembling? And if the answer is no, that we manage to remain immune to such nonsense during the hours we spend each week watching television commercials, are we then insensitive to all those other communications to which we should attribute real meaning—as well as to those we know we must discount, in self-defense?

Politics, Media, Advertising

The rhetoric of television advertising has transformed business communication. It has also brought a revolution to the political scene. Political tacticians may have been calculating opportunists since long before Machiavelli. The arts of advertising give their cynicism a frightening ferocity. Political messages are a small part of all advertising, but they have a disproportionate share of advertising's impact on society.

The indifference and jaded skepticism with which viewers regard television advertising in general embraces political advertising as well. It colors their view of candidates and, inescapably, of the whole political process. By one account, Abraham Lincoln jotted down his text of the Gettysburg Address on the back of an envelope. It is now taken for granted that a president's more memorable phrases are crafted by hired flacks.[48]

American political advertising never seems to have had much intellectual content, if nineteenth-century election campaign posters are any indication. If the "image" of today's candidate is the contrived creation of copywriters and producers of commercials rather than the genuine projection of a personality, what is one to make of "Honest Abe," "Old Hickory" and other similar synoptic characterizations? A rare newspaper advertisement tries to lay out a candidate's positions on significant issues and approaches the complex policy matters with which government officials must contend. But television commercials can register only one point at a time—either that the candidate is competent and righteous or that the opponent menaces civilization as we have known it. Thus political advertisements, with their flag-draped heroes, are often the most dishonest ones on the tube.

These commercials are designed by the same rules that apply to consumer goods advertising. They also use adorable, happy tots, soaring music, slice-of-life scenes from real landscapes, sincerely delivered off-hand testimonials from ordinary folks, richly intoned voice-overs, vacuous concepts. These generally undistinguished advertisements are lost in the great sea of product messages that fill the airwaves, sharing their brevity, their disjointed juxtaposition, their general mindlessness.

In a presidential election year, messages on behalf of candidates running for local and state offices (many of them avoiding party identification) may carry a weight comparable to that of the national campaigns themselves, but all their slogans and exhortations are sandwiched among the usual assortment of product claims. Can the viewers consider the claims of candidates to be any more credible than those of competing brands?

Politicians are in awe of television's ability to make and unmake both them and their rivals. This awe expresses itself in a reliance on television advertising as the main instrument in campaigning. Within the parade of intrusions into the nation's comfortable nightly viewing habits, the political commercials represent relatively minor reinforcements of messages that have already had ample opportunity to register.

Former New York State Comptroller Edward Regan, arguing against underwriting political campaigns with public funds:

> Let me tell you [about the] best commercial we ran. We're standing in Union Square Park. This commercial had to do with the soft side of the comptroller's office. So there's this group of actors standing in kind of a semicircle, and the camera's running around panning them. And at one point, the camera just caught these marvelous looks just coming out of these faces, old and young, well dressed and, you know, and they were just radiating up to me, and there was a voice-over saying what we were talking about. It was the best single shot of any commercial that year. You know what this was about? I told them, to break the ice, to start the conversation, who my nephew was. My nephew is the hottest casting director in New York City. And they went wild with me. . . . And you want taxpayers' dollars to go for that?[49]

American politics has become an offshoot of product marketing. Even before the emergence of political consultants who were essentially specialists in creating television commercials, big agencies created electoral campaigns for presidential candidates. In the mid-1950s, agency cynics working on election campaigns began to refer to their candidates as "the product." Years later, George Bush was described as a "line extension" of the Reagan presidency.[50]

Often an agency acquires political clients because of the political involvements of existing corporate accounts. In some instances, agencies have sought to establish political links that might strengthen their hold over existing clients and be regarded as an attraction for new ones. Sometimes, in the case of candidates for the presidency or Senate, agencies wanted to win connections with individuals who would be powerful friends in the future. Occasionally, assignments reflected the political ambitions and contacts of agency principals. (Edward Ney, the former chairman of Young and Rubicam—which worked on the Reagan and Bush presidential campaigns—was appointed ambassador to Canada. Another Republican ad man, Sig Rogich, received a lesser plum, the ambassadorship to Iceland). And always, as with any piece of new business, an agency would be interested in the commission or fee it would earn from the added billings, even though experience showed that the credit rating of political accounts was often questionable and media asked for their money up front. In recent presidential election campaigns, as the political activity of agencies became controversial, creative and media functions have been moved to ad hoc organizations staffed by individuals on leave from their regular agency employers. (In 1992, the Republicans set up "The November Company," headed by the chairman of Ammirati and

Puris. It included such executives as the president of D'Arcy Masius Benton and Bowles/North America and the chief creative officers of Bozell/New York and McCann-Erickson/New York.)

In an election campaign, agency account executives and management supervisors work with candidates and their advisors, with the political consultants and the party machinery, to develop plans and to coordinate the work of specialists. Temperamentally the liaison and administrative types are much less likely than writers, artists, or researchers to be troubled by ideological qualms. They are drawn into the candidate's entourage, with all the ensuing personal and emotional attachments that create convictions where there were none before.

Gene Jones, creator of Nixon's campaign commercials:

> I'm a professional. This is a professional job. I was neutral toward Nixon when I started. Now I happen to be for him. But that's not the point. The point is, for the money, I'd do it for almost anybody.[51]

As early as 1956, science fiction carried warnings of the advertising men who "merchandised" presidential candidates like toothpaste, with the help of sinister pollsters. Polls identify key target groups of "swing voters" who might be susceptible to persuasion, by appeals directed at their hopes and fears rather than by reasoned discussion of public policy issues. The content of cynically prepared and mendacious political commercials (like those featuring the killer-rapist Willie Horton, used by George Bush in 1988 and then turned against him in 1992) has itself become a matter of campaign debate. And campaign debate has degenerated into a repetition of points already crystallized into tag lines for commercials.

The very nature of television—its emphasis on the human countenance, its difficulty in handling abstract ideas—has transformed the nature of presidential politics. Gerald Ford's TV advisor, John Deardourff, said explaining complex issues through commercials was a waste of money; their function was to convey the personality of the candidate. Confirming this proposition, Robert M. Teeter, Reagan's pollster and Bush's 1992 campaign manager, conducted research that used videotapes of politicians in action—including unfamiliar Canadians—without any clear indication of their substantive views. Respondents rating unknown figures evaluated them in the same way as those who knew their actual positions and performance.[52] Image superseded ideas.

The rise of political consultants changed the relationships of agencies and their political clients; it coincided with the emergence of television as the primary weapon in electoral contests. As consultants assumed control over the shaping of the candidate's public *persona*, they took over the creative role of the agency, hired their own research firms to study policy issues, campaign themes, and candidate reputations, handled their own production of commercials, and employed outside time-buying services to allocate media budgets. Consultants are now engaged in the overall shaping of campaign strategy and the formulation of candidates' policy positions, activities that once evolved from the maelstrom of organizational politics rather than as a sideshow of show business.

Although many political consultants entered the scene as producers of commercials, they recognized early in the game that their candidates needed coaching for every televised occasion (and for nontelevised occasions too, though there were hardly any of those any more). Candidates employ "spinners" (or "spin doctors") to weave tales that favorably interpret the debates and developments in the campaign for television audiences and news reporters. On a lower level, members of Congress produce "interviews" for local stations in their districts, with "questions" that can be dubbed in by the station's own newscaster. The Republican Campaign Committee had a camera crew on the lawn outside the Capitol each Wednesday for this purpose.

Presidents have plunged into the details of their campaign advertising with as much amateurish dedication as the head of a soap company might summon for the commercials for a new detergent. Richard Nixon wrote H. R. Haldeman on December 1, 1969:

> When I think of the millions of dollars that go into one lousy 30-second television spot advertising a deodorant, it seems to me unbelievable that we don't do a better job in seeing that Presidential appearances always have the very best professional advice.[53]

Roger Ailes, the strategist behind the Willie Horton commercial, candidly critiqued Bush's television delivery technique. ("There you go again with that fucking hand. You look like a fucking pansy!"[54]) He expressed his underlying strategy on a number of occasions:

> News is who has the hottest attack ads and who can get the highest ratings. What would a journalist rather cover—new TV ads or the latest proposal to change the capital gains tax?[55]

> The media has no interest in substance. . . . There are three ways to get on the air: pictures, attacks, and mistakes, so what you do is spend your time avoiding mistakes, staying on the attack, and giving them pictures. You do that and you're guaranteed the lead story on the evening news. . . . If I were to talk about world peace, pollution, ethics, no matter how good my programs were, I'd be a guaranteed loser.[56]

> The reality is that every successful politician in the history of the world had people around to make them look good. Who do you think told Caesar to wear the purple cape? Who do you think told him he needed six horses pulling a chariot instead of just four? Why do you think he rode through Rome denying he wanted to be king? Who do you think thought that up, him? C'mon![57]

The philosophy expressed in such statements may be rooted in ancient principles of pragmatic politics. The techniques of executing them are those of the skilled manipulator of modern communications tools. The substance of political messages is subordinated to the virtuosity of these techniques. Principles count for less than the packaged aura, just as product marketers "sell the sizzle, not the steak." Thus the arts of advertising sway the nation's fate.

Advertising and National Values

Whether it promotes candidates or consumer products, advertising is not an extraneous intrusion into the flow of information and entertainment. It is itself an important element of media content and has a significant impact on what we think and how we act, as consumers and as citizens.

At the end of the last chapter, I noted that the Marxist critique of the media system failed to offer anything better as a replacement. The same may be said of the Marxist denunciation of advertising. As the twentieth century draws to its close, the collapse of the Communist order in the Soviet Union and Eastern Europe has brought a fresh realization of the economic value of advertising and of the merits of the free media system it supports. With a loss of confidence in the ability of human beings to realize socialist ideals has come a remarkable rediscovery of market doctrine—a rapid acceptance of the notion that the pursuit of individual self-interest may unintentionally yield social benefits.

Karl Marx insisted, correctly, that consumption has important political consequences. When the Berlin wall was breached in November 1989 and hundreds of thousands of East Germans were able to sample life in the West, they quickly exhausted the supply of bananas and oranges and headed for hamburgers and soft drinks. It was the consumer goods of the West that they identified with freedom, even though the corrupting influence of these possessions had been the theme of forty years of indoctrination. They thronged to see the creations of Hollywood, expressions of a fantasy world in which Rambo, Mickey Mouse, Colonel Sanders, and Ronald McDonald were all icons of equivalent potency. As audiences flocked to American movies, the East European film industry collapsed, its state subsidies eliminated.

In post-Soviet Russia, Coca-Cola has cachet. At the height of the Cold War, Communist propaganda in Europe faked Coca-Cola advertisements showing the Crucifixion, with the caption, "Christ on the cross would have suffered less if he could have had a Coke." But advertising had long attracted special venom from Marxist ecclesiastics. The 1941 edition of the *Great Soviet Encyclopedia*:

> Hullabaloo, speculation, and a mad race for profits have made advertising a means of swindling the people and foisting upon them goods frequently useless or of dubious quality.

The upheavals in the Communist countries at the end of the 1980s were prompted by rising dissatisfaction with the system's inability to meet the population's material needs. Under socialism, higher priority than in the West was given to certain public goods (like subway systems and ballet companies). But these were no substitute for the goods that people consumed individually. After 75 years of Soviet power, the yearning for VCRs, Cardin ties, and other appurtenances of degenerate capitalist materialism is no less avid than in those nations where the cult of consumption has long been enshrined.

Does this then mean that, apart from a few surviving hunter-gatherers and many landless peasants inured to the most dismal expectations, people universally share the same desire for bigger houses, richer diets, more intriguing gadgets? A look around tells us that they do not. Some prefer to trade leisure for income; others labor altruistically in low-paying jobs that reward them with approval or affection. Still others concentrate their energies on the acquisition of wealth to the point that they have no time left to spend or enjoy it. Such variations may arise from differences in personality or from the importance that different subcultures assign to the ownership of personal property. They do not seem to bear any relationship to the amount of individual exposure to advertising messages that present consumption as an ultimate value.

In the late fall of 1944 I entered the city of Aachen, Germany, as a young soldier. On the side of a large building that had been badly damaged by shellfire was an enormous painted billboard. It showed a happy housewife holding a package of soap flakes, with the slogan, "Wash *must* be cared for by Persil!"[58] At that very moment, a few hundred miles away, the Nazis were busy converting children to ashes—and were even (falsely) rumored to be using human ashes to make soap. The incongruity of that billboard remains in my memory primarily in its juxtaposition of the grim realities of twentieth-century life with the conventional pleasant fantasies in the marketer's dreamworld of contented housewives and sparkling white laundry.

Unlike such countries as Japan and West Germany, the United States has been living in the present, borrowing against the future, and saving very little to preserve its resources and the physical plant of roads and buildings on which the common weal depends.[59] How much of this suicidal tendency can be accounted for by the continual glorification of consumption?

In many countries, perhaps in most around the world, the pressure to acquire and to consume seems minimal, compared to what we take for granted in the West, especially in the United States. Partly this disinclination reflects the inertia of tradition, but mostly it is because unproductive economies are incapable of satisfying an already existing demand at prices that the public is able to afford. Neither a scarcity of purchasing power—as in the impoverished countries of South America, Africa, and Asia—nor a scarcity of goods—as in Russia—signifies an absence of the appetite for consumption.

Deep in the Amazon jungle, members of isolated tribes sit on the dirt floors of their grass huts, wearing T-shirts bearing the seals of American universities. Their diet is meager; their life expectancy low. Would they like more T-shirts, blue jeans, transistor radios, Coca-Cola? The question answers itself.

Near the tip of the Northern Cameroons, in the heart of West Africa, I once met a French physician who operated a hospital at a remote outpost in the bush. She spoke feelingly of the tribulations and struggles of her patients. Would these people be better off, I asked her, if we of the West had never come along to disturb their traditional ways with all the complexities and complexes of our turbulent civilization? She said, "I have never yet met anyone who did not want to make life better for himself and his children."

But what makes life better? Is it designer jeans rather than an animal skin, dinner at La Tour d'Argent rather than over a campfire? Is it a Mercedes in the garage, membership in the country club, a first-class passage to Tahiti? Or is it clean air and clear streams, highways without potholes, streets without homeless beggars? The most devastating criticism of the effects that commercial communication has on our values is not that it puts great stress on the acquisition of material goods and by implication devalues contemplation, spirituality, sociability, and aesthetic pursuits. Rather, it is that advertising is dedicated overwhelmingly to persuading us to acquire possessions for our individual selves, and thus scants society's resources for the more valuable things we use and need in common.

The institutions of advertising perform its specific minor corporate tasks of persuasion, oblivious to its larger social effects. These effects arise not just from ads themselves, but from the way advertising shapes the substance of most media.

4

Paying the Piper, Calling the Tune

What advertisers say matters less than their influence on the media that carry their messages. At the height of the turmoil over Vietnam, the diplomat-scholar George Kennan drew a rather tortuous connection between "student bewilderment and unrest" and "the problem of the advertiser and the mass media." He posed a rhetorical question:

> Does anyone seriously believe today that the advertiser is a fit person—a person fitted by purpose, by function, by dedication—to bear what amounts to at least half of the total responsibility for the education of American youth?[1]

There is no such person as "the advertiser." As we saw in the last chapter, advertisers come in all shapes and sizes and have differing objectives. Their presence is felt in a number of ways: They sometimes directly seek to get media to say what they want said or to avoid saying what might damage them. Some sponsor broadcast programs, like soap operas, whose scripts they control. Occasionally, facing pressure themselves, they try to get media to knuckle under. Much more significantly, their budgeting decisions determine the fortunes of publications and programs.

Media assume their form and substance under the pressure of competition—more for advertising than for audiences. As advertisers define their markets in terms of particular target groups, media accommodate them by becoming more specialized. Advertisers do not act in concert to exert their collective economic weight. However, in pursuing their individual and separate interests, they tend to play by the same rules. Those rules, sometimes based on mistaken premises (as we shall see in the next chapter), govern the media system. Key points:

- Advertisers rarely try to buy journalists to slant news in their favor; more often they try to suppress news they don't like.

93

- They are sensitive about the environment for their messages and edgy about controversy.
- When advertisers yield to vigilante pressure, media producers veer toward self-censorship.
- Advertisers shape content directly when they sponsor broadcast programs. They shape content indirectly — as in the case of televised sports — by supporting media that meet their marketing requirements.
- The virtual end of local press competition shows how advertisers determine the life and death of media, with serious consequences for society.

Corrupting the News

The crudest form of advertiser influence on media content has been the subornation of what purports to be honest and disinterested news reporting to serve a private interest. Occasionally one comes across cases of out and out corruption: The Dominican dictator Rafael Trujillo paid the Mutual Broadcasting radio network $750,000 in 1959 and sent $2,000 a month to Hearst's International News Service. Newspapers in debt to the Teamsters gave favorable coverage to Jimmy Hoffa. Most cases of venality are less open and shut.

In the nineteenth century, newspapers that proclaimed their mission to be public service cited the diversity of their advertising base as the foundation of their editorial integrity. Advertising freed the press "from pecuniary dependence upon cliques and monopolies," in the words of Volney B. Palmer (who founded the first American newspaper representative firm in 1832). Editors fought and largely won the battle to separate "church and state" — to keep the news function free of advertiser influences.

In defiance of this precept, the occasional subversion of the press by advertisers' demands continues in an uninterrupted tradition, and has been exposed by successive generations of muckrakers. There is a long history, in periodical publishing, of using the news columns to support advertising messages. Almost any issue of the *Columbia Journalism Review* contains a "dart" directed at a paper that shamefully runs a puff piece to back up an advertiser's promotion. Fresh examples turn up all the time in what are widely regarded as reputable publications.

Corporations, whether or not they are major advertisers, intrude their commercial or corporate interests into the news media directly through their routine public relations efforts, a corrupt practice only when press releases are published (in whatever disguise) as a *quid pro quo* for paid advertising. Products and the companies that make them are often interesting to the public and are legitimate topics for news coverage. Publicity handouts have for many years been a staple element of editorial content in newspapers and magazines, not only on consumer subjects but on everything else. Supplementing the contrived news embodied in conventional press releases, public relations firms and advertising agencies routinely prepare and send out, by satellite, "video news releases" (VNRs) that are aired as "news" by dozens and even hundreds of stations with millions of viewers. Ostensibly on subjects of general interest, they embody plugs, usually most unobtrusive, for clients and their products.

A former editor of *Harper's*, John Fischer, reported that "only three times in 14 years of editing this magazine did I run into anything that could be called advertising pressure, and in each case it was trivial."[2] *Harper's* has long been a periodical of unexceptionable integrity. Many other editors might take advertising pressures so much for granted that they do not even recognize them when they are there.

For many years newspapers were owned by manufacturers and mining interests, especially in plant towns. Newspapers owned by railroads failed to report railroad wrecks. The public sometimes seems indifferent to such connections. Veco International, an oilfield services company employed by Exxon to handle the big 1989 Alaskan oil spill, bought the *Anchorage Times* that same year. A poll showed that 26% of Anchorage residents were "more likely" to read a paper associated with the oil business and 24% "less likely," while 50% said it would make no difference. (The *Times* was sold to its competitor in 1992, and ceased publication.)

The public's blasé attitude is understandable. In an era of monopoly newspapers, which are often regarded as public utilities, Americans appear to be complacent in the face of press opinions they do not share. Only 9% say they would stop reading a paper if they disagreed with its editorial policy, and 8% claim that they *have* stopped reading a paper because of its partisanship or bias.[3]

Local advertisers are not likely these days to try to get publishers to editorialize on behalf of favorite candidates or causes, though they may occasionally lean on them to keep a story of personal interest off the front page. Publishers discussing their biggest frustration agree that it is facing advertiser friends' requests to soften news reports when "my kid's in trouble." Internally, business office intervention is more apt to occur in areas that directly relate to the newspaper's revenue stream than on larger political or social issues.[4]

A century ago, a pioneering study showed that Nebraska papers were selling news columns to advertisers.[5] This practice is not so remote from the fairly recent notion of "adding value" by providing an advertiser with extra favors. *Better Homes and Gardens* printed 3.4 million copies of its cookbook in a special edition for Kraft, in exchange for eight pages of advertising.[6] The same erosion of the rules is evident in the broadcast industry. NBC transformed its broadcast standards department (which monitored the acceptability of ads) to make it responsible for developing exploitable product tie-ins and reduced its staff from sixty to twenty.

Allen H. Gerson, vice-president of program marketing and administration:

> What we want to do is to try to find new kinds of things that we can offer to our sponsors to make network television advertising even more attractive.

Greed is sometimes laced with naïveté. After General Electric acquired NBC, its board chairman suggested that since authors interviewed on the "Today" show "must sell a lot of books," their publishers could be charged for such appearances.[7]

Newspapers and magazines are periodically the targets of indignation and pressure by advertisers who, in the worst of cases, want only their side of the story told and, in the best of cases, are expressing (sometimes legitimate) objections to biased and antagonistic coverage of their interests. William D. Dyke, former mayor of Madison, Wisc.:

> How many times have we wondered why it is that the advertiser will go back and buy a full page, week after week, and watch the columns of the paper be used to destroy the business that is supporting it?[8]

A realtor in Nampa, Idaho, who had succeeded in getting the local editor fired, told *The New Yorker*'s Calvin Trillin: "If it's bad for our business, why should we advertise? . . . It's our business to be optimistic about the community."

Nine out of ten newspaper editors (in a 1992 survey of 147) were aware of attempts by advertisers to influence the news by withdrawing their ads or threatening to do so. More than a third reported that such an attempt had been successful.[9] Larger papers are understandably more successful than smaller ones in standing up to such pressures.

• As an example of the kinds of problems that the press sometimes faces, consider the case of Nordstrom's, a retailer that made striking gains in the 1980s because of its reputation for intensive customer service. The Seattle-based company was the subject of an investigative report in the *Wall Street Journal* in 1990, which recounted, in detail, charges of unfair labor practices. Both the *Seattle Times* and the *Post-Intelligencer* subsequently ran their own stories, describing the charges made by disgruntled employees. Nordstrom's pulled its advertising from both papers in protest. The chain was a major advertiser, and its revenue was critical for the newspapers, especially at a time of business downturn.

• When the Charlotte, N.C., newspapers ran a Sylvia Porter column on used car dealers, the local dealers boycotted the paper. Similarly, when WCCO-TV in Minneapolis ran a consumer report, a Ford dealer grumbled,

> We vote with our dollars. If I'm out trying to tell a good story about what I'm doing and paying $3,000 for 30 seconds, and someone's calling me names, I'm not going to be happy.[10]

• A television program on "Banks and the Poor" was previewed by representatives of the American Banking Association, and many public television stations were consequently pressured locally to keep it off the air.[11]

The style of such pressure varies from the most subtle wining, dining, and wooing to the most brutal and direct intimidation. During the course of Senate hearings that eventually gave rise to the Fair Packaging and Labeling Act of 1966, the Grocery Manufacturers Association invited sixteen magazine publishers to a meeting on "the facts of life covering advertising-media relationships." Paul Willis, president of the G.M.A., said,

> We suggested to the publishers that the day was here when their editorial department and business department might better understand their interdependency relationships as they affect the operating results of their company; and as their operations may affect the advertiser—their bread and butter.[12]

Magazines and newspapers evinced decidedly little interest in this consumer issue.

The president of the Pennsylvania Retailers Association wrote to newspapers in his state during the 1991 recession, suggesting that they build consumer confidence: "We think, 'Employment Up' [as a headline] is better than 'Unemployment Down.' "[13]

Even respected publications and successful broadcasters give way to these kinds of influences:

• When the Amalgamated Clothing Workers picketed Marshall Field's for selling imported merchandise, an ad prepared to explain their action was rejected by all four Chicago newspapers, for which Field's was (and, for the two survivors, still is) a key advertiser.

• The Florida Fruit and Vegetable Association protested a 1970 NBC documentary that showed the plight of migratory agricultural workers, and threatened that it would ask the FCC to investigate "whether such licensee is adequately discharging its responsibility so as to warrant its continuing to be a licensee." Coca-Cola, whose Minute-Maid subsidiary is a major factor in the business, shifted all its network billings out of NBC, which had changed the script, but not the visuals or the message of the show.[14]

• A supplement on heart disease, proposed by the American Heart Association, was rejected by the *Reader's Digest* in 1986 on the grounds that no revenues would come from the large food advertisers owned by the tobacco conglomerates.[15]

• A television series prepared by the National Audubon Society included a program critical of the clear-cutting practices of the logging industry on Federal lands in the Pacific Northwest. Representatives of the timber industry warned away prospective advertisers on Turner Broadcasting, including Stroh's (which had promised $600,000 for the series), Ford, and Exxon. The program was shown without commercial advertising.

• A 90-minute CBS documentary on hunting, "The Guns of August," lost over half a dozen advertisers in 1975, when the National Rifle Association brought its gunfire to bear. The network substituted public service commercials, but ran the program.

• Eastman Kodak objected to an issue of *Time* devoted to the history of photography, which raised the prospect of filmless pictures in the future.[16]

The instances I have just cited stand out for their singularity, and some of them are ancient history in an industry where "last season" seems an eternity away. But there are institutional reverberations in each such case. The most important effects are not in the accommodation or resistance to the specific advertisers, but in the longer-term influence on corporate definitions of what is and what is not permissible subject matter.

Advertising pressure does not just affect media coverage of news and public affairs; it hits other advertising:

• In April 1988 RJR Nabisco withdrew more than $70 million from the DFS Compton agency after it created an ad for Northwest Airlines, promoting its shift to a no-smoking policy.

• Advantage/Quik Fit, a company with a stop-smoking system based on audiocassettes, had its ads refused by *Time, Newsweek, Sports Illustrated,* and *Us* magazines. Riley McDonough, the advertising director of *Us,* remarked that "it would put us in an awkward position to run an antismoking ad in the same issue as cigarette ads. To be honest, it's purely an economic question, not one of phi-losophy."[17]

Media have long had internal rules over what types of products to accept for advertisements and what restrictions to place on advertising copy. (These may include unsubstantiated claims, unfair attacks on competitors, or dangerous prod-ucts.) Only 9% of newspapers, with 4% of the circulation, refuse ads for handguns, but 32% (with 37% of circulation), refuse ads for abortion services.[18]

For years, the networks refused to accept advertisements advocating one side on controversial public issues. A weakening ad market caused them to change this stance in 1990, though they still drew the line on such hot topics as abortion and gun control. A spokesman for General Electric's NBC commented, "It's not a free-for-all. We still have to be vigilant that the deep pockets don't gain control over the issues."[19] The commercial broadcaster fears not merely that a particular advertiser may drop advertisements from a program, but also that the discomfort and expense of dealing with letter campaigns and boycott threats will poison long-term client relationships.

Some advertisers have stood their ground courageously behind stars involved in controversy. After the "See It Now" program in which Edward R. Murrow exposed Senator Joe McCarthy, CBS management's reaction, according to Murrow, was: "Good show. Sorry you did it."[20] But his sponsor, "Chief" Irving W. Wilson, Chairman of Alcoa, told him: "I wouldn't ask you not to do such programs, but I would hope you wouldn't do them every week." Murrow said, "Neither would I." Alcoa dropped its sponsorship a year later.

In rare instances, a media organization has been known to abandon the field altogether rather than compromise its integrity. The New York Times Company sold off eight medical journals after a boycott by pharmaceutical companies who objected to an ad in the newspaper. These advertisers were of little significance to *The New York Times* itself, but their support was vital to the journals. This episode illustrated the extraordinary vulnerability of specialized publications and the difficulty they face in serving their readers by being informative, objective, and critical while maintain-ing their revenue base.

General consumer publications might be expected to have an easier time of it. This is no longer true as they become more dependent upon outcast categories of advertisers, who, for one reason or another, have fewer media options than most. Articles on the health effects of smoking only rarely appeared, over a 7-year period, in the magazines that accept cigarette ads.[21] The two leading tobacco companies, Philip Morris and RJR Nabisco, are also leading forces in the food and beverage businesses.

Cosmopolitan's Helen Gurley Brown:

> We just don't say rotten things about our advertisers. There is very little to warn our readers about, because advertisers' products are so good.[22]

However, a physician who wrote a health column for *Cosmopolitan* reported a "big fight" when she included smoking as a risk factor in a health checklist, "because they didn't want to offend their advertisers."[23]

The same Mrs. Brown:

> Who needs somebody you're paying thousands of dollars a year to come back and bite you on the ankle?[24]

That is a very good question, but it is also a good answer to the thesis that the free workings of the media market always advance the public interest.

Content and Advertiser Sensitivities

Advertisers have every good business reason to avoid environments unsuited for their messages. The emotional tone that is set by a publication or broadcast influences the public's attentiveness to the ads and receptivity to persuasion. During the Persian Gulf War, four out of five people did not oppose advertising in the middle of news coverage, although three out of five agreed that "light-hearted, upbeat commercials" were inappropriate.[25] Commercials continued to interrupt the reports from the battle zone, although some advertisers briefly reduced their volume or changed the tone of their messages.

William Croasdale, a senior vice-president of the Backer Spielvogel Bates agency:

> Commercials are full of music and happiness. They have a lot of comedy in them. Everything is upbeat. Sponsors don't want to shift from a general discussing soldiers killed in action to 'Double your pleasure, double your fun.' It's jarring.[26]

In television, as in radio before it, advertisers avoid disturbing and painful settings. Precisely because the environment for ads is thought of as a natural frame, they prefer the bland and noncontroversial, whether or not this character coincides with the decision-maker's own tastes. Bob Shanks, then vice-president of ABC, said a program should not move viewers "too deeply": "Ruffling, it is thought, will interfere with their ability to receive, recall and respond to the commercial message."[27]

Another observer, Paul Espinosa, comments that

> any issue which is likely to divide, and thus diminish the audience is viewed as a topic to be avoided.[28]

Actually, viewers do not appear to carry over their critical judgment of a program's content to make a negative judgment on its advertisers, even though sponsors have always assumed that the reverse—a positive transference—happens in a favorable way when they are listening to or watching something they like. A 7-day ABC miniseries, "Amerika," portrayed what life would be like after a Soviet occupation. Nearly half the viewers found the show boring, and one in six found some aspect of it offensive. But their attitudes toward the sponsors did not change.[29]

Individual advertisements are perceived in a context that often embraces incongruent and contradictory messages, from direct competitors and from other products. This occurs almost routinely in print—where some advertisers welcome the attention it arouses—and not uncommonly in broadcasts within the same programming period, sometimes even within the same cluster of commercials and accidentally back to back. Of all the commercials in a prime-time network hour, 42% are in direct conflict with a competing message in the same period.[30] On one occasion, a single network program carried commercials for five different brands of soft drinks.

Every advertisement performs in a communications context that can alter its meaning. No airline expects newspapers to suppress the news of an airplane crash, but advertising contracts normally stipulate that airline ads should not be run near such a news story, or should even be switched to another day. From this quite rational business practice a direct thread leads to an old and classic case that illustrates the conflict of reconciling creative integrity and legitimate business self-interest.

• In 1959, the American Gas Association sponsored a television drama series called "Playhouse 90." When the script of an episode dealing with the Nuremberg trials made repeated references to the gas chambers in the Nazi death camps, Lennen and Newell, the advertising agency, demanded and got changes in the script. A Lennen and Newell executive:

> In going through the script, we noticed gas referred to in a half-dozen places that had to with with the death chambers. This was just an oversight on somebody's part. . . . We raised the point with CBS and they said they would remove the word "gas" . . . and at the last minute we found that there were still some left in. . . . The show went on the air where the word "gas" was deleted by the engineer.[31]

From the standpoint of the client and the agency, this made perfect business sense. The damage to public information and to creative autonomy was beside the point. The validity of the sponsor's anxieties in this case may be seen by the experience years later in the exceptionally bizarre juxtapositions that occurred during commercial breaks on the miniseries "Holocaust," which appeared in the spring of 1978 on NBC. There were commercials for pantyhose and roach killers. After victims were told that the gas chambers they were about to enter were "disinfecting areas," a message from Lysol talked about its efficacy in "killing germs." A sequence that showed Nazis enjoying photographs of their mass murders was followed by a commercial for Polaroid cameras.

• Advertisers have always been sensitive to the intrusion of disturbing or competitive programming elements. Alcoa, a major supplier to trailer manufacturers, changed the locale of a play called "Tragedy in a Temporary Town" from a trailer lot to a shanty mining town.[32] A Civil War drama sponsored by Chrysler managed to avoid mentions of Lincoln. A Ford-sponsored program eliminated the Chrysler building from a shot of the New York skyline.[33] And pictures of real camels were forbidden on the Camel News Caravan, as were cigar-smokers.[34]

As Chairman of the FCC, Newton Minow encountered other bizarre instances of advertiser interference with program content: When two tobacco companies had similar programs, one insisted that the heavy be shown smoking filter cigarettes; the other wanted the villain to smoke nonfilters.[35] According to Minow, "An electric company wanted a different title for Kipling's 'The Light That Failed.' As for Edith Wharton's bleak tragedy, 'Ethan Frome,' the agency inquiry was, 'Couldn't you brighten it up a little?' "

In the face of unexpected incongruities, the advertiser's actions in many cases seems entirely justified. Quite understandably, a Puppy Chow ad was pulled off an episode of "Little House on the Prairie" in which wild dogs chased a girl. In other instances, advertisers simply make judgments on matters of content unrelated to their products, sometimes because of their own opinions and sometimes in deference to the opinions or threats of others.

Vigilantes, Boycotts, Self-Censorship

Advertisers not only influence media content directly; they are vulnerable to pressure from outsiders with axes to grind. More often in the realm of entertainment than in journalism, media managements have repeatedly been led to self-censorship by advertisers acting not so much out of their own convictions or self-interest as in fear of vigilante groups. Self-appointed guardians of morality—like their counterparts and allies on the political far right—have shown themselves adept in the use of sophisticated techniques of persuasion, including boycotts and threats of boycotts against advertisers. One fundamentalist preacher, Donald Wildmon, argued that he was going after 10% of the advertisers:

> All they do is buy cpm [cost per thousand, the arithmetic measure of advertising "efficiency"]. That is all they care about. We're saying, hey, when you make a decision, please, don't make it entirely on cpm. We know where you're coming from, that you've got to get your cpms, that you've got products to sell and all that, but remember, we're your customers and you have a competitor and we can do business with your competitor.[36]

Huge corporations (Coca-Cola, McDonald's, General Motors, Chrysler, General Mills, Campbell Soup, Ralston–Purina, Bristol Myers, American Home Products, Johnson & Johnson, and Sears) have canceled commercials on shows allegedly contaminated by sex or obscenity. ("Saturday Night Live," for example, had made repeated use of the word "penis" for comic effect.[37]) Even impeccably honest and serious programs like ABC's "Nightline" have been singled out as "offensive." The lists of blacklisted programs include "Geraldo," "Phil Donahue," "Benny Hill," "Divorce Court," "Saturday Night Live," "Inside Edition," and "The Dating Game.") Pepsi-Cola canceled a $5 million commercial after the singer Madonna released a music video that showed burning crosses, stigmata, and love scenes with a saint-like figure.[38] General Motors dropped its sponsorship of the miniseries, "Jesus of Nazareth," in 1977 when fundamentalist groups objected to the portrayal of Christ as a human.

Programs have also been blacklisted on political grounds. In 1991, an unnamed advertiser pulled out of an episode of "Murphy Brown" that included snide remarks about Wildmon and his ally, Senator Jesse Helms. (There was no such timidity when the program counterattacked against Vice-President Quayle a year later.) One advertiser refused to have commercials appear on any program produced by Norman Lear.[39]

The question raised in such incidents was not about the merit of the objections, but whether the advertiser's judgment of politics or propriety was to prevail over that of programming professionals. Procter and Gamble refused to sponsor an ABC movie with a rape scene that was considered gratuitous, but remained in an NBC program with a rape scene that was thought to have "redeeming social value." Just before the Moral Majority pressure group was scheduled to announce a boycott of sponsors to whose programs it objected, Owen Butler, P & G's chairman, told the Academy of Television Arts and Sciences

> "while we stand firm in our conviction that we must not let our programming decisions be made by threats of boycott, we have simultaneously made an intense effort to listen very carefully to what the vocal critics, as well as the general public, have to say about the kinds of television programs we sponsor.[40]

P & G had itself earlier been the victim of a boycott campaign led by mysterious defenders of Christianity who purported to believe that the company's century-old crescent-moon trademark was a symbol of Satanism.

Advertisers were actually paying a premium price for positions on "clean" programs.[41] When some pulled their commercials out of shows that had been targeted by the vigilantes, others stepped in to take advantage of the resulting bargains. An agency media director commented, "advertisers who are able to provide some flexibility are achieving pricing benefits."[42] Their flexibility made business sense. Although the agitation of pressure groups is highly effective in dealing directly with advertisers, there is no indication that it works with the public, which responds to advertised products on their own merits.[43] Instances of capitulation may serve the selfish interests of individual advertisers, but they do advertising itself no service. Its credibility depends to a very large degree on the integrity the public ascribes to the media in which it appears.

The screws have also been applied to media managements by (often self-appointed) representatives of minority groups clamoring for redress of sometimes well-justified grievances. Blacks, Latinos, Indians all have legitimately protested their exclusion or demeaning depictions in the past. And new and sometimes ridiculous complaints from unexpected quarters have created extraordinary sensitivities. The word "gypped" was dropped because it offended Gypsies. The Tlingit Indians made a demand for representation through a quota of TV characters.[44] An association of blind people protested the way a blind character in a TV show was depicted. Programs dealing with homosexuality and teen-age suicide were threatened with boycotts by homosexual activists, but have also (for no mysterious reason) failed to attract advertisers.

Self-censorship represents a more pervasive and insidious influence on the substance of media than any direct advertiser pressures. Even when media withstand attempts at intimidation, their managers must always think twice when potentially controversial or objectionable topics arise. The individual components of the media system operate by their own historically determined rules. In those sectors governed by the traditions of journalism rather than those of show business, there is a strong need for professional autonomy, a built-in resistance to pressure of any kind. Professionalism, by definition, implies a dual dedication to craftsmanship and to public service—a point to which I shall return before we are through. It is the glory of American mass media that this dedication persists to a very high degree. But it is always constrained by the business necessities of survival, and the rationalization for compromise is always the need to live and fight again another day.

Sponsorship

Except for advertisements themselves, the presence of advertisers is nowhere more apparent than in broadcast programs with which they are directly identified. In this respect, broadcasting has gone immeasurably beyond the power of print. Advertising posters represented a direct communication from the advertiser to the consumer, while advertisements in newspapers or magazines conveyed their messages as part of a complex visual environment. There the meaning of an individual ad was filtered through the reverberating meanings of the other ads and editorial items that surrounded, preceded, or followed it. The perception of the ad was further colored by the readers' relationship to the publication itself and their identification with its subject matter and its tone.

As rival newspapers and magazines clamored for advertisers' business, they stressed their believability, the loyalty of their readers. Advertisers still regarded each advertisement as an individual message directed at prospective customers, but they placed their ads recognizing that they would be received in context. To a degree—but only to a degree—that context could be determined by the choice of publications. When sponsors owned broadcasts, the context was totally under their control. To this day, when corporations sponsor radio symphony broadcasts or dramas on public television, their public relations motives reflect the same survival instincts that once led Roman nobles to endow spectacles in the Colosseum.

Although business self-interest underlies all such programs, the motives of those in the corporate hierarchy who stand behind these efforts and who administer them are far more complex. Dispensing funds is an exercise of power, translatable into personal perquisites—entry into elite circles, opportunities to socialize with the talented and famous, the chance to implement one's own tastes on a scale that would never otherwise be possible.[45]

Sponsors no longer wield the power they had in the 1930s, when less than half the radio network time was sold out. For that reason, says broadcast historian Erik Barnouw, "in the sponsor-controlled hours, the sponsor was king. He decided on programming . . . (and) was assumed to hold a 'franchise' on his time period or periods."[46] Programs like Twenty-Mule Team Borax's "Death Valley Days" were created and produced for advertisers by their advertising agencies.[47]

How does the advertising sponsor's attitude differ from that of the Renaissance princeling with a court composer on the payroll, or of a Russian count with a retinue of serf painters and musicians? For such traditional patrons, the presence of servant or dependent artists was part of the essential embellishment of life. If the court required a master chef in the kitchen and a master armorer to keep the weaponry bright, did it not also require its own masters of the arts to beautify the surroundings, to record achievements, and to help idle time pass agreeably?

Advertisers similarly borrowed glory from their media presence. In sponsoring a program they were getting much more than the opportunity to say "a few words" about the product. They were essentially buying the right to associate themselves in the public mind with a certain kind of experience, with a cast of characters whom listeners found congenial, with a setting or a style of entertainment that attracted them. The manufacturers of Hellmann's Mayonnaise (with their "Happiness Boys," Billy Jones and Ernie Hare) and the makers of Pepsodent (with "Amos 'n Andy") spent (what were for the time) very large budgets in the conviction that they were making human connections with consumers, quite apart from the specific benefits they were promising in the commercial copy.

The sponsor basked in the favorable aura of the show. To offset the inevitable annoyance caused by commercial interruptions, positive identification was heightened by using the show's leading personalities. They stepped out of character to deliver commercials; their photographs adorned point-of-sale promotional placards; they made personal appearances at sales meetings and even at public events. They were company spokesmen. ("Jell-O again!" the comedian Jack Benny opened each broadcast.)

The erosion of the sponsor system came first in nonnetwork radio programming. Local advertisers with modest spending money were lured to the medium through the sale of individual spot announcements whose prices dropped as air time approached. The radio spot market became an auction, in which station representatives negotiated deals with advertising agency time-buyers, wielding virtuoso haggling technique.

The first years of television carried forth the radio sponsorship tradition, with a comedian like Ed Wynn now visible under his Texaco Fire Chief helmet. The popularity of "The $64,000 Question" in the late 1950s was a commercial triumph for Revlon because its sponsorship heightened brand awareness and familiarity. Its commercials were in no way unusually convincing, but they reached a bigger audience than anticipated.

In those glory days of quiz shows, a sponsor could determine which contestants should stay in the game and which should be cut off, by posing impossible questions. ("Stiff him!" ordered Revlon's Charles Revson.) It was, in fact, the public revelation that the quiz shows had been rigged that prompted the networks to assert their control over programming.

Program sponsorship on television did not fade away because advertisers lost the conviction that it had value altogether separate from their commercials. Rather it was because the escalating production costs of television made it impractical to maintain an exclusive identification with a particular show. The new ratings-dependent philosophy of media-buying put a premium on diversifying audiences. Roughly half the viewers of any given program would watch the next weekly episode, but an altogether different show at another time period might produce a lower level of duplication. Advertisers eager to maximize their "reach" were intrigued by the networks' offers of "scatter plans" that enabled them to spread their commercials among different kinds of programs at different hours of the day.

While the total amount of television advertising expanded steadily, both local and national spot advertising grew faster than the networks' share—long before cable made further inroads. In network television, exclusive sponsorship became rare. The advent of program syndication created new opportunities for corporations to produce their own shows. Advertisers became involved in complex deals that entailed the barter of programming rights in exchange for air time and the sale of commercial positions.

When programs had exclusive sponsors, advertisers were concerned with their qualitative aspects in a way that no longer exists. What was important was the rub-off from the excitement, good feeling, affection, or other sentiments evoked in the audience; the numbers were secondary. Later, when messages were scattered around among programs, the purchase of commercial time had to be reduced to bureaucratic efficiency, with reliance on cost formulas, survey data of often dubious validity, computers, and armies of underpaid clerks.

Sponsored programming was down but not out in the 1990s. General Motors was still working with the N.W. Ayer agency to produce its own "Mark of Excellence" programs, while it "underwrote" others on public television. General Foods, Chrysler, Coca-Cola, and other large advertisers produced made-for-TV movies of which they were sole sponsors. George Mahrlig, director of media services, Campbell Soup Company:

> Advertisers are seeking to identify with properties and have involvement in a property from a strategic standpoint for the company's image—billboard sponsorship and all that. And these people are realizing back-end potential.

Or, to put this into plain English, advertisers who produced programs had the chance to earn some of their investment back later through video, foreign rights, and especially the enormously expanded market for rebroadcasting, or syndication.[48] In 1994, Procter and Gamble had six television soap operas, which it produced itself and for which it set its own standards.

Sponsors and Soap Operas

Nowhere has the identification of sponsor and programming been more openly apparent than in the world of the soap opera. It was proclaimed in the opening line of the daily episode: "And here's Oxydol's own Ma Perkins again." The listeners were, literally, the buyers of soap, and cleaning dishes and washing laundry were supposedly high on their minds as they listened. *Broadcasting* magazine in 1935 described "Today's Children" (sponsored by Pillsbury) as "homey drama that appeals to 'just folks,' the mothers, the homemakers, the flour users of America."[49]

The relationships among corporation, agency, and soap opera producers were complex and intimate. "We do our best to help and guide the writers, but we don't dictate to them," a P & G executive explains benevolently:

> Nine times out of 10 or even, say, 99 out of 100, I think our writers look at us as part of the team. I don't think they ever feel we're businessmen coming in from Cincinnati to tell them how to do their jobs, because we don't do that.[50]

The original radio soap operas were geared to the pace of the then typical full-time housewife, who filled her morning with domestic tasks, flitted in and out of the room where the radio was located (usually the living room, where it occupied the place of honor), and often missed episodes alogether. Plots were elemental and moved at a glacial pace, with languorous pauses in desultory dialogue. They carried the listener endlessly forward from one episode to the next. No resolution was ever in sight.

Soap operas dealt in fundamental passions and with the intimate domestic problems of love, jealousy, illness, and death. Characters were introduced and dispensed with as actors moved in and out of favor. (More recently, on "Dynasty," a character was rendered comatose by brain surgery so that a high-priced actress could be cut off the payroll. This cost-saving tactic reversed the procedure used several years earlier, when a popular character reemerged a year after his death, which was explained away as his wife's bad dream.)

While prime-time drama (first in radio, then in television) dealt with the intrusion of external forces into individual lives, soap opera plots were spun within a confined and predictable framework. Their configuration and even the selection of characters were manipulated to attract audiences that fit a desired consumer profile.

The sanitized romances of radio soap opera gave way to the sexually explicit daytime television soap operas of the 1970s, whose content became steamier than prime-time drama. From a focus on the tangled family relationships of earlier days, soap operas evolved into a preoccupation with sexual connections in all conceivable forms. Their production formulas were applied to formats 1 hour and even longer, and their ingredients, narrative form, and style were increasingly extended to prime-time.

With expanded resources, television soap operas—once a low-budget format—have acquired fancier sets and are often shot on-location. However, the endless raveling and unraveling of human relationships that make up the plot lines have never been transferred successfully into a motion picture format, where they would have to survive closer scrutiny and engagement than they receive through television's less compelling mode of communication.

The principal characters, notes *New York Times* critic Walter Goodman, have such names as Egypt, Chelsea, Crystal, Sable, Misty, Thorne, Tod, Ridge, Brooke, and Darla.[51] The themes are endlessly repeated: lost children, sudden or expected inheritances, deadly operations.[52] Body ailments are a staple element of soap opera story lines,[53] making the medical profession a highly visible source of their cast of characters. (In the first 5 years of "Marcus Welby MD," the actor Robert Young got more than a quarter-million requests for medical advice.[54])

Programs produced by soap companies naturally had to fit corporate preconceptions of what the audience would find acceptable. While kinky sex was perfectly all right, abortion was an unmentionable topic.[55] The intimate involvement of soap operas with their corporate sponsors has left them peculiarly vulnerable to pressure.

Soap operas were invented and are continued as a format that serves advertisers' purposes. As in every other domain of broadcasting, the decision-makers prefer to believe that they are merely surrogates for popular demand, reflected in the size of the audience. But the audience comes because the programs are there, and it is the advertisers who own them and put them there.

Televised Sports

The reciprocal relationships among advertisers' interests, the broadcasters' desire to please them, and the evolution of the public's interests are well shown in the growth of televised sports. We have just observed that daytime soap operas efficiently reach women consumers who have always predominated in the broadcast audience. Advertisers of products directed to men, like beer and shaving cream, have looked for comparable opportunities to target their messages, and have found them in sportscasts.

Sports, like politics and the arts, can no longer be considered an autonomous sphere of human activity. Our direct experience with each of these realms is now inseparable from the mediated contacts and perceptions we get through television. Americans have an abiding involvement in sports, both as participants and as spectators. We can trace the antecedents of this avocation back to the original Olympiads, though the popularity of individual sports has changed over time.[56] The presence of more sportscasts has heightened the level of visibility and interest, creating masses of fans where formerly there were only occasional onlookers. Millions of home viewers have been added to the crowds of live spectators at games and matches, stimulating many of them to attend the actual events and to pursue their new interests by reading about them.

While talk about sports teams and players has long made up an important part of American conversation, its decibel level has been raised by the commercially induced influence of television.[57] When people observe the interaction and performance of athletes, the sophistication and skill of their judgments increases, as does the possibility for disagreement, which makes endless opportunities for discussion.[58] Acquaintances and strangers alike can talk about mutually known subjects and personalities, with little risk of exciting strong emotions. Because of television's accessibility and because viewing is so often a family activity, women have become a significant component of the audience. Television has broadened the range of interests by covering minor sports like fencing, soccer, stock-car racing, and karate. Tennis and golf, which formerly appealed only to elite minorities, and kinetic, plebeian, like wrestling and ice hockey, have transcended their earlier social class affinities. Athletics have provided new channels of opportunity for long-excluded racial minorities and changed the way they are perceived both by themselves and by the white majority.

As a result of this growth in interest, both professional and amateur sports have been transformed into huge and highly profitable industries. (Football teams typically get two-thirds of their average income from TV.) Fueled by advertisers' demands for male audiences of the youthful, vigorous, affluent kind that sports telecasts are assumed to attract, both the on-air and cable networks have escalated the prices they are willing to pay for broadcast rights. Originally they were convinced that advertisers had an inexhaustible willingness to pay more and more. Later they became trapped in competitive bidding motivated mainly by the fear of weakening their overall programming lineups and losing a valuable share of the viewers. As a result, they incurred hundreds of millions of dollars in losses, despite the incredible load of commercials (which occupy 29% of the time).[59] As internetwork competition raised the stakes, players' salaries rose accordingly, thus radically changing the economics of the sports industry.[60]

The style and structure of sports have changed because of the necessities imposed by television. Time-outs and other breaks are taken to accommodate commercial pods. The timing of games has itself been determined by the broadcast schedule. The expressive style of players—formerly almost invisible to the grandstand audience—is now seen by millions in closeup and is inevitably restrained and modified as a result. Uniforms have been designed to make them more attractive on the tube. Broadcast commentary on the games increasingly dramatizes the personal rivalries among athletes, to heighten the dramatic tension. Daily press coverage has followed suit. The competitive structure of professional baseball was altered in 1994, since televised post-season games had become an important source of additional revenues. The National and American Leagues were each separated into three divisions, permitting an additional series of playoffs.

America's fascination with professional sports personalities and teams, quite genuine, represents a mighty social force. But the evolution of this preoccupation cannot be understood except as a byproduct of the networks' search for advertising revenues. The prizes glitter for *them*. (A single 30-second commercial on the 1994 Superbowl broadcast cost $900,000.) The creation of sports manias illustrates the social consequences that follow when media content is maneuvered to serve advertisers' marketing needs.

Producing Media Content to Serve Advertisers

An ABC executive:

> The network is paying affiliates to carry network commercials, not programs. What we are is a distribution system for Procter and Gamble.[61]

Cyrus K. Curtis, founder of the Curtis Publishing Company:

> Do you know why we publish the *Ladies Home Journal*? The editor thinks it is for the benefit of the American woman. That is an illusion, but a proper one for him to have. But I will tell you the publisher's reason. . . . To give you people who manufacture things that American women want and buy a chance to tell them about your products.[62]

The influence of advertisers is not only felt directly in sponsored broadcasts, occasional stabs at news reports, or efforts at censorship; it is expressed more subtly in the way media formulate their content to maximize advertising income. Once upon a time, editors started publications with a vision of how to satisfy some distinctive public interest. The vision might be grand and sweeping, when the capital requirements to found a great newspaper or magazine could be met. They might have had the narrower purpose of supporting a political cause, of giving a voice and an identity to an ethnic or occupational group, or of catering to the perennial human urges for diversion, inspiration, solace, and titillation. (This old spirit is not wholly dead. A proposed new magazine named *Rapture*, which was to carry no advertising, explained its specialized mission: "Women have been given no sanction to express their sexuality in a normal healthy manner. There is more to sex than sex.")

The motives of media innovators have been both noble and crass, in every possible combination. But their translation traditionally began with a conception of the editorial product, an aspiration to make it distinctive, and a reliance on the judgment of the marketplace of prospective readers. A very different kind of impetus generally prevails in the initiation and operation of media today.

Alan Cohen, NBC's senior vice president of marketing, asks, "What can NBC do to help [a company launching a new luxury car] besides just selling advertising?" and suggests that the answer is to create an event

> that can be broadcast with a promotional tie-in. Even creating a show about how to buy a luxury car, which the auto company could sponsor. . . . We could use an existing show, and the program could tie into the topic. We wouldn't necessarily do it with news.[63]

Advertisers do not hesitate to rise to such occasions. Campbell Soup's George Mahrlig:

> We're looking for opportunities for vignettes, where we can surround our commercial with interesting programming to sustain the viewer's interest and then mug him with a commercial.[64]

Special issues and advertising sections now represent about 10% of all magazine advertising. A fifth of *Reader's Digest's* advertising pages and a fourth of *Business Week's* are in "advertorials"—advertisements embellished with puffery disguised as pseudo-editorial matter.[65] A special issue of *Fortune* had Chrysler as the only advertiser.

No medium has been more influenced by advertising considerations than newspapers. Advertisers increasingly use them not for the credibility their messages assimilate from the surrounding editorial matter, but simply as vehicles for distribution. Advertising circulars, or inserts, which account for a fifth of newspapers' retail advertising, have changed their production economics. (More than half the money an insert advertiser spends for a newspaper advertising schedule goes to the printer—not to the paper, and a small number of big printers control much of this business.) The growth of inserts has also changed the appearance and content of newspapers from the reader's perspective.

Circulars that are tucked into daily newspapers do not have the same organic relationship to their editorial content as conventional run-of-press advertisements.

They can just as easily be delivered through the mail or stuffed into free papers ("shoppers") that have no editorial independence. Insert advertisers are prepared to judge newspapers against other media simply by their cost of delivery. The inner-city readership of afternoon papers holds few attractions for them. Many large traditional retailers (like Detroit's J.L. Hudson and New York's Stern's) have given up their downtown locations to concentrate on suburban shopping malls. Mass retailers grew by avoiding central-city locations altogether and concentrating on malls or free-standing suburban real estate. They typically demand selective distribution, only to the areas near their stores, weakening the newspapers' function as a voice of the entire community. Metropolitan newspapers have thus been encouraged to move into zoned editions, not only for advertising, but also, in many cases, by producing editorial products that can compete with local weeklies and shoppers for reader interest.

In the 1980s, newspapers turned to a greater editorial emphasis on conveniently packaged regular feature sections designed to appeal to readers' utilitarian and avocational interests, but also capable of serving advertisers' needs. In some instances they were openly removed from the control of the editors. (In 1991, the Raleigh *News and Observer* put its Sunday automotive and real estate sections under its advertising department.) The acquisition of high-speed inserting equipment encouraged many publishers to increase their use of occasional special-themed sections designed to attract specific kinds of advertising, with editorial or pseudo-editorial matter prepared by the advertising department or by free-lancers, or sometimes just picked up from advertisers' handouts. Most of this advertising represented new business, so there was every indication that the trend would continue in spite of strong skepticism on the part of editors.

Such "advertorials" fit in with yet another significant trend, which is the ever-larger proportion of newspaper editorial content devoted to feature material rather than hard news. To get the correct perspective on this, we must note that—keeping pace with the advertising—American newspapers have grown enormously in bulk—by over half in the number of weekday pages and double on Sunday, over a ten-year period that ended before the onset of the business recession at the start of the 1990s. The press is printing more real news, especially local rather than national world news, which many editors now incorrectly seem to feel has been preempted by television. But the overall balance of newspaper content has drifted more and more in the direction of entertainment, with packaged sections that carry imaginative labels like *Living, Life Style, Life* and *Style*. Spurred by the challenge of falling readership and aided by computerized makeup, newspapers entered a period of highly creative experimentation and innovation in design and content. Greatly increased use of graphics and shorter news items also reflected editorial attempts to match television's pelletized digestibility, though there is no evidence that this strategy has been successful.

Inevitably, marketing requirements have clashed with the ethos of professional journalism. When Beverly Barnum, manager of market research for Harte-Hanks Communications, told a group of editors that newspapers were a marketable product, like toothpaste, a rejoinder came from Richard Smyser, editor of the *Oak Ridger* in Tennessee:

What's rolled from Gutenberg to Goss
You see as so much dental floss . . .

But Bev, if tricks that sell Ipana
Can fatten the amount of manna
In envelopes our paycheck comes in
That's something we can sink our gums in.

Target Marketing

Advertisers seek to be efficient by choosing media whose audiences' characteristics resemble those of the customers they want to reach. This old and commonsense practice has been given a new name: "target marketing." In an earlier era, advertisers often began with the conviction that everyone might be a potential prospect for what they were selling. Today's philosophy stresses selectivity.

Two contradictory forces have been at play in the definition of marketing targets. On the one hand, there was a revival of the theory that human beings are at heart all alike as consumers, whether they live in Ecuador, Mali, or Finland. As a byproduct of business concentration there was a great growth of multinational operations in the corporate, agency, and media worlds. This was rationalized through the lip service commonly paid to "global marketing" as a concept.

The idea of advertising on a worldwide scale was hardly novel. Companies like Unilever, Shell, Exxon, and Coca-Cola, and agencies like J. Walter Thompson and McCann-Erickson had been doing it through much of the twentieth century. Most of these organizations had long ago learned to exchange good ideas across borders. They knew how to strike a balance between the need to standardize where standardization made sense and the need to be responsive to the unique cultural, economic, and political demands of each national market. Now it was being said that people are fundamentally the same the world around, so that a single advertising campaign, perhaps with minor adaptations, would work anywhere. This was nonsense, of course, but the advertising business has always had a high level of tolerance for nonsense.

The notion of global marketing ran contrary to the increasing tendency for marketers to emphasize the distinctions among people within a given country. Advertisers are highly conscious of how audience numbers vary between men and women and among various age and income groups. Familiarity with these facts leads them to pursue a conventional wisdom about how different publics can be "delivered": college-educated men, with Sunday afternoon football games; high-school-educated women, with daytime talk shows. The stereotypes are not inaccurate, but they lend themselves to simplifications.

It is simply not true that there is no accounting for taste—in attire, architecture, films, or reading matter. Straightforward demographic categories have proven to be the best predictors of what media people turn to, as well as of what goods they buy, but variations in taste obviously reflect combinations of forces that go well beyond these conventional designations. "Psychographic" measurements of personality, which became popular in market research in the 1970s, actually turn out to be secondary indicators of demographic differences.[66] Marketers use statistical techniques that cluster census tracts or postal zones to attribute the predominant attributes of age, race, or income to all the people who live there. This practice is convenient for some analytical or planning purposes. However, it overlooks the rich variety of personality, living habits, and interests among people who exhibit apparent homogeneity.

Markets are being differentiated along narrower and narrower dimensions— smaller local geographic units, more restricted definitions of age and socioeconomic status, more exotic categorizations in terms of personality and life style.

The emphasis on target marketing prompted the growth of specialized media. Advertisers were moving to "segment" the market either in terms of purchasers' social characteristics or of their motivations for using a product—the various kinds of "benefits" they got from its use. In contradistinction to the long-prevailing philosophy of mass merchandising, a brand or a store rarely sought to appeal to "everyone"; it tried to differentiate itself by appealing to a particular kind of customer—even when its competitors produced an almost identical product. Since most advertisers are interested in the same attractive targets, the lucky (rich, young) people who fall under this heading are subjected to a barrage of messages out of all proportion to their importance in the total market for most products.

Media have been described as "demogenic" if their audiences seem to have a desirable profile. (The term "demogenic" is just one of many barbaric neologisms that regularly crop up in the vocabulary of marketing and rapidly disappear.) In the early 1980s, for example, advertisers concentrated an extraordinary amount of attention on the so-called "yuppies" (young urban professionals), a group that acquired identity with the campaign of Senator Gary Hart in the 1982 presidential primaries. On one occasion BBDO's top television expert described NBC as the "yuppie network." (At that time, the much publicized and sought-after urban professionals and managers under 35 actually accounted for only 1.5% of the whole adult population.)

Media corporations devised publications and programs that would correspond to such artificial and sometimes wholly imaginary definitions. Between 1975 and 1993, the total number of consumer magazines grew from 1,018 to 2,318; 543 new ones were started in 1991 alone. Magazines have traditionally defined individuals' personal identity. (There is even an *International Journal of Terrorism*.)

Only three of the top ten circulation magazines are also among the top ten in advertising revenues. Publications that are started up today must still attract readers, and must still do so by establishing some unique difference from the choices that already exist. But the process characteristically begins with an appraisal of advertising opportunities rather than with an editorial concept. Following the vogue terminology of package goods marketing, the publisher looks for a "market niche," an as yet unoccupied (or perhaps uncertainly or inadequately occupied) position of specialized subject matter or appeal that corresponds to a target for certain kinds of advertising. The creative task becomes one of devising an editorial formula that will attract readers from this target audience, and, if possible, reinforce the impact of the advertisements by placing them within a supportive environment of words and pictures. Editorial fantasy (expressed through fiction in bygone days) moved into the area of consumption: home, food service, travel. (Travel magazines were described as "an excellent avenue for niche marketing to the upscale."[67])

- To illustrate this transformation: The founders of *Parents Magazine* in 1926 started with the idea that new mothers wanted practical advice on child care. In an era of high infant mortality, they may have been brushed by the idealistic desire to raise the level of parental knowledge. Many years later, *Parents* was a minor property of the German Bertelsmann conglomerate. The editor of a new rival, *Parenting* magazine, Robin Wolaner, gained her editorial experience at *Penthouse* and *Viva*, which featured nude male centerfolds. Restricting her aim to parents who were "children of the 60s", she sold a $3 million joint venture participation to Time Warner.[68] (It takes so much money today to start up a magazine that few would-be editorial entrepreneurs can manage the funding on their own. Venture capitalists want the assurance that there is a firm, experienced, professional hand at the tiller. This preference opens the way for the giant publishing conglomerates to expand their involvement, often with only modest capital investments.)

Major magazines have long offered geographically targeted editions. Some, like *Time*, have aimed editions at specially defined publics, such as physicians. Specialization was taken farther by the advent of "geodemographics," which used census data to identify postal zip code areas whose residents had particular social characteristics. *American Baby* magazine often runs 100 versions of the same issue, with a total circulation of 1.1 million.[69] *Newsweek*, in 1992, used the new technology of selective binding to prepare eight-page sections designed for readers' individual interests, at an extra charge. *Sports Illustrated* provided readers with hundreds of customized inserts carrying news of their favorite sports and teams. With computer technology and improved automated printing, binding and bundling methods, magazines can inkjet customized messages on to their pages.

Just as magazines and weekly newspapers are commonly inaugurated to meet advertising opportunities, television programs are often created to fill specifications that are set by the competitive demands of the advertising market. As in the magazine business, the costs of entry are extraordinary and dictate caution in estimating the prospective advertising support. (An hour-long prime-time network program costs $1–1.3 million to produce.)

On television, the scheduling and arrangement of programming is geared to the advertiser's convenience as much as it is to actual viewing habits. To illustrate — young children watch TV every day of the week. Yet two-thirds of all commercial TV stations carry no children's programming on weekdays,[70] because cereal and toy advertisers prefer to focus on Saturday morning.

Networks making up their schedules plan and place individual programs to attract specific kinds of viewers. In a given time slot on a particular evening of the week, knowing what is to precede and what is to follow, making their best guesses as to what the other networks are likely to do, they set up their requirements in terms of the desired demographic descriptors that will provide maximum strength for the schedule and be most salable to advertisers. Prognoses are easily made from the historical record: A sitcom, a game show, a cops and robbers series — each will deliver its predictable ratios of young women and older men, of rich and poor, of urban blacks and small-town whites. The pilots (samples of proposed series) provide a large array of choices within each genre, but the judgment and guesswork go into selecting the winners, not into predicting the characteristics of the viewers. If the choices are deemed inadequate, new ones can be concocted to formula. President of a film studio, formerly a television network programming head:

> At the network, I used to be able to say I want a show for the 45–64s or for the young
> marrieds, and I'd have a dozen proposals or scripts on my desk the next morning.
> Here if I ask for something like that, I draw a blank. They've got plenty of script
> outlines, but you have to look at them first and then figure out who's going to pay to
> see the movie.[71]

On the air and over the cable, "narrowcasting," rather than broadcasting, has
become the order of the day. The array of choices has widened because of the growth
of stations and channels, but the choices are designed to the specifications of
advertisers, not of the public. Cable channels are differentiated by programming that
is geared to particular kinds of viewers (defined overtly by ethnicity or gender, or
more subtly through content that attracts viewers of a certain age or social class).
Advertisers understand very well the differences between viewers of ESPN, the
Weather Channel, Arts & Entertainment, MTV, and the Nashville Network.

Targeting also transformed radio. The number of commercial radio stations
multiplied enormously, reaching about 12,000, by 1994. They survived economically
by forsaking the mass audiences of radio's Golden Age and by concentrating on
narrow and specialized strata of the public, primarily by adopting musical styles that
conformed to the taste of a particular age group, social class, or ethnic segment. The
"top 40" hit tune format, with its mixture of genres, gave way to stations whose
selections were locked into a particular musical type. Recordings were selected for
broadcast through a practice known as "negative programming" to produce minimum
aversion among the targeted group of listeners and meet advertisers' requirements.[72]
A broadcasting executive:

> We did shrink our teens by intent and we have improved the 25- to-49-year-old
> figures by eliminating hard rock.[73]

Deregulation brought the virtual elimination of the hourly news bulletins that had
long characterized radio, leaving the air open for a nonstop output of music,
commercials, and call-in talk shows. (These appeal to a proletarian audience eager to
ventilate its repressed anger. People who might be tongue-tied on television have no
hesitation in expressing themselves on the telephone.[74]) Because of their two-way,
participatory character, talk shows with minute audiences were prominently mentioned during the 1992 election campaign, and were naively described as an "alternative" to the "old media" by which politicians communicated with the public. The
shows are in many cases an outlet for extremist sentiment and outrageous nonsense.
(WLIB's "Gary Byrd Experience" proclaims that "Beethoven was black" and that
"AIDS was created by white people."[75])

Music remains radio's preeminent component, but its audience (in part reflecting
the impact of advertisers' preferences) is by no means identical with the tastes tallied
at the cash register. Rock had 26% of the audience in the top 100 radio markets, and
classical music stations had 1.7%.[76] But of all retail spending on recordings, 43% was
for rock and 5% for classical.[77]

The targeting practices that advertisers had imposed on radio came to prevail in
the record business, as Serge Denisoff relates:

The specter of advertising "targeting" bode an ill wind for the record industry. Playlists and format changes usually followed directions hatched by Madison Avenue.[78] [One radio station rock music] formula consists of time segments, such as a quarter- or half-hour period, in which a specific pattern of popular tunes is logged and played. A segment may begin with a current hit, followed by a recent hit, a golden oldie, a newcomer, and so on. Often these selections are color-coded . . . so the disc jockey can't go wrong. At many stations the format is so precise that each record is logged by a program or music director on a log sheet and timed along with commercials and announcements. While this rigid, formalistic procedure eliminates much of the deejay's creativity, it ensures a definite "sound" for the station.[79]

Broadcast satellite technology made it easy for radio stations to set up ad hoc robot networks of their own. In the 1970s and 1980s a number of new "turnkey" radio networks sprang up, using broadcast satellites. Typically the turnkey networks charged affiliates a programming fee that ranged from $1,000 a month to a $1 million a year. They also sold 1 or 2 minutes of national commercial time per hour. In the case of some, like Transtar, the network's name was not mentioned on the air, and time references were to minutes after or before the hour, so that listeners had no clue that they were not listening to a local broadcast. Locally recorded announcements could be fed in automatically to breaks triggered by inaudible beeps in the network feed, so that the station could be operated with no programming staff.[80]

In the days of the crystal set, radio had been the most intimate of all media; the transistor revived this personal character. Now it was being transformed into an automated mechanism. Music, the art that perhaps pulls most closely at primal human emotions, was churned out on order to conform to specific advertising sales goals.

Advertising and Media Survival

The most important influence that advertisers have over media content is not in the direct pressure they sometimes apply. It arises from their power to spend their money where they think it will most help them. The life and death of individual media vehicles hangs in the balance of these decisions.

Do the themes and personalities of broadcasting reflect advertisers' personal appetites and prejudices? Probably not nearly to the same degree as their business judgments. Like other people of their social class, advertising decision-makers watch far less television than the average person.[81] Peter McColough, the former president of Xerox, moved his company toward greater use of selective media and television programs of quality, but he pointed out that this was possible because the products were not sold to a broad consumer market:

> To imply, however indirectly, that a General Foods should spent $1 million on a production of "Rosenkrantz and Guildenstern" that might reach eight million viewers, while one of its competitors is spending the same amount with scattered commercials on "Lucy" and "Gomer Pyle" to reach 17 million people . . . is not only asking for a high order of social responsibility. It is also asking for economic suicide.

Proclaiming that "commercial television is above all a generalized merchandise medium of enormous cost," McColough said, "it's built to pander to the general taste, not to prod it."[82]

Unlike broadcasting, publishing is a costly manufacturing venture, which can be ruined by a relatively small drop in advertising income. (It costs at least $100 million to start a mass weekly magazine. A newspaper printing plant can cost up to half a billion.) Great magazines with millions of readers and newspapers with hundreds of thousands have been forced out of business for lack of advertising support. The newspaper supplement *This Week* was distributed in the early 1960s by forty-two newspapers with a combined circulation of about 10 million. By the end of the decade it was out of business, as its food advertisers deserted it for television, where such massive numbers were commonplace.

In the face of the new competitive pressures, magazine publishers struggled to keep their audience figures high. Battling by ground rules that were not their own, the giant weeklies in the 1960s found themselves ground through the mill of an impossible economics. *Life* could not cut its costly 8 million circulation (which produced 30 million readers per issue) without giving advertisers the impression that it was on its way down. To keep the circulation figures up meant confronting horrendous postage and promotion costs. Martin Ackerman, then president of Curtis Publishing (owners of *The Saturday Evening Post*):

> To get seven million subscribers you have to mail out ads to 50 million people offering them all sorts of giveaways. . . . You end up offering them the magazine for one-half or one-quarter the [newsstand] price. Thus magazine publishers give their products away today.[83]

The give-away of the doomed mass magazines was of course no different from the give-away of broadcast programs. In both cases large audiences were acquired and measured. But the departure of advertising meant that the magazines' readers were deprived of their singular voices. The *Post*, in a last, desperate effort to retain advertising revenues, changed its editorial style and dropped half of its subscribers. In explanation, a trade ad showed a happy couple with a child striding through the woods. The headline read, "The Colin Edwards are too far out," and the text continued,

> They miss by a mile, six and one-half miles to be exact, since they live beyond the boundaries of one of the 370 U.S. counties where the *Post* now concentrates. The *Post* is distilling down its circulation to the rich A and B markets [as Nielsen defines them], where the bulk of U.S. sales are concentrated. We are getting out of the boxcar number business and into station wagon statistics. . . . We are in the process of refining our circulation to match the advertisers' best markets. Focus on them. Forget the rest.

Although the copy indicated that the *Post* would now concentrate on the *crème de la crème*, *Life* made a deal to take up the subscriptions the *Post* was dropping and logically insisted that these be a cross section, not the less desirable half. The resulting division of the circulation list between the two magazines was done at random, county by county. There was a rash of indignant letters from people who had been readers for as long as 40 years. However, there were only minor repercussions when the *Post* finally gave up the ghost, largely from subscribers who wanted their money back. Most of the mail was destroyed unopened.[84] Advertisers were the ones who counted, not readers.

Advertising Dominance and Newspaper Survival

Advertisers' judgments determine the health and even the survival of media, but these judgments do not necessarily correspond to what is in the social interest—specifically to the survival of vigorous, independent, and competitive journalism.

The rule of dominance, which applies throughout branded packaged goods marketing, gives an edge to the leader in any product class. (Among other advantages, the leader can buy advertising more efficiently than the competition.) A variant of this rule is that the leading vehicle, in any medium, attracts more advertising than is warranted by its actual share of the audience. For example, in the 1988–89 broadcast season, NBC, with a 26% prime-time share, got 30% of the ad dollars. CBS, with a 20% share, got less than 20%. A loss of audience share means that fewer people see the network's promotional announcements for its shows, which has a spiraling negative effect on audience size, further reducing the share.

Advertisers, seeking efficiency, go with a winner, who presumably offers economies of scale. The process has had especially adverse effects in the medium that carries more advertising than any other—daily newspapers. Great papers have died even though hundreds of thousands of people were willing to pay for them and read them faithfully each day; they died because advertisers reduced their schedules. The total amount of advertising spent in most major cities is more than enough to support competing newspapers, if only a small shift were to take place in media allocations.

Advertisers—following the rule of dominance—have increasingly dropped second newspapers from their schedules. Classified advertisers all want to place their ads in the paper with the biggest classified section, even though these ads are more carefully perused in a thinner paper. It is not necessary for a newspaper to have a strongly selective social class appeal in order for it to achieve preeminence. The *Washington Post*, after the demise of the *Star*, became the surviving monopoly paper of Washington, a role it essentially maintains (with by far most of the advertising) even since it acquired the *Washington Times* as a new competitor.

Despite the presence of a large impoverished black population in the District of Columbia, the *Post* is read on an average day by 59% of the adults in the metropolitan area, giving it a degree of universality that transcends any restrictive social class appeal. It fills the basic utilitarian information functions that are met by any monopoly paper in the country, but at the same time it operates with the style and gravamen that befit its role in the nation's capital. The *Post*'s readership or advertising success probably would be in no way diminished if it were edited at the level of the *Pittsburgh Post-Gazette* or the *Kansas City Star* (respectable but hardly outstanding newspapers). Yet the excitement and verve it instills into the life of Washington and the political influence it exerts on the national and world scenes would be immeasurably less.

The *Post*'s importance, like that of the *New York Times* and the *Los Angeles Times*, was the creation of its owners and of the great editors that they selected and supported in the face of both economic and political adversities. But while it is only fair to pay homage to the likes of Katherine Graham, Arthur Ochs Sulzberger, and Otis Chandler, their achievements as publishers depended on the inclination of advertisers to rush in the direction of the leading newspaper. The *Washington Star*, the *New York Herald Tribune*, and the *Philadelphia Bulletin* were also distinguished family-owned newspapers with long histories and admirable editorial spirit. All retained the loyalty of hundreds of thousands of readers up till the end, but the end was determined by advertisers and not by quality, importance, or reader interest.

The *Philadelphia Bulletin*'s circulation fell from 641,000 in 1970 to 434,000 when it folded in 1982; its ad linage dropped from 34 million to 20 million lines. In 1981, the similarly doomed Los Angeles *Herald Examiner* had a third of the *Times'* circulation, but only one-fifth as much advertising. Its ad director, David Feldman, commented,

> No one wants to take the long-term view and look at the return of their investment over time. Most of the media buyers are young and very mobile, and no one in that position wants to make a radical move where someone might say they did the wrong thing. They want a safe haven, something they can put on their resumé, so they make a safe call.[85]

Robert McCormack, then ad director of the *Washington Post*, contended that "concentrating" on the leading paper was in the advertiser's interest: "If an advertiser can get the coverage he needs with one paper, he's not going to buy two. You don't have to be a genius to figure that out." The *Philadelphia Bulletin*'s ad director, Robert Keim, said bravely, "The advertiser isn't responsible for the product or how we sell it. And we can't expect to run around with a tin cup, saying 'Help me!' " Joyce Reynolds, vice president of Philadelphia's big store, Wanamaker's, agreed that

> there is that mentality here of wanting to go with a winner. It's very unwise thinking, but in many areas you're dealing with very unsophisticated advertisers. A lot of smaller companies without access to media people will make the decision to go with the stronger paper without realizing that, ultimately, it's not the wisest decision to make.

About a fifth of the readers in two-paper markets read both papers. Advertisers regard such duplication as wasteful, even though newspapers could argue that it gives their messages a redoubled effectiveness.

An alarming attrition of newspaper voices was also occurring in cities where the surviving two papers were published by the same owners. These morning-evening combinations came in many shades of editorial autonomy. In some instances—Milwaukee is a notable example—separate newsroom staffs competed as vigorously as though they were working for different publishers, and two different editorial pages espoused opposing points of view. At the other extreme were papers that were merely updated from the morning to the afternoon edition, with a change of name and headline typeface. The morning papers, with easier nocturnal delivery schedules, served wider hinterlands than the afternoon papers that concentrated on the central cities, and they therefore profited from the growth of the suburbs, while the declining fortunes of the afternoon press followed those of the cities themselves.

Although most commonly owned papers offered advantageous combination rates to advertisers, these were not seen as much of an incentive by the major retailers using preprinted inserts. Quite sensibly, they wanted these circulars to get the widest possible distribution rather than a double delivery to the same households.

Many publishers struggling with the economics of their afternoon papers felt that by killing them off they could strengthen their morning products, expanding the total amount of editorial space, assigning reporters to cover new beats, and offering the afternoon paper's best features to a wider audience. When these fading afternoon papers were merged, there were, inevitably, circulation losses, but most of their readers eventually gravitated to the morning editions. There were, needless to say, substantial savings in production and distribution expense, and therefore greater profit for the owners. And so the process of consolidation was emulated in one town after another, which further reduced the number of daily newspaper titles.

Retail advertising was newspapers' main revenue source; it was also an extremely important source of reader interest, because merchandise news is one of the paper's most appealing features. The continuing health of newspaper retail advertising, as retailers were the first to say, depended on newspapers' faltering ability to deliver the mass market of readers on whom stores depend for their traffic.[86]

Retailers go to each others' cocktail parties; they work from the same lore, make similar evaluations, and take the same advice. The press critic A.J. Liebling once said that the fate of America's competitive newspapers was in the hands of "a few dry-goods merchants." Between the old-time merchant and the newspaper publisher were personal bonds that cemented their business relationships. They served on the same community boards and had mutual acquaintances. They had a common stake in the economic well-being of the city from which they derived their fortunes, and both understood their interdependence. Even when they moved in different social circles, each was a meaningful figure on the other's horizon. These personal relationships had much the same character in small towns and in huge cities, and they held true in competitive situations as well as in monopoly markets. In most cases it was the publisher whose family represented old money and who enjoyed membership in the more exclusive clubs. In some cases, publishers thought their status too exalted for them to mingle freely with parvenu merchants. Department store principals and their highly paid sales promotion executives often complained that the publisher never called to invite them to lunch. The reason was not always snobbery. Some publishers, reared on the editorial side, were uncomfortable with the very idea of selling advertising and considered entertaining customers to be a more appropriate assignment for their underlings.

The nature of these relationships was altered by the transformation of ownership in both the newspaper and retailing industries. Corporate managers in either business were apt to see their present locations as way stations in their careers rather than as lifetime commitments based on a family inheritance. In either case, both the corporate ethos and human nature continued to demand community involvement and friendly customer-vendor contacts. But this involvement was perforce more perfunctory than in places that held ancestral gravesites; the contacts were harder-edged and more brittle than those that were once expected to endure forever.

Both in general merchandising and in the grocery business, a smaller number of large chain organizations account for a growing percentage of the entire retail business. Newspapers, like other media, find them tougher customers with which to do business. When a functionary of Sears negotiates advertising page rates with a functionary of Knight-Ridder, sentiment does not enter.

In the late 1980s, large retail companies entered a difficult period, after years of expansion that outpaced the capacities of the market. Some, like Sears and K-Mart, underwent substantial changes of merchandising philosophy, switched their media allocations, and reduced their dependence on consistent newspaper advertising for specific items. These two giants were replaced at the top of the heap by a newcomer, Walmart, whose business had been built with an advertising-to-sales ratio of 0.5%, compared with 5–6% for the traditional department stores.

Department stores—once newspapers' mainstay—had undergone extensive restructuring as a result of mergers and acquisitions. The expensive borrowing required for this purpose brought enormous pressure on expenses, including advertising budgets. It led to bankruptcy in the case of several of the biggest department store groups.[87] Within a few years, some of the best-known names in American retailing history faded from the scene. Retail failures severely affected newspapers that depended on them; for example, the *New York Daily News* suffered when Gimbel's and Ohrbach's vanished.

Since a competitive daily press is a life-enhancing force for a city, surely its preservation is in the interest of businesses that depend for their own survival on the city's economic and social health. Competing papers keep their advertising rates down—other things being equal—and are therefore more desirable negotiating partners for a business with a long-term stake in its customer base. But department store managements faced their own pressures for short-term profit and were disinclined to consider the long-term consequences of their advertising policies.

In 1970 newspapers had 39% of consumer media advertising expenditures; in 1980 their share was 36%; in 1992, 32%. At least some of the erosion may have been because fewer salespeople from rival newspapers were knocking on retailers' doors. But mainly the problem was growing competition from direct mail, free-distribution weeklies, and city magazines. Retailers and other local businesses moved away from their traditional price and item advertising in newspapers to promote store "image" and shifted more of their promotion into broadcasting; by 1993 they were spending almost as much in radio and television as in newspapers.

Markets that housed three, four, or even half a dozen metropolitan dailies at the start of the twentieth century have seen the same story of failure and merger repeated over and over. In 1993, only a single central-city paper was left in Los Angeles, San Diego, Dallas, Buffalo, Cleveland, Pittsburgh, New Orleans, Kansas City, Richmond, Knoxville, Little Rock, San Antonio, and Miami. In most of the few remaining competitive cities, second papers struggled for survival, kept alive in spite of often prodigious losses by owners impelled in some cases by a sense of public responsibility, tradition, and loyalty to the staff, in other instances by vanity and the hope of political advantage, or by sheer inertia. Fewer than fifty independently edited newspaper Sunday magazines were left by 1994.

The Newspaper Preservation Act of 1970 exempted failing newspapers from the antitrust laws by permitting them to set up joint production and business operations with their competitors, while preserving separate editorial management. This kept second papers alive in such cities as San Francisco, Seattle, and Cincinnati, but it did not avert the demise of the (Newhouse-owned) *St. Louis Globe-Democrat*, the (Cox) *Miami News*, (Hearst's) *San Antonio Light*, (Scripps-Howard's) *Pittsburgh Press*, or the *Knoxville Journal*. In all these cases the owners had more to gain, under the terms of the joint operating agreements, by letting the papers go under than by keeping them alive and draining their share of the agency operation's profits. In spite of these experiences, joint operations seemed to be the best hope for the survival of important papers like the *Detroit Free Press*.[88]

Newspapers scrambled for sustenance by devoting increasing attention to smaller accounts, by cultivating new categories of advertising, by offering more flexible part-run and zoned advertising options for advertisers who would formerly have considered the metropolitan daily to be too expensive, and by seeking more revenue from subscribers and from electronic delivery of their information resources. But the potential in these areas did not match the business they had lost.

As all this happened, the mix of newspaper advertising revenues changed. The softening of display advertising—retail and national—raised the importance of classified, which had been relatively free from competition and which now accounted for 35% of ad spending in newspapers. With growing competition from telephone yellow pages, specialized free publications, cable, audiotex, and teletext—and with a major new threat looming from telephone company information services—newspapers' preeminence in this type of advertising was no longer assured.

In the early 1990s, less than two-fifths of the American population had access to two or more locally published daily newspapers. (In 1978, the proportion was nearly three out of five.) The resulting monopoly pricing structure does not serve advertisers' interests, but that is beside the present point. As I shall spell out in Chapter 7, it is a disaster for the public.

The attrition of competition in the daily press illustrates the significant social and political effect of advertising decisions. These decisions have even wider repercussions since, as we saw in Chapter 2, the content and operations of advertising media are tightly entwined with the media that depend directly on the public. This chapter has described how media shape themselves to fit advertisers' interests. Advertisers' preoccupation with audience size has unfortunate consequences. It arises from commonly held and often mistaken assumptions about how media communicate.

5

Advertising by the Numbers

Just as fewer large organizations own and operate the media, more and more of their advertising income is derived from fewer sources. Advertising's great power over the media system is exercised by a relatively small number of people and institutions who operate by unwritten rules of questionable validity. Control has become steadily more concentrated among the clients who pay for advertising, the agencies that create and place it for the corporations whose advertising is most visible and highly charged, and the research organizations that supply the information on which advertising decisions are based. The research itself provides the basic rationale for advertising decisions, but it is commonly used in disregard of its limitations, which deserve close scrutiny. This chapter describes the extent to which advertising power is concentrated and then evaluates the consequences. Key points:

- Creative flair and judgment give advertising persuasive force. As large companies dominate, the human relationships of a personal service business are replaced by impersonal bureaucratic procedures.
- Bureaucrats try to operate "scientifically" and thus become dependent on marketing statistics.
- They demand "accountability" for their advertising expenditures, but effects are hard to measure.
- Computer technology demands a constant input of fresh data, which become steadily less reliable and available from fewer sources.
- Statistics dependency creates an obsession with audience size as the indicator of meaningful communication—which it is not.

Managing the Advertising Function

Who spends all the money? There are no more than 10,000 people (excluding clerical workers) in all the agency and corporate media departments that place billions of dollars of advertising billings and fuel the main components of the nation's media system. By 1992, in the United States, the five largest national advertisers accounted for 25% of all national spending in consumer media; the top four groups of agencies represented 36% of all agency billings.[1] The eight top supermarket chains had 26% of total food store volume.

Corporate giants are peculiarly subject to cost-cutting pressures forced by the heavy borrowing that makes them giants in the first place. In many cases, they feel impelled to pare advertising budgets to improve their showings on the bottom line. Large advertisers — retail and national — and their agencies negotiate with media from a position of great strength. They are highly knowledgeable about media economics and have a keen sense of how far their demands can go. In the huge bureaucratically run international enterprises that control today's advertising, it is harder than ever for any individual media vehicle — a station, a newspaper, or a magazine — to get a hearing.

The giants do most of the elbowing and jockeying. On the selling side, the multimedia conglomerate has an advantage. The buying of broadcast time has long been done through intense bargaining. Magazines have come to regard their rate cards as only starting points for negotiation; promotional and merchandising incentives are said to "add value" to the space that is sold, in what is in effect a kickback arrangement. Newspapers have also become considerably more flexible in their pricing policies. As price pressures on the media continued to mount, there was a real danger that "adding value" could move beyond such innocuous practices as positioning ads advantageously or offering merchandising support. It could compromise editorial integrity.

Great shifts have occurred in the power balance among the players in the marketing arena. Companies expand into each other's traditional territories. In packaged goods marketing, the mainstay of television advertising, the number of competing brands has greatly increased — from 10,000 stocked by a typical supermarket in 1980 to 18,000 ten years later.

New brands and line extensions intensify competition for the limited amount of shelf and display space at the point of sale. Marketers' attention has shifted from the struggle to influence the consumer to the primary battle to get products into the stores in the first place. The retailers who control access to the ultimate consumer have had manufacturers dancing to their tune. But retail organizations have themselves been in a state of extreme disarray, partly because of the process of agglomeration, through buyouts and mergers and partly because of shifts in consumer purchasing patterns.

The relations of advertisers and media were transformed long ago by the emergence of advertising agents as an important independent force in the media business.[2] Agents originally represented newspapers in remote locations and collected their 15 percent commission before transmitting the rest of the money. One hundred years ago, when agencies became responsible for choosing among media and for writing and designing the ads, their functions became differentiated from those of the media sales representatives. The advertising agency was now expected to act in the client's interests rather than the medium's. The fixed commission structure encouraged creative ingenuity because it held out the promise of reward commensurate with the growth of the client's business.

The character and operations of agencies have changed considerably since Theodore Dreiser described them in his novel, *The Genius*, before the first World War. Advertising agencies are not merely providers of ingenious copy and engaging illustrations; they are themselves mighty institutions of corporate America.

Just as attorneys or accountants may be willing to handle the affairs of clients of whose merits they may be privately doubtful, the advertising agency does not usually take it upon itself to question the virtues of those who are willing to retain its services, as long as their activities are lawful. The willingness of advertising professionals to apply their skills to any product, regardless of its nature, is not so much an expression of cynicism as of craftsmanship. On any account, work is broken into bite-sized chunks, with copy, art, production, media planning, and research all contributing elements. The time-buyer negotiating with station representatives, the casting director hiring actors for a commercial—such specialists are oriented to their immediate tasks, not motivated by any grand vision. Occasionally creative or research types of independent mind may beg off an assignment to a cigarette account, hoping that no permanent blemish will mar their records; whether or not it does will depend on their supervisors and on the size and character of the agency. A large agency with a diversified client roster values its creative and professional staff too highly to risk alienating them unnecessarily; someone else will always be ready to do the job.

Agencies have the admirable social function of questioning their clients closely about the competitive quality of what they produce, and thus driving them to constant improvement. It is not the spirit of public service that impels advertising professionals to work in this way. They are using what they know to earn a living, and it is simply unthinkable to give forth with anything less than their best efforts. In the feverish atmosphere of agency operations, the staff rejoices when a new account is won, mourns and trembles when one is lost, and tackles each job, day by day, as a challenge to its talents. In a long-standing relationship with a client, personal bonds and loyalties are forged on both sides, even when they take an ambivalent love-hate form.

The stock in trade of the account executive (the huckster, the man in the grey flannel suit) is the ability to command the client's confidence. The legendary lunch-time martinis gave way to mineral water in the 1980s, but the account executive's wise counsel and good fellowship remained indispensable. The corporate advertising director and the agency management supervisor may detest each other, but their fates are entwined, and they are likely to display a public friendship, marked by continual socializing at agency expense, even though they may disparage each other to their own associates.

As is the case with every other form of media content, those who create advertising must work to meet deadlines and timetables to which the muse is not always responsive. A continuing preoccupation of the business executives who run advertising enterprises has been the problem of how to foster the artistic temperament and at the same time harness it within the budgetary and scheduling constraints that business requires.

With the coming of radio, the creation of advertising and the management of media schedules became more complex, technical, and specialized, and the structure of agencies changed accordingly. In the era before marketing became a well-known term and an accepted discipline, the agency worked in close harness with the client's management and sales department to set sales objectives and to plan new product introductions.

To fit their expanding role, agencies developed specialized departments for research,[3] sales promotion, merchandising, and public relations. The standard commission no longer proved adequate to meet the clients' growing demand for more services. Agencies began to charge extra for them and to set up subsidiaries that could demand special fees without raising questions in the client's accounting department.

As the cost of marketing services grew, it was inevitable that more and more corporations felt they could operate these functions internally without the need to use an outside agency. Corporate marketing staffs appeared and expanded, corporate media departments and house agencies proliferated. Corporations developed their own sales promotion and public relations facilities and farmed out assignments to creative "boutiques" and to media buying companies that originally arose to bargain for broadcast time. Clients tended to deal directly with outside research services themselves and to rely increasingly on syndicated and prepackaged research. Retailers lagged behind manufacturing and service corporations in this process, but they took much the same route.

The result of all this was a squeeze on agency income. The percentage of U.S. advertisers paying the agency the full 15% commission fell from over half (52%) in 1983 to about a third (35%) by the early 1990s. Commissions now accounted for only 40% of agencies' gross income, compared to 65% in 1960. Some advertisers said they would pay their agencies based on performance, as though their own advertising could carry all the responsibility for a product's success or failure, and competitors' activities did not enter into the equation!

While agencies were weakening, clients' corporate headquarters were moving out of the central cities where managers had the opportunity for casual contact with colleagues, competitors, and opposite numbers in other types of enterprise. In their new self-contained, hermetically sealed rustic exurban office parks, corporate advertising professionals were remote from disturbing contact with urban problems and urban culture. Their thinking was less likely to be stimulated by the unexpected. More and more conversation became inbred shop talk. But in the meantime their power increased. Agencies followed the corporate exodus from the city centers. Over half of agency billings had historically been concentrated in New York City, the nation's creative capital; this proportion had dropped to 38% by 1994.

While the advertising vice-presidents of big corporations engaged in serious wheeling and dealing, the persons who influenced or controlled media decisions within their agencies were often overworked novices. The compensation paid to advertising practitioners shows enormous disparities. At the start of the 1990s, DMB&B was offering a senior creative person on its newly acquired Burger King account a 5-year package that (with an annual base salary of $400,000 plus benefits) added up to $10,570,000.[4] By contrast, the entry level salary for an assistant media planner at Young and Rubicam was $13,000. A senior planner earned $25–35,000.

At publicly held agencies driven to show greater profit, corporate cost-cutters sought to eliminate expensive professional talent in creative and media departments. Management attention was diverted to the financial issues associated with take-over attempts, leveraged buyouts, and overindebtedness, away from any serious interest in the clients' advertising strategy. In an atmosphere of retrenchment and uncertainty, morale suffered, and the founts of inspiration threatened to dry up.

All these changes were bound to affect the quality and effectiveness of the advertising that was turned out. If big advertising bureaucracies tend to be cumbersome and therefore produce more than their share of bad ads, the dynamics of competition might force them to change or to atrophy and give way to aggressive newcomers.

One consequence of the changing power relationship has been a deterioration of the trust that binds all the players in the game together. As business relationships become more impersonal, it is harder than ever to sustain the traditional human relationship between agency and client principals in what is quintessentially a personal service business. Instead of judgment, there is an increasing reliance on foolish formulas. This is unfortunate, because advertising is communication; it depends on creative impulses, on intangibles that cannot be read on computer printouts.

Scientism and the Concentration of Advertising Power

The media system is enchained by statistics of sometimes dubious validity that obscure the real consequences of its messages. Magazines are dropped from a schedule if their "reader profile" shows signs of aging or impoverishment; television programs are yanked off the air if their ratings fail to meet expectations. Research is not just a means by which the media are attuned to the changing sentiments of the audience. It is a powerful force in its own right. And it is increasingly relied upon to justify the activities of corporate bureaucrats rather than to provide insight into the communications they control.

The exercise of power may appear rational and even benevolent if it follows rules that are perceived as "scientific." What a big advertiser does may seem more acceptable and legitimate if its actions are considered to be governed by impersonal and objective criteria rather than by whim and emotion, by guess and by gosh.

Large organizations pride themselves on their efficiency. In practice, this means that they tend to operate mechanistically, with lots of procedures and systems. Their managements place a premium on hard numbers, which they believe will somehow translate into the hard numbers they expect to see on the bottom line of the quarterly earnings statement.

Corporate bigness based on borrowing brought a more intense focus on immediate results, a concomitant reluctance to plan and invest for long-term results, and a greater demand for accountability. Carcasses of projects and careers litter the battlefield after every corporate merger and takeover. In spite of the standard rhetoric about "trimming fat," size engenders bureaucracy by its very nature. There is a reliance on stock recipes in media planning and buying, and a dependence on ever-growing quantities of marketing data presented in formalized fashion to fit them.

The managements of large companies are inclined to believe that an advantage of their size lies in their superior information resources. As the amount of information increases, there is no commensurate growth in the ability to use it intelligently. The ease with which numbers can be manipulated in the computer era drowns marketers in facts and discourages the pursuit of wisdom.

Operating procedures, as well as common articles of faith in conventional wisdom, tend to be shared among similar competing organizations, fostering homogeneity. Protesting and disclaiming all the way, large companies gravitate toward the use of set methods, in evaluating advertisements and in selecting media. When it comes to allocating their advertising funds, they prefer the well-trodden highways. The relentless pursuit of audience size fosters conservatism and discourages genuine innovation, both among advertisers and their agencies.

The publisher of the *New York Globe*, Jason Rogers, commented in 1919 on the agency-client relationship. He distinguished between the outlook of the advertiser, dealing in tangible products and services, and the agency, whose domain was the intangible realm of communication and persuasion:

> The main reason for the lack of straight thinking on advertising by the average advertiser is psychological. He has been trained to think of advertising as something apart from his business. He has been told that it is something that cannot be handled by business men. He has seen advertising handled by men outside of business—an alien race to commerce—a race of men peddling what to him seemed dreams, and which he yet realized were actualities when used by other business men. Not thoroughly understanding advertising, he handed it over to a man outside his organization. In most cases, once he allowed his advertising to be handled by an organization apart from his business, he grew to consider advertising itself as being apart, something alien and foreign, a magic force which, working entirely apart from the business, would have wonderfully beneficial results.[5]

The view of advertising as a "magic force" was almost opposite to that of the great copywriter Claude Hopkins, who wrote in 1923 that "enormous advertising is being done along scientific lines. Its success is common knowledge."

Nearly 100 years ago, a flyer for a New York agency unequivocally proclaimed, "Men may look forward to the day when advertising will be what it has long deserved to be, one of the world's greatest sciences." The phrasing of the statement may seem dated, but it conveys an attitude that still infuses a lot of advertising practice. A key executive from a large packaged goods company recently called advertising evaluation "more of a science than it ever was"—which may be damning it with faint praise. There *is* growing pressure to approach advertising as though it could be managed scientifically.

"A lot of the fun has gone out of the business," said Bob Jacoby, former chairman of Ted Bates, after he deposited $110 million as his share of the agency's sale to the large British firm, Saatchi and Saatchi. Fun is what the agency business has been and what makes advertising successful. It is harder for large agencies to create great advertising as their clients spur them on to be more scientific.

At one point, the trade press reported that the Saatchi and Saatchi agencies among them accounted for one out of every five dollars spent in U.S. network television. It is unlikely that the brothers Saatchi (who founded the business in London and eventually had to cede managerial control) sought to impose a guiding hand of corporate philosophy upon the time-buying practices of all their individual offices and affiliates. But could any television network, in its programming decisions, be unresponsive to the prevailing philosophy of Saatchi and Saatchi or any other giant of the agency world?

What is that philosophy? Very simply put, it is that the best programming is the kind that delivers the maximum number of advertising "exposures" at the lowest possible cost. Buying is done—or rationalized after the fact—in terms of statistical abstractions. This is encrusted with all kinds of pious qualifications. Every agency media director would claim that the quality of the vehicles used is important, that he is not after "mass" but "class"—the youthful "achievers"—and that the "demographics," or audience characteristics, have to be right for the product. But in the real world of media buying, these principles evaporate.

The big audiences for which advertisers tend to go are attracted to content that aims for the middle range of intelligence or lower. To the degree that advertisers deviate from the rule that more is better, they tend to move in concert to capture the same target groups of the population: rich (or, as they are now called, "affluent") people, who buy more of almost everything, and young people, whose consumption habits are presumably still malleable and who have long useful lives as consumers yet ahead of them. The premium placed both on youth and on purchasing power represents an inherent contradiction in terms.

When advertisers try to be selective, they often find that this approach does not really work, because selectivity cannot be reconciled with their own criteria of economy. (Specialized media have a higher per-capita audience cost than those that are more generally diffused.)

Prime-time television is the mass medium par excellence in the eyes of national advertisers. Its audiences are in such a state of perpetual motion that differences in their characteristics are in most cases small from program to program. (In selling advertising time, an enormous emphasis is placed, of course, on these small differences.) Regardless of who the target of advertising is, the underlying premise remains the same—a message sent out is assumed to be a message received and taken to heart.

Although advertisers seek to plan their media schedules "scientifically," selecting media to match audience characteristics with consumption habits, their principles are at odds with the facts of life in a world of intense horse-trading. The buying and selling of advertising on an opportunity basis leads to widespread disparities in the judgments made by different advertisers in the media marketplace. On one program that was condemned for its portrayal of homosexuality, some advertisers paid $100,000 for a spot, others—who held out for a last-minute bargain—$40,000.

In 1991, General Motors and Time Warner entered into an $80 million contract that involved promotional use of magazines, cable, video, films, and books. This was not a mutually exclusive arrangement. Time Warner had made similar deals with Chrysler and Nissan, and General Motors had made one with CBS Sports guaranteeing exclusive automotive sponsorship of the NCAA basketball games for a seven-year period. Deals like these underscored the fact that advertisers were buying what they called "tonnage" at the best prices they could get, in spite of all their pontification about targeting. A growing proportion of national advertising—6% in 1993—was bypassing agency media departments and was funneled through independent media buying services whose specialty was bargaining for rating points. The money that changed hands was tangible, the communication a chimera.

Evaluating Advertising Performance

Advertising is a form of rhetoric, a persuasive endeavor, but it is ruled by numbers. Large companies are obsessed with the notion of accountability, but a creative work's monetary value is difficult to measure exactly, even when it is sold directly to the ultimate consumer. When it is sold to advertisers, the task of assessment becomes even tougher. In the advertising-supported media, consumer research has encouraged the perception of audiences as commodities for sale. Communications in similar as well as totally dissimilar media are thus evaluated by the same criteria of efficiency and productivity that are used to measure the output and sale of merchandise.

Ratings and other audience research data are often regarded as substitutes for box-office receipts, but no advertiser wants these numbers for their own sake in the way that film-makers or book publishers count their take. The advertiser wants to sell the product, and usually assumes that it will sell in proportion to the number of people who are reached by the messages. (There is, by the way, an intervening, and crucial assumption—that the messages have a positive persuasive effect. That assumption is wrong, since many advertisements are totally unconvincing and others are actually counterproductive.)

Audiences have been measured with great care because measurement of advertising's effects on sales— which is the criterion that advertisers really want to use—is extremely complex, difficult, and expensive. What happens in the marketplace reflects what competitors do as well as what a given advertiser does. If maximizing the audience also maximizes the effect, *The National Enquirer* (circulation 3.8 million) would be a vastly more influential medium than *The Washington Monthly* (circulation 34,500). It is not.

Most advertisers are sophisticated enough to know that what counts is not the overall size of the audience, but the number of prospective customers it includes. Whether or not advertisers restrict their aim to particular targets or extend it to the whole population, they value the measurements of audience size out of the conviction that these numbers are acceptable surrogates for what is otherwise very hard for them to learn—namely, what rate of return they are getting from their advertising investment. For this reason, the raw numbers are usually translated into indices of comparative efficiency, like reach and frequency, gross rating points, and cost per thousand. (Reach refers to the percentage of the public covered by an advertising schedule; frequency, to the average number of times an average person is potentially exposed to the messages; a single gross rating point is equivalent to 1% of the public reached, for the first time or on any subsequent occasion. The cost per thousand refers to the cost of getting the message to a thousand people in the whole population or in any given target group.) The resulting numerology has an awesome impact when it is displayed in brightly colored bar charts on the desktop terminals of media buyers or is embodied in stacks of printouts on the desks of corporate brand managers.

Why don't advertisers rely directly on sales results to evaluate their advertising? Some do, of course, when they can see an immediate response from a special offer, as direct marketers can when they check returns from a catalogue, mailing piece, or television sales pitch (with "operators standing by"). Retailers like to think they can check the yield from an ad that features specific items at a special price. But retailers also know that customers come into their stores for many reasons that have nothing to do with their ads, that customers brought in by an ad buy other items in the store, and that many of them will never end up buying the advertised merchandise once they have taken a good look at it. Moreover, the sales results attributable to a retail ad can never be sorted out from the environment of directly competing ads and the effects of the weather.

Effects are even more difficult to trace in the case of national advertising, because it is rarely prepared in the expectation of influencing an immediate sale on the spot; it is intended to create a favorable impression or to add to existing, previously formed favorable impressions that might influence a purchase at some time in the future. Technology has made it possible to determine exactly what quantities have been sold at what price. While this capability has introduced revolutionary new methods into the pretesting of advertising, it has also produced data in quantities too great for routine advertising evaluation. Figures on sales volume or market share reflect the effects not only of advertising but of pricing, distribution, promotion, and the quality and packaging of the product itself.

Advertisements do not communicate individually nor in isolation. If there were only one detergent commercial on the air and only one shoe ad in the newspaper, it would be relatively easy to determine how well each had done. In reality, it is not easy at all, and the problems confronting researchers become more difficult as messages and media channels multiply.

Research and the Computer

The field of market research has always been pulled in two sometimes contradictory directions—the professional objective of serving society and the truth, and the business objective of earning a profit and making it grow. This inherent tension is directly affected by the trend toward corporate concentration, which has transformed research as well as advertising. In the go-go years, many market research companies were acquired by conglomerates with no special sense of their founders' original professional ethos.[6] The five biggest companies did 55% of the $2.3 billion market research business in 1992.[7] (The largest company in the field, Dun and Bradstreet's A. C. Nielsen, Inc., had 23% of the total.[8])

A relatively small number of firms that practice audience research continuously and on a large scale are the principal arbiters of what the American public reads, sees, and hears. It is no slur on the personal merit or integrity of the people who manage these firms to say that in many cases they are almost totally uninterested in the content of the data their corporations generate, in the methods used to generate them, and in the standards that govern the process, except insofar as these may be related to their targeted profit goals. These managers understand that they must staff their businesses with professionals who do have some concerns for content, methods, and standards, and that these researchers must be given some latitude to do what they want. But they judge them by the financial results, rather than by the excellence of what they do or the knowledge they generate. What is essentially a humanistic social science has been transformed into an assembly line of repetitive and largely meaningless statistics.

John C. Holt, the chairman and CEO of A.C. Nielsen, and executive vice-president of Dun and Bradstreet, provided a rare insight into the thinking processes of the new generation of corporate research manufacturers in an address to the 1988 annual conference of the Advertising Research Foundation. He informed his listeners, "A single woman, 22 years of age, living in New York is very different from a woman 42 years of age with four children, living in Los Angeles where purchasing patterns are much, much different." It is hard to imagine a pioneer researcher like Percival White in the 1920s or a research entrepreneur like Alfred Politz in the 1950s impelled to utter such a self-evident platitude to a professional audience.

Holt went on to reveal his organization's mission.

> I well remember late one night, toward the end of a long conversation I was having with one of our customers, when he paused and said: "You know, Jack, when all is said and done, my job is to sell more soap. And your job is to help me do that by continuing to give me accurate information—information with integrity."

Needless to say, information collected with integrity can be utterly worthless if the wrong kinds of measurements are being made or the wrong interpretations drawn from them. It is precisely the search for meaning, for knowledge, that distinguishes the research analyst from the collector and processor of data.

Though the analysts are a hardy, and even a necessary breed, it is the producers of data who are taking over. There may be nothing inherently bad in this, if we assume that the invisible hand of the marketplace will inevitably point its thumb down to what is stupid or just plain wrong. How long does it take, however, for stupidity and error to be detected, and how much damage can it do in a media system whose informational and cultural diet is largely produced, distributed, and consumed on the basis of market-research-generated information?

The capital demands for entry into the research business have taken a quantum jump since the advent of the computer. The machine was already in evidence in advertising agencies by the late 1960s, but it was off in a back room and, like a caged beast, had to be approached warily and only by its trained keepers. As terminals spread to almost every desk, it became possible for anyone and everyone to gain access to vast amounts of marketing data and to manipulate these in relation to possible alternative strategies. This diminished the uniqueness of the research professional's role. Large agencies began to eliminate their research departments altogether, replacing them with planning groups, made up of apprentices who, as the expression goes, "crunch" numbers. The primary users of the data are no longer researchers, but media buyers and salespeople, brand managers, and other corporate or agency functionaries for whom the numbers serve a wholly instrumental purpose.

As more media and account people become dependent on research-generated data, they develop an overwhelming urge to take quality for granted and to be deeply resentful of any nitpickers who suggest that the data might be not only imperfect but sometimes irrelevant. Since decision-makers want research to reduce uncertainty, the presence of competing and therefore inevitably conflicting bodies of information are an annoyance rather than an advantage.

Sampling, interviewing, data processing, and report production all routinely make use of expensive equipment that would have been unimaginable 40 or 50 years ago. This has changed the character of survey research, but surveys in all their forms represent a diminishing part of the total research output. A growing part of what is generally classified as marketing research is derived from scanner data, the metering of television sets, statistical modeling and other computer-based techniques that are costly to set up and maintain. Thus the advantage has steadily grown for organizations with substantial financial resources.

The universal use of the computer in business prompted a desire to crowd the maximum amount of information onto a single spreadsheet, and thus to squeeze an ever-greater variety of facts about product and media consumption out of a given database. Advertisers have become more and more obsessed with the idea of the "single source" – the dream of getting all the information on what individuals buy and on all their media experiences from one giant research service, so that cause and effect can be clearly measured.[9] Presumably such a service would end the deplorable present necessity of putting together the data derived from different research organizations, with all the inevitable inconsistencies that result. The underlying premise is that the quality of information from a single source could be equivalent to what can be obtained by specialized studies that focus on just one subject at a time. The premise is incorrect, but good judgment, experience, knowledge, and common sense are commonly overruled by the desire for convenience.

Research users increasingly demanded data produced in a continuing and predictable format that lends itself to the tracking of change over time, data that complied with standardized systems and procedures. More and more of the information relied upon both by advertisers and media to measure product movement, brand share, audience size and characteristics, and the like represents repetitive syndicated facts ground out by large research factories. Needless to say, large research companies are usually positioned to exercise the economies of scale required to produce and organize these types of simple statistics in great quantities.

The effect of all this has been to further the process of concentration in the research business. There has been a steady diminution in the number of viable services that measure the same phenomena by different methods. In 1994, A.C. Nielsen was the only source of national data on the grocery market and of national and local television audience ratings. Arbitron was the only surviving source of radio ratings, Birch-Scarborough Research the only firm supplying local newspaper audience figures to a national format. Magazines had two competing services (SMRB [Simmons Media Research Bureau], and MRI [Mediamark Research Inc.]) producing different, and often very different audience statistics.

The principal effect of the phenomenon I have been describing is the redirection of research from analysis to manufacturing, from an intellectual enterprise to an administrative one. The reduction of competition has reinforced this tendency. In times past, the very inconsistency of data from different sources stimulated a great deal of reflection, discussion, and experimentation in the domain of methodology. This discussion was inseparable from thought about the meaning of the data themselves.

The power of research derives from its almost universal acceptance as an impeccable indicator of what works in the marketplace – of products, media offerings, and political ideas. But this effort is increasingly dedicated to the sterile measurement of appearances rather than to penetrating the dynamic essence of the public's thoughts and moods. There is little left of the tradition of going out and talking to people, one at a time, trying to get a direct sense of what they are saying, and then taking whatever numbers these conversations yield and trying to interpret what they really mean. This evolution explains why the citation of research findings almost always has a conservative effect, since figures that show what people do generally confirm the judgments of those who provide them with the wherewithal to do it. To consider the potential for change, one must look beyond mere description. Meaning is secondary when research is an instrument of power rather than of understanding.

Research as an Instrument of Power

The entire structure of modern marketing rests on data. An enormous enterprise is now dedicated to the collection and sifting of innumerable numbers that track the shipment of merchandise, its sale through the stores, its share of the market, its actual use by consumers, its familiarity and reputation, the characteristics of its customers, the distribution and impact of its advertising. This research is conducted by many methods, some as deeply personal as a one-on-one intensive interview, some as apparently impersonal as a metering device attached to a television set or a computer record of the company's own factory orders. In no case is the human element entirely absent. In many instances, the human element, with all its attendant uncertainties and resulting imprecisions, is overwhelming.

Uncertainties and imprecisions have their place in making managerial judgments. A business executive may consider the risks of unforeseeable external events or competitive actions that could make plans go awry, but the plans themselves must be based on the best available intelligence. Whatever is quantifiable must be assigned an appropriate numerical weight. There is no room for probability theory in the final equation, any more than there is in preparing a balance sheet.

In the business world, survey research data are commonly imbued with the same definitive character as the numbers the accounting department uses to make up a payroll, tally production, or calculate profit or loss. Most survey researchers would regard those as really hard numbers, though they look softer when examined closely. When it comes to assessing imprecision in corporate data, the statistical tolerances that arise from survey sampling error are only the tip of the iceberg. Even the most solid-seeming, automatically collected numbers crumble, when we look at them under the microscope.

Perhaps the hardest numbers to be found in business are returns on investment or net earnings. Shipments of goods from the factory can be inflated by special promotions and be advanced or delayed for accounting purposes, to show up in one calendar period rather than another and thus make the books look good to financial analysts.

Just as manufacturers' shipment figures can be flawed, so can the measurement of sales at the retail level. Store audits and supermarket scanning records, even when they are collected from perfectly drawn samples of stores (which never happens) and reinforced with large financial incentives, are subject to massive problems of incompleteness: uncooperative store managements, equipment failures, data losses.

• The president of McCann-Erickson once got a panic call from the head of Nabisco, a major client: the Ritz brand's share of the dry cracker market in the Pacific region had plummetted. Big executives of the agency flew out from New York to investigate why consumers were turning away from the brand. The data that had evoked this flap were not just penciled jottings on a work sheet. They were in a very official-looking, beautiful, hard-number bar chart, and they bore the name of A.C. Nielsen. No one ever did find out what had caused the squiggle, but it was indeed a squiggle—an erratic aberration caused by human error or some chance occurrence in Nielsen's sample of audited stores.

More recently, data based on scanning product bar-code symbols have provided an accurate measure of sales at the checkout counter, but these data must still be assembled properly from a cross-section of stores to produce valid projections. At the outset, not all stores had the necessary equipment to create such measurements, and it was difficult to control the sample to make sure it was representative. Jerome Greene, a prominent statistician, used a complicated computer weighting system to produce nationally projectable sales figures. They were resisted by manufacturers who insisted that the numbers were wrong because they differed from Nielsen's, the accepted yardstick. These large corporations were never willing to make independent assessments of market size because they had such a tremendous investment in the accumulated trend information. Improvements in research are always inhibited by the fact that any change in method creates problems of comparability with the existing data for which there is a historical record. (A similar case occurred some years later, in 1991. *Billboard* introduced a new, greatly improved system for measuring sales of record albums, based on bar-code readings at store checkout counters. It immediately ran into strong objections, because the trend lines were off.[10])

For years, the whole established structure of American network television has been based on the Nielsen ratings, which used an "audimeter" attached to the set to measure the number of households tuned to a program. Nielsen's power over broadcast programming decisions was heightened in 1975, when it began to get metered data fed back immediately by telephone rather than by mail, and launched an overnight ratings service covering the major markets. Three years later, Marvin Antonowsky, then program chief of NBC-TV, explained his decision to take a new series off the air after only three episodes. Although the star, Lee Grant, had called him "the mad programmer," Antonowsky insisted, "Everything happens very fast now. The business has changed. Fast input makes possible fast output."[11]

Nielsen's household meters were automatic recording devices. Its new people meter (introduced to meet a competitive threat from the Maxwell-owned European research giant, Audits of Great Britain) required family members and visitors to press buttons to identify their presence, just as the diary had required them to record their viewing conscientiously. The resulting figures turned out to be significantly lower than the ratings produced by the previous methods. As Nielsen switched the basis of its reporting from the household to the people meters, its ratings dropped.[12] This created consternation at the networks, whose advertising charges were based on a guaranteed audience size. Millions of dollars and enormous efforts were expended to investigate the disparity. It seems most unlikely that similar trouble would have been taken if the new numbers were higher rather than lower.

In radio too, the ratings are all-important, although radio measurements are far more primitive than television's. Only half of the commercial radio stations get regular Arbitron ratings. A New York FM radio station with an Arbitron rating of 4 or 5 had revenues of about $15 million in 1994, to which each additional Arbitron rating point could add $3 or $4 million.

Radio station WAKY in Louisville at one time had a Nielsen share of 5, a Pulse share of 29, and a Hooper share of 42. Comparably wild incongruities have long existed in magazine audience measurement. Research firms invariably produce numbers that differ—sometimes substantially—from each other and that are internally inconsistent between one measurement period and the next. Discrepancies have ranged up to 50% between MRI, which averages its audience figures every 6 months, and SMRB which does not average. *People*, with 3.3 million circulation, was shown by MRI to have an audience of 35.2 million, while *Family Circle*, with 4.9 million circulation, was said to have 28 million readers.

Because of the disparities between these two leading audience services, most advertising agencies adjust their data, magazine by magazine, using judgment and intuition. There has always been the solid reference point of audited circulation to fall back upon. Broadcasting has no similar gold standard to apply. Differences in methodology that may appear insignificant to the average person result in wide disparities when they are projected into numbers of viewers. They acquire real impact when they are reflected in advertising budget allocations.

Measuring the size and composition of audiences is not the only way to compare media. One research service, TvQ, rates television programs on the basis of audience opinions. Television systems in France, Britain, and Canada conduct surveys of how program quality is assessed or "appreciated." In the United States, the Markle Foundation spent over $2.5 million between 1980 and 1985 on research and development of Television Audience Assessment's model ratings system, which measured both program "appeal" and "impact" through a viewer diary technique. But broadcasters and advertisers have shown no interest in qualitative measures that require interpretation and reflection on what they mean. By contrast, straight measurements of the audience appear to be unambiguous. They are definitive, but not necessarily accurate.

The Problem with Surveys

Why are the measurements imprecise? A substantial part of marketing data is derived in one form or another from contacts with the public. In the era of the dual wage-earner household, interviewing has become much more difficult. A generation ago, market research was done largely through personal interviews, with men contacted in the evening and women in the daytime. Today, most of the interviewing is done by telephone in the evening, at about a third the cost of a personal contact. The growing number of answering devices (in 46% of the households by 1992[13]) complicates matters further and raises the incredible specter of automatic interviewing machines, with questions recorded on tape, speaking to answering machines with their own recorded instructions. Harassed respondents are apt to cut long interviews short, and the rise of telephone sales solicitation (rechristened "telemarketing") further raises the level of public impatience.

Less and less research comes from customized studies that examine each marketing problem as a unique case. (Actually, more of the customized research is made up of group interviews and shopping mall studies of often dubious validity.) Paradoxically, an insistence on economy in research has been coupled with a professed need for greater and greater quantities of collateral information derived from the same survey respondents. This has lengthened interviews and reduced the public's cooperation rate. Thus the data became mushier the more they were depended on. Successfully completed personal interviews (after repeated callbacks) typically constituted about two-thirds of the original planned sample in 1994, compared to four out of five in 1967; telephone interviews were completed with about half the designated respondents. In 1990, 36% of the public reported that they had refused an interview.[14] A 60% completion rate from an original probability sampling design was now considered acceptable, though it would not have been a few years earlier.[15]

Difficulties are multiplied when an initial interview is made mainly for the purpose of getting respondents to cooperate in more arduous tasks, like filling in diaries or other self-administered questionnaires, using a special credit card to shop for groceries only at one particular supermarket, or submitting to the continuing presence for several years of the equipment that meters television set and VCR operations. Of the Nielsen Television Index's initial sample, only a little more than a third are included in the final figures.[16]

Inevitably, people who become respondents differ from those who are inaccessible or refuse to cooperate. Cooperators in television surveys are more likely to be heavy viewers, cable subscribers, and members of large families.[17] In commercial surveys, there are usually a limited number of call-backs to unanswered or busy numbers, compared to the 109 attempts that have been made, in at least one government-funded survey, to get to a designated respondent. Professional researchers have tackled these problems seriously, and have resorted to statistical techniques that allow them to correct for the difficulty of reaching some kinds of people.

Surveys once relied on quota sampling, with interviewers instructed to contact specific numbers of people of each sex and in designated age and social class groups. The probability sampling procedures that acquired currency after World War II were considered more scientific because they removed the choice of respondents from the individual interviewer's control in favor of a predesignated selection based on random numbers. Because of the decline in cooperation levels, research firms now use computer models that adjust raw survey numbers to conform to the Census description of the population. These produce corrected projections, but in effect revive the old quota procedure at a different level.

The numbers emanating from reputable market research companies represent the best information available to answer the perennial questions that business executives ask as to how they are doing, who their customers are, and how they can best be reached. But the numbers, not infallible, deserve none of the reverential awe with which they are customarily treated. They are less apt to inspire unquestioning faith when there are different, conflicting sets of data available from competing research suppliers. But this is less and less likely to happen, as specialized research becomes more costly and thus more monopolistic.

The fact that the media industry's most important statistics are uncontested has had alarming consequences, since it has only increased the certitude with which they are imbued, and thus made them more crucial in all the decisions made directly by advertisers or made by media in anticipation of advertisers' wishes.

The Tyranny of Audience Measurement

Research helps to shape the kind of media system that advertisers find congenial rather than what the public would create if left to its own devices. The kinds of audiences advertisers want do not exactly run parallel to the distribution of real audiences, of their present tastes or potential tastes. The size of audiences shown in the records of past history is ordinarily used as a guide to future planning, both by the advertisers and by the people who run the media. In network television, advertisers have for years received guarantees that their accumulated audiences would reach a minimum size, as measured by A. C. Nielsen. The networks must deliver "make goods"—additional commercial positions—if their actual ratings fall below their earlier estimates.

Fifty-five percent of network advertising is sold "up front" in the spring, before the fall programming season starts, usually at a better cost efficiency than the advertiser would get later in a "scatter buy," taking whatever may be left over. Estimates of the ratings that the new programs will achieve derive from the performance of similar programs in the past. For national advertisers who rely mainly on television, the networks' up-front buying deadlines force early decisions on their budget allocations and plans for other media as well. (The remaining commercial network time is sold at negotiated and often reduced prices in the "scatter market.") Thus television's income depends on the use of safe and familiar formulas of content that meet advertisers' expectations. What breaks the mold can also break the bank.

In broadcasting, the preoccupation with ratings is all-consuming, and is manifested in the high rate of program turnover, which transforms the relative handful of long-term survivors into legends. Television series are abruptly terminated not because viewers have rejected them but because they are not delivering the guaranteed number of gross rating points to the advertisers. Program production is geared to the kind of values with which advertisers feel comfortable. Ratings are generally regarded as the only meaningful measurement of a programs's success. Former NBC programming executive Paul Klein:

> Why is the rating so important to us? Why do we hold our breath every day when we
> come to work? Because our pricing, our scheduling, our budgeting, our jobs all are
> dependent on our ability to predict this number with reasonable accuracy. If we miss
> in our forecast, it costs us money—either "lost opportunity" money through under-
> pricing, or "make-good" money [*i.e.*, rebates on schedules that fall short of pro-
> jected audience size] through over-pricing.[17]

A rating point is worth $140 million to a network, on an annualized basis. Each
rating point on a network show brings in over $8,000 for a 30-second spot, and there
are seven such spots in a half-hour show— a substantial proportion of them split into
15-second units. A hit like "The Cosby Show" at its peak was worth over $100 million
a year to the CBS network.[19]

With this kind of money at stake, it is no wonder that minor blips in the
measurement of media audiences are treated as though they represent the reality of
viewer presence and attention, rather than being artifacts of highly fallible methods
of collecting, assembling, and projecting statistics. NBC's "Today" was said to have
slipped "noticeably" over the preceding year, when its rating dropped by a percentage
point.[20] (This was of course a meaningless number, given the statistical margin
of error.)

Every November, February, May, and July, Nielsen measures the size and
demographic characteristics of program audiences in all the television markets.
(Arbitron did so too before it withdrew from the field in 1993.) These four "sweep"
months have attained inordinate importance for local stations. The networks have
always beefed up their programming and their promotions in those months in support
of their affiliates, sometimes with expensive miniseries (like ABC's $100 million
"War and Remembrance," which lost $20 million), sometimes with made-for-
television movies.[21] Offering promotional incentives to viewers during sweeps is
outlawed by an FCC rule, but other forms of "hypoing" (artificially boosting the
numbers) are widely practiced. There is a continuing clamor to keep the audience
numbers high, even from the agencies who want to impress their accounts. Lawrence
Friedman of the N.W. Ayer agency, advises broadcasters:

> Whatever else you do, promote! The more firmly entrenched you are in the minds of
> your market's diary keepers, the more likely it is that they will remember you when,
> as happens so often, they fill out several days' worth of viewing from memory.[22]

The struggle for ratings is not necessarily a hindrance in the eyes of all those who
are caught up in it. Some consider it a spur to excellence and innovation, like a writer-
producer who told communication scholars Jay Blumler and Caroline Spicer:

> It could be that all the competition forces people to be more creative and unusual and
> forces the network and cable services to take more of a chance. Or it could be that in
> scrambling for the ratings they want [they] will produce more of the same. . . . It
> could go either way.[23]

Perhaps it could go either way, but in practice it gravitates in the direction of
uniformity.

Beyond Statistics

In pursuing audiences, don't advertisers encourage the media to be responsive to the public's preferences? No. The concern with audience measurement arises mostly from a misguided notion of how communication works and a willingness to equate its impact with mere physical presence. Why shouldn't the count of set-tuning or people-viewing be the appropriate indicator of whether or not a program serves the advertiser's purpose as a vehicle for the company's messages? The answer is simple. In communication, as in everything else, the meaning of an experience has very little relationship to the amount of time that we spend on it: brushing one's teeth or making love, feeding the cat or breaking a leg, seeing a great movie or seeing a bad one. Yet recordings of time spent, rather than of intensity and meaning, govern all commercial evaluation of broadcast programming.

Communication cannot be quantified in any meaningful way because its very essence is symbolic. It is possible to enumerate events, but it is impossible to count experiences. Because each is qualitatively unique, they do not add up and they cannot really be compared. One does not ask which is better, "Tosca" or "The Magic Flute?" — let alone, which is better, "Tosca," *War and Peace*, or "The Night Watch" — because each of these works of art is incomparable. Nor can one compare advertisements in this way.

How many copies were sold of Einstein's book on the theory of relativity? If anyone knows, nobody cares, because we do not measure the value of ideas by that criterion. Technical publications that serve an extremely restricted number of readers may nonetheless have great intellectual importance. An abstruse paper in a journal of theoretical physics may be read and understood by only a handful of specialists, but they are the ones who can use the information, and their institutions are willing to pay for it. But if they were *not* willing to pay, would it be correct to argue that such publications were not worthwhile, since the market had rejected them?

I once asked the long-time editor of a highly influential small literary review what its circulation was. He said he did not know. He certainly did not care to know. I got the same answer years later from the director of a university-supported cable channel when I asked him about his ratings. In both cases these men worked on the assumption that what they were disseminating had to be judged on its own merits, and judged by some standard other than the immediate willingness of the public to spend its money or time. There was an era when newspaper editors may have played by the same rules, if their papers had an established place in the market, by virtue of their history, distribution, or monopoly position. They knew that people would continue to read no matter what, and that the most important thing they could do for the readers was to exercise their own judgment about what was important for them to know about. But this philosophy is hard to jibe with the principle of giving the public what it says it wants.

Since advertising media succeed or fail by the numbers, their managements are obsessed with the constant need to make those numbers go up. When they are managed for this purpose, their content is geared to build audience size rather than to meaningful expression. Concentrated power over advertising decisions is more pernicious when those decisions are based on mistaken premises. From this combination stem the ailments of commercial culture, to which we turn next.

III

FLAWS AND FAILURES OF COMMERCIAL CULTURE

6

The Pursuit of Sensation

Endlessly chasing the audience numbers, advertising media gravitate toward established formulas of entertainment, toward the lowest common denominator of taste. Commercial culture as a whole is laced with infantilism and insipidity. It thrives on fictional clichés that are guaranteed to produce satisfaction every time. It favors the vulgar, the mean, and the hackneyed, and shies away from experiment and variety.

This chapter lays out the evidence that supports this sad thesis. It considers the less appealing characteristics of commercial culture and raises the question of whether or not they simply reflect the democratic response of the market to regrettable mass preferences. This forces us to ask what standards of judgment should be applied, and by what right. Television demands close examination, because it occupies so much of the public's time. Do media influence the way we act? If so, how are the effects to be determined? We shall look at what television does to children and at what media violence and sex mean for adults. Much of what we find awry can be explained as a by-product of the preoccupation with audience size. Key points:

- Popularity is not the proper criterion to judge mass communications; the people who produce them know what is good and what is not.
- Violence and sex are exploited in the competitive struggle for audiences, in which media supported by advertisers and by consumers are interdependently engaged.
- Media activity in itself can affect the audience and is inseparable from the effects of media content.
- Antisocial content in mass media has antisocial effects, though the proof is not the kind that lawyers insist on.

Innocent—and Not-So-Innocent—Pleasures

The media system is permeated by a sensationalism that seems to become progressively more blatant as national mores change; in turn, it has had profound effects on the national mores. There is nothing novel about the exploitation of prurient and sadistic instincts. What is disturbing is the scale on which this can now be done and the cynicism applied to the task. The outrageous coexists with the most dismal banality. Great works of art, literature, or drama are apt to arouse anxiety, irritation, or grief; commercial culture thrives on the happy ending. The innocent but idiotic refrain of dubbed laughter on the comedy sound track exemplifies a studied inanity that even staunch defenders of commercial culture find it hard to justify.

Headlines of supermarket tabloids:

Dead Mom Gives Birth in Coffin
Princess Di Raped by Skinheads from Mars
A Space Alien Made Me Pregnant
Cat Eats Parrot—Now It Talks
Son Kills Father and Eats Him[1]

Press release from Fox Broadcasting, synopsizing a new television show:

Marcy loses her wedding ring down the pants of Zorro the Great, a male exotic dancer.[2]

Newspaper headlines:

2 Teen-Age Children are Held as Plotters of Father's Murder
Madman Sears 2 with Acid in Subway
Says Hotel Forced Her to be Sex Spy
Kinky Hubby's Into Bondage
Arizona Bishop Jailed Over Shootout

Record titles:

Screaming for Vengeance
Children of the Grave
Bad to the Bone
Maneater
Paranoid

Names of rock groups appearing on MTV:

The Dead Kennedys
3 Teens Kill 4
Sadist Faction
Rash of Stabbings[3]

Television programs:

An Eye for an Eye
Destroyer
Shark Bait

Juggernaut
The Howling
Peeping Tom[4]

Such colorful specimens are hardly representative of the nation's mass media output, but they occur often enough to arouse revulsion and signal deliberate exploitation. A vice-president of Twentieth Century Fox Film, describing the possibilities in a new syndicated program, "Famous Jury Trials":

> There's a tremendous reaction to rape or murder. Everybody wants to look over everybody else's shoulder. It has great women's appeal.

This forthright pronouncement encapsulates the principal objection that can be made to commercial culture on moral and aesthetic grounds: It represents deliberate pandering to the worst instincts of the crowd. Disdain for the habits, manners, and tastes of the masses is in a long line that stretches back to Plato and Aristotle. To the old argument that the common is also commonplace and coarse, a new dimension has been added by a media system in which popular culture is manufactured for profit, and by rules that have little to do with the instincts or principles of creative expression.

A Puritan strain in the critique of popular culture has ascribed its derelictions to a kind of original sin, a natural tendency of the public to gravitate toward the most debased forms of amusement. In England, *Livesey's Moral Reformer* complained in 1833,

> The extensive circulation of newspapers is a sure criterion of the *mental* activity of the people of this country, but by no means of the advancement of moral principles and virtuous habits. This is certain from the circumstance, that the most licentious papers usually command the largest sale. . . . The press is degraded by adventurers, who constantly prostitute their talents for gain. Knowing the depraved taste of our immoral population, they suit their article to their readers, and are thus openly, and with an unsparing hand, sowing and watering the seeds of moral deformity.[5]

Religious and political elements often were conjoined in nineteenth-century England with disparagement of mass amusements, as the social historian John Golby observes:

> In many respects the socialist critique of popular culture echoed that of the rational recreationalists. Whereas the latter wished the people to become Christian, domestic and rational in their recreations, the former hoped they would become socialist, communal and rational, but both berated popular culture for its hedonism and cynicism. . . . Imprisoned within the attender at the music-hall, the spectator at the football match and the reader of *Tit-Bits* was, they believed, a worthy socialist trying to get out.[6]

The use of the term "mass" in connection with media now carries with it only the implication of vast numbers rather than an evaluation, pro or con. For Marx, the masses were nothing less than oppressed humanity, salt of the earth, and the phrase "toiling masses" became a stock item in twentieth-century Marxism's arsenal of clichés. But "mass" was a pejorative term to the early Victorians, summoning up the image of unwashed multitudes, of a volatile political temperament and inferior appetites.[7] The phrase "mass culture" continues to carry these connotations of popular tastes threatening humanity's enduring heritage. Nineteenth-century American critics attributed the high metropolitan crime rate to penny periodicals. The *Contemporary Review* blamed the publishers, saying that the masses were content with literary junk because "there is nothing better, of the very cheap kind within their reach."[8]

Revulsion at mass media and their popular culture has often reflected a deeper abhorrence of large-scale industrial civilization in all its aspects: The critic John Cowper Powys:

> One's normal days in any large city, and in most small ones, are continually spent amid architecture that is no architecture, pictures that are no pictures, music that is no music, and sights, smells and vibrations that are just the very things to loathe and abhor which the culture of half your lifetime has been sensitizing you and refining you.[9]

Mass media have been viewed as a narcotic, deflecting the public from serious confrontation with life's real problems, or even exacerbating those problems. Henry James:

> The reading of the newspaper is *the* pernicious habit, and the father of all idleness and laxity.[10]

Thorstein Veblen complained that mass culture's bread and circuses deflected the masses from revolution.[11] But Benito Mussolini used just this point to provide the guiding spirit for his own Fascist revolution:

> All belief is extinct, we have no faith in our gods, no belief in the Republic. Great principles are no more. Material interests reign supreme. The multitude demands bread and amusements.[12]

Whatever the political function of commercial culture, the heart of the complaint is *not* that it is simplistic, foolish, and deadening, but that it does not have to be that way. This presupposes that other, better criteria of judgment should be applied to it than those of the market.

Are Sales the Measure of Success?

I have already argued that audience size is not a good standard for evaluating advertising media. In the case of media for which the public pays directly, isn't the market the appropriate judge of excellence? No. Sales are hardly an infallible measure of the value of any form of expression. Appreciation may be a better yardstick of achievement. So may be evidence that people have been persuaded to do something. The sales of Thomas Paine's pamphlets were probably less important to him than the actions they incited. For a contemporary Nobel-prize winning novelist, the honor may compensate for a life-long failure to get on the bestseller list.

The influence of a message is not a function of the amount of money that is paid for it. A modest number of books sold in hardcover will bring in a bigger dollar return for the publisher and author than a substantially greater number in paperback. Television programs often earn more in syndication than in their original broadcasts. Films that fail at the box office can have hugely profitable second lives on television and as videocassettes.

There are ambiguities in attributing cause and effect, as well as in measuring financial performance. Sales do not simply reflect the merit of a communication, even when we define merit as appeal to the paying public. They respond to the vicissitudes of the market—the number and kind of competitive offerings made at the same time. They reflect promotional budgets and skills, and the serendipitous effects of timing, as subjects and personalities achieve topicality in the news, as current fashions and tastes swell or wane, reinforcing or diminishing particular interests. And sales are a function of distribution and access.

Hit films and records and best-selling books do not attract audiences just because of their inherent merits, but because people want to share experiences with their peers. A film that is booked only into a few art theaters in major cities and university towns will never find a theatrical audience among the mass public. Books that can be obtained only on special order will not sell like those in booksellers' window displays. A book, a record, or a movie can win no audiences at all if people have not heard of it, and it will not get into the stores or theaters unless distributors know that it will be advertised and promoted on a suitable scale. Advertising-supported media also spend millions to advertise in other media, mainly to attract audiences, but media that rely directly on the public promote more heavily.

As with any other consumer product, media that derive their income from direct sales to the public must first pass the scrutiny of a relatively small handful of purchasing agents—"gatekeepers," to use social psychologist Kurt Lewin's term. Their judgments are presumed to arise from their experienced intuition of the public's predilections, but these judgments are often not merely imperfect but bad. Error and caprice enter the gatekeeping process at every stage: the state of a literary agent's schedule that determines her willingness to take on an unknown author, a junior editor's decision to pass on a manuscript or reject it out of hand, a reviewer's decision to review or not, a producer's decision to raise additional funds or to cut the budget, a film theater chain's decision to raise the admissions price. All of these essentially accidental branching points in the life of a media product affect its financial success, if not its very existence, but they may have nothing at all to do with its ability to arouse a response from its ultimate audience.

Even if financial payment is accepted as the main criterion, its definition is not clear-cut. Is it to be measured in the initial compensation for a work, in the return over a lifetime, or with allowances for posthumous success? Paul Gauguin lived from hand to mouth while he painted masterpieces that bring millions on today's art market. But this, it may be argued, is an exceptional case. Karl Marx:

> Milton, who wrote *Paradise Lost* for five pounds, was an unproductive laborer. . . . [He] produced *Paradise Lost* for the same reason that a silkworm produces silk. It was an activity of his nature.[13]

But a hack commissioned to produce something for sale, is productive, Marx thought, because he is producing capital. Marx noted another peculiarity of the market for cultural goods that defied the conventional mechanisms of pricing: "Desire increases with increasing price. Thus, in the upper reaches of the art market the individual demand curve is the inverse of the classical demand curve."[14]

A century and a half later, this observation is echoed by the art dealer Klaus Perls:

> Is there any intrinsic value? No. It's all fantasy. Prices can go to $40 million, and so what? Why not higher? Any amount of money can be justified.[15]

Sotheby's invented the fine-arts auction in 1958. High prices did not drive away customers; they attracted them.[16] Just as the value of a painting in today's art market is surely a dubious indication of its merit, the earnings of a best-selling novel have little to do with its quality as an enduring contribution to literature.

The domain of the arts is itself today inseparable from the world of media hype. Financial rewards are a product of fantasy, fashion, and promotion as well as of the ability to touch public sensibilities. If profits also correspond to excellence, that may be no more than a happy accident.

What is Good, True, or Beautiful?

Media managements are apt to insist that they follow the public's criteria of acceptability rather than their own personal instincts. The notion that there are independent yardsticks or standards of judgment is today often considered absurd, an attempt by individuals of a particular gender, race, and social class to impose their values on the rest of humanity, which happily does not share them.

To deny any qualitative differentiation of tastes is like denying differences in the validity of opinions. However sincerely held, the conviction that the earth is flat does not have the merit of the belief that it is round. Slavery and cannibalism have their own rationales for those who engage in these practices, but that does not deter the rest of us from making our own moral verdicts on the subjects. The opinion that members of a disliked minority should be denied the vote or access to certain jobs or perhaps to life itself does not warrant consideration equivalent to the opinion that all men are created equal and endowed by their Creator with certain inalienable rights. Naturally what I have just written represents opinions, with which members of the Flat Earth Society or the Ku Klux Klan would disagree. I must go on the assumption that the reader accepts not only the inevitability of deviant opinions, but the fact that many of them do not make sense and are unacceptable.

Tastes, too, are matters of opinion. To argue that one cannot argue about taste is like saying that one cannot dispute opinions or consider some right and some wrong. Robert Hutchins wrote:

In order to believe in democracy we must believe that there is a difference between truth and falsity, good and bad, right and wrong, and that truth, goodness, and right are objective standards even though they cannot be experimentally verified. . . . Our intellectual leaders have been telling us . . . that nothing is true which cannot be subject to experimental verification. In the whole realm of social thought there can, therefore, be nothing but opinion. Since there is nothing but opinion, every-body is entitled to his own opinion. . . . If everything is a matter of opinion, force becomes the only way of settling differences of opinion.[17]

There are indeed standards by which we can identify and judge the meretricious, the incompetent, the unoriginal, the dull, the degenerate, the maudlin, the ugly— even if there are some people whom they beguile or even inspire. The standards are forever in dispute, the applications even more so; yet we do not have to assign the same weight to the good and the bad, the real and the phony.

Taste is not merely opinion; it is also a matter of definition. A Danish radio station played music by Haydn, Schubert, Beethoven, Mozart, and Mendelsohn, once identified in the newspaper listing as "popular music" and another time as a "classical concert." It drew a much larger audience on the first occasion, though listeners stayed with it to the same degree under either label, once they had tuned in.[18]

How do we judge the quality of any expression? Samuel Johnson, David Hume, and George Orwell agreed that "the test of time" determined whether a creative work had merit. This test may allow us to pass judgment on artistic expressions of Johnson's era and Hume's, perhaps of Orwell's half a century ago. But what guidance does it offer us for evaluating current work? This question underlies the continuing debate over government funding for the arts, just as it is used defensively by media representatives confronting their critics. As the prevailing standards change, works that were formerly on, or even over, the fringe become accepted.[19]

Is there a universal test for excellence, or for good taste? The formulas of commercial culture can be defended on the grounds that they reflect majority tastes and that criticism of them represents nothing more than another minority view. Paradoxically, such arguments for cultural relativism typically come from the same quarters that denounce commercial culture as the imposition of false values upon the public for the benefit of society's ruling elite.

A president of the Modern Language Association, Houston Baker, argues that cultural choices are "no different from choosing between a hoagy and a pizza," and that "if tomorrow publishers decided that it was no longer possible to publish Charles Dickens, then Dickens would no longer be part of the canon of English literature."[20] In this view, established literary reputations essentially emerge from an old-boy network rather than from the inherent merit of the works themselves. Robert Peters, a conceptual artist, proclaims, "One person's music is another person's noise." The assumption behind this inane aphorism is that there is really no distinction between music and noise.

The advocates of cultural relativism consider traditional aesthetic criteria to be meaningless and criticize the critics of popular culture as undemocratic elitists. "Elitism" is widely regarded as a term of opprobrium so severe that it can only be countered by flat denial, even being disavowed by the heads of the National Endow-ments for the Arts and for the Humanities. The elitism under criticism is not that of a closed and self-perpetuating social class, but merely a category that embraces the constantly replenished pool of cultivated talent without which any society must degenerate.[21]

The denial of absolute standards rejects Western elite culture, *vis à vis* the arts and lore of other societies; it also implies that traditional elite culture is in no sense superior to the popular culture of the moment. (Elite or high culture represents either the enduring heritage of human achievements or the carefully guarded support system of ruling-class tastes, depending on how you look at it.)

Relativist philosophy accords well with the acceptance of the market as the arbiter of mass media content. To the degree that communications of any kind may be assigned different rankings, those that enjoy the greatest popularity may be assumed to have the greatest merit, since all human expressions are deemed to have equivalent validity.

In contrast, the poet and critic Helen Vendler points out,

> The canon, in any language, is composed of the writers that other writers admire, and have admired for generations. The acclamations of government, the hyperboles of marketing, the devotion of dons, have never kept a writer alive for three or four hundred years. It is because Virgil admired Homer, and Milton Virgil, and Keats Milton, and Stevens Keats that those writers turn up in classrooms and anthologies. . . . And writers admire writing not because it keeps up some school-masterly 'standard' but because it is 'simple, strenuous, and passionate' (as Milton said)—strenuous, imaginative, vivid, new.[22]

Not all the practitioners of commercial culture would reject such traditional criteria of excellence and integrity—in principle. In practice, they would argue, what is to be admired is what succeeds with the customers.

One Culture, Two, or More?

Commercial culture is generally identified with popular culture, although the two are by no means identical. Popular culture embraces the constantly changing figures, styles, and icons that, at any given moment, are generally familiar, attract wide audiences, and fill time and casual conversation.

Mass culture, say its critics, is characterized by a pervasive passivity.[23] By contrast, creating the traditional popular arts of everyday life once entailed active public participation. The practitioners of folk culture are often assigned to their craft by family, caste, or village tradition rather than by unusual personal skill.[24] Folk and elite cultures alike may be subject to commercialization (or in other societies, like China, to political exploitation by the state). Popular culture is not altogether without its enduring components (witness the persistence of nursery rhymes), while elite culture too has its fashions, fads, and movements.

Popular culture draws upon the traditional structural forms of elite culture. But format (drama, for example) should not be confused with substance (the actual convolutions of plot and depictions of character). Popular culture everywhere represents an amalgam of indigenous and international elements; elite culture is often described as having a "universal" quality. A market for elite culture does not exist naturally; it is sustained, either as a matter of public policy, by educational institutions and public broadcasting systems, or by enlightened management of the privately owned mass media. In every world capital, great newspapers play a catalytic role in upgrading taste and in developing widespread cultural interests that might not otherwise be activated.

Elite culture thrives when its public expands; this can happen only if it is physically and economically accessible. Mass media expose people to elite cultural experiences in ever-growing numbers.[25] But these occasional exposures are tiny relative to the extensive daily contacts that almost everyone has with mass culture in all its manifestations. The audience for elite culture in the United States is remarkably small, compared to the huge audiences for popular entertainment. (The average public television program is viewed nationally in 1.3% of the households.) Next to the "adult" videos in my neighborhood video store is a "culture" section, where cassettes can be rented at half the regular rate, presumably because of the slow turnover.

Naturally, people who watch the arts on television are more likely to attend live performances, and attendance is closely linked to educational achievement levels. An educated elite has different preferences and tastes from those of the unlettered, presumably because education means knowing better. This is a longstanding distinction; differences between high and low tragedy and comedy were already established in Greek and Roman theater. (Aristotle's esthetic and poetic theories reflected criteria of taste that were no doubt different from those the majority of Athenians found embodied in their popular entertainment.[26])

The symbols of popular culture that grip the public's imagination transcend their commercial origins. Thus they are left free to be judged on their own merits rather than by their sales, box office receipts, or audience ratings. Who is to judge those merits? The elite standards used by critics are often totally at odds with those of the mass publics the media serve. No medium attracts more hostile commentary than television from many of those who know it best. Yet television, as it is, enjoys widespread public approval.[27] Does this disparity of public and specialists' judgments arise from the fact that it is the task of critics to criticize or from the inherent difference in the social-class perspectives they bring to bear on the same content? There may be a little of both involved. But in the long run, the advantage goes to the critics, since their task is to remind media producers of their own standards of accomplishment. Commercial culture, it must be remembered, can find any level it wants.

Changing Standards

Prevailing notions of good taste have undergone constant change throughout history, and indeed vary widely among different societies. Our media system is unique in its tendency—and its capacity—to manipulate social standards in the pursuit of its commercial interest. The attempt to capture larger audiences has impelled media to press farther and farther against currently acceptable boundaries of propriety, and thus to move back the boundary posts themselves.[28]

Media standards are set not so much by censors as by those who produce content and have their own sense of the limits that cannot be transgressed. Newspapers and most magazines have resisted the temptation to intrude four-letter words or explicit sex into their columns (though they have become increasingly willing to be tolerant in straight news reporting). When they self-consciously refer to their responsibilities as "family" publications, they are expressing not only the conservative proclivities of their managements, but also a perception of their civic mission.

Pressures on the government-franchised and -regulated broadcast media have always been more potent than those on print or film. Program producers gear their content to what they believe will arouse the greatest public response. Rosalyn Weinman, NBC's head of broadcast standards and practices:

> We view our job as trying to help the producers. . . . We're really trying to help them do what everyone wants to do: attract the most, offend the least.[29]

The program acceptability standards set by the networks in part reflect changes in popular mores; in part they are set arbitrarily. (The CBS program practices department rejected an episode of "Maude" [produced by Norman Lear] that involved spouse-swapping when it was produced for the 1974–75 season, but let it run in 1976.[30] In 1993, NBC cut a masturbation scene from "Saturday Night Live" but permitted a skit in which Britain's Prince Charles had his head transferred to a tampon to "get closer to" his girlfriend.[31])

Enforcement of the acceptability rules was sharply curtailed at the close of the 1980s by budget cuts. Those standards were of declining significance as the networks lost audience, and as every conceivable form of vice, in depiction and language, could be encountered on cable channels.

In 1991, ABC's highest rated "movie of the week" was a violent and sadistic film called "The Tracey Thurman Story", which advertisers avoided. ABC's Bob Iger said,

> We're programming to what we perceive to be the tastes and desires of the American public. If that means stories about AIDS, homosexuality or abortion, so be it. That's our pursuit and our right. There seems to be a great reluctance from advertisers. We lose millions a year over this.[32]

This seems doubtful, given the ample opportunity for advertising on other types of programs, even on ABC.

Networks are quite capable of making courageous decisions when the issue at stake is not entertainment but public information, where different conventions and rules apply. In 1978, ABC's Helen Whitney produced a documentary, "Youth Terror–The View From Behind the Gun," which interviewed a young man who repeated the words "motherfucker" over and over. The network's top brass assembled to judge the suitability of this interview, the climax of the film. Chairman Leonard Goldenson said, "I don't see how we can cut the language," and the film went on the air. Nineteen stations refused to carry it.[33] In this case, what was at stake was honesty in the portrayal of reality. Many changes in mass media mores cannot–even with great generosity–be put under that heading.

Film in the Age of Television

The heightening of sensation in film and television content reflects the present interdependence of these media, even though one is supported by consumers and the other—until recently—by advertisers. Their mutual dependency reflects their intense competition as well as their common personalities and business interests. Radio was not a direct competitor of film as television was to become. Rather radio reinforced the movies' appeal, used their stars, their imagery, and their formulas. In contrast, television, which provided a cheaper, more readily accessible source of entertainment, changed America's movie experience. In 1946 the average American (including children) went to the movies twenty-nine times a year. By 1985, per capita movie attendance had declined to a rate of five times a year, and it has continued to drift downward slowly since then.[34] Movie experience changed again with the advent of cable television and the videocassette recorder.

Television occupied over twice as many hours of the day for the average person as radio did in its Golden Age, thus greatly enlarging the total amount of time spent with the media. The already well established formulas rapidly became a major part of everyday experience in a way that had never existed in the past.

As film competed with television for audiences, production costs escalated, first in the process of vying for stars who could command their own price and a share of the gross, and then for scripts. At the start of the 1990s, Hollywood was veering away from films based on a name star and a simple plot to more complex plots that required a more literary origin. This increased the competition for options on new novels and escalated their prepublication prices, sometimes to the million dollar level.

A generation earlier, the studios had moved to color productions as their standard, to emphasize the difference between films in the theater and the black and white images on the tiny tube. The theater screen became wider and larger. Multichannel sound (later stereo and Dolby) was introduced, and three-dimensional projection techniques were tried and abandoned. Casts became larger; locales, more exotic, and budgets, ever more extravagant.

Most important, Hollywood dramatically changed the content of the films themselves to differentiate them as much as possible from the blander programming material permitted by television network censors. Violence became both more prevalent and more gory, sex progressively more explicit (especially after court rulings that restricted censorship), vulgar and obscene language more commonplace. Violence, sex, and obscenity often seemed to be introduced gratuitously, not as an essential component of the plot or character depiction, but to titillate the audience in ways that had once been forbidden by the office of the Motion Picture Association's director, Will Hays, and that the self-imposed codes of television still discouraged.

First general principle of the 1930 Motion Picture Association of America Code:

> No picture shall be produced which will lower the moral standards of those who see it.

The Hays Office's rigidly enforced production code was effective as long as the principal producing firms and the theater chains had common or closely associated ownerships. The code lost its teeth as a result of the forced divestiture of distribution facilities, competition from television and foreign films, the rise of independent producers, and the shifting of judicial standards of obscenity. In the 1960s, Supreme Court decisions on censorship raised the boom on the use of obscenity, nudity, and explicit sexual references in both print and motion pictures. Popular tolerance moved in parallel fashion.

• When Hollywood lowered the barriers imposed by the old MPAA (Hays) Code, new problems were created for film promotion. Some newspapers set limits on suggestive copy and illustrations in advertisements for pornographic films; others refused to take them altogether—even mere listings of the title and cast. One prominent publisher rejected any advertising at all from a certain distributor who specialized in this kind of film. Would he extend this policy as a punitive measure if the distributor switched exclusively to films intended for general family audiences? He was troubled by this question but insisted that he had a perfect right to refuse even legitimate advertising from someone of whom he disapproved. A publisher's right to print only what he chooses to print is fundamental to the freedom of the press. But what of the theater owner's right to peddle his product, or the public's right to know about it? The argument that alternative means of communication exist, while true as a legal abstraction, has no bearing on the market realities of information flow in a one-paper town. There are far more serious issues involved here than the promotion of dirty movies or the censorship of one medium by another.

As more marginal films appeared, and "frank" or "adult" scenes and foul language became more commonplace, the fear of a renewed popular reaction led in 1968 to the creation of a new film-classification system designed to restrict juvenile attendance, rather than to modify content directly. The film ratings system was set up to protect children rather than the public at large, but it puts the burden of enforcement on parents, who must take their own steps to comply with the restrictions.

Of the films rated in 1986–69, 6% were given an X for their sexual content. In 1985, only one film was rated X. Erotic films were still being made, but they simply bypassed the ratings system altogether and slipped into their own channels of distribution. In 1968–69, 32% of the films rated received G ratings, which meant they were approved for a general audience of children as well as adults. A dozen years earlier, every film released by Hollywood might have qualified for such a rating. By 1985, only 4% of the films were rated G. It was widely believed in the industry that this rating discouraged attendance. (In spite of the prevailing assumption that a restricted rating is good box office, the handful of G-rated movies do better.[35])

In 1990, the film industry went to a different rating system that somewhat blurred the former categories. Of the 621 films rated in 1992, only 3% were rated G, and another 14% PG (recommending parental "guidance" to ward off the obscenities or nudity shown); 18% were rated PG-13; 63% were R; and the remaining 1% were euphemistically labeled NC (not for children). The availability of pornographic videocassettes sharply reduced attendance at movie theaters specializing in X-rated movies, forcing substantial numbers of them to close down.

When MPAA president Jack Valenti invited him to chair the film ratings board, Richard Hefner's reaction was, "My mother didn't raise me to count nipples." After nineteen years as chairman, he said,

> We are in deep trouble. . . . I am saddened by what we do to ourselves in the media today. . . . The ratings system is designed purely to protect the asses of the motion picture industry against censorship. . . . I am appalled by most of what I see when I look at films. I wish the roof would open up and swallow the people who make the films and distribute them. . . . It is counterproductive, the way we create anti-social attitudes in the form of the garbage we spew forth in the media.[36]

To meet the competition of television, feature films became increasingly venturesome, testing the limits of what the audience would find acceptable, and defying conventional wisdom and morality. The changes in film content facilitated and legitimated the changes that took place during the same period in standards of language use and sexual mores.

Film and television content mirrored the transformation in values, but through a distorting lens. As always, the media also provided new role models and guidance for behavior. The changes in sexual attitudes and practices were facilitated by the universal exposure, through films and television, to subjects and scenes that had long been accessible only in secret, or with difficulty.

Television network programming practices also changed in direct response to the examples set by theatrical film-making. In spite of recurrent government protests and investigations, violence remained an important element of prime-time TV drama. After one Congressional inquiry, the television networks restricted its depiction, but as the scenes of mayhem moved off-camera, they were replaced by even more frightening images of terrorized or screaming victims.[37]

Behavior and speech that had been adopted by the film industry as a defense against television became staple fare on television itself. The effect was to drive motion picture content farther and farther beyond its former limits. Hollywood's current output wallows in gore, in contrast to the bygone epoch of the Hays Code, when it showed what the critic Stephen Farber calls "bloodless and painless" murder. He suggests that "this kind of 'tasteful,' antiseptic violence is in the long run more dangerous than the graphic brand of violence on movie screens today."[38] The anxiety created in the audience by suspense is probably far more damaging than the horror evoked by the actual sight of bodies mangled with all the art of studio makeup.

Just as film and television content are inextricably related, so are they with the content of popular novels, which are often concocted and marketed by literary agents with their film adaptations in mind. Between 1966 and 1988, violent and anti-social themes in best-sellers increased by two-thirds.[39]

Even more disturbing than the mayhem that fills screens large and small is the indifference to established codes of morality. To do what television could not do, Hollywood abandoned a fundamental theatrical convention that long antedated the movies themselves: punishment or retribution to wrongdoers. For the first time in the history of fiction, antisocial actions were glorified in those films whose heroes were criminals and whose villains were the forces of justice, depicted as incompetent, mean-spirited, and vindictive.

First film and then television fiction made criminal activity seem commonplace and its perpetrators sympathetic.[40] Wrongdoers inhabit splendid domiciles and move through glamorous surroundings. More and more typically, they successfully avoid the traditional painful consequences of their actions and instead survive to live more happily ever after.[41] Feature films show characters smoking marijuana or sniffing cocaine and enjoying it or joking about it. Civility and obedience to the law are commonly portrayed as antiquated and ridiculous.

Exploiting Eroticism

The exchange of sex for money is called prostitution. The exploitation of sexual imagery for profit is not so clearly defined. Commercial pornography is a big business. Some 165,000 people are employed in producing or selling it. It is a classic example of a pure response to market demand. The rewards can be gratifying. "Deep Throat" cost $25,000 to make in 1972 and grossed over $50 million.

The appeal of the salacious is formidable, timeless, and universal.[42] The telecommunications revolution makes it more accessible. On Nynex alone, there are 11 million calls a month to 1,000 "information services" offered on 350 lines. Forty percent are for "adult" services.

Definitions of pornography—sexual depictions "with no redeeming social value"— are hard to pin down, in the courts, legislative chambers, or practice. In the filming of "The Misfits" in 1961, the film's director, John Huston, feared objections from the Catholic Legion of Decency to a scene in which Marilyn Monroe embraced a tree. He traded it off for a bedroom scene that had been shot in two alternative versions, one of which showed the actress bare-chested. Frank Taylor, the producer, pointed out that

> because I had used the bare-breasted version we had a negotiating posture, and after we'd bargained for two hours, the church agreed that if we covered Marilyn up we could have the tree. All of which proves that pornography is in the eye of the beholder.[43]

The public's feelings on the issue are ambivalent, to say the least. As in many polls on First Amendment issues, snap answers to generalized questions often yield a majority in favor of censorship. While 80% feel that "people should have the right to purchase a sexually explicit book, magazine or movie," 65% say that community authorities should be able to prohibit such sales.[44]

There are pornographers like *Screw*'s Al Goldstein who regard their labors as a sacred vocation. Lesser pornographers like to depict themselves as fulfilling a useful social function, even with such magazines as *Aroused, Lace and Flesh, Simmer, Heat, Frill*, and *Shriek*. One publisher, Edwin A. Schnepf, says he is "supplying a service" to fill "a definite need." "If a guy can't satisfy himself with sexual means sanctioned by society, what harm is there in providing him with the material— whatever it may be—that does meet his desires?"

Joseph Steinman, distributor of porno videos:

> There are some people who would like to frequent sex theaters, but for various reasons they don't: They're either ashamed to be seen going in, they don't want to

take their wives with them, or whatever. This way, they're able to see the X material in the privacy of their own home, and it doesn't seem so distasteful to them.[45]

Allan R., copy editor for a group of "fetish and violence girlies":

What the hell, it's a living. And it's not that bad. Within the limited format, there's room for some experimentation and creativity. The pay is good, the atmosphere is relaxed, and the work isn't very demanding. I could do worse.[46]

• The publisher of the porno magazine *High Society* (circulation 600,000), Gloria Leonard, kept in touch with her market by starring in at least one hard-core video each year. She offered a choice of 4,000 recorded telephone messages, delivered by subjects of her photographic essays. An example: "Meet me and I'll lick your lollipop."[47]

There is even a "topless radio" talk show, "Feminine Forum." The raunchy *Penthouse* and *Playboy* are America's leading magazine exports, aside from those magazines with international editions, like *Reader's Digest* and *Time*. The publishers of these magazines have long since left their original formulas behind them and gained the appearance of respectability behind corporate facades, applying the doctrines of "line extension" and "synergy." Playboy Enterprises moved into cable television. *Penthouse*'s parent, General Media Corporation, which published the respectable *Omni* and owned the title to the once-literary *Saturday Review*, entered the high-tech era with CD-ROM disks that combined print and video. (There was the prospect that high-tech pornography might eventually be transposed into "virtual reality.")

• Pornographic films accounted for a high percentage of sales in the early stages of the videocassette market (an estimated 70% as recently as 1978). By 1992, the proportion had settled down to 10–15%,[48] perhaps because so little was left to the imagination in films that carried MPAA ratings.

Much of the sexuality in mainstream entertainment—like much of the violence—follows purely commercial directives and is usually unrelated to the inherent requirements of plot or characterization. Orion Pictures inserted sexually explicit scenes into "Johnny Be Good," a film rated PG-13 for theatrical release, so that the video could be rated R, and presumably enjoy greater sales.[49] The cover art for paperback books has for years been designed to suggest erotic delights that are invisible in the text itself. The cover of the 1944 Pocket Books edition of Dashiell Hammett's *The Maltese Falcon* showed three hands reaching toward a statuette of the bird. For the 1977 edition, the cover showed a woman undressing, while a man behind a sheer curtain fingered a high-heeled shoe, with a pair of panties on his lap.[50] Since the mid-1980s, made-for-TV films have featured homosexuality, rape, prostitution, and mothers and daughters who shared lovers. In January, 1984, ABC presented the first program featuring incest. Alfred R. Schneider, ABC's vice-president for policy and standards said, "Within the past year we began to allow a man to lie on top of a woman. We are reaching the point of physical motion under the covers of a bed."[51]

Extramarital sex became a principal preoccupation of daytime serials. Sexual innuendos and "jiggly" breasts were casually introduced into prime-time comedy programs. Masturbation and homosexual sex were topics for both comedy and drama. In 1991, the televised Senate hearings on Supreme Court nominee (and later Justice) Clarence Thomas and the rape trial of Senator Edward Kennedy's nephew, William Kennedy Smith, brought matter-of-fact references to sexual organs and sexual intercourse to a nationwide audience of all ages. Later came the case of Lorena Bobbitt, who became a celebrity after she snipped off her husband's penis.

Language on-screen became saturated with gratuitous vulgarity that had previously been confined to the netherworld of speech, and thus crept into more common usage. Obscenities began to come easily to the lips of guests on late-night talk shows. A content analysis of R-rated movies in 1991 found a "major obscenity" every 2½ minutes.[52] To question such practices may be regarded as Pecksniffian prudery, but the debasement of language disguises a deeper ill, which is the degradation of human relationships.[53]

Cable, whose content is unregulated by the Federal Communications Commission's broadcast obscenity rules, was quick to shed the major networks' restrictions on off-color scenes and language, particularly on public access channels. HBO and other pay cable networks strove to titillate audiences with themes, words, and images they would never see on CBS, NBC, ABC – or even on Fox. This development, in turn, led the major networks to modify their own criteria of acceptability.

In general, television focuses on the joys of sex, not its problems. A typical network hour in 1988 had one or two mentions of sexual intercourse and nine or ten other sexual innuendos, but no mentions of birth control. References to sexually transmitted illness occurred only once in 10 program hours.[54] While adultery was now depicted much more commonly than in the past, no moral judgment was passed two-thirds of the time. Prostitutes were portrayed sympathetically, as victims of an unjust social order. In the 1990s unorthodox sexual practices and (with the growth of the AIDS epidemic) sexually transmitted diseases have become everyday subjects of media content, accepted as part of the normal business of life. Does all of this induce the slightest effect?

The Fictional World of Television

The fictional world of television, to which the American public dedicates a substantial part of its waking time, is one that differs markedly from that in which the same public spends its workaday life. It is inhabited by very different kinds of people and ruled by very different values. In this respect it is not distinguished from the imaginary worlds of other media. What really matters is the sheer pervasiveness of this fictional experience.

Dramatic programming in broadcasting has used a familiar assortment of genres, some providing unique situations and characters, as in feature-length films (including those made for TV), most of them using off-the-shelf themes, backgrounds, and personalities that maintain continuity – and therefore, a stable audience – from episode to episode: the serial drama, action series (with police, spy, mystery, or Western themes), and situation comedies. There is an extraordinary similarity of subject matter across different program types.[55]

What is the world of TV fiction like? It is an unusually violent place, but the violence is blissfully unattended by pain and suffering. Television's people drink alcohol fifteen times as often as water (which is not, after all, a social drink), but they smoke only in old movies. In daytime serials, they are preoccupied with health problems, though their ailments are exotic rather than commonplace; in the evening they turn remarkably healthy and trim. Virtually all of them either have perfect vision or wear permanent contact lenses. They bed down with prostitutes more often than with their spouses; in fact, their sex lives consist largely of extramarital affairs, with considerable dollops of violence and rape.

Fictional characters interest us precisely because they are different from us in certain critical respects, though not so different as to make us lose our capacity for identification and empathy. All forms of fiction, from the earliest legends to the present day, deal with atypical characters and scenes. The figures of the stage, of novels, films, and television dramas, have never depicted a true cross-section of society.[56] Nearly three-fourths of television prime-time characters are male (typically in their late 30s to early 40s), and men account for nearly nine out of ten of the college graduates and professionals. Television's elderly often tend to be senile or sinister, its blacks are comics; its workingmen, buffoons. Its women still often tend to pretelevision stereotypes; nearly three-fifths of them are shown simply in terms of their private lives. The world of work shown on television is glamorous; routine service and factory jobs are in the background or invisible. Lawyers outnumber plumbers, forty-four to one. Businessmen are commonly shown as criminals.[57]

Constant exposure to television's imaginary characters, settings, and situations molds the public's expectations of the surrounding reality.[58] The fantasy distortions of TV fiction are transferred into everyday life, and conduct depicted by television is easily taken to be acceptable conduct, even when it includes the antisocial.

Although televised fiction teaches no significant moral lessons in the tradition of the Greek theater, it does teach a large number of minor ones—often in contradiction to the standards of conduct to which society pays lip service—simply by virtue of its constant reiteration of the same formulaic characterizations and dilemmas. And by constantly diverting us from unpleasant reminders of the human condition, it restrains us from dealing with them too closely at the same time that it protects us from feeling their full force.

If the world of the mass media—especially that of television, the most pervasive medium of all—is permeated with unreality, does this not inevitably affect the public's judgment, its ability to see and cope with things as they are? It is easy to fall prey to the notion that what is out there is out there, that the reports of reality can be blotted out by a change of channel, just like the entertainment on the television set.

The Appeal of Violence

Violence and sex—the two aspects of American commercial culture that generate the greatest popular and legislative concern—are significant ingredients in the recipe for success in building audiences. On the stage, the essence of dramatic conflict is in the

clash of personalities and values, but in film and television, psychological confrontations are outnumbered by graphic portrayals of physical conflict. Corporal punishment, or the threat of it, takes a prominent part. Even the video footage of a tennis
match is more exciting and enjoyable to viewers when accompanied by an audio
commentary that describes the players as bitter enemies than when it describes them
as friends or ignores the relationship altogether.[59]

"Violence is as American as apple pie," said the 60s black militant, H. Rap
Brown. It has surely been part of the scene since Columbus landed in the Caribbean,
and it has been reenforced by centuries of armed combat. America's high rate of
violence reflects both its past history and its present urban problems, but the content
of mass media has also helped to shape our violent national character, through a
process that starts early in life. And the violence in American mass media arises from
the impersonal forces of the market as well as from the human appetite for sensation.

Newspapers and television news programs daily confront us with reports and
images of a perilous world, beset by wars, catastrophes and crime—a world incon-
gruous with the one most Americans know firsthand. When people are asked what
they remember in the news, murders and murderers are mentioned far more than
foreign wars.[60] In fact, homicidal maniacs were seven times as memorable, at the
time, as the bloody war between Iran and Iraq. Disturbing news reports and images
are strongly reenforced by their fictional counterparts, which make horror seem
commonplace and thus acceptable. (Televised imagery described as real arouses
more attention and produces more aggressive feelings than when the identical scene
is described as fictional.[61])

The deadpan violence that pervades today's audiovisual media descends from the
bloodthirsty traditions of the Roman colosseum, long preserved in such amusements
as bearbaiting and dogfighting. Samuel Pepys attended public executions, for kicks,
and huge crowds gathered to witness hangings until well into the nineteenth century.
The spirit lives on in cockfighting and bullfighting (which are banned in the United
States) and in wrestling and boxing matches (which are not). One person in five
thinks it would be a good idea to televise executions.[62]

Jacket copy for a "slasher" videocassette, *Filmgore*:

> A cosmic cavalcade of bloodthirsty thrills from the most violent movies ever made!
> An entertainment extravaganza of extreme exterminations, devastating decimations,
> and delicious decapitations!! . . . An endless orgy of unimaginable atrocity at an
> incredible velocity—the most sanguinary sensations ever splashed and splattered
> across the savage screen.[63]

The U.S. murder rate (one every 22 minutes, doubled since 1960) is eleven times
higher than Japan's and four times higher than Europe's.[64] Even so, the rate in prime-
time network television is 1,000 times higher than in real life.[65] Commercials for
theatrical movies and promos for television programs are especially violent. TV
murders do not result from quarrels—as they overwhelmingly do in the real world—
but in the course of another crime.[66] Property crimes are underplayed, since burglary
does not usually make for high drama. Although in reality only 5% of all arrests are
for violent crimes, over half of all illegal acts shown on television involve violence.[67]

Antisocial content pervades television programming of all types.[68] Violence directed at innocent bystanders is also now a stock feature of comic films, in which mass annihilation, torture, and mutilation are presented as legitimate causes for amusement. Films increasingly make fun of the destruction of innocent life, as *The Wall Street Journal*'s Robert Knight has inventoried: In *Prizzi's Honor* "an innocent woman is gunned down by mistake in an elevator. (The reviews said this was a comedy, right?)" In *A Fish Called Wanda*,

> an inept killer is crushing a woman's pet dogs to death; we are supposed to laugh at his inability to kill the woman herself, which he finally does when she has a heart attack. . . . In *Batman*, innocent people die grotesque, agonizing deaths while "Joker" Jack Nicholson cracks one-liners.[69]

Specialized media cater to the interests of sadists and individuals with aberrant sexual preferences, but it is the infusion of violence into mainstream media that is most troubling. More brute force is actually shown in sexual encounters in mainstream films than in outright pornographic films.[70] When violence becomes commonplace, it no longer arouses revulsion. Thus a public accustomed to heavy dosages of fictional violence is inured to aggression in real life. Repeated exposure, with no adverse effect, produces a counter-conditioning reflex—a desensitization to anxiety-provoking stimuli.

The exploitation of violence in the media is not an unconscious sequence of unrelated actions on the part of its producers. It is deliberately designed to attract audiences, and when it works, it is appropriately rewarded. The makers of "Texas Chain Saw Massacre" were signed for a five-picture contract by Universal. Orion Television Syndication advertised its "Crimewatch Tonight" program in the trade press with ads headlined "Profit from Organized Crime" and "Crime Pays."

The Marquis de Sade:

> In the final analysis what are the two principal mainsprings of dramatic arts? Have all the authors worthy of the name not declared that they are terror and pity? Now what can provoke terror if not the portrayal of crime triumphant and what can cause pity better than the depiction of virtue a prey to misfortune?

Violence and sex were deliberately injected into NBC's programs on orders of Robert Kintner, the network's president in 1959. A former head of programming, David Levy, says, "There was nothing casual or accidental about the policy," and notes that the secretary of the program board was told to delete the directive from the minutes. "We don't want that kind of stuff in our records."[71] It would be hard to find a media executive who *publicly* espouses the use of violence for its own bloody sake, but it is often defended as a part of everyday life and as a necessary device to maintain audience interest. According to CBS's 1985 program standards,

> a CBS television program is a guest in the home. It is expected to entertain and enlighten but not to offend or advocate. CBS entertainment programs are expected to conform to generally accepted boundaries of public taste and decorum. . . . As a component of human experience, the dramatic depiction of violence is permitted. . . . It should not be gratuitous, excessive or glamorized. Violence should not be used exploitively to entice or shock an audience.

Speaking in less unctuous tones, Frederick S. Pierce, then president of ABC Television, told the House Subcommittee on Communications[72] that programs

> that contain incidents of violence . . . have a legitimate place in a diverse program schedule. The best-made programs of this type have very large audiences, and the mail we receive commenting on these programs is both heavy and overwhelmingly positive. Throughout history, the essence of some drama has been conflict, and in such works violence has always been one means to resolve conflict. . . . We require that where programs contain conflict as a natural and dramatic consequence of plot development, it be responsibly portrayed and its consequences depicted. Gratuitous violence serves no useful purpose.

The CEO of one media conglomerate, who describes himself as "very comfortable with what I get," was asked about violence in the media. He answered,

> violence – that's greed. That's capitalism. If that's what the public wants, just give it to them. *The New York Times* and the *Washington Post* have the editor give the reader what the editor wants to see. I don't see that. I want to give the public what the public wants to see.[73]

A question may even be raised as to whether viewers identify the aggressive acts that they see on television or in the movies as violence.[74] People's reactions on the subject are characterized by an ambiguity that suggests a conflict between the id and the superego. Only a third of the public identify programs employing violence, sex, gross language, or bad taste with poor quality. Less than a fourth dislike or avoid specific programs because of such features, and of these only one in five claims to take any specific action, like switching from an advertised brand.[75]

While half of the public acknowledge[76] that "I personally enjoy watching some entertainment programs featuring violence," three out of four agree that "violence on TV entertainment programs stimulates dangerous behavior in some adults." Two people in three think there is a relationship between violence on television and "the rising crime rate."[77] Three out of four say that graphic violence is shown "just to attract viewers" rather than to make a point.[78]

Is the public correct in its view that televised violence carries real-life consequences? To answer, we must confront the larger question of media effects. Before we come to those, however, we should consider another aspect of the sensationalism that media cultivate in their quest for audiences.

Media Experience and Media Substance

What do mass media do to people? Objections to them on aesthetic, moral, or political grounds are surely less compelling than charges of specific damage to public safety or well-being. The rest of this chapter considers how they have shaped the American scene and the American character, including its less admirable features. We must consider both the effects of their content and the effects of the activity – or lack of activity – they entail.

Media certainly occupy a great many hours. In particular, television, the supreme embodiment of commercial culture, eats up a substantial amount of the public's disposable time, though the amount has not changed appreciably since set ownership became almost universal. (Though daily set use in the average TV home grew from 5 hours in 1960 to over 7 hours in 1993,[79] the increase was offset by a decline in the number of viewers per set.) It should be noted that overall viewing levels (and ratings) are always inflated by those households in which the set is almost never turned off, and that the time spent in the presence of television is not necessarily a valid indication of its impact.

Viewers follow the path of least effort, watching those programs that make the fewest intellectual demands, that provide easy relaxation. Within these limits, however, they seek a range of content to avoid boredom. For this reason, every network and station program department—including even those of specialized cable networks—seeks a balance of different program types, including some of above average intellectual level or aesthetic merit. Television is bland and lacks real variety, but programs of quality may well be overrepresented in their share of broadcast time, relative to their actual appeal to the public.

As the medium that commands by far the greatest investment of the public's time, television has come in for an exceptional amount of criticism, partly because of regret that it has not lived up to its great potential for enlightenment. Edward R. Murrow remarked once, "If TV can merely 'entertain, amuse and insulate,' it's nothing but wires and lights in a box." He confessed to his sponsor "I wish we could uninvent television."

In the Pilkington Report, prepared by a British commission that investigated the state of the medium,

> It was put to us that in television as elsewhere, one man's meat ought to be another man's poison; that too often viewers were offered neither meat nor poison, but pap— because, presumably though no one likes it at least no one will get indigestion.

Looking back 30 years after a memorable speech he delivered as chairman of the Federal Communications Commission, Newton Minow (who later became a director of CBS) said television was still (as he had earlier described it) a "vast wasteland," though it had improved in its range of choice, in its educational broadcasts and in its news programming. "Prime time entertainment shows still tend to underestimate the intelligence of the viewer."[80]

George Gerbner, a communications scholar who believes that American tastes and preferences are today cultivated mostly by television, argues that

> the more viewers watch . . . the fewer basic content choices they have. . . . Many of the most typical content patterns of life on television—action structure, casting, social typing, and fate—are common to most types of programming and news. They are inescapable. . . . The more viewers watch television, the more they share common conceptions of reality.[81]

Gerbner's last statement is no mere assertion; it is amply supported by research evidence. The "common conceptions of reality" to which he refers are imposed by media managements in their constant quest for larger audiences.

One recurrent criticism of all media is that, because they consume so much time and attention, they overload the senses and strain mental functions, creating a passive outlook toward life. They may just as easily be criticized for reducing the stimulation people get from direct human contacts.

What are the consequences of the sheer *time* expenditure on television? There is some indication that the prolonged passive inactivity of viewing inhibits reflection[82] and leaves its traces on personality, just as the tube's dominance over conversation has its subtle effects on the intimacy of family relationships. As we saw in Chapter 3, the fragmented, disjointed nature of communication that is subjected to constant commercial interruption may have altered patterns of perception and learning. It is not altogether true that the medium is the message, though the medium is undoubtedly one of the messages and maybe one of the most important. But Marshall McLuhan was correct in calling attention to the psychological effort required to assemble meanings out of the flow of electronically driven light impulses bombarding the cathode ray tube, and in speculating on how these mental processes differ from the act of reading.

Incoherence may be innate in the special vocabulary of video, regardless of how it is programmed. Editing and camera techniques—cuts, pans, zooms, closeups, and flashbacks—are taken for granted by an experienced viewer. Children now master them as a normal part of the process of cognitive development, much as the infant at an early stage penetrates the mystery of peek-a-boo, but television's rapid pace and frequent cuts and shifts seem to stymie their learning. Psychologists Fred and Merrelyn Emery assail television's "inability to instruct as distinct from its ability to inform,"[83] and conclude that it

> not only impairs the ability of the viewer to attend, it also, by taking over a complex of direct and indirect neural pathways, decreases vigilance—the general state of arousal which prepares the organism for action should its attention be drawn to a specific stimulus.

After a 13-year study in which people recorded their moods throughout the day in response to electronic beepers, Robert Kubey and Mihaly Csikszentmihalyi found that

> people report feeling more passive and less able to concentrate after they view television. The passivity spills over into how they feel after viewing. A kind of inertia develops, and it becomes more and more difficult to get up and do something active. In other words, viewing leads to more viewing.[84]

Paradoxically, the more people watch, the less they enjoy it. Activities that engage other people are enjoyed more than television viewing, which generates the same level of emotional affect as work and doing chores. Next to resting, it is the least active of all "activities," most resembling "idling" and daydreaming. After watching TV, viewers find it more difficult to concentrate, are less activated, and don't feel as relaxed or as well.

The mere activity—or rather, nonactivity—of viewing appears to have physiological side effects. People who watch television a lot are in worse physical shape than light viewers.[85] During the past 20 years, obesity has increased considerably among children—especially boys, who are more responsive than girls to TV ads for candy and soft drinks.[86] Thus the physical and psychological effects of television content interact with those produced by excessive viewing.

IQ scores are substantially lower among children who spend more time viewing. So, by a smaller but consistent margin, are their school achievement levels.[87] Television does not affect homework,[88] but it seems to slow down the acquisition of reading skills, displaces reading practice for at least some children, and has a negative effect on creativity and the imagination.[89]

Most significantly, the character of the particular programs viewed has no bearing on the findings, for children or for adults. Perhaps the mainstream content of television has an increasingly homogeneous character that seems to blur the distinction between program types. In short, while media content and character are hard to separate, the substance is far less important than the viewing experience itself.[90]

A similar observation may be made about the kinetic popular music of recent decades, based on repetitive drumbeats and dedicated to motion rather than to mood. Because of its electronic sound, rock music is qualitatively different from the popular music forms of an earlier era. Music played at full blast through stereo headsets can damage the eardrums of its devotees, but it may have more serious numbing effects. Laboratory mice raised listening to arrhythmic drumming are viciously aggressive, move aimlessly, and have trouble finding their way out of a maze.[91] By contrast, mice reared with classical music show no difference in learning or memory abilities from mice reared without sound. (There is some indication, moreover, that mice respond differently to different compositional techniques, preferring Mozart to the atonal style of Schoenberg.)

By its amplified nature, rock—in whatever permutation—dominates its environment, imposes the will of the performers upon the audience, and subordinates whatever melodic line it has to technique. Rock and rap lyrics are deliberately aggressive; they stretch the limits of coarse obscenity and cry out violent expressions of hate. (Words spoken or sung are more easily tolerated than they would be in writing.) This outpouring of strong rebellion against established conventions—personal, social, and political—is commercially contrived, not spontaneous. The lyrics, drowned in percussion, are followed even more mindlessly by their impressionable public than the "moon," "swoon," and "croon" of an earlier era. The physiological effects induced by the mechanics of amplification can in no way be separated from the psychological and social effects of the messages the music carries—not only to its devotees but to the many others upon whom it is involuntarily imposed.

Audio or video, media dependency reflects the direct impact of technology on human behavior and not the sins attributable to commercial culture. Addiction to television, stereo headsets, comic books, or other media anodynes, like addiction to substances, has causes that go deep. Yet media's power over people is inseparable from the motives that lead those who own them to strive for the largest audiences they can get. Commercial culture can hardly be altogether absolved of blame for the consequences of media exposure.

Media as Change Agents

If mere exposure to the media has effects, what of their messages? Consider the *Communist Manifesto* or *Mein Kampf*. *Uncle Tom's Cabin* did not bring on the Civil War, but it had a profound influence on attitudes toward slavery.

Numerous studies of newspapers and of certain types of magazines, books, and radio programs have illuminated their positive, life-enhancing, and socially adaptive functions. Television has also prompted some research of this style into what has been called its "pro-social" influence (for example, how it broadens intellectual horizons and teaches children cognitive skills). But far more money and effort have been devoted to investigation of the harm it can do.

Some scholars hold to a theory of "powerful effects," and others maintain that media merely reinforce the workings of primary social institutions: family, school, church, workplace. The "minimal effects" theory is exemplified by former FCC chairman Mark Fowler's flip characterization of TV as "a toaster with pictures." (He is actually not that far off the mark, at least for a substantial minority of viewers, who say they use TV as a "background.") But only a fraction of the exposure to media is on this incidental level.

Debates have raged for years regarding the specific effects of media violence on children's behavior and of pornography on sexual mores. In such public confrontations, media advocates have generally argued that their effects are minor: that the public does not imitate what it sees or reads about, that antisocial aggressiveness is caused by family and environmental conditions, and that the added impact of the media is negligible. The television industry's contention that its social effects are small is in marked contrast to its eagerness to assert its sales power for advertisers, of which there is abundant evidence. Betty Hudson, NBC's senior vice-president for corporate communications, was questioned about the idea of incorporating nutrition advice in children's programs, to offset the effects of the voluminous advertising for sweets. She insisted that such "counteradvertising is not effective."[92]

Advertising has long been endowed, both by its practitioners and by unsympathetic observers, with attributes of power that exaggerate its true capacities. Over a century ago (in 1887), Thomas Smith, in his *Advertiser's Guide to Publicity*, wrote, "Like the Nasmyth steam hammer, advertising can be used with crushing, irresistible force."[93] (Smith, incidentally, urged advertisers to appeal to "the greatest number of people who can be persuaded.") Indeed, the hundreds of millions of dollars it costs advertisers to evaluate their ads are spent on the unspoken premise that any individual message is so powerful that its persuasive effects can be detected and measured. Yet the advertising establishment indignantly rejects the thesis that all these messages have an effect in the aggregate: that they determine the overall shape of consumer demand, that they create demand that might not otherwise exist.

Advertising in general *does* work; it adds to purchases of the advertised brands. Does it also add to consumption of the advertised products? Hard evidence that this happens is hard to come by.

• Research done on behalf of the British tobacco industry found that the volume of cigarette consumption, while highly responsive to pricing, was not at all dependent on the total amount of cigarette advertising in a given period of time. The American tobacco industry has used this evidence in defense against charges that its ads persuade people to smoke. The cigarette companies insisted that their advertising is intended to change brand preferences rather than to get people to use tobacco in the first place. In 1985, faced with the threat of a restriction on the broadcasting of beer and wine advertising, the brewers commissioned a similar study, which came up with similar results and produced similar arguments.[94] (In both instances, the changes in advertising budgets were small relative to the huge continuing expenditures.)

It is relatively difficult to prove that advertising has a long-term effect on other forms of behavior, apart from consumption.[95] Joseph Klapper, the longtime director of CBS's Office of Social Research, suggested that media are less influential in changing opinions that people absorb from their environments and stations in life than in providing them with opinions in areas where life circumstances have not provided them with any.[96] But what can these areas be, since one's environment provides predispositions to pass judgment on all conceivable subjects?

Noone has ever seriously argued that media content is a more significant influence on children than family upbringing or peer group pressure. The media are now so firmly woven into the fabric of American culture that their effects are almost impossible to disentangle from all the other influences on patterns of conduct and thought. The values they promulgate have already been incorporated to differing degrees and in different ways in the subcultures of various parts of the population.

Consider the changes in sexual mores. They were induced by a variety of complex forces: the new technology of contraception; the massive entry of women into the work force, with the consequent alteration of sex roles, household composition, and living patterns; the coming of age of the postwar baby-boom generation, whose sheer size put pressure on existing institutions and whose rebelliousness was spurred by the strains of the Vietnam War. The proportion of 15-year-old girls who had had sexual intercourse nearly doubled between 1971 and 1986.[97] It is impossible to say in what measure the media were cause, in what measure effect.

Motion pictures had been scored for their effects on the sexual knowledge and practices of the young long before the advent of television. A 1970 presidential commission on pornography waffled its conclusions: "The data do not appear to support the thesis of a causal connection between increased availability of erotica and the commission of sex offenses; the data do not, however, conclusively disprove such a connection."[98] After the release of the report there was more pornography and less research on it. Fifteen years later, under the Reagan administration, the Attorney General's Commission on Pornography was given a budget of $400,000—so small as to guarantee that its investigations and conclusions would also not be definitive.

Rape became a more commonly reported crime in the 1980s, at the same time that it assumed high media visibility. One out of four college men say they would or probably would rape if they could "get away with it"; the proportion goes up dramatically if the term "forced sex" is substituted for "rape." Rapists are heavy readers of sex magazines, though there is no indication of causality in this correlation.[99] Rapists are attracted by the violent depictions, not the erotic aspects, of pornography, and the linkage of pornography and violence is more lethal than either alone.

A rapist to a victim:

> I know all about you bitches, you're no different; you're like all of them. I seen it all in the movies. You love being beaten.

One notable study found that men became more aggressive toward women after an erotic film clip than after a violent one.[100] Generalized emotional arousal, not sex specifically, seems to be what counts. With erotic as with violent content, the more often the contact, the less the excitation. Repeated exposure does not lead to greater enjoyment of the material but promotes insensitivity to victims of sexual violence. Revulsion diminishes and disappears.[101]

One need not dwell on pathological cases to document the contention that people are affected by how the media depict sexual interactions. After looking at sexually provocative women on television shows like "Charlie's Angels" or in magazines like *Playboy*, male college students found their own girl friends less attractive. Thus there are consequences, in the most intimate human relationships, of the media's steady output of messages that tell us how some people behave, and by implication, how we too might or even should behave.

Substantial changes in courting and sexual conduct, in the acceptability of social deviance, and in the use of obscene language have all accompanied changes in patterns of family interaction and in personal goals. All of this has been coterminous with the age of television. If television has been an element in these changes, it has been joined by other media.

The years of television have coincided with a vast increase in social pathology in the United States. Crime, delinquency, illegitimacy, divorce, drug and alcohol abuse, mental illness, and suicide arise from the stresses of a society that has undergone remarkable and rapid change. These ailments particularly afflict the economically disadvantaged, as do milder manifestations like interpersonal aggressiveness, mistrust, family tension, and inferior school performance. But it is the disadvantaged who have been most drawn to television entertainment both as an inexpensive pastime and as an easy form of fantasy-fulfillment. (Blacks watch half again as much television as other Americans.)

Any attempt to establish the effects of television must control for the fact that wealthy, well-educated, self-confident people spend less time viewing than poor people whose lives are stressful and empty. Social class relates closely to psychological traits that are associated with, and perhaps reinforced by, viewing: anxiety, loneliness, and a lack of purpose.[102] (Heavy smokers are likely to be TV addicts, too.) Poor, less-educated, and divorced or separated people are especially inclined to use television to avoid dark moods that come from being alone and having time on their hands. These patterns heighten the complexity of tracing connections between television viewing and the indicators of social disintegration.

There is no conclusive way to compare adult behavior and beliefs before and after television. Even if there were accurate benchmarks, we could never be sure that television in and of itself was the cause of the change. After all, the attributes of American television that are most criticized—its commercialism, violence, vulgarity, and stereotyping of character and population groups—were firmly established in American mass media long before it arrived on the scene. Television has merely intensified public exposure to the dismal aspects of commercial culture.

In short, the impact of television, or of the mass media in general, is hard to record with scientific precision. It might be compared to that of water dripping on a stone. Any individual drop might not leave a detectable trace, but over time a long succession of drops would wear away an impression. Though the obstacles to measurement are formidable, and perhaps insurmountable, the effects of mass media have generated a very large amount of empirical research—disproportionate, in fact, to the appropriate rank of this important subject amidst the panoply of social issues deserving study. The evidence has been hard to translate into social policy.

Measuring TV's Effects

Mark Fowler:

> If I am asked, "Do broadcasters have a responsibility when it comes to the special child audience upon which their license renewal will depend?" the answer, I think, should be no.[103]

The greatest public and legislative concern over the impact of the mass media has always centered on children, impressionable creatures who lack the judgment required to distinguish the merits or validity of what they are exposed to. Attention has at various times focused on the harmful influences of the movies, of comic books, and of the lyrics in popular musical recordings. The criticism has a number of facets, related to learning ability, the distortion of reality, and the specific subjects of violence and sex. As usual, television has been at the center of the criticism, comment, and study. There is good reason for this, as Cedric Cullingford points out:

> When children talk about their interests, without any soliciting about television, it is firstly clear that television is a most important part of their lives. It is, by far, the most mentioned commodity. But it is nearly always part of a larger pattern of play, of domestic details, of the texture of family life. Other activities are not excluded, or replaced."[104]

Not excluded or replaced, I would agree, but inevitably diminished. Children spend an enormous part of their time in front of the tube, an average of about four hours a day, by some estimates.[105] In an era of working mothers, when television is widely used as a substitute for parental supervision, childhood viewing habits have inevitably reflected those of adults. The more television the parents watch, the more their children watch. Children differ from adults not only in what they view, but in how they view it. Adults are bored by repetitive content; children enjoy it. Adults see programs as wholes, with beginnings, middles, and ends; children do not.[106]

Children's programming on television is intended as diversion rather than instruction, with a few notable exceptions in public broadcasting. Fiction represents 80–90% of all children's series. The Saturday morning cartoons are violence-filled, crudely rendered, and heavily loaded with commercials.

The character of children's programs may not be altogether to the point. By the age of nine or ten, most of the television a child sees is adult programming. (Conversely, many adults also watch children's programming, with or without children present.) With the deregulation of broadcasting in the Reagan years, the networks could disregard the presence of the vast juvenile audience after 8 p.m. According to NBC's chief programmer at the time, Brandon Tartikoff, "heavy adventure with acts of violence, jeopardy and threatening action" were now allowed.

Television addresses children directly with a substantial flow of commercials for toys, sweets, cereals, and soft drinks. But children watching adult programs are exposed to a much greater volume of advertising that is not intended for them, and that becomes a powerful formative influence. They are also exposed to a kind of violence different from the knockabout zapping of cartoons.

I have just pointed out that the households where children and adults spend most time watching are those where learning is least valued, family tensions are greatest, and aggressive behavior is more common. If we compare heavy and light *adult* viewers of dramatic programming (with its heavy component of violence), we anticipate that the heavy viewers will be more aggressive—and they are. We may suspect that a consistent and heavy dosage of television violence boosts their existing aggressive propensities. If we took pains to factor out the attributes initially associated with heavy viewing, could we establish the effects of several years of *additional* viewing in raising the level of aggression to an even higher point? Such a demonstration would require an extraordinarily complicated and costly experiment and exceed the practical capacities of applied social research. The same questions might well apply to the *juvenile* audience.

In one expensive and elaborate effort, a group of NBC researchers tried to investigate what additional television viewing, at different levels, did to the behavior of school-aged children who at the outset already had widely varying degrees of preschool television exposure.[107] With the best of intentions, the samples were not large enough to prove the case that the additional television made a difference, since the heavy-viewing children were already more aggressive to start. NBC touted the conclusion that this conformed to the "null hypothesis" that additional TV watching did not make a difference. What was really shown were the limitations of the survey budget.

The sheer amount of television children watch might be expected to have consequences for their learning abilities and behavior, as I have already shown they do. But what of the actual content of the television programs they look at? How do children interpret the world they see on television and reconcile its features with what they see at home and in the everyday life around them? The eminent child psychologist Jean Piaget observes that children before the age of seven are egocentric and thus unable to understand reality. The images in fairy tales seem real for them because they accord with their fantasies.[108]

Whether children interpret the television violence they see as "fantasies" or "real" is very much influenced by the context and by whether the violence shown is justified by some rationale.[109] They imitate powerful and successful figures more than weak and unsuccessful ones. Children who are most aggressive in their attitudes (particularly the most avid viewers, from disadvantaged backgrounds) are most likely to regard what they see on the tube as similar to real life. The imaginary world of television has the power to overwhelm the world the child observes directly.[110] The evidence generally confirms that television is an influence on the way children behave, and violent television makes them behave badly. Most of this violence is embedded in the adult programming that youngsters freely watch.

A substantial body of social research supports the commonsense conclusion that antisocial media content encourages and channels antisocial behavior, both in children and in adults.[111] The media bring aberrant forms of behavior into general awareness. They provide models of behavior for disturbed individuals, whether these get their ideas from books, like *Don Quixote*, or from films, like juvenile delinquents whose lawyers try to blame producers for their clients' crimes. After the assassinations of President John F. Kennedy, his brother Robert, and Martin Luther King Jr.,[112] the number of threats a year against the lives of prominent government figures jumped more than fivefold. The number of homicides increases significantly after publicized prizefights "in which violence is rewarded" and drops significantly after publicized murder trials, death sentences, life sentences, and executions "in which violence is punished." Suicides increased after Marilyn Monroe's death.[113]

The response to violence depends on its context; it varies for individuals with different capacities for fantasy. Barrie Gunter, a researcher for British commercial television, suggests that "the practised daydreamer can turn to fantasy activity to work out or resolve anger-arousing problem situations, whereas the inexperienced daydreamer is more limited to the direct behavioural expression of aggression."[114] But the qualifying effects of individual personality, like those of the interpretation or context for violence, should not obscure the central point, which is the link between media content and violent actions.

Laboratory experiments show that exposure to media violence produces aggressive feelings or actions; it also increases tolerance for violence committed by others. A comprehensive review of the voluminous literature on the relationship between aggressive behavior and viewing television violence demonstrates what the distinguished authors call "a bidirectional causal relation"—that is to say, a two-way connection.[115] What can be convincingly seen in the psychological laboratory is hard to replicate in the infinitely more complex conditions of real life—but the connection is there, all the same.

Social scientists seek to understand the subtle relationships between different kinds of media experience and subsequent behavior. Government commissions look for "proof," using the metaphors of jurisprudence. Why is it so difficult to extract causal proof from social field experiments? Given the absence of a smoking gun, broadcast industry researchers have continued to insist that "there is no consensus among researchers regarding the relationship between television and aggression, and a spirited debate continues within the scientific community."[116] The senior scientific advisers to the National Institute for Mental Health—which had squarely affirmed the relationship—called this statement

a shallow attempt, ostensibly for public consumption, to focus on only one portion of the NIMH review, rehash industry attacks on independent research of the past ten years, ignore or distort both the evidence presented in the NIMH report and the consensus of the field, and present conclusions that obscure the issue and deceive the readers.[117]

Reinforcing this strong position, the Council of the American Psychological Association in 1985 passed a resolution stating that "the conclusion drawn on the basis of 25 years of research and a sizable number of experimental and field investigations is that viewing televised violence may lead to increases in aggressive attitudes, values and behavior, particularly in children" and urged the television industry to reduce "direct imitable violence."[118]

Social science is a dynamic body of knowledge and theory that represents current understanding of human beings and their relationships. It must constantly confront new evidence that appears inconsistent with what is already known or believed, and assimilate that new evidence by refining its theories or improving its methods. By contrast, applied social research is always conducted with pragmatic ends in view; it is intended to guide the policy-maker. In social science, no statements can ever be accepted as final; in policy-making they must be, as a basis for taking action.

In 1993, the networks yielded to congressional pressure and introduced, as a two-year experiment, a "parental advisory" label preceding programs that, in *their* own judgments, were unsuitable for young children to watch.[119] But this accommodation was accepted with great indignation, as a strictly pragmatic act. At the press conference announcing the new system, Howard Stringer, president of the CBS Broadcast Group, noted that "Julius Caesar" had violence and that "tragedy ends in death." MPAA's Jack Valenti, who also participated, placed the burden of responsibility upon parents,[120] thereby evading the main point—that violent shows are most often viewed in the very households where television is used as a babysitter and where parental control is least likely to be exercised.

Under pressure from Attorney General Janet Reno[121], the networks also appeared to be accepting the idea of an independent evaluation of the violence levels in their programming. Meanwhile, the cable industry prepared a plan to rate programming violence, shift violent shows to late evening hours, and introduce an electronic control system that would allow parents to block unacceptable programs.

As the experience of the motion picture industry has shown, labeling violence tends to enhance, not lessen, its presence. Production and programming practices have not changed, notwithstanding the best scholarly evidence and judgment, simply because it is widely believed that the ratings depend on the existing prescription. But the evidence does not support the contention that violence and sex are essential to capture the audience's interest.[122] Action and sound are sufficient to mobilize attention; literary history confirms that there are an infinite number of ways to arouse an audience; shifts in programming formulas do not affect viewing levels in the aggregate. Violence prevails because it pays off and is therefore in style, not because it satisfies intense innate human cravings.

Does the quality or character of what the media disseminate really matter at all, as I have been arguing in this chapter? There is little scientific proof to back up the broad-gauge criticisms of commercial culture's preoccupation with material possessions, or of its standards of intelligence and taste. Those criticisms may resonate at a gut level, but their truth cannot be demonstrated. By contrast, the evidence quite conclusively shows that media sex and violence influence social behavior, although they do so in a way that interacts with more direct and powerful interpersonal forces. In recent years the spotlight has focused on television, but no medium of communication can be blamed for the way it is controlled and used. Sensationalism is a salient feature of commercial culture. It is driven by the race for bigger audiences. Its consequences become even more pernicious when it intrudes into the sphere of journalism.

7

The News as Entertainment

The pursuit of audiences increasingly forces journalism to assume the guise of entertainment. Thus it departs from its proper functions, to report accurately on the world around us and to raise the issues that arouse public concern and require government action at every level—from local trash collection to international diplomacy. That function is vital to democracy, but incompatible with concentrated power over the news media. Can news monopoly be discouraged while liberty of expression is maintained?

The routine processing of daily news is governed by the public's appetites and advertisers' perceptions as well as by the professional pride of journalists. Like every other aspect of commercial culture, the news flow also responds to the media policies laid down by a government that disclaims the existence of media policies.

In theory, the evolution of a multichannel electronic media system seems destined to foster the multiplication of perspectives on the news. In practice, choices are steadily being constricted, as the daily press loses its competitive character. Our knowledge of reality becomes murky when we no longer have the chance to see it from different points of view.

This chapter focuses on the two principal news media, television and daily newspapers, and on the changing practices of journalists as they struggle to maintain their audiences. The increased flow of information has not improved the public's familiarity with current events. Journalists—especially in television—struggle with the questions of how to evoke public interest in the news and of how news itself should be defined.

In the past 20 years, television has become the news medium on which most people say they principally rely. This response seems to reflect the vivid impact of major televised news stories, rather than the coverage of the routine affairs that make up most of the day's events and that remains the unique province of the press. Forty million people watch network television news each night, while nearly 120 million read a newspaper in the course of a day. I have already touched on the growing difficulties that face the daily press; this chapter goes into these more deeply. Key points:

- The state of public information has not kept pace with the greatly increased exposure to news.
- With all its great resources and formidable talent, television journalism has been forced to conform to the rules of show business. It gives us a vivid first-hand view of great events, but that view is often fragmentary and distorted. Those who report the news sometimes overshadow what they report on.
- Television coverage has itself become a force that shapes the events on which it reports. Inadvertently for the most part, but sometimes less innocently, television news can evade the truth and thus adulterates the public's judgment, the ability to see the world clearly as it is.
- The limitations of television news accentuate the importance of the daily press. When newspapers disappear and lose readers, nothing takes their place.

Information-Rich but Ignorant

History is studied by schoolchildren and college students. News, current history, is exposed, in one form or another, to nearly everyone, but it is woven into the entertainment that fills the mainstream of commercial culture. As a result, our almost universal and instantaneous access to important information is not translated into a willingness to use it.

Americans display a naive reluctance to draw connections between what they perceive as compelling social necessity and what they consider to be in their immediate self-interest. (For years—until energized by President Clinton—they overwhelmingly rejected proposals to increase taxes and wanted no reduction in government social programs, though they regarded the budget deficit as a major national problem.) A low rate of political participation accompanies ignorance of basic facts and issues of public debate, and the persistence of abysmal superstition.[1] (Forty-two percent of Americans say they have had contact with the dead.[2] Nearly half think humans were created in their present form about 10,000 years ago. And 57% of those who own cats confide in them about important matters.)

Voting turnout in the United States is the lowest of any major democracy. It steadily declined, from 63% of those eligible in the 1960 presidential election to 50% in 1988, before recovering to 54% in 1992.[3] A turnout of only half the voters in presidential elections seems at odds with the enormous public exposure to television news, to campaign news in particular, and to the preelection debates.[4]

There are plenty of anecdotal indications of the American electorate's imperviousness to the political information to which it has ample access. Although the quantity of news about Congress has grown enormously in the last half-century, Gallup polls since 1942 show no particular trend, attributable to television, in the proportion of people who can name their congressional representatives. Over a period of two decades, an average of 56% are unable to name any candidate for

Congress from their district or for the Senate from their state.[5] At the start of the 90s, over half the public did not know that the Democrats were a majority in Congress.[6]

The same impenetrability applies on other subjects. In spite of the vast quantity of news reporting in broadcasting and in the press, the public exhibits an extraordinary ignorance on personalities and issues that are continually brought to its attention.[7] When the Pentagon Papers were the main item of news in all media, 45% of the public said they had neither heard nor read about them.

The public's poor ability to play back information that is constantly paraded before it may be an indication that the media have low impact. More likely, the explanation is that people do not retain facts they do not consider to be meaningful or useful. The average viewer of a network newscast recalls only 1.2 of its 20 news stories, when interviewed later in the same evening. Half recall no story spontaneously.[8] What is not remembered is not necessarily forgotten. The information may be activated when a new episode of the same story surfaces on another occasion. However, it is evidently not salient enough to be put to any active use. There is no clear-cut message delivered all the time by all the media that defines what news the public should keep uppermost in mind. Not surprisingly, therefore, at any given moment it is rare to find public consensus as to what is the most important current news story.[9] Different choices reflect the differing judgments of news organizations as well as individual propensities to relate to particular topics.

In fairness, it must be noted that surveys showing large areas of public ignorance are almost invariably presented without benchmarks by way of comparison.[10] The state of public information in the days before news media must have been rudimentary and confused. But with all the vast machinery of contemporary news-gathering at its disposal, a very substantial part of the population manages to remain oblivious both to the oft-repeated facts and to their implications. The mass media cannot be blamed directly, but they seem to fall short of what they should achieve. Here a distinction must be registered between print and broadcasting. Viewers of TV news are no more familiar with the subjects dealt with in the newscasts they watch than nonviewers, while readers of newspapers are better informed on public issues than nonreaders. The problem is, there are fewer of those readers, year after year.

Defining the News

Why is honest journalism so essential for a society that aspires to be democratic and orderly? Pragmatically, our lives are organized around the assumption that we know what goes on in the real world around us. We know it partly through our own inspection and experience, and partly through what we are told by those we trust. Mass media have extended the penumbra of accepted sources well beyond the circle of individuals and institutions whom we know first-hand. Lead article in the *San Francisco Examiner*, July 15, 1918:

> London. British forces, after landing on the Murman coast, have occupied the town of Kem on the White Sea, says the *Frankfurter Zeitung*, according to a Rotterdam dispatch to the *Daily Telegraph*.

We tend to be skeptical of any report that reaches us through a devious route. When we know that a story has gone through many hands, we usually suspect that it may have changed in the telling, though we are also inclined to assume that some essential element of truth remains. Our knowledge of what goes on in the world comes to us through a series of filters, of varying degrees of density, color, and distorting effect. Every item of news that comes our way in the mass media has inevitably passed through such a filtering procedure, less obvious than in the 1918 dispatch just cited, but no less powerful. The filters occur in the complex organizational processes that intervene at every level of rewriting, editing, selecting, cutting, headlining, and positioning. The filters are already present in the minds and eyes of reporters observing and organizing information.

Journalists must capture interest and attention and at the same time convey essential facts. What is important is not always interesting.[11] Much of news reporting has always represented the recounting of minutiae of only transitory importance. Big news stories are inevitably complex; they require description from multiple vantage points, information assembled from different sources, and the analytical skill to synthesize it and make sense of it all.

What takes a news report outside the category of the routine is its ability to arouse empathy. We learn and absorb most quickly the information to which we can relate. Journalists must engage the emotions of the audience even at the risk that individual striking events may be confounded with more general truths. Particular instances of tragedy can evoke emotion, outrage, and indignation, while events on a much larger scale fade into an impersonal summary of history.

- Televised interviews with a half-dozen Muslim women raped in the Bosnian civil war carried far greater impact than a United Nations tally of 20,000 such victims. Earlier, the death of 100,000 refugees in Ethiopian resettlement programs was reported in a 2-1/2-inch item on an inside page of *The New York Times*.[12] During World War II, the *Times* ran a front page account of a group of Jewish girls who committed group suicide when they were placed in a Nazi brothel. At the same time, reports of mass murders of tens of thousands were buried in 1-inch items on back pages, either because they were just statistics or because they were unsupported by details.

It is harder to ignore the vivid visual reports of television, which show us victims of war and catastrophe. Scenes of fleeing refugees or starving children arouse strongly sympathetic feelings—as long as they are confined to occasional vignettes. Prolonged coverage of human suffering would bring rapid flicking to a different channel. Gruesome footage of soldiers dismembered and in agony never got on the air during the Vietnam War.

The arousal of "human interest" is one of the most highly valued skills of journalism, and it is accomplished by many of the same techniques that the novelist or short-story writer uses to create empathy, suspense, and emotion. It does so by playing on universal relationships and sentiments. Former NBC News president Reuven Frank:

> Every news story should, without any sacrifice of probity or responsibility, display the attributes of fiction, of drama. It should have structure and conflict, problem and

denouement, rising action and falling action, a beginning, a middle and an end. . . .
The picture is not a fact but a symbol. The real child and its real crying become
symbols of all children.[13]

Anecdotal accounts enter into the news to the degree that there are not more
important things to show or to write about. Reports of war are generally accounts of
objectives taken or positions lost, interspersed with the statistics of battle losses.
Rarely are the stories infused with the human touch, and they are covered because a
reporter happens to hear about or observe them.

Many elements of news media content are the product of accidental or random
events rather than of deliberate planning. A speaker at a public meeting hurls a racial
epithet in the course of a heated exchange irrelevant to the main business proceedings. If no reporter were there, a handful among the several dozen people in the room
might have been sufficiently exercised to tell friends about it. As it happens, there is a
reporter present, as a result of a very marginal decision by the metropolitan editor.
The reporter considers the epithet newsworthy and quotes it in an article that is
brought to the attention of several million readers. There are vigorous counterat-
tacks. A controversy has been created out of what may or may not have been a "true"
news event—out of scale with the fast judgments made by the reporter who wrote the
article or the editor who gave it emphasis. News becomes what media choose or
chance to print or to air. Any event seems more important on a slow news day than
when much is happening.

• The 1,500-word letter that first told the story of the My Lai massacre
in Vietnam was sent by a former soldier, Ronald Lee Ridenhour, to President Nixon,
Defense Secretary Melvin Laird, three senators, and twenty members of Congress. Only his home-state representatives replied. The letter was sent in March
1969; an Army investigator talked to him in April; by June Ridenhour was convinced
that the story would be covered up, and took steps to make it public. The news
did not break in the press until November.[14] Top executives of the leading wire
services independently volunteered comments that the story had been squelched
at high levels in the military.[15] While they agreed that the press should have got-
ten on to it long before it actually surfaced, they also stressed its superficial similarity, on the basis of first reports, to many other discredited atrocity stories involving
civilian deaths in the heat of combat. The cry of "Wolf!" had been sounded too
often; the gatekeepers had become blasé. No one intimated that the news media
had joined with the Army to suppress the matter. Perhaps what is most important
in this grim episode is that a free press eventually *did* bring the story into the
light.

An important statement or revelation goes unreported because there are no
reporters present and then receives front-page play when it is repeated on another
occasion by a speaker whose name carries greater recognition value. People interviewed by reporters generally express themselves more freely than they might if they
were committing their words to paper for deliberate quotation at a later time. They
expect that personal asides, hesitations, idiosyncrasies of speech, and obscenities
will be eliminated from the story as it appears in print. Verbatim quotation may be

used to make a statesman appear like an incoherent idiot. When Barry Goldwater ran for president in 1964, an aide told reporters, "Print what he means, not what he says." It is precisely in the search for meaning that news media play their most essential role, but also where it is easiest for them to go astray.

Is the News a Bore?

Ratings rule television, and news programs are no exception. Large numbers of viewers avoid serious content when they have the alternative of being amused. A CBS special report on the night of the 1988 New Hampshire primary got only 8% of the viewing audience, while 39% tuned in to ABC's coverage of the Winter Olympics.[16] In New York, nearly half the election night viewers in 1992 were watching something other than the network broadcasts of the returns.[17]

Viewers are not just indifferent to the broadcast of special news events; they can be indignant. CBS interrupted a professional football game for 15 minutes to show the flight of Apollo 8, the first live television broadcast from space. Within an hour, the network had received 2,000 calls of protest, including one from a man who said he hoped that the astronauts would never come back. Years later, his wish was fulfilled. When the space shuttle Challenger exploded on January 28, 1986, the networks switched their regular programming to news coverage of the disaster. ABC received 1,800 calls, 80% of them complaints about the preemption of favorite soap operas.

Viewers find politics boring, says Howard Stringer, president of CBS News. David Burke, his predecessor, senses an "unwanting to know" among the public. If television news were to "put on the hair shirt and say, 'Look, sit down, I'm going to talk to you for a while about the Federal deficit and you're going to like it,' well, they won't. They'll turn it off."[18]

News analyst Eric Sevareid, at a CBS internal postmortem on the 1976 campaign coverage:

> Why must we make the functioning of democracy, which is the most boring political system on earth, why should we try to make it unboring? One of the great fundamental civics lessons in the democratic society is to teach the discipline in enduring boredom.

His colleague, Mike Wallace:

> Did it ever occur to you that you drive people away from your civics lessons by overcoverage?[19]

The dilemma posed in this exchange would confront broadcasters under any media system, but it is particularly acute when management judges news programming by its audience size rather than by its professionalism.

The steady reader of a great newspaper or news magazine is conscious of history raging and inching forward on a hundred different fronts. The viewer or listener to broadcast newscasts is treated to a limited number of isolated stories. (CBS typically considers thirty-six stories, including sixteen from its own correspondents, to get twenty for a 21-1/2-minute show; commercials and promos fill out the half-hour.) Even in the networks' most gilded days, their news staffs always worked with limited budgets, and the number of crews in the field was extremely small in relation to the number of stories occurring on any given day, throughout the world. What television news displays on the air reflects the news judgments that deploy its camera crews. There is a tendency to concentrate resources inefficiently on the main story that happens to be breaking at any moment. At the peak of the Lebanese civil war, the three networks had a total of twenty-six camera crews in Beirut. Now they are more likely to rely on one of the independent international video news services.

Newspapers are full of incidental nonsense that occupies odd bits of available space and that readers can avoid with a glance. There is no equivalent mechanism by which to evade the meaningless and ridiculous items that fill air time on television newscasts. President Bush's dog Millie was mentioned in more evening TV network news stories than the secretaries of energy, education, agriculture or veterans' affairs.[20] Even though they husband every second of time, producers character-istically waste many minutes on street interviews. In international reporting, camera crews seek out English-speakers, especially those who speak the language fluently and fast. These are inevitably drawn from an educated, well-to-do, and often opinionated minority. American viewers thus get the impression of foreign nationals as being just like them.

In the absence of exciting breaking stories, television news blows up trivia to epic proportions, if they lend themselves to suspense. In the fall of 1988, attention was focused on a massive $1 million international effort to free two whales trapped off Northern Alaska by the Arctic ice. The Eskimos involved in this rescue effort were having whale meat for lunch.

When Roone Arledge became head of ABC News in 1977, he announced that he would quicken the pace by putting on more stories, but at the same time would miraculously manage to leave room for "more background and perspective."[21] This miracle has still not taken place. Network news departments are staffed by talented, seasoned, well-informed journalists, but their skills are confined by program for-mats and by the constant need to maintain high levels of audience interest.

Television, with its stringent time and scheduling limitations, is generally resi-stant to extended reportage and commentary. Any television newscaster or commen-tator, anyone interviewed on a talk show, even any participant in a panel discussion, is highly conscious of the sweep-second hand of the studio clock and is under pressure to say what must be said swiftly, economically, without hesitation. This makes serious issues difficult to discuss in all their complexity and at the length required to understand their nuances and subtleties. C-Span has attempted to do this, but its audiences are tiny.

The opportunity for politicians or other news-makers to say anything substantive or meaningful has become more and more attenuated. The "sound bite" in broadcast news (whose average length went from 43 seconds in 1968 to 9 seconds in 1988[22]) derives from the montage of commercials, with their rapid succession of briefly presented images.

It is patently impossible to present an intelligent news analysis in a few seconds, or even in a few minutes. The problem also arises for experienced reporters, who must spend precious moments of their brief field reports explaining who and where they are and signing off at the conclusion. It applies all the more to laymen confronted with a camera and sound crew. Reasoned discussion is best carried out in print.

As more television time is devoted to the news, more time is spent watching it (since, as we have noted, viewers watch what is placed before them). The average adult's weekly consumption of television newscasts rose from 45 minutes in the early 1950s to over 4 hours at the start of the 1990s. Much of the television news audience is made up of people who are present simply because they keep their television sets on a good deal of the time.[23] A third of news viewers tune in to a newscast because of the show that precedes or follows it.

Although news programs are more highly regarded by viewers than entertainment shows, their holding power is no greater.[24] Only one viewer in ten cites "news quality" as the reason for watching.[25] Much of the viewing occurs sporadically rather than as a matter of invariable routine. At the height of the Falklands War, among those who had seen any of twenty newscasts on ten weekdays, only 5% had seen four or more. The press described the public as "glued" to their TV sets.

Broadcast news, on-air and through cable, presents an increasing number of alternative channels to get the headlines, and news-viewing has suffered. Between 1983 and 1993, the combined ratings of the three early-evening network newscasts fell by 23% in cable households but only by 10% in non-cable households. Most of the time spent watching news on television is with local news programs, which give individual stations their identity and account for 40–50% of their profits.[26] These newscasts typically handle only a handful of photogenic stories each day, specializing in fires, accidents, and crime. Only 15% of their time is devoted to national and world news.[27] The "news team" members (always balanced to include a woman and a "minority") chortle over nothing, engage in idiotic, time-wasting banter, and seek to impress viewers with their charm and bonhomie rather than with their grasp of the affairs they talk about.

Richard O'Leary, president of ABC's owned and operated stations, defends "happy talk" news as "human and informal, compared with the old-fashioned newscasts in which people talked the news down from the heights."[28] Los Angeles' KTTV launched "Metronews, Metronews" in 1976, as a "newscast for people who hate newscasts." It was dedicated to lots of laughs.

Much of local television news is produced by individuals whose main interest seems to be the medium, rather than the substance of the news itself. Only 14% of news producers, compared to 52% of television news reporters, say they went into TV news because they enjoy journalism.[29]

Increasingly, the networks were adopting some of the attributes of local news programs, but at the local level, news no longer had the allure it once had. The race to apply new technology—from tape recorders to helicopters—added to operating costs.[30] More and more stations dropped their late evening newscasts in favor of comedy reruns or talk shows.[31] A station that substituted "Wheel of Fortune" for the network news saw its ratings go up. In 1986, ABC moved its network newscast in New York from 7:00 p.m. to 6:30 (when there were fewer sets in use) and replaced it with a game show, "Jeopardy"; the other network-owned stations followed suit. Bill Fyffe, WABC-TV's station manager, said, "We'll make a better profit. That's part of the reason for this business."[32] This was intended as wry understatement.

Intense pressures to cut back on news built up at the networks, each of which, in the early 1990s, was spending $300–350 million a year on its news operation. News generally costs less to produce than entertainment, but by the networks' accounting methods, their news programs were all unprofitable or just broke even; such features as ABC's "20/20" and CBS's "60 Minutes" turned a profit. For managements, news increasingly appeared like an expensive luxury. In the early 1960s, remembers Jay McMullen, a former CBS producer, "we were never told to think about ratings, think about whether this is going to make money or not. News departments were operating kind of like public utilities."[33] The pioneer broadcasters' understanding that the news divisions gave the individual networks their character and prestige was not always shared by their successors. CBS Chairman Laurence Tisch:

> There is a widespread attitude in the industry that maintaining news quality requires that cost management and budget levels be left entirely in the hands of journalists. It is pure fiction to imply that the independence of the news depends on its economic autonomy. No one ever suggested that the editorial budgets of *The New York Times* or the *Washington Post* or *Time* or *Newsweek* are sacrosanct from the business review of the publisher.[34]

The difference, of course, is that news is the business of newspapers and news magazines, while in broadcasting it is of secondary importance. Broadcast news operations had indeed become ever more expensive. Camera crews and overseas bureaus ate up corporate profits. (It cost $250,000 a year to maintain a correspondent in Tokyo, on top of the salary.) Valuable newscasters commanded higher and higher wages, which put an economic squeeze on the whole news function. (Until Barbara Walters was hired by ABC from NBC in 1976 at $1 million a year, top newscasters' salaries rarely passed $150,000.[35] Fifteen years later, Diane Sawyer was to earn $7.5 million under a 5-year contract with ABC.)

The decline in network news ratings through the 1980s (they stabilized at the outset of the 90s) coincided with an economic turndown and placed great demands on news managements to cut costs. All three network news organizations underwent series of massive bloodbaths that thinned the ranks of senior professionals. They closed many of their own bureaus at home and abroad and relied on their affiliates to cover domestic stories outside Washington and New York. The survivors on the staffs were pressed to become more productive. Correspondents were sometimes asked to supply material for so many network shows that they did not have time to cover stories.

The well-compensated Barbara Walters commented that the presence of too many newscasters on a broadcast could create problems:

> If we have too many people, we may find that people don't relate to any of them. We have to be be sure that in our search for briskness and for depth that we realize that this is a medium in which people relate to other people.

The preferred solution, inevitably, was to move news production closer to show business. Symbolizing this transformation, music was introduced into TV newscasts in the 1970s. It is used not only to identify a particular newscast, but to create an air of excitement that may be lacking in the news itself. A retired CBS newsman told a congressional committee in 1988

> We were ordered to add glitz. We were told to feature a celebrity interview at least every half-hour and if we did offer issue-oriented segments, the watchword was to give more heat and less light, the idea being that a noisy shouting match was a much better ratings draw than any reasoned debate.[36]

Newscaster Dan Rather:

> They've got us putting more fuzz and wuzz on the air, cop-show stuff, so as to compete, not with other news programs, but with entertainment programs, including those posing as news programs, for dead bodies, mayhem and lurid tales. "Action, Jackson" is the cry. Hire lookers, not writers. Do powder puff, not probing interviews.[37]

On-air promo for KCBS-TV News, Los Angeles:

> Real live sex slaves and their captors! Quick, turn to Channel 2![38]

Television as Intruder

Television is not an invisible spectator of the events it reports; it is an important part of the action. Phenomena we observe are altered by the very fact of observation (as Alfred North Whitehead and Werner Heisenberg pointed out in a different context). Malcolm W. Browne, a photographer, who stood by while a Buddhist monk methodically burned himself to death as an act of political protest in Saigon:

> Frankly, it never occurred to me to interfere. I have always felt that a newsman's duty is to observe and report the news, not try to change it. This attitude may be subject to criticism, but that is how I reacted and how I would react again.[39]

This bizarre abnegation of human impulses was taken up in the motion picture "Medium Cool," which begins with the hero, a TV cameraman, phlegmatically photographing an accident victim before he summons aid, and ends with an unknown child photographing the cameraman's own death.

Television news, with its crews and equipment, intrudes heavily into events in which the main focus should be on the actual participants. International meetings sometimes degenerate into circuses. (The Reagan–Gorbachev summit in Geneva in 1984 was covered by 3,500 news people.) Television news operations carry a high level of political influence merely by their coverage of events, through their ability to create instantly familiar personalities, to produce a widespread perception of crisis, and thus to force political decisions at a more rapid pace than they might otherwise take. Television stations were among the first objectives of revolutionaries in the East European coups d'état of 1989.

On the slum streets of American cities, flamboyant demagogues (an H. Rap Brown or Abbie Hoffman in one generation, an Al Sharpton or David Duke in the next) skillfully capture the spotlight through outrageous utterances or acts. The very indignation they arouse stimulates the audiences the media seek. The promise of instant fame through media coverage spurs troubled individuals to commit insane actions that alter the course of history.

Arthur Bremer, to FBI agents, after his arrest for shooting George Wallace:

How much do you think I'll get for my autobiography?[40]

The attempted assassination of President Reagan, by a young man (John Hinckley) who wanted to impress a movie actress, followed the model of John Lennon's murder. In both cases, the assassin, like John Wilkes Booth, thought of himself as engaged in a theatrical act. (Stephen Sondheim's failed 1991 musical comedy, "Assassins," actually made presidential murderers and would-be murderers into entertainment personalities.)

Prison rioters now characteristically demand that their side be heard on the television news. A Vietnam veteran in Cleveland held twelve persons hostage until his demands were covered on TV. Television has been held responsible for racial violence and urban unrest and rioting.[41] In the lethal Los Angeles riots of 1992, local viewers were graphically shown where the action was, and told that the police were nowhere around. Many regarded this information as an invitation to participate.

Television news stimulates international terrorism, since it draws public concern and attention to the uncertain fate of victims. Thus it stymies governments when they should be free to act privately and without public pressure. Television was an active participant in every crisis involving hostages in the Middle East, broadcasting statements made directly by the terrorists, including statements made by the hostages that served the terrorist cause. Because of its eagerness for visual documentation, television broadcasts whatever the captors and their mouthpieces wish to dissemi-nate, regardless of whether or not it contains anything truly newsworthy. The Carter presidency was paralyzed during its last year by the Iranian hostage crisis. The continuing suspense story dominated the news for weeks; it was high drama in the familiar pattern of serial entertainment. Howling mobs were assembled in Teheran each day for the delectation of the U.S. television audience. Shouting "Death to America" on cue whenever the cameras appeared, they turned the ordeal of the Embassy hostages into a nightmare for the administration.[42]

When Lebanese Shiites hijacked a TWA flight in 1985, killing an American passenger in cold blood, television interviews were conducted both with them and their hostages. Terrorists who had perpetrated monstrous acts appeared like reason-able, even sympathetic, human beings with legitimate grievances. During one such incident, ABC's "Good Morning America" anchorman interviewed Lebanese tribal chieftain Nabih Berri by telephone and asked, "Any final words for President Reagan this morning?" Of course this sort of thing is done in the name of satisfying the wants of the audience.

ABC's Roone Arledge:

> If I had my way we would never cover hostage families, but there is a human interest element there that exists.[43]

In this instance, "human interest" is a code term for ratings.

The Newscaster as Celebrity

In all media, editors' judgments of what is news depend on public familiarity with the protagonists. Television, with its heavy use of the headshot or closeup, makes the news a matter of personalities rather than of political and social movements or of ideas. Its reporters now often overshadow what they report on. Like the actors and interlocutors who are also a recurrent presence on the television screen, they appear to be familiars of the domestic environment. Television presents an endless parade of cheerful chatty people who call each other by their first names on first encounters. As eavesdroppers on this intimate society, viewers are expected to share the general sense of camaraderie. It is inconceivable for anyone summoned to appear on a talk show to address the host in any other way than as a close personal friend. This kind of familiarity is taken for granted, even with any television personalities whom a guest may not know. (The presumption of intimacy has been taken over throughout society in routine relationships that were traditionally governed by formal rules of etiquette. Addressing strangers by first name has become commonplace in American life, as has the second-person familiar in formerly formal European societies.)

Ever since the days of Samuel Pepys, journalists actively participating on the scene have made the news seem like a personal experience and thus more inviting. Long before television, newspapers made celebrities of their reporters and columnists; they sold more copies when readers had a feeling for the individual who was telling a story. Radio featured newscasters as varied as Richard V. Kaltenborn, Gabriel Heatter, Walter Winchell, and Edward R. Murrow, whose characters and styles were registered just by their voices.

With television came the newscaster as superstar, by far better known than most of the news-makers themselves. Singing movie stars may provide performances of greater intensity, but the images of television newscasters enter the home with much greater regularity. The equanimity with which they survey the world horizon, the dispassion and polish with which they read their scripts, instill in the viewers a far greater sense of confidence than they have in any mere politician.

The trusted newscaster is a parental figure who may be depended upon to stay in place even as the transient news-makers of the day move on. Before Watergate, CBS's Walter Cronkite had the trust of 73% of the public, President Nixon, 57%. Critic Michael Arlen describes Cronkite's interview with presidential candidate Jimmy Carter:

> It was a strangely endearing scene: one of those carefully arranged candid moments in the lives of great men. Cronkite, though, was unmistakably the grander presence. He was the sage, the Fisher-King. How often had he seen these mortals come and go, questing after votes, or peace, or war, or even after the moon and outer space?[44]

The daily format of the news, with familiar personalities at an appointed time, offers the viewers reassurance that everything is basically OK, no matter how disturbing the news may be.[45] Some viewers endow newscasters with the power to manipulate the events they report on. During the Watergate hearings, CBS newsman Daniel Schorr received phone calls from viewers asking him to get rid of boring witnesses and to bring back "that nice John Dean."[46]

The response of viewers to newscasters has become more critical to the success of a program than the professionalism with which the news itself is covered and packaged. Forty percent of the viewers of network programs and 20% of viewers of local shows refer to the anchor as the reason for viewing.[47] A promo commercial for WMAQ in Chicago shows two women overcome by excitement when they spot a reporter at the next table in a restaurant.[48]

Since the newscaster's personality is so crucial to the ratings on which success depends, it inevitably becomes a matter of research and then of manipulation. Research consultants are called in to raise ratings by changing costumes, redesigning sets and hair styles, and "personalizing" the newsroom.

• When Christine Craft was dismissed from her job as anchor of KMBC-TV in Kansas City in 1981, she was told (as she later put it) that she was "too old, unattractive and not deferential enough to men." She was criticized for lacking "warmth and comfort" and for being too casual in her dress, and was given a "clothing calendar" to make sure she did not wear the same clothes more than once in three weeks.[49] Steve Meacham, a news consultant, conducted interviews in which he solicited audience responses by asking, "Is she a mutt?" and "Move her back to California? If we all chip in, can we buy her a ticket?" When Craft sued the station, its general manager told the court that appearance was "at the top of the list" of qualifications. A news consultant commented, "I think we are moving more into the Ken and Barbie school of local news, where the most important requirement for an anchor is to be young and goodlooking."[50]

• Not every newscaster is equal to the strain. Chris Chubbuck, an anchorwoman on WXLT in Sarasota, committed suicide on July 15, 1974. She announced her intentions on the air: "In keeping with Channel 40's policy of bringing you the latest in blood and guts in living color, you're going to see another first—an attempt at suicide."

The Persian Gulf war, the first reported visually in real time, was "hosted" personally by the newscasters, and brought to the public by courtesy of their government. NBC and CBS sent their anchormen into Saudi Arabia resplendent in color-coordinated safari outfits. They reported news from a front that was many miles away, based on press briefings that might just as easily have been turned over to them in Washington or New York. Their reportage lost all semblance of the antiseptic objectivity that had been the traditional tenet of print journalism, as they spoke of the "bravery" and "professionalism" of "our forces" and of their personal pride in the American victories. ABC's Peter Jennings spoke of the "brilliance of laser-guided bombs." CBS's Charles Osgood called the bombing of Iraq "a marvel" and referred to "picture-perfect assaults." NBC's Tom Brokaw said of civilian casualties: "We must point out again and again that it is Saddam Hussein who put these innocents in harm's way."[51] (This kind of partisan stance—which has no counterpart in newspaper reporting—has antecedents, like Walter Cronkite reporting a rocket launching: "Go, baby, go!")

Satellites brought live reports of aerial bombardments and surrendering prisoners into American living rooms, giving the events of battle an immediacy that had never previously been possible. The war was treated in the manner of a game whose outcome was uncertain, and military strategy was discussed with the style of experts discussing rival athletic teams, faced with such questions as, "What is going on in Saddam Hussein's head?" The coverage carried themed titles, theme music, and fast montages of planes, tanks and battleship guns. An announcer warned of "Scud missiles aimed at Saudi Arabia. After the movie."[52]

Former NBC News president Michael Gartner:

> It's unreal to be watching a war unfold like a football game. You get so wrapped up in covering it that you forget it's a war and you have to stand back sometimes and say, "My God, this is a war."[53]

Politics as TV Spectacle

Wars arrive somewhat unpredictably; national elections, on a regular schedule. American politics has been converted into a sector of the entertainment business. In 1992, Bill Clinton sought to break away from network news by playing the saxophone on "The Arsenio Hall Show" and by appearing on MTV and "Larry King Live," but this campaign tactic would not indefinitely substitute for mainline news coverage during his presidency.

The networks' handling of politics derives from their pursuit of higher ratings; on the other hand, political campaigning has been altered by its preoccupation with network news. The results are familiar: the protracted reporting of the primaries, the interminable ordeal of candidate interviews and debates, the tedious spectacle of the conventions (largely abandoned in 1992 for lack of popular appeal), the polls that show who is ahead, and finally the election night exit polls that announce who has won before the votes are actually counted. What sustains popular interest in televised politics is no longer the clash of principles but the mystery of the outcome. It is not political concern or anxiety that prompts the public to pay attention to poll results and pundits' prognostications; it is suspense. As the horse-race aspect of campaigning has come to predominate, the focus in televised presidential debates has been on "who won?" rather than on what was elucidated.[54]

Coverage of candidates, mainly positive in the 1960s, became mostly negative by 1992, as it focused more on campaign controversies and less on issues. News stories became less descriptive and more interpretive, as journalists, rather than candidates, increasingly set the tone.[55]

While politics increasingly abandons the domain of ideology, it has become assimilated into the unending stream of televised amusement and must compete for attention with far livelier and jollier contenders. Many viewers resent the intrusion of election coverage into their otherwise constant diet of fun and games. During the

1980 conventions, the networks' share of prime-time viewing declined from 85% at the outset to 50% at the close. They abandoned gavel to gavel coverage in 1988. In 1992, even their highly abbreviated broadcasts got less than half of the viewing audience, competing with old movies, syndicated reruns, and the other miscellany available on independent stations and cable channels. The conventions themselves are physically dominated by the networks' booths. As in televised sports, the timetable, pace and actual content of the proceedings are orchestrated to meet television's needs.

As the boundary lines fade between the stage, the mass media, and real life, politicians, who make their presence felt on television, are perceived as show business personalities and are judged by the same criteria. The links were already well established before television arrived at its present preeminence in the conduct of campaigns. Politics has always been a form of theater, in which charismatic figures play roles, mouth lines written by others, and appeal to crowd emotions to win attention and rapport.

Clayton Moore, who played the Lone Ranger in 200 programs during television's early days, was once sued by Lone Ranger Television, to prevent his appearance at county fairs and shopping centers wearing a leather mask and white hat. A lawyer for the plaintiff said, "It's our mask. By wearing the mask, Moore is appearing as the Lone Ranger. But in spite of what Mr. Moore feels in his heart, he is not the Lone Ranger. We own the Lone Ranger." Like actors, politicians sometimes seem to have difficulty in distinguishing between their real selves and their imaginary roles. Presidential contender Jesse Jackson played the part of himself in a prime-time situation comedy before becoming a talk-show host.

This interchangeability of roles works in reverse too. Visible personal identity, established through motion pictures and later television, has made stars widely acceptable as authorities in areas that have nothing at all to do with their stardoms. In the 1930s, Hollywood talent developed what in those days was called a political consciousness (with subsequent dire consequences in the McCarthy era). The principle was at that time firmly established that actors could draw large numbers of people to political rallies, persuade them to sign petitions and send in contributions, and provide a dull candidate with an aura of glamor.

Charlton Heston, mayor of Carmel, Cal.:

Truly, I would rather play a senator than be one.[56]

His fellow actor, George Murphy, got to play one in Washington. Ronald Reagan, promoting Marlboro cigarettes, was in a tradition of actors who converted their familiarity to the public into credibility for product endorsements. When Reagan became the corporate spokesman for General Electric he was still the journeyman actor fulfilling a mercenary assignment, but his memorized script took possession of him and provided him with a readymade conservative philosophy that was easily converted into a political career. Reagan never really fully abandoned an infusion of the imaginary world he inhabited as an actor into the all-too-real world of national politics. As president, he interrupted Cabinet meetings devoted to very serious subjects with references to film plots that seemed à propos to him. He was given to interjecting lines from old movies into his public utterances. From "The State of the Union" he got the manly sentence, "I am paying for this microphone," which he used effectively in debating George Bush during the 1980 presidential primary race.

Dan Rather:

> The Reagan people saw the whole campaign as a movie. . . . They thought as movie directors do, of shooting sequences—we have our star, this is our sequence, now how . . . do we want the shot framed? The Mondale people—at best—saw it as a series of quick sound bites.[57]

Kukrit Pramoj played the role of the prime minister of "Sarkhan" alongside Marlon Brando in the film version of "The Ugly American." Some years later, he became the actual prime minister of Thailand.[58] Actor-politicians have been notoriously successful in both Brazil and India. In the United States, a number of radio talk-show hosts ran for Congress in 1994, although success had evaded television preachers like Pat Robertson and Jerry Falwell, who also tried to translate their show-business cachet into political careers. (Robertson managed to convert his take from the faithful into a cable empire and, briefly, ownership of the bankrupt United Press International.)

If the political system and the media system are now closely entwined, print journalism as well as broadcasting is affected. Once the timing of presidential press conferences was geared to the exigencies of early evening network newscasts rather than to newspaper deadlines, newspaper editors began to question the significance of their own work. The conviction of television's supreme primacy led to a diminished interest in newspapers' role of explaining, on the record, complex points of public policy that defied exposition in a few seconds of video footage. Thus political news, the enormously important though often tedious task of sifting through the manifold functions and processes of government, became ever less of a priority for the daily press.

Faked News and Docudrama

The public can never confuse the print journalist's notebooks with the reality they sketch. In television the distinction is not all that clear. Just as newspaper reporters make judgments as to what is newsworthy, able television journalists reassemble what the camera records to convey what they judge to be the true meaning of events. It is only a step away from these necessary steps of selection and editing to a radical reconstruction that incorporates what the camera never caught at all.

News reporting easily confuses confection and reality. Robert Thompson describes a BBC correspondent in Vietnam who usually visited

> trouble spots in a fairly relaxed manner, to interview knowledgeable people on the spot and then to have a quiet look around himself. At the end of this he would record a short five-minute objective summary of the situation as he saw it. At the time of the Tet offensive . . . he complained that he was just being dragged around by the

cameraman and would probably get shot. He could only comment on the pictures which the camera could take and had little idea what was going on anyway. When he got to Hue and saw American aircraft dive-bombing the citadel still held by the Vietcong, all he could think of saying into the microphone was: 'My God! It's just like watching television!'"[59]

If a trained observer on the scene finds it hard to distinguish the real and the imaginary, how infinitely more difficult it is for the media audience, which is constantly expected to make rapid switches from one realm to the other!

The limited horizon of the television camera has a selective and therefore a distorting effect in its depiction of reality. Television imposes technical requirements that put great power into the hands of those who light, shoot and edit film. An instrument in human hands, the camera can make the unimportant seem dramatic and vice versa or make the simple appear complex. It can flatter or degrade the personalities who parade before it. (A televised individual in motion, photographed from a slightly low angle, is more often judged as "active" and "potent."[60]) A similar process of control occurs in the editing process, which reconstitutes what the camera has actually recorded. The "unique perspective" of television, its penchant for distorting reality through the selective focus of the camera eye, was first noted by sociologists Kurt and Gladys Lang in a study of General MacArthur's reception in Chicago after President Truman recalled him from the Far East Command.[61] The Langs compared the impression of mass enthusiasm conveyed by the television cameras that accompanied the General's cavalcade with the reports of live observers, who found comparatively little public excitement.

The effects of communications very much depend on conventions, on the audience's expectations, on its empathy with the protagonists, on the extent to which it can anticipate the outcome, on the degree of its uncertainty about the deeper meaning of what is presented. Tension, apprehension, awe, and terror arise from a combination of words, intonations, and visual appearances. Changes of viewpoint create dramatic excitement. In literature, the close of a chapter can bring on a new setting, a new set of characters, a switch in time. In film and video, through the cinematic device of montage, the audience can be jolted into awareness of many facets and levels of meaning inherent in a given set of events. Rapid shifts of visual and auditory images, switching of themes and subjects — such devices automatically convey the complexity and multilateral nature of experience.

Television news producers deal simultaneously with alternative camera displays of ongoing action reported live. They must rapidly select and edit fresh video clips for a newscast. They are less apt than producers of news *documentaries* to use tricks of artful juxtaposition. Documentarists distinguish good guys and bad guys through timing, placing sequences, splicing tape, using close-ups, and selecting protagonists to represent points of view. They introduce drama into what might seem dull if it were reported straight. More like artists than journalists, they manipulate images to arouse the emotions of the audience. The technique, if not the subject matter, is exactly like that of comedy producers who dub in laughter and applause or prompt the studio spectators in order to stimulate the responses of the unseen public and get the ratings up.

Only 10% of the news footage exposed gets into a typical story, and inevitably it is selected for its dramatic effect. In preparing the controversial CBS documentary "The Uncounted Enemy," Mike Wallace's 2-hour interview with General William Westmoreland was cut to 5 minutes and 38 seconds on the air.[62] An officer's response to an interview question was doctored to make it appear that he referred to American intelligence reports as "crap" when he was actually referring to outdated South Vietnamese Army reports. The producers spliced answers to hypothetical questions to make it appear that they referred to specific questions about Westmoreland.[63]

Interpreting reality is one thing; distorting reality is another; fabrication is something else altogether. Television news has, since its earliest years, occasionally slipped into the fallacy that distortion is justified to convey an essential truth, hiring political "demonstrators" and "revolutionaries" and staging events for the cameras to recreate what may actually have happened earlier or elsewhere.[64] Such incidents are no more typical of television network news than the newsgathering practices of the supermarket tabloids are of daily newspaper journalism. But the constant cost pressure on the network news departments sometimes leads them to the thin edge of impropriety.

The Unreality of "Reality Television"

Facile reinterpretations of history, embodied in popular motion pictures and TV programs, are easily mistaken by the public for depictions of historical facts. Don Hewitt, the executive producer of CBS News's "Sixty Minutes," suggests sardonically that the average person's knowledge of history is filtered through fiction. "I thought Hamlet was a real prince who said 'To be or not to be.' All I know about the French Revolution is what I read in *A Tale of Two Cities*."[65] He is right, of course, in the sense that our impressions of real people and events are shaped by our exposure to artistic conceptions as much as by objective reports.

Readers are unlikely to confuse the musings of Tolstoy's Napoleon or of Alexander Solzhenitsyn's Lenin with a true historical record, no matter how convincingly they are presented. It is difficult to mistake a written fiction for a work of nonfiction, but visual imagery has the power to create a sense of ambiguity about the reality of events.

In film, as in the theater, fictional representations of real historical personalities take on a compelling character, and audiences may be inclined to take the script's conception literally. David Wark Griffith's "Birth of a Nation" warped later generations' view of the Reconstruction Era. Rolf Hochhuth invented the myth that Churchill ordered the death of General Sikorski, and a pair of lesser playwrights rewrote the espionage trial of Julius and Ethel Rosenberg to make them innocent victims rather than traitors.

• In the same tradition, but in glorious blood-stained color, Constantin Costa-Gravas's film "Missing" described the fictional case of a young American killed during the overthrow of the Allende government in Chile in 1973; it alleged that the U.S. government conspired in the overthrow and possibly ordered the character's execution. Replying to rebuttals and protests by the State Department, the director argued that he did not pretend that the film was a documentary. "Don't ask a film director to be a political technician. Either you give two points of view or you say, 'Here is what I think. I draw my own conclusion.' "[66]

• A later film, "Mississippi Burning," about the murder of three young civil liberties activists, misrepresented crucial facts in the unraveling of the case and erroneously portrayed the FBI, under J. Edgar Hoover, as a defender of the civil rights movement.

• When a *New York Times* critic, Richard Bernstein, objected to the distortion of the historical record in "Fat Man and Little Boy", a film about the making of the atomic bomb,[67] the film maker, Roland Joffe, objected strongly:

> Behind his heroic posturing in defense of historical objectivity, [he] is in fact defending a partisan interpretation of history. The "official view" of these events that would have us believe, with Panglossian simplicity, that there is no other.[68]

The other version, presumably, was in the wholly fictional fabrications that were devised to support Joffe's "nonpartisan" interpretation of history.

• A similar defense was offered by Oliver Stone, producer of "JFK," a film fantasy that attributed President Kennedy's assassination to a conspiracy by Lyndon Johnson, the CIA, and the military establishment, all bent on expanding the war in Vietnam, with the connivance of former Chief Justice Earl Warren.[69]

Time Warner, which distributed "JFK," came under fire, but there was nothing new in this case of a large corporation's cold-blooded exploitation of public gullibility in its pursuit of profit. This particular dereliction seems no more egregious than the other types of sensationalism that permeate mass media content. A different and more serious issue of responsibility arises when docudrama leaves the movie theater and becomes a staple of television network programming. Now several other factors weigh into the discussion: the proper use of the public franchise; the sheer size of the audiences exposed; the heightened possibility for confusion created by the dissemination of fictionalized reenactments of history within the framework of a respected news medium.

The television docudrama stems from a genre with a venerable history. Soviet agitprop films specialized in reenactments of the scenes of the Russian revolutions and civil war. Their sharply drawn caricatures of the original events made the morality of the opposing sides seems as grainily black and white as the photography itself. In the United States, radio carried notable replays of history, through such programs as "The March of Time," and much later, "You Can Hear It Now." But these programs sought to dramatize what the historical record indicated, not to rewrite the record itself. Some television programming has continued to follow this path, with varying degrees of embellishment.

• "The Atlanta Child Murders", a 1985 CBS docudrama on the killings of 23 young blacks in Atlanta, aroused strong indignation from Mayor Andrew Young and other city officials. The producer decided to reopen the question of the convicted killer's guilt, even though no new evidence had surfaced to cast any additional light on the case beyond what had been presented in the original trial and the subsequent appeal. Although the murderer was convicted, and the verdict later upheld, producer Abby Mann had his own opinion. He insisted that "I don't believe Wayne Williams's guilt was proven." Kit Andersen, CBS's "director of dramas based on fact," said she did not read the entire trial transcript, but had "read most carefully those aspects that were included in the screenplay."[70] Naturally, the mere reconstruction of the facts would have made for less compelling entertainment than the intimation that there was an unresolved mystery and a miscarriage of justice. But this fictionalized rewriting of the history of the case created the dramatic experience that millions of viewers would take away with them.

What is perhaps most significant about such incidents is the spirited justification of the distortions. Hugh Whitemore, writer of a docudrama on the Chambers-Hiss case, accused critics of falling into "the trap of believing that documentary films represent an entire and complete truth." In effect he was saying, let the viewer beware; the ambiguity between the real and the fictional was transformed into a standoff between truth and falsehood, with equal legitimacy ascribed to both.

Twentieth-century totalitarian systems have promulgated lies to serve their political objectives. The manufacturers of commercial culture also confound the make-believe and the real world, sometimes with ignorant sincerity, more often with their eyes wide open. If their amorality is merely in the service of the market, is the market the appropriate means to judge the truth?

An infelicitous term, "Reality Television," has been used to describe all of the diverse programming that is neither straightforwardly informative, like the news, or manifestly fictional. It covers all the new types of pseudodocumentaries, doc-udramas, and other forms of entertainment that present fictional recreations of real events, dramas in which the names of real people and sometimes the guise of real happenings are used to mask the scriptwriter's imagination.

The ambiguity of fact and fiction has been evident even at the level of the production arrangements within the television networks. While news divisions were producing docudramas, the entertainment divisions bypassed the networks' own news professionals by hiring outside journalists. The NBC program, "Yesterday, Today, Tomorrow," which presented reenactments of news, was switched to the control of the entertainment division in November 1989. Michael Gartner, then head of NBC News, insisted that

> everything we did was fair and accurate. We just couldn't surmount the issue of viewer confusion. Journalistically, I had no problem whatsoever with anything we did.

Gartner's acknowledgment of viewer confusion was based on several focus group interview sessions, to which he referred as "statistical evidence."[71]

• A few months earlier, Felix S. Bloch, a U.S. foreign service officer, was accused of having turned a briefcase containing secret documents over to a Soviet diplomat. ABC News simulated this episode for its "World News Tonight," with crosshairs superimposed on the screen to suggest that the tape had been shot by surreptitious surveillance. After a delay, a title flashed on the screen to signal that the scene had been staged. Joanna Bistany, vice-president of ABC News, insisted that "the reporting was impeccable." A year later, Bloch's guilt had still not been proven in court, and the government eventually dropped its suit.

ABC News' own Sam Donaldson found this simulation deplorable. "People who saw that story are liable to say: 'I know Bloch's guilty. I saw him pass that briefcase.' Of course, they didn't see that at all." At this time, CNN was the only television news organization with a policy that ruled out such reenactments. CNN's Ed Turner pointed out that the other networks' news producers were impelled to make their stories "more visually compelling," since they were being judged in the context of entertainment programming.[72]

• NBC's "Dateline NBC" (one of the new "news magazines" introduced by the networks to handle feature stories in greater depth than the newscasts permit) faked a road accident to demonstrate the vulnerability of General Motors trucks. Gas jets were ignited under a vehicle to ensure a colorful explosion, but this fact was not mentioned in the 1993 broadcast. When GM sued NBC News and withdrew its advertising from the network, an apology came forth quickly, the producers were fired, and Gartner (who bore no direct personal responsibility in the incident) resigned abruptly.[73]

The problem of staged simulations had occurred in more important contexts. During the war with Iraq, a 2-hour special on ABC, "Heroes of Desert Storm," interspersed documentary material and reenactments.

Don Ohlmeyer, the producer:

> When we show a tank being blown up, what's the difference whether it was news footage or whether we blew it up ourselves?

If the very producers of such programs often seem to enjoy the delusion that they are conveying the truth, is it any wonder that the viewing public is misled? After all, the recreation of recent history may be said to be no more fictional than the contrived performances of real politicians and crowds for the television cameras, as we observed in Chapter 3.

Nicholas J. Nicholas Jr., initially Time Warner's co-CEO, said shortly after the giant new company was established that

> the journalism business has very much become as much entertainment as it is journalism. The line between them has become blurred.

He went on to disparage fears of the merger's threat to journalistic integrity as

> the latest variant of Gresham's Law: the debased currency of entertainment will drive pure journalism, an intrinsically more valuable activity, out of the marketplace and corrupt the whole process of fact-finding and truth-gathering. . . . [This] requires us to presume that the public has the intelligence of a high-school sophomore and

that given the choice between news and entertainment, it will usually choose the former only if it's dressed up in the clothes of the latter.[74]

Regrettably, this assumption is correct when news is presented within the framework of what—in the case of television—is perceived as an entertainment medium. Yet when television packages serious, even gruesome, subjects in the form of entertainment, it can generate a huge audience and leave a strong residual impact.

• Murder on a monstrous scale has been good show business long before Steven Spielberg's "Schindler's List" became a hit. Audience promotion for the 1978 docudrama series, "Holocaust," included an ad with the headline, "Heinz Mueller's story: He knew being a prison guard meant privileges—and one of them was the prisoners' wives." A summary of one episode in *TV Guide* read like an item in *Soap Opera Digest*: "Fighting alongside Russian partisans, Rudi and Helena take time out to get married. Meanwhile, Karl and two fellow inmates are tortured by Nazis." Fictional figures in the "Holocaust" series appear to have been imbued by viewers with the same reality as historical personages who were also depicted. (The same confusion applies on other occasions. At the Academy Awards ceremony in 1989 an actor explained that his hair was cropped short because he had just flown in from Auschwitz, where he was making a film. This got a big hand.)

The criteria applied to such ventures are not those of professional historians, or even those of journalists, but the box-office instincts of show business.

Barbara Hering, assistant general attorney of NBC in charge of docudramas:

My desk is like a veto. I don't go out and research the subject. I read a script and say, "Support this."[75]

Eighty percent of news on TV is what editors would call "soft" rather than "hard" breaking news; it is made up of features or stories planned ahead of time. As news audiences declined, titillating topics (like a baseball player's illegitimate children) were introduced to spice up the usual journalistic formulas. WCBS-TV in 1980 ran reports titled, "The Last Taboo," "Beyond the Pill," "Teen Age Suicide," "Child Molesting," and Battered Parents."[76] The CBS Evening News covered a confrontation between a congressman and the mother of a 13-year-old with whom he had allegedly had an affair. The weeks of the ratings sweeps brought forth a spate of such stories.

Just as mutually exclusive categories of news and features in newspapers are hard to define, television news, talk shows, and documentaries overlap. Are the morning breakfast shows, "60 Minutes" and the Ted Koppel show to be classified as news? While 48% of the public identified NBC's "Today" as news and 29% called it entertainment, 46% could not classify "Yesterday, Today, and Tomorrow," which used reenactments of real events.[77]

• In 1993, each of the networks ran its own vivid dramatization of "The Amy Fisher Story," about a teen-ager who shot the wife of her middle-aged lover. In one case, the victim cooperated; in another, the assailant. All three reenactments of this sordid and petty incident won large ratings.

The "news magazine" format, since it first appeared in the late 1980s, featured celebrity hosts whose reputations in some instances had already been made as newscasters. They purported to interview, and often managed to victimize, members of the studio audience or celebrities. The features presented on these programs were selected for their entertainment value and, in some highly publicized instances, used actors for dramatic reenactment of actual events as the producers imagined them. One former reporter turned entertainer, Geraldo Rivera, suffered a broken nose in a brawl with teenagers. His "documentary" on Satanism got the highest rating recorded for a 2-hour program of this category. Rivera's producers lured guests by placing ads in the personals column of *New York* magazine: "Real Life 'Sea of Love': If your personal ad has led to a NIGHTMARE, please call. . . . Cash paid for stories."[78]

*Barbara Walters got Jimmy and Rosalyn Carter to tell her if they slept in the same bed.[79] On one occasion the talk show hostess Oprah Winfrey interviewed a psychotic who said she was Jewish and that she had been forced to participate in a rite of sacrificing children.[80] Far more outrageous incidents had occurred in the past. In the mid-1950s, an episode of "This Is Your Life"—in which guests unexpectedly faced figures from their pasts—brought the pilot of the Enola Gay (which dropped the bomb on Hiroshima) together with scarred victims of the bombing who had been brought to the United States for plastic surgery. Their reunion was interrupted by commercials for nail polish and shampoo.

Criticism of such practices was called "unbecoming elitism" by talk showman Phil Donahue in a televised round-table discussion of the subject led by producer Fred Friendly. Rivera asked, "How much of this stems from the fact that the advertising dollar is finite?" And Don Hewitt insisted, "Come on! It's all about money." They were correct about show business, but not about journalism.

The Unique Functions of Newspapers

An honest, vigorously investigative press is an important counterpoise to television's evanescent news collages. The *New York Herald*'s James Gordon Bennett once warned of the impending effects of the telegraph in words that might serve equally well in the era of broadcast news and videotex:

> Mere newspapers—the circulators of intelligence merely—must submit to destiny, and go out of existence [while] the intellectual, philosophic, and original journalist will have a greater, a more excited, and more thoughtful audience than ever.[81]

No matter what wonders of data display or retrieval may be created by new electronic technology, the printed word will remain unique and essential to civilization. Text communicates with an efficiency that audiovisual communication cannot match. It lets people select the messages that are relevant to them and reflect on their meaning. In contrast to broadcasting, print permits us to linger upon a thought, or upon an image, and to return to it if necessary—something that cannot be done if the words or the images are constantly changing. It lends itself to the abstraction that is necessary to the thinking process and to making sense of vast amounts of information.

Newspapers continue to practice journalism with a scope and depth that television cannot match. The very size of a metropolitan paper's news staff, the resources it has at its disposal, the amount of space it dedicates to an enormous variety of separate items and subjects—all give it an unusual power as an overseer of public affairs.

The time is long past when American newspapers of a highly political cast vied to attract readers through sensationalism rather than statesmanship. In another age, newspapers established identity and won loyalty through their zealous advocacy of principles and causes.

Wilbur F. Storey, owner of the Chicago *Times*, 1861:

> It is a newspaper's duty to print the news and raise Hell.

Few contemporary dailies would dare to promote themselves, as did the *New York Sun* in 1870, as

> the Great Organ of the People. As such it will continue to uphold with all its might that which is good and true, while it will fearlessly expose knavery, corruption, and imbecility in high or low places wherever their practice imperils public safety or private virtue.[82]

A crusading newspaper, by definition, has a sense of political mission that is almost impossible to sustain in the era of local monopolies. To a degree, alternative weeklies still fulfill this function at the local level in major cities, but their readership and influence are necessarily limited—because they do not have a daily presence, because their hard news content is limited to their own investigative efforts, and because they lack the solid retail and classified advertising base that attracts readers to the general press.

Uniquely among the media, newspapers provide an integrating force that binds a community together through commonly shared information. As population has moved from city to suburb, the notion of community itself has changed. The weakening of newspapers bespeaks the disintegration of civic ties. It is both a cause and symptom of the progressive erosion of the nation's moral and political cohesion.

Newspapers have lost much of their regular readership, especially among young people. More than four out of five people still read a paper, but fewer do so as a daily habit. In 1970 four out of five people read a newspaper on a typical day; in 1993 only 63% did, and few of them (15%, far fewer than in the past) read more than one paper.[83]

There are many reasons why Americans read daily newspapers less often than they used to. They are under more time pressures; they live outside the central cities where papers are published; they can watch the news on television. Another important reason is that there are simply fewer newspapers around. Readers no longer identify with their local paper to the degree that they could when they had choices, and when the one they chose represented their personal politics and interests.

Press rivalry activates readers. When a paper goes down, many of them never switch to the survivor. The social consequences are enormous. As the economic base of newspapers is weakened, so is their ability to cover public affairs in depth, with integrity, and from a variety of viewpoints. Complacent survivors are irresistibly drawn toward the gently flowing mainstream or even to the shoals of mediocrity, and the public is left without alternative reports and opinions on what is going on.

The scale of the decline is not easily gleaned from the bare statistics, which track the drop from 1,745 dailies in 1981 to 1,570 in 1993.[84] While most of the papers that disappear, like most of those that start up (usually as converts from weekly or semiweekly publication) are in small communities, the real impact has been felt in the metropolitan markets that house a large (77%) and growing share of the nation's population.

Have other print media moved into the gap? The arrival of USA Today in 1982 provided a new alternative on a national scale, along with the Wall Street Journal and the national edition of The New York Times. Suburban newspapers grew and prospered; some became giants themselves.[85] But the circulation of national and new suburban dailies did not begin to approach the levels of the metropolitan press they had helped to displace. Other media have not really substituted for the functions once served by competing local daily newspapers. Weeklies and, to some extent, shoppers distributed free in selected neighborhoods, provide coverage of community news with a detail that dailies do not match, but the paid weekly press has lost readers, and shoppers (which had risen to over two-thirds of total weekly circulation by 1993) are, for the most part, not read very attentively. Their exclusive dependence on advertising limits the integrity of their reporting as well as its scope. As for nonprint media, public access channels on cable television often offer time to local news-makers or would-be news-makers, but they reach a minuscule audience. Radio news, since the Reagan administration's broadcast deregulation, has dwindled to a trickle. There are no real replacements for the local daily press.

The Need for Press Competition

Knowledge and political wisdom depend on the clash of ideas. On the national scene, there are sufficient media vehicles around to ensure that some outlet can always be found for the other side of every story. On the municipal level such opportunities exist in fewer and fewer places. No appraisal of the American media system can avoid the critical question of whether daily press competition can be revived.

It was once exceptional to find a single daily paper, or a combination of morning and evening dailies, holding unquestioned dominance in a particular city or town. Today, local monopoly is the rule. Since newspaper operations require a very high capital investment relative to their variable operating costs, the larger newspaper in a competitive market can always operate most efficiently. (The main reason, as I showed in Chapter 4, is the advantage the lead paper enjoys in advertising.) John Busterna, a scholar of newspaper economics, suggests that this creates a "natural monopoly" and that "there is no economic basis for wanting to punish the most cost-efficient firm in a market."[86]

It is true that certain types of media industry may, by their very nature, tend toward a monopoly that is easily acquired by someone with the imagination to be there first. Political scientist Ithiel De Sola Pool:

> Once an organization has compiled a bibliography of all the chemical journal articles of the past 20 years, no other sane entrepreneur will attempt to duplicate that massive effort.[87]

While this type of situation may exist in specialized fields of information, it is hard to accept the idea that monopoly is "natural" in an established mass medium like the daily newspaper. Busterna believes, in fact, that newspaper monopolies in larger markets are not inevitable, and could be overcome by government action. For example, "the government could regulate advertising and subscription rates like a public utility so that monopoly pricing and profits can be avoided." Or it could separate the ownership of printing presses from the ownership of the news-gathering and information functions.

In fact, separation of the printing from the editorial functions (a kind of "vertical disintegration") is the essence of newspaper joint operating agreements; these invariably also give the printing organization control over the business aspects of the paper—advertising and circulation—including pricing.

• Before a joint operating agreement (JOA) was allowed in Detroit, between Gannett's *News* and Knight-Ridder's *Free Press*, critics argued that both papers kept their rates artificially low in order to bring about the losses that would make a JOA possible. The administrative law judge who recommended against the JOA determined that "the objectives of dominance and future profitability were pursued by both papers (and their parents) in the belief that failure too had its reward in the form of JOA approval." (The attorney general ultimately approved the joint operation anyway, and the combined operation proved far less successful, financially, than anyone had expected.)

Competition sets higher editorial standards and makes for greater quality than can be achieved on a monopoly paper by even the highest-minded management and most dedicated staff. When there are rival newspapers, there are bound to be conflicting interpretations of the same news stories, whether these are of local or international import. During the Spanish-American War, the *New York Herald* story of an engagement was titled, "Antonio Maceo Loses a Battle," while the *World* said, "Maceo Chasing Spanish." Years later, a front-page story in *The New York Times* read, "300 Vietnam GIs Saved After 24-Hour Mauling," while the *Herald-Tribune* headed the identical wire service dispatch, "*U.S. Cavalrymen Track Down Elusive Guerrillas, Kill 159, Many Wounded on Both Sides.*"[88] The truth is more likely to emerge eventually when there are two such disparate reports than when there is only one, even the right one. The *New York Herald-Tribune* is no more. In 1994, there were more daily newspapers published in Chinese in New York City than in English.

Publishers bemoan the waste involved in having two reporters covering the same story, but the presence of two makes it less likely that significant facts will be ignored, that distorted or biased accounts will go uncorrected and uncontradicted, that questionable judgments will be rendered both on the news and on the institutions of the community.

Anton Chekhov:

> What would you say if a newspaper reporter, because of his fastidiousness or from a wish to give pleasure to his readers, were to describe only honest mayors, high-minded ladies and virtuous railroad contractors?

While a given reporter's news judgments may be highly professional, in most cases, in a monopoly newspaper market, the public has no access to alternative reports of controversial local stories. Moreover, only one editorial judgment is made as to whether or not an item is newsworthy and deserves to be reported at all. This is a serious enough problem in the public's perception of the facts of life in the surrounding world; it becomes even more serious in the realm of opinion—criticism of the arts and cultural events and editorial comment on local affairs.

Warren G. Harding, when editor of the Marion, Ohio, *Star*:

> Boost, don't knock!

Few daily newspapers in the United States today intrude a publisher's personal philosophy into the news columns in the manner of the outrageous Manchester, N.H., *Union-Leader*. Still, publishers, like other media proprietors or managers, experience no difficulty in infusing their outlook into the editorial product, since journalists drift quickly into an articulation of management's views and may come to adopt them as their own.[89]

The loss of the second newspaper in a city inevitably leaves the survivor stronger and sometimes better as well as more profitable. The *Philadelphia Inquirer* has a larger editorial staff now than both it *and* the *Bulletin* had when the *Bulletin* was still alive. In 1980, the *Cleveland Plain Dealer* ran 850 news items each week, the *Press* 970. In 1983, after the *Press* folded, the *Plain Dealer* was running 1,073 items.[90] The *Raleigh News* and *Observer* added five pages of news after the evening *Times* was folded. But these expansions hardly compensate for the losses of news space in the vanished papers.

When its competitor goes down, a surviving paper, almost inevitably, loses its edge. American newspapers generally lack the sharp political orientation that traditionally has characterized the European press. A paper that is conscious of its role as the voice of the entire community is necessarily more cautious about the possibility of giving offense and is likely to be politically less outspoken than one that speaks to and for a segment of the public. The same process applies in the domain of cultural commentary.

In-depth coverage of national and international news is accessible from ever fewer sources through the press. At the start of the 1990s, three out of five dailies carried the Associated Press wire, and a declining number subscribed to the United Press International, which had undergone a series of reorganizations and retrenchments. Only two dailies in five carried a supplemental wire service, though this proportion had tripled between 1960 and 1985.[91]

The attrition of newspaper competition reduces the public's access to information of all sorts that is never carried in broadcast media because of time limitations. (The text of a half-hour newscast would fill about five columns of a newspaper page). Perhaps even more significantly, it reduces the public's exposure to considered editorial reflection on the issues of the day. Broadcast stations rarely editorialize, and when they do, their views are expressed briefly and in fleeting form. Sunday morning panel discussions on the networks may be of high quality, but they attract small audiences. This makes it all the more critical that newspaper editorialists continue to struggle to enunciate thoughtful opinions on the difficult questions of public policy. While only one reader in four reads the typical editorial (or the typical news item, for that matter), editorials can enter the general stream of public discourse in a way that no other medium manages to do, and their reasoned character makes them a force with which public officials must contend, and whose words and thoughts they are often inclined to adopt as their own.

Ideas, I argued earlier, are not to be judged by the number of people who hold them, nor is the validity of knowledge to be gauged by the number who choose to partake of it. Fortunately, there is ample room on the American media spectrum for the expression of every conceivable kind of idea and, in fact, for the display of incongruent or conflicting ideas within the bounds of the same media vehicle. Unpopular ideas and recondite knowledge are disseminated through innumerable book and magazine publishing houses, through public broadcasting and cable. There is a great difference, however, between the mere existence of such channels and easy public access to them.

Deviant opinions and unwelcome facts are not equally accessible to the public at large, because so many of them are disseminated only through media of obscure reputation and minor reach: little magazines, countercultural weeklies, public access cable channels that almost nobody watches. Only rarely does a television news report or documentary arouse a full-scale rebuttal, in the style of Senator Joe McCarthy's pathetic riposte to Edward R. Murrow's crushing expose.

Similarly, letters to the editor of a newspaper or magazine rarely carry the length or weight required to offset the original reporting to which they respond. Newspapers and magazines, quite properly, decide what letters to print. The idea of a "right of access" to the press has been proposed,[92] and supported by the American Civil Liberties Union. But this suggestion would pose a serious threat to newspaper economics, be impossible to enforce in practice, and conflict with publishers' First Amendment rights to print what they want. The proposal has never lifted off the ground. Letters and rejoinders are vital for a free press, but are not a substitute for a healthy variety of media voices. We saw earlier that the decline of newspaper competition is, in large part, the advertisers' fault. It is bad news.

Much of this chapter has concerned television news at the national level, but the news that concerns most people most closely is the news that is closest to home, for which newspapers are the primary source. If newspapers are less effective and important than they once were, it is not so much because television news has taken away their readers as because television has taken more of the advertising dollar.

The success of Ted Turner's Cable News Network, with its around-the-clock worldwide services, has deepened the public's reliance on broadcast news. C-Span, with its live coverage of public hearings, meetings, and congressional deliberations, has provided extraordinary access to the routine operations of government as well as to news in the making. Television news would not be the mighty force it is if it were not staffed by professionals of great ability and integrity. The disintegration of journalistic standards that I have described in this chapter results from management's unrelenting preoccupation with the audience ratings on which advertising revenue depends. In the process, the reality of news-reporting has faded into the make-believe world of entertainment.

8

Believing in the Make-Believe

The mind which has feasted on a luxurious diet of fiction has small taste for the insipidity of truth.   SAMUEL JOHNSON

The commercial culture we absorb in such massive doses envelops us in make-believe and distracts us from the realities of current history that urgently demand our attention. The world we know and cope with directly faces more and more intrusions from the wider world that media open to us. This secondary experience strengthens our collective chances for survival if it equips us to deal more intelligently with disquieting information. The chances are weakened if the media divert us from the truth or leave us incapable of discerning it. They often do both, churning forth an incessant jumble of fiction and fact, whose elements are hard to sort out.

We saw in the last chapter that television journalism is increasingly tempted to adopt fictional devices. This chapter extends the discussion of how the real is often confused with the imaginary. It seeks the origins of the confusion in the literary distinction between narrative and drama, and suggests that photography and its offspring, film and video, lend themselves to distortion and ambiguity because they appear so patently to extend the audience's own senses directly. Key points:

- Tenuous boundaries separate fact and fiction. What distinguishes honest reporting, in journalism or in writing history, is the quest for truth rather than the claim to have found it.
- Fantasy experience differs from that of real life, and dramatic audiovisual fiction differs from written narrative.
- Fiction's power derives from its capacity to convince its audience that it resembles reality.
- Reading requires more exercise of the imagination than audiovisual fiction, which occupies ever more time.
- Photography, in both still and motion picture forms, creates illusions that are not routinely recognized as such.

Fictions and Facts

News media propagate collective illusions, which differ from the fantasies in which individuals indulge. By second nature we accept the selfish interests and beliefs of those groups with which we identify. People live zealously, or through mere habit, by ideologies that set blinders for their attention, their information priorities, and their judgments of what is true and what is not. Monstrous misperceptions of reality give rise to even more monstrous acts, and monstrous acts are justified by reconstructions of reality.

George Orwell's hero, Winston, is kept busy rewriting the *Times*' original reports of Big Brother's speeches, so that his inaccurate predictions are revised to jibe with what actually happened.

> As soon as all the corrections which happened to be necessary in any particular number of The Times had been assembled and collated, that number would be reprinted, the original copy destroyed, and the corrected copy placed in the files in its stead. This process of continuous alteration was applied not only to newspapers, but to books, periodicals, pamphlets, posters, leaflets, films, sound-tracks, cartoons, photographs—to every kind of literature or documentation which might conceivably hold any political or ideological significance. Day by day and almost minute by minute the past was brought up to date. . . . All history was a palimpsest, scraped clean and reinscribed exactly as often as was necessary. In no case, would it have been possible, once the deed was done, to prove that any falsification had taken place.[1]

1984 came and went, but in 1989, a few weeks after the events in Beijing's Tienanmen Square, a young Chinese woman who had brought food to the student demonstrators and had witnessed the subsequent massacre, denied, to an American reporter who had also been there, that anything had happened.[2] Such fulfillment of Orwellian prophecies represents only one of the many forms of distortion that enter into our perception of the world around us. Most human beings are content to organize their lives around religious myths, secure in the faith that, while legend may not conform to historical fact, it embodies deeper truths about life's meaning. Willingness to reject the usual criteria of what is literally true characterizes new secular religions as well as traditional ones. "If you don't have the facts, make them up," was the operating philosophy of Communist activists during the 1930s.

Heinrich Heine's *Lorelei* was attributed by the Nazis to an "anonymous" author. History has long been invented, with forged documents like *The Protocols of the Elders of Zion,* false news reports like those routinely emitted by Goebbels' propaganda ministry, and in recent times, paranoid burrowing in archives to "disprove" the Nazi murder of the Jews.[3]

It is one thing to revise an accepted interpretation of facts, and another matter to deny facts altogether or to invent them in the service of a new interpretation. Trofim Lysenko falsified laboratory results in support of the Marxist-Leninist doctrine of dialectical materialism, as interpreted by Josef Stalin. Was this violence to biological truth qualitatively different from the distortion of the historical record through the "confessions" extorted by torture in the Moscow trials? It was not, but the latter kind of falsification is harder to prove, because history is based on human testimony, which is notoriously subject both to innocent error and to willful deceptions.

In the interest of truth, Western scholarship and journalism follow the tradition of pursuing evidence, periodically rearranging and reassessing it as new documents are uncovered. A distorted version of the facts, proclaimed by a high public official, receives news coverage because of the official's position, while an accurate depiction by some lesser figure will get no coverage at all. If there are many separate channels for news, there is also far more likelihood that truth will out while the issue still matters. But why should the truth matter when fantasy is so much more pleasant and so much more readily accessible?

Reconstructing Reality

What differentiates fantasy from the real? Consider the relationship between our direct sensory experience and two other realms: those of stored learning and of the imagination. We see, hear, and feel what is within range of our eyes, ears, and fingers, and anything beyond that range (including the color and shape of the chair in which you are now sitting) has to be supplied out of memory. We pay attention—that is, we organize our immediate sensations into meaningful patterns—by applying memory to interpret what we see, hear, and touch. In our imaginations, we combine memories in ways that have not occurred specifically in real life. The exercise of artistic imagination does this in ways that are compelling and absorbing, that can recreate that experience for others.

There is no clearly defined boundary point where the straightforward depiction of reality moves into the realm of the imaginary. Ancient Roman sculptors modified and idealized the features of emperors and statesmen when they rendered them in stone or bronze. Early Renaissance painters did the equivalent when they began painting members of the Holy Family after real-life models rather than as stylized representations in the Byzantine fashion. Every painter of actual human faces and figures, or of buildings and of landscapes, has had to subordinate the extraneous elements of the subject matter to fit the formal requirements of design and color balance, and to capture truth that would be obscured by a literal transcription of reality.

In literature, the transition from memoir to novel is more a matter of degree rather than of sharp discontinuity either in intent or in execution. The novel emerged when the technology of transportation and communication vastly increased the amount of available information about actual events and conditions in places remote from the reader's direct observation. Cervantes, in describing Don Quixote's obsession with the romances of Amadis of Gaul, avowed the importance of distinguishing the real world from the fantasy realm. Novelists seek essential truths of human experience, often based on their own lives and observations, sometimes (as in the case of Emile Zola) setting out with explicit journalistic or sociological aims, but always coating the facts with a veneer of dissimulation.

Hans Castorp, Stephen Daedalus, and the narrator of *A la Recherche du Temps Perdu* may be nothing but fictional disguises for their creators' autobiographical reflections, but we know better than to regard these fictional heroes as real persons whose real activities are being recounted. Not even the most thinly disguised *roman à clef*, in spite of its prefatory admonition that the characters bear no intentional resemblance to anyone living or dead, can be taken as an accurate, objective description of the doings of real characters, living or dead. Fiction can penetrate to the heart of human contacts and conflicts better than memoirs, history, or journalism (all of which may be written at varying levels of candor, completeness, and competence), but fiction's technique and intentions are different.

If descriptions of the world and its creatures—in depth and in context—must be subjective, how can the audience penetrate to the truth of experience that it cannot test directly through its own senses? The answer is in part determined by the medium through which this experience is conveyed.

All telecommunications force leaps of the imagination. Unlike the telegraph, the telephone did more than convey a message; through its vocal cues it facilitated, with great immediacy, the imagining of the person at the other end of the wire. With radio, this process is applied to the exercise of fictional imagination. In motion pictures and television, the gap that must be covered by the imagination is reduced to what an uninstructed person might consider to be the vanishing point. To a small child, the patterns of light and dark on the television screen are real people, somehow miraculously reduced in size and placed within the box. In a media-saturated existence, even adults may find it hard to distinguish what is real from what is not.

Words Spoken and Written

Fiction in dramatic form dominates commercial culture. What explains its hold upon our psyches and our time? The answer must be that it tells us important things about ourselves. All creatures communicate, if only to sense each other's presence as objects of food, sex, or danger. Only humans tell stories. Unlike birdsong or the screeching of monkeys, storytelling transcends the boundaries of immediate experience. Stories are both real and unreal; they must be rooted in what we know for ourselves, but they use that knowledge to penetrate into mysteries that can only be imagined.

Fiction once entered most people's lives by word of mouth, as legend. Stories were told by the hearth of an evening, in the marketplace by a professional storyteller, in a house of worship by a priest or shaman, to children by elders at bedtime. Listeners by the fireside saw legendary figures in the dancing flames; the story in the telling was invested with a reality that stemmed more from its vivid stimulus to the imagination than from the literal reenactment of mythic roles.[4]

Fiction holds our attention because it permits the imagination to reorganize our own lives and relationships, because it expresses and releases the emotions that we feel toward those significant other persons whose contacts make us human. Fiction confronts us with the painfully tender delights of uncertainty, with the recognition that the course of every life is full of branching points from which there is no return. And fiction, because it transports us from the constraints of external reality to the boundless inner reality of our fantasies, allows us to evade the pressures of the here and now; it entertains us. The tales that hold our interest have protagonists whose traits are extraordinary, or who are placed in extraordinary situations, or who are undergoing experiences that have extraordinary importance because of the way they illuminate enduring human urges, emotions, or relationships.

For the child who has only recently discovered and mastered language, words are a way of transcending the bounds of the visual universe within which his movements are confined. The world of make-believe is one that the child can control, a world reorganized and simplified and orderly, in which his own presence is central to the action. The fascination of the story lies not in its outcome, which is well-known, but in the reconstruction of the imagined details from the bare bones of the plot. While the familiar words can be repeated over and over, the child cannot be bored as long as they keep stirring up fresh contemplations of the nuances, fresh evocations of meaning and possibility. (The picture storybook may actually hinder this process. "Illustrations direct the child's imagination away from how he, on his own, would experience the story," writes the child psychologist Bruno Bettelheim.[5])

A child learns to differentiate reality from appearances, her own face from the face she sees in the mirror. So she learns to sort out the stories that reflect the real world from those that represent the imaginary.[6] Just as children learn to distinguish between the truths that parents tell them and the fairy tales they also tell, so they learn to distinguish between the media representations of reality and those that are fictional. We reluctantly surrender our belief in the reality of Santa Claus and Mickey Mouse; most Americans retain their belief in an anthropomorphic God and in the Devil. Children by the age of six know that a baseball game on television is the real thing and that a soap opera is just a play. Advertisements are in a more ambiguous domain; they speak of real things, but the motivations behind them are self-interested and therefore suspect.

A child can interrupt a bedtime story, told or read, to have a choice episode repeated: "Tell me again how . . ." As adult readers, we do not ordinarily go back to reread the parts of a story that stir us, but we can slow down or even stop momentarily and let them settle into our reveries.

Drama is always fictional, and always embedded in the dimension of real time. Written narrative may or may not be fictional. It can be vastly entertaining when it reports what is real—as journalists, historians, and other social scientists try to do. Factual journalistic accounts of what has actually happened come under the heading of stories, if they have identifiable human protagonists, and involve a series of events in which an ambiguity, problem, or conflict is presented and ultimately worked out. Fictional narratives always adhere to certain conventions; the characters and the setting must be introduced, relationships must be described, obstacles must arise out of the existing equilibrium, and some resolution must be found.

Accepting the fantasies of one's group enhances the ego, since it reassures the individual that we do not stand alone. The fantasies we create for ourselves are ego expressions in a direct sense, insofar as they permit us to reorganize what we know of reality into an imaginary form that is more satisfying to our needs. The projection of oneself or of one's own surrogates into this reassemblage of experience is what gives personal fantasy its power. It is the secret of emotional involvement, which makes the difference between mass media communication that is ignored and communication that is compelling.

We are more strongly affected by the situations we live through than by those we know at second-hand, and more by those that are real—or perceived as real—than by those we understand to be imaginary. The interest aroused in us by fiction takes on an altogether different coloration when we mistakenly accept it as fact and may be impelled to act upon it as such. Walt Whitman:

> The true use for the imaginative faculty of modern times is to give ultimate vivification to facts, to science, and to common lives, endowing them with glows and glories and final illustriousness which belongs to every real thing, and to real things only.

We are inclined to accept the essential reality of what we know to be fictive if it arouses chords from our personal experience. When spectators identify with imaginary characters and situations, their mood of diffuse excitement is displayed emotionally in their subsequent behavior. Television viewers who identify with a character are more affected emotionally by a program than those who do not, whether they believe the depicted situation is real or fictitious.[7]

While journalistic accounts of real-life happenings can arouse us, they often do so precisely because the stories are unfinished and we are left hanging on the outcome. At other times, as in most fiction, the tale is brought to a conclusion, with all the loose ends tied. Since most news stories deal with matters that are remote or comparatively unimportant, we tend to be disengaged from them. But fictional drama is designed expressly to maximize an emotional commitment. To paraphrase Aristotle's classic description in the *Poetics*, we feel better after our feelings have been brought to a state of tension and then released by a resolution of the problem that has been set before us.

The distinction between narration and drama developed only when words were written down. It was not the same as the distinction between the straightforward recording of prose and the recitation of poetry, with its metric cadences and multiple layers of meaning. Both narrative and drama have their common roots in epic poetry, declamations in which the bards repeated the words of gods and heroes and assumed the appropriate persona as the saga unfolded.

The flowering of written fiction did not come at the expense of drama declaimed in the theater. Evidently these two different channels of creative expression serve different functions for their audiences, even though they deal with the same human connections, conflicts, and passions. The traditional unities of time and place that set limits on the playwright's freedom and the practical limitations of time make most plays shorter than most novels. Until the invention of the motion picture, dramatists operated under a variety of practical restrictions—in the number of characters, the number and frequency of scene changes, and in the audience's expectation of an unambiguous conclusion.

The critical difference between print fiction and theatrical fiction is that the reader is in control. We accept textual word-images as a selective or distorted refraction of reality. By adjusting the reading pace, the imagination operates without hindrance. Playgoers can walk out of the theater, just as they can set down an unsatisfying book, but the effort is considerably greater (except when film drama is translated into home video form, where remote controls and fast-forwarding make it easy to extricate oneself). In drama, unlike fiction written to be read, the tangible presence of actors on a stage clearly differentiates the real from the unreal.

The theater director Tyrone Guthrie writes,

> Even the most realistic productions of the most realistic plays are not fully realistic . . . [but] a play can be so absorbing that you are temporarily quite lost to reality. . . . Is this illusion? I think not. Has it not often been your experience, when reading a book to be thus rapt? But does it therefore follow that you are apt to mistake figment for reality? Does the rapt beholder of Leonardo's 'Virgin of the Rocks' think that he is really in the presence of those holy beings, that he is really in that golden and brown landscape?[8]

No spectator has ever permanently confused the stage Hamlet with the original Prince (though some, transfixed, have been known to mount the stage to intercept an act of villainy in progress). In the theater, our interest in the substance is inseparable from the pleasure we take in the presentation.

Technique of performance arouses the empathy that makes a dramatic experience memorable. A great play may be produced with stunning impact on a bare stage, so that our imaginations supply scenery and costumes. But a play's ability to arouse suspense or even deeper emotion, to illuminate, exalt, or divert, always depends on the ability of the director and actors to interpret the author's words to good effect.

This mediation is absent in narrative fiction, where we ourselves must supply the interpretation. This requires a cognitive, thinking process, rather than the apperceptive, holistic acquisition of meaning that occurs both in real life and in dramatic experience. (To put this in psychophysiological terms, reading activity is centered in the brain's left hemisphere, the dramatic experience, in the right.) The feelings engendered by compelling drama may have such great power that we are impelled to convey them to others after the spectacle. The dramatic experience is a collective one; it is usually shared and social. We vent our responses by talking about them (a left-brain activity), and we can (in our right hemispheres) individually repossess the images that impressed us. All this happens after the event.

In reading fiction, however, the process is much more complex, because the (left-brain) activity that makes sense of printed symbols triggers imaginative responses (in the right brain), and it is precisely these that force us to interrupt or slow down our reading pace. Reading is not inherently a more absorbing activity than being present at a dramatic presentation. However it entails the simultaneous use of different centers in our brains, and is thus inherently more demanding of us. Readers of a novel or short story must use their fantasies to fill in all the background details the author leaves in obscurity, to endow the characters with their own projections, to explain the missing elements of the plot. Viewers of film or television are left little room for maneuver; what you see is what you get.

Imagination works differently when we *read* fiction than when it is recited to us or *enacted* before our eyes. The vastly increased part of *dramatic* fiction in our lives, through film and video, and the corresponding decline of *narrative* fiction in printed form, means that *less* rather than more of our time is dedicated to the exercise of imagination.

History as Fiction

"What is truth?" asked jesting Pilate. The question keeps being asked, both with irony and bewilderment. Poetic fiction penetrates to essential truths, while an array of indisputable facts may be totally irrelevant to reality. Christopher Marlowe, in "Doctor Faustus", dealt in legend; Shakespeare, in "Richard III", transformed historical reality into legend. We accept both works as evocations of the human adventure, without reflecting on their factual basis.

For the Greeks, history was the account of specific and nonrecurring events; it registered their timing and sequence, but in a manner quite different from the recording of successive rulers and dynasties, as practiced by the Mesopotamians and the Egyptians. Greek history related aspects of the human experience from which future generations could learn useful lessons. Its authenticity was expressed in its avoidance of the poetic diction that designated the *Odyssey* and *Iliad* as works in which the recollection of actual happenings had been greatly modified by the imagination. History evolved out of a tradition of oral storytelling in which the kernel of accurate reporting about actual events was embedded in a surrounding of fantasies that served as metaphors for deeper truths or for fears or unfulfilled wishes.

By contrast, poetic drama was the appropriate vehicle for the presentation of great themes about perennial human relationships. Aristotle contrasted the historian with the poet who is concerned not with specifics but with the "universal event". The classicist Eric Havelock writes that a

> metaphor applied by Plato to the psychological situation of the poet and the audience is that of the dream from which both of them, bewitched by the images which pass before them, like sleepwalkers have to be awakened before they can become aware of "what is."[9]

Myth, a form of fiction, evokes the recurrent themes of human development and confrontation with natural forces. Myths provide explanations for the phenomena in life and nature that we do not fully understand; they provide insights, or at least the illusion of having insights, into human behavior that would otherwise appear to be without meaning or motivation. The distinction between history and myth is difficult to draw in the stories passed down to us from ancient times; much historical scholarship has been dedicated to untangling the buried debris of real events from the encrustations added by court poets or religious disciples.

The tales of medieval travelers presented curious mixtures of genuine ethnological reportage and fantasies of men with heads growing out of their stomachs. It is not clear that the public for these voyagers' stories distinguished, or even sought to distinguish, between the factual and fictional aspects of what they heard or read. (Even today, a substantial part of the American public still appears unable to make such distinctions. Seven percent think that Elvis Presley might still be alive,[10] and substantial numbers are ready to accept the reality of visitors from outer space.)

Fiction, and especially drama, concentrates on the extraordinary. It distorts reality by emphasizing the dramatic and the bizarre. Writing history has changed from an emphasis on events to trends, from the singular and the heroic to the general and mundane. The historiographer Hayden White argues that historians and writers of fiction have similar aims and use similar forms and techniques of discourse. Reacting to the myths stirred up by the French Revolution, he says, early-nineteenth-century historians began

> to identify truth with fact and to regard fiction as the opposite of truth. . . . They were captives of the illusion that one could write history without employing any fictional techniques whatsoever. . . . They did not realize that the facts do not speak for themselves, but that the historian speaks for them, speaks on their behalf, and fashions the fragments of the past into a whole whose integrity is—in its representation—a purely discursive one.[11]

Writing fiction and writing history are both creative reorganizations of experience. In either case, the author seeks to satisfy the need for engagement, to find the connection that makes the readers feel that the story is relevant to their own lives.

To say that history and fiction obey common rules of narrative discourse is to bypass the critical distinction between them, which is the professional historian's need to remain restricted to the actual evidence before applying imagination, interpretive skill, and rhetorical flourishes. Novelists are free to make up facts; historians should not, nor should they change the facts to improve the story. This last point becomes particularly noteworthy at a time when history is being reinterpreted and historical icons (like Christopher Columbus) are shattered to fit the needs of transient political agendas.

However valuable it may be to place new perspectives on the historical record, there is no way to substitute the everyday routine of common people for the landmark events that have traditionally made up that record. Every member of the human race had unique experiences on the day that Neil Armstrong landed on the moon, but it was the moon landing that is history, not the unsung exploits of the rest of us.

All media view the world from the narrow and narcissistic perspective of parochial interests. For Luxemburgers or Trinidadians, Luxemburg or Trinidad are the centers of the universe and are accorded an importance in their news media that far outweighs momentous events in remote places. Americans rock and roll while thousands starve or are slaughtered in the Sudan. Both occurrences—dance and destruction—represent reality. Does this mean that one cannot be described except with reference to the other? Reality is always segmented, so that the same events take on different dimensions and meaning from different perspectives. In fiction, novels like *Rashomon* or Willkie Collins's *The Moonstone* use the device of telling the same story from the vantage points of different characters, like the conflicting testimony of opposing witnesses in a lawsuit. Journalism, for good and sufficient practical reasons, generally aims to give a single observer's synthesis of what many observers might see. This kind of abstract summary can be made more easily in print than with the visual images that selectively illuminate the infinite aspects of a single day, hour, or moment.

Hundreds—even millions—of realities sum up what the world is all about at any given moment. Who can describe them all? By the doctrine of historical relativism, one person's account of an event is inherently no more credible than another's and, in 1994, the official Libyan or North Korean view of the international scene has the same degree of informedness and integrity as that of the Canadians or the Swiss.

Current debates over these matters have philosophical roots that go back to Plato, but our principal concern must focus on the question of objectivity, as expressed both in science and in journalism. Karl Marx taught that individuals cannot divest themselves of their own social class origins, nor of the prevailing habits of mind imposed by a class-dominated social order. If that is so, claims to objectivity are pretentious, since reports of any kind must always be put into perspective, and the critical question is, whose perspective will prevail. This point of view assumes that all witnesses or reporters have equally honorable and valid motivations.

The writer of fiction is preoccupied with the subjective inner reality in the minds of the protagonists. The historian and the journalist set out with the objective of reflecting external reality. Thucydides, in his first book on the Peloponnesian War, writes:

> I have made it a principle not to write down the first story that came my way, and not even to be guided by my own general impressions; either I was present myself at the events which I have described or else heard of them from eye-witnesses whose reports I have checked with as much thoroughness as possible.[12]

This still seems like a useful precept, though it is increasingly ignored.

Journalism and Literature

Journalists share the difficulty of historians in distinguishing their personal visions from the demonstrable facts they report. Historically, they started out as men of letters. Their accounts of the life around them were expressions of artistic impulses — to communicate some of the essence of their time. What they themselves observed was inseparable from their commentary on events, personalities and customs — the very stuff of literature. In setting forth their accounts and their opinions, they self-consciously adopted the best literary style of their era, for they were writing for friends and intellectual equals. The journals of Boswell, Addison, and Steele can still be read with pleasure as part of the most distinguished English writing of the eighteenth century. Oliver Goldsmith the journalist is at one with Oliver Goldsmith the novelist, applying the same talent to write fact and fiction.

A handful of newspaper columnists in the contemporary United States, and many in Europe and Latin America, still carry on the tradition of urbane, literate personal journalism, imbued with the writer's biases and private enthusiasms. The crossover from news-reporting to creative writing is a familiar landmark on the career paths of many well-known American writers. Ben Hecht:

> It was as natural for a police reporter to start writing a novel or a play as it was for an ant to climb a grass blade.[13]

Moving from reporting to writing fiction was a step up the social scale. Archibald MacLeish (himself both an editor of *Fortune* and a poet) said of Ernest Hemingway at the *Toronto Star*, "So he wasn't a writer yet. He was a journalist." But the American press, which in its time employed Karl Marx, Walt Whitman, Mark Twain, Theodore

Dreiser, Jack London, Hemingway, and Tom Wolfe, has been generally averse to the encouragement or display of literary talent. In part this attitude reflects the ascendancy of the doctrine of objectivity, with its goal of eliminating bias and merely personal interpretation of "the facts." This principle became central to the notion of journalistic professionalism in the nineteenth century, as American newspapers moved away from advocacy.

With the rise of "New Journalism" in the 1960s, reporters freed themselves from the long-standing convention that they should write only about what they knew had happened, or at least about what they had been told. Magazine articles have depicted composite or imaginary characters as though they were real. Clay Felker, then editor of *New York*, said he edited out an acknowledgment to this effect in one publicized instance because "it got in the way of the flow." Truman Capote described his 1966 book, *In Cold Blood*, as a "nonfiction novel," which blended "the art of the novelist together with the technique of journalism, fiction with the added knowledge that it was true." Capote spent three years in his research for the book, but he reconstructed dialogue that the people he interviewed could not have heard and described thoughts and emotions that were never expressed. A number of popular books since then have used similar methods of reporting undocumented conversations or the private thinking of individuals with whom the authors never spoke.

Separating conjecture and opinion from dispassionate reporting is still dismissed by some critics as a "ritual" that exists within a social context in which terms like "truth" are vague and arguable. As in Western scholarship, objectivity in journalism is indeed a state of mind. Its essence is the *quest* for dispassionate truth, not the *claim* to truth. If its accounts are subject to amendment, amplification, adumbration, and retraction, it is because the quest is essential, while the record itself is in constant transformation.

All reporters endow events with their own distinctive perspectives and have it within their power to interpret them so as to change the very reality reported. Investigative reporting aside, the claim to be disengaged from the subject matter is no more than a pretense. Journalists have made as well as reported news, from Stanley's expedition to find Livingstone to Herbert Matthews's foray into the Sierra Maestra to interview Fidel Castro. Emile Zola, in the Dreyfus case, exemplified the writer who takes on a great cause and influences the events of his time. Norman Mailer, political activist courting arrest *On The Steps of the Pentagon*, became Norman Mailer, journalist-novelist transcribing his personal experiences into reportage. Jean-Paul Sartre, polemicist and "judge" at the "Vietnam War Crimes Trial," and Ilya Ehrenburg, anti-Nazi propagandist, are in the tradition of the writer *engagé*. Emulating Gabriele d'Annunzio, conqueror of Fiume, Benito Mussolini the journalist became Mussolini the ideologist, the politician, the Fascist dictator.

Talented journalists, no less than authors of fiction, summon their passions to infuse vitality into their descriptions of events. The discouragement of literary pretensions by contemporary American newspaper editors in part reflects the spiraling cost of newsprint and the prevailing editorial belief that excess verbiage should be pruned to make the most of a limited amount of editorial space. More recently, too, it arises from the judgment that busy readers are impatient with lengthy articles and that they have been conditioned by broadcasting to take their news in brief, pelletized form.

The excess adjectives and adverbs that the careful editor deplores may be precisely those that give color and vitality to an account, that make it memorable, that raise it from the level of routine reportage. The essence of literary art is in the overtones and undertones of additional meanings that can be conveyed by particular selections and arrangements of words. Staunching the flow of those words can constrict the vision to which the writer seeks to give form.

Images captured in writing must be attended to in order to make their impact. For this reason, great broadcast journalism, in its rare occurrences, is apt to be a derivative of writing (as in Edward R. Murrow's news reports or Eric Sevareid's commentaries, which they carefully scripted before they delivered them). And so the media format shapes the message.

Pictures Do Not Lie?

Visual imagery, presented directly rather than through verbal evocation, now dominates both our fantasies and our understanding of the reality beyond our immediate ken. Photographs are always seen in context. Whether published or exhibited in a gallery, they are usually accompanied by text or titles that tell us how they are to be interpreted. The early silent motion picture could not have served as a dramatic vehicle without the captions that periodically appeared to frame the imagery.

Printed photojournalism has a memorability and a psychological impact that video journalism achieves only in rare moments. Many of the still photographs commissioned and published in the heyday of *Life* and *Look* were works of art. They combined extraordinary sensibility, technical skill, and the instinct or accident of being present at the scene at the right moment. These photographs (a prototype might be Robert Capa's Spanish Loyalist militiaman caught at the moment of being shot) derived their power from their ability to arrest the reader, to generate reflection, to stimulate empathy. They create a kind of involvement that is difficult to achieve with an ongoing pictorial narrative, complete with voiceover, when no prior selection has been made of the particular frame that captures the quintessential meaning of what is being shown.

The heroic tradition of photojournalism continues—at the Associated Press, individual newspapers, and a handful of magazines and photo services—but it is limited by the constriction or demise of the great magazines that supported it in its prime, that provided editorial direction, logistical support, financing, and encouragement. Issues of *Life* and *Look* were each perused by tens of millions of people; their striking images thus achieved the massive dissemination that we now associate with an extraordinary television event. Without them, our perception of the world is different today, notwithstanding the ubiquitous presence of moving images on the television screen.

Memorable scenes have been recorded by television: the shooting of President John Kennedy's assassin, Lee Harvey Oswald, the execution of a captured Vietcong lieutenant during the Tet offensive, the little naked girl fleeing a napalm attack on a Vietnamese road, the crowds chanting "Death to America" outside the U.S. Embassy in Teheran and cheering freedom atop the Berlin Wall, the police beating of Rodney

King, which precipitated the Los Angeles riots of 1992. These images are remembered not just because they are striking in themselves but because they have been shown so often.

Photography in all its forms, including video and motion pictures, has expanded the boundaries of ambivalence between technical manipulation and our instinct that seeing is believing. Throughout history (at least until photography stimulated the birth of impressionism, which in turn led the way for post-impressionist abstraction), painting has combined elements of realism and of the imagination. Painters have invested their canvases with allegory, symbolism, and displays of fantasy and fancy, while at the same time, they depicted human beings, animals and landscapes or other settings that conformed to the literal representation of the real world. An intensely realistic style of painting was already the norm before the invention of photography, suggesting to some historians that the invention itself was no more than a necessary response to the historical demands of the moment. But no one could have mistaken *trompe l'oeil* for the real thing. And the earliest of photographs were themselves soft, fuzzy, static, and vaguely dreamlike. The confusion remains, up to the trick photography of the computer age.

In the 1930s, the tabloid *New York Graphic*, notable for its use of green paper and for publishing the Buck Rogers comic strip, attracted attention, and some controversy, for its use of composite photographs. In these, lurid crimes were vividly reenacted with the use of paid models, on whose torsos the heads of the real *dramatis personae* were superimposed. The faces of unpersons like Leon Trotsky were long absent from the "historical" images of the October Revolution in Soviet museums. New technology has brought marvelous new possibilities to perfect such crude photographic retouching techniques. The magazine *Spy* used a cover photograph that seamlessly placed the head of Hillary Rodham Clinton atop the scantily clad body of a model in the leather trappings of a dominatrix, complete with whip.[14]

While respectable newspapers and news organizations forbid altering news pictures, advertising photographs are routinely retouched. Advertising is a significant element among the innumerable ambiguous mass communications that blur the line between fiction and reality. Advertising is real, because it deals with the most humble appurtenances of everyday life, and yet it is unreal, as we saw in Chapter 3, because of the idealized characteristics of the people shown using the products, the artificiality of the settings, and the deliberately created fantasies—the artifice that would not be allowed in photojournalism.

Advertising art now uses digitized photographs, broken down into tiny units called pixels, which can be manipulated on the computer to produce distortions of astonishing realism. Computer graphics, employing digital processing and electronic palettes like the Paint Box, can manipulate moving as well as still images to recreate the visual evidence of history. George Wedding, director of photography, *Sacramento Bee*:

> We turn the pages and in one photo spread, we ask the reader to accept the picture as real, as accurate, and in the next spread we ask them to recognize digitally enhanced photos. Our readers are flooded with spectacular images, and we're asking them to make distinctions they may not be able to make.[15]

At first glance, there appears to be something shocking about the reconstruction of a still photograph; it is tampering with "reality." No such sense of shock is evoked by the editing of movies. Computer-generated wizardry in film animation—a technique first developed in making TV commercials—has made it possible to have live actors interact with cartoons and puppets, even with the recreated dinosaurs of "Jurassic Park."

Computerized graphic techniques permit photoengravers to produce a print of a Giotto fresco that is faithful to its original fourteenth-century colors rather than to its present weathered appearance. Can such an application of technology be condemned out of hand? When the libraries of old black and white films were ransacked for television, the computerized addition of color tints was intended to ease the shock for an audience accustomed to a full-color video world. The film industry and its buffs emitted loud protests against the indignity of "colorization," but the technique could not be stopped.

While the performance of a play represents a continuous expression of effort by its cast, audiences have long been accustomed to the idea that a motion picture represents an assemblage of numerous rehearsed attempts to find perfection. By repeating a scene, the director can select among interpretive nuances and overcome the ineptitude of stars who may be handsome but untalented. The same type of manipulation has been commonplace in recorded music since the invention of magnetic tape.[16] Audio recordings represent selected pastiches of repeated renditions. In music videos, dancers gyrate and mouth the words sung on someone else's audio recording. Though this practice has aroused some indignation, it has a long line of antecedents in Hollywood.

If it is acceptable for a singer to prerecord a number and then lip-synch it for a motion picture, why is it impermissible to use separate performers—a singer and an actor—to achieve an even better effect, with appropriate screen credits at the end of the film? Is there anything less moral about this illusion than about any other contrived illusions, in film or on the stage?

The world of illusion requires artful dissimulators, but audiences must participate in the artifice by a "willing suspension of disbelief," as William Wordsworth put it.[17] Photographic illusion depends on the audience's unconscious acceptance of conventions imposed by technology. Sound film altered the relationship of the spectator to the action because it eliminated the need for pantomime and therefore changed both acting style and camera technique. (Closeups were less important when it was no longer necessary to see the character mouthing the words.) Sound introduced psychological subtlety into the depiction of character and stepped up the pace of films. Sound made it more difficult to daydream on other subjects while watching the screen—or indeed to slumber altogether.

But with all the great changes in cinematographic style over the course of the twentieth century, there is no indication that any change took place in the spell that films cast over their spectators. Watching film or television, the audience can hardly be unconscious of the medium through which an original reality is being brought to its presence. It is aware of the processes of filming or recording, of projection and electronic transmission. Viewers may understand rather well how direction, editing, makeup, and special effects create illusions and drama. But even for sophisticated adults, film and video shot in natural settings create an illusion of reality as the stage never could.

Film eliminates the barriers of the imagination that separate the audience from the live action on the stage. The boundaries disappear because the screen is an optical frame rather than a purely psychological one like that separating live actors from the audience. Because the direct evidence of our eyes and ears is so compelling, the illusion of reality can be maintained whether we are seeing documentary depictions of the world as it is or the enactments of fantasy. But film also interposes new barriers because it communicates indirectly and requires the audience to fill in details.

Public access channels on cable television and the growing prevalence of home video cameras also blur the difference between the intimate and the remote, giving in the first instance an illusion of mass exposure and in the second instance a sense of permanence to what is essentially private, transitory, and trivial. In either case, an invisible line has been crossed between the real and the imaginary.

Much of our time is spent observing and empathizing with imaginary presences, readily confounded with the personalities of the real world. We saw in the last chapter how the confusion of fact and fiction affects the practice of journalism, and we have just seen how photographic technology heightens the ambiguity. It would be simplistic to blame commercial culture for the blurring of the line between truth and fantasy, since the line has never been clear. But we cannot overlook the fact that the media system is overwhelmingly dedicated to dramatic fiction and that journalism has been steadily subordinated. The social consequences may disturb us, but these are irrelevant to the way media are run. Commercial culture is produced to meet the demands of the market. However, it creates the market whose demands it meets.

IV

DYNAMICS OF COMMERCIAL CULTURE

9

The Manufacture of Taste

Manifestations of banality, sensationalism, and corruption in commercial culture might be excusable if they reflected the low intelligence or poor judgment of those responsible. Too often they arise from a studied and often cynical condescension, and are justified as a necessary response to popular demand. Public tastes are purposefully manipulated, simply as part of the normal operation of the media system. Tastes are neither spontaneous nor immutable; they are provided to the public ready-made. Media's content reflects what their managements choose to offer rather than instinctive public preferences. Managements use their best judgments of what will succeed in the marketplace. As a result, all mass media use tried and hackneyed devices to win audiences of predictable dimensions. There is no reason to assume a malevolent intent behind the process. It is the consequences that count.

This chapter deals with the origins of cultural preferences and the variations among them, and with the motives and misgivings of those who create media content. Producers justify the discrepancy between what they produce and what they like themselves by saying that they merely follow where the market leads. But do they? Key points:

- People gravitate toward what is familiar, though their tastes are not altogether predictable.
- What is easily accessible and heavily promoted becomes familiar—as the popular music industry illustrates.
- In commercial culture as in the arts, there are high moral expectations of talented people, but an uncomfortably high proportion of media content is created with a detached disdain for its public and rationalized as a response to that public's low taste.

The Appeal of the Familiar

Tastes and preferences are not innate; they are inculcated by social habit. The public likes what is familiar, and what is familiar is what media managements choose to present. To grasp the full significance of this chicken-egg proposition, we must go back to one of the oldest debates in the human sciences—over nature and nurture. How much are our lives shaped by biological inheritance and how much by our surroundings and upbringing? The answer to this perennial question carries strong implications for the domain of taste.

A huge accumulation of research in experimental social psychology supports the assertion that preferences are governed by what is familiar. Reviewing the evidence, the psychologist Robert Bornstein suggests a simple explanation of why

> it is adaptive for adults to prefer the familiar over the novel. . . . Who was likely to survive longer, reproduce, and pass on genetic material (and inherited traits) to subsequent generations, the cave dweller who had a healthy fear of the strange and unfamiliar beasts lurking outside, or the more risk-taking (albeit short-lived) fellow who, on spying an unfamiliar animal in the distance, decided that he wanted a closer look?[1]

Another psychologist, Edward Titchener, explains the liking for the familiar by the pleasure of recognition. But it turns out that this is not the explanation, since repetition of subliminal stimuli—those which cannot be consciously recognized—is also effective. People selecting among abstract shapes in the psychological laboratory prefer a peculiar-looking polygon that has been repeatedly shown to them at a speed that makes it totally unrecognizable, even though they are unaware that they have seen it before.[2] They accept, and by implication, are "persuaded" by meaningless messages that they cannot understand.[3]

Pleasant exposure is better than unpleasant, of course, but even neutral exposure strengthens the sensation of familiarity, whether it relates to a media vehicle, to advertised merchandise, or to a business establishment. The consumer seeks the assurance that what is about to be consumed is of predictable character or content. Prior exposure produces a sense of acquaintance. That is why standardization is the essence of consumption, both for goods and for media. We have confidence in what we know, and we like it.

There is some merit in the argument that the intellectual level of media content merely corresponds to the level of popular demand, just as there is merit in the proposition that genetic structure always sets bounds for environmental forces. But a comparison of cultures, and of social differences within cultures, reminds us of how powerfully those environmental forces mold attitudes and values.

Tastes are governed by custom and modified through exposure. Preferences in media content, as in everything else, are inculcated at an early age and sustained by what is offered and easily affordable in one's surroundings. People reared in societies outside the Western musical tradition respond to tonalities that Westerners find strange and even abhorrent, and find what we consider to be the best of our own music confusing and even irritating. In the United States, the enormous social class differences in taste clearly arise from differences in social experience. Different levels of school achievement are associated with different lengths of exposure to aesthetic complexities, in music, literature, and art. Even more significant differences in values are imbued through the family and peer relationships that teach us where we fit in the social order and what activities and ideas are acceptable to it.

Giuseppe Verdi may be regarded as a figure of popular culture in twentieth century Italy, just as William Shakespeare may have been one in nineteenth-century America.[4] A society in which enjoyment and connoisseurship of opera is almost universal rather than the possession of an elite demonstrates that taste is not altogether a matter of individual intelligence, sensibility, or formal education. (The mass of Italians who roar or whistle their reactions to operatic performances in small provincial houses have been educated to pass judgment on what they hear and see, in the same sense that they have been educated on matters of dress, cuisine, and interpersonal conduct.)

The social order shapes predilections for different varieties of media content. Individuals high and low in the social scale take the individual media in widely varying doses, and they gravitate to very different elements within the scope of what each medium has to offer. Seeking information takes effort. Better-educated people have more information needs, but they are also better skilled at the techniques of getting what they want.

If a preference for *The National Review* over the *National Enquirer* reflects social class rather than genetic predisposition, is radically altering American social structure the only way to exchange their relative popularity levels? In fact, the nation's educational system has been engaged in this rather daunting enterprise since the beginnings of the Republic, with a remarkable degree of success. Americans rich and poor share the illusion that they belong to the "middle class," because they share the homogenized experiences of mass media culture.

Upbringing and life experience shape affinities and values, but people who live in identical, adjacent housing units may have radically different interests and living styles that reflect idiosyncrasies of temperament, sensibility, and interpersonal influences. Such differences may be linked to birth order (being an only, first, middle, or youngest child in the family), to physical appearance, medical history, or early childhood experience.

A shrewd social psychologist, knowing someone's sex, age, occupation, educational level, area of residence, ethnic origins, and family situation, may be able to make pretty good inferences about the kind of things that that individual likes to read, watch, and listen to. Pretty good, but imperfect. It is precisely the unpredictable elements in taste that permit successful cultural experimentation. From such innovations emerge the fads that change the direction of taste.

Our preference for Franz Josef Haydn over John Cage may be derived from significant personalities around us, just like the more fundamental preference for chamber music over *salsa* or polkas. But most of us would probably insist that there is an undistillable residue of ourselves that enters into the matter, one that cannot be explained by the influence of our parents or of the kids on the block.

Every individual harbors a characteristic assemblage of cultural preferences, but few people exhibit the kind of internal consistency that seems to be inherent in such classifications as "highbrow" and "lowbrow." Just as there is a continuum of aptitudes rather than a sharp distinction between those who can and those who cannot, so there are many gradations of cultural integrity and complexity. One person's "highbrow" is another's "middlebrow" or even "lowbrow." The reader of *The Economist* may sneer at the reader of *Time*, and in turn be sneered upon by the reader of *The National Interest*.

What specifically is elite and what is popular is constantly being redefined, the cultural historian Lawrence Levine points out. (Wolfgang Amadeus Mozart wrote his father, "As for what is called popular taste, do not be uneasy, for in my opera there is music for every class, except the long-eared.")[5] The same works attract different audiences at different points in history, and are perceived and interpreted differently. The most trivial, mindless, and crude artifacts of popular culture acquire the patina of "nostalgia" with the passage of time; they become the subjects of historical reminiscences and even of serious scholarship.

A reader of Marcel Proust and Thomas Mann may prefer jazz to the works of Francis Poulenc and Arnold Schoenberg. A lover of classical music cannot love it all uniformly; some admirers of Johann Sebastian Bach detest Johannes Brahms. But these self-evident statements still assume that the taste patterns are consistent. This is patently not so. The audiences for rap music and for poetry recitals are distinctive and different, as are the audiences for their mass media counterparts. Yet few people in contemporary America manage to compartmentalize their lives so as to avoid all contact with uncongenial expressions of taste.

Within any form of cultural expression, no one can live with only one genre, finding happiness exclusively in late eighteenth-century Austrian chamber music, or in the songs of Stephen Foster, or even in acid rock. In music, films, television programs, or reading matter, the audiences for masterpieces and for trash are not mutually exclusive, "Audiences . . . can and do enjoy bad films," writes the anthropologist I.C. Jarvie, "and they are perhaps even necessary to them as a canon against which to see, and recognize as such, better films."[6]

Us, the entertainment weekly, in a trade ad showing the bodybuilder-movie star Arnold Schwarzenegger, runs a simple and stark text: "There are times when people just aren't in the mood for Kafka, Sartre, or Kierkegaard."[7] Everyone, no matter how limited the opportunities, requires some occasions for diversity in cultural diet. That is why newspapers and magazines normally carry articles on a wide assortment of topics, often aimed at different levels of information, intelligence, and interest.

The programming practices of the television networks have also been built upon this premise. There is no significant category of television viewers that watches only situation comedies or only talk shows. A schedule is fashioned for any evening with a sequence of programs of different genres succeeding each other, on the assumption that the audience can be held only if there is a constant change of pace and style and subject matter. It needs variety, as well as consistency, in its media diet. It dotes on diversion, but it will accept some instruction along the way.

The Churning Audience

Media producers do not slavishly pursue market currents, yet the fierce competition for audiences leads to endless imitation. For years, the three major television networks have been closely matched in the ratings race, and about one-fifth of the public say they "enjoy" each of them.[8] As their ratings fell and competition became more intense, the networks devoted more and more of their prime-time schedules to feature films and miniseries.

In reality, the audience is in constant turnover ("churn," the industry calls it). Although viewers select half of all programs in advance, they switch in and out to pursue more appealing alternatives. Less than half the viewers of a typical 1-hour show watch it to the end.[9] The more options, the more fickle the audience. Viewers in cable households switch channels more often than those in areas without cable; pay-cable viewers switch most often. In the face of this tremendous audience mobility, the networks offer a constant procession of new programs, which viewers judge rapidly and often harshly. As individual programs change, television drama also undergoes perpetual motion in its dominant genres. Sexy singles alternate with sagas of family life. Cowboys and space explorers yield to cops and robbers, who give way to sitcoms.[10]

Media output is governed by the size of the available pool of talent, energy, and moral force. Sometimes this is a simple matter of supply and demand, with larger compensation attracting people of greater ability who produce work of a higher order. Often it reflects nothing more than the ability of a particular genre to stimulate interest among the limited supply of qualified contributors.

America is the land of forgotten crazes—the yo-yo, the hula hoop, the Davy Crockett coonskin and the Pet Rock. Within a given constellation of tastes, there is room for fads and fashions to come and go, and a need for superficial variety in the formats and styles through which the same system of values is expressed.

Chasing the audience, commercial culture must be continually inventive in its specific content, while it adheres to proven and conventional structures and formulas. It is victimized by fashion at the same time that it sets fashion, since it must follow the popular styles that the public already accepts while it seeks to formulate new ones. This makes commercial culture fiercely competitive, with each media vehicle constantly on guard lest others preempt its franchise.

While editorial and production subjects and techniques are subject to constant fads and vogues, fundamental taste patterns do not change markedly or often. In part, the shortage of talent and of fresh creative inventions makes it necessary to recycle the same themes over and over. According to one analysis, a little over half (55%) of 945 prime-time situation comedies and dramas that were aired between 1950 and 1987 were "more or less" original ideas.[11] A closer look would show less rather than more.

Collections of elementary story plots have been published for many years; now there are a number of computer programs (IdeaFisher, Plots Unlimited, The Idea Generator and Collaborator) that facilitate literary creation by allowing a writer to use different combinations of characters, situations, settings, and denouements. A scriptwriter can organize plot elements and characters, classified by genre and category. Plots Unlimited offers 13,900 possibilities, such as, "A, trying to expose treachery, falls in love with B, suspected of the treachery." Computer programs also suggest "lead-ins" and "lead-outs" that add complexity to the situation.[12] Thus the entertainment industry's search for the new and different leads it back to the accepted formulas that merely wrap the soothingly familiar in the guise of novelty.

Distributing and Promoting

How does the public's penchant for the familiar jibe with the media's incessant quest to innovate? To the accusation that giving the public what it wants forces a reliance on the tried and true, the ready answer is that media operators constantly search for new material, new ideas, new talent. Their scouts frequent little theaters, nightclubs and standup comedy cabarets; they scour obscure magazines to find unknown writers of promise. They want to be on the crest of fashion and yet stay ahead of their competition. Essentially what they hope to catch are the emerging trends that will swell into mainline entertainment; they have no desire to move the main line or to switch to another path themselves. Innovation characteristically alters the surface of media content rather than enhancing its capacity to convey and deepen human experience.

Why should not audiences left to their own devices gravitate naturally toward a higher level of talent and complexity in media content? Media habits are far more than an expression of personal tastes, however these originate. What audiences choose or buy reflects what is available to them and what they believe is popular because it is familiar.

Much if not most of the mass communications that come our way represent choices that other people make for us, whether it is the text the teacher assigns us at school, the television program our spouse wants to watch, the film that happens to be playing at the local movie on the night we have scheduled to go out, or the only daily left in town. We usually retain the option of avoiding such exposure altogether, but then we must pay a price: flunking out of school, getting into a domestic argument, forfeiting a night out on the town, remaining ignorant of whether property taxes are going up or down.

Among the marketing precepts that govern the output of commercial culture is the rule that a product cannot be sold unless it is accessible to the consumer. Distribution entails more than the physical presence of the product at the point of sale. It means that the product has a visibility that gets attention, because of the convenience or salience of its position or the sheer volume of merchandise on view. Display is integral to distribution, but it is also a means of communication, and therefore, like advertising, a form of promotion. Where extensive advertising precedes the introduction of a new product, consumer inquiries prompt retailers to request shipments of it. Normally, however, manufacturers must struggle to open the channels, to get their merchandise where customers can find it. They pay for the privilege of getting a hearing from supermarket buying committees, and pay "slotting allowances" as tribute to chains to get shelf space in the stores.

Cultural products face the same challenges. Periodicals selling their copies one at a time must get them into places where readers can find them. This task has become more difficult as the number of newsdealers has diminished, as urban crime and vandalism create new hazards for vending machines, and as supermarkets set limits on the number of publications they carry (both because of space shortages and because of the paperwork entailed in making returns). Subscriptions, the principal distribution method for most newspapers and magazines, have presented growing problems of a different order: for magazines, a steady escalation in postal costs, for newspapers, increased turnover in juvenile carriers and a decline in the quality and timeliness of customer service.

Changes in distribution patterns have changed the content of print media. Newspapers that expand their circulation territories to encompass growing suburbs must broaden their editorial coverage as well, sometimes at the expense of the central city. Other newspapers, cutting back on their costly distribution to rural hinterlands in their states, have correspondingly retreated on the news side.

Off-beat, experimental, and foreign films have never generated their full potential audiences in the United States, because of the difficulty of getting theatrical bookings outside of a handful of art cinemas and university film clubs. Film distribution depends on the judgments and prejudices of theater owners (who in turn may be responsive to the local mores). In broadcasting, distribution is a matter of the time of day as well as of spectrum frequency allocation and signal strength. Programs aired at odd hours have limited distribution, in effect, if they are transmitted while most people are asleep or at work.

"Where a show is placed," says TV consultant Michael Dann, "is infinitely more important than the content of the show."[13] The same program aired in a different time slot may have a vastly different rating, depending on the changed competition and on the total size of the viewing public at one time or the other. (A 6 p.m. show that averaged a 43% share among women under fifty dropped into the low 30s when it was pushed back to 4 p.m. These tactics develop their own vocabulary. By the principle of "counterprogramming," each network tries to schedule a program of a different type than the competition offers in the same time slot. In "hammocking," a new program is placed in the "saddle" between two established hits, or "tent poles.")

The broadcasting networks, from the beginning of radio days, have faced affiliates' resistance to some of their programming feeds—on the grounds that they are highbrow, avant-garde, offensive, or boring. In businesses whose profits depend on sales, it is natural to produce what the widest possible number of potential customers will buy.

To compensate for the fallible judgments of impresarios, producers, and editors, media content is shaped to fit the existing desires of the audience, assiduously studied through market research. Editors are urged to "listen to their readers" and to produce publications that are "market-driven" rather than to listen to their consciences and to follow their best professional instincts.

What customers will like can never be predicted exactly either on the basis of lore or experience or through consumer research, especially in the field of communication. Research helps to identify probable losers, but an enormous number of factors interact in complex ways to produce a winner.

Media choices are not made on the basis of taste alone, or because of the relative affinity or distance we feel toward the various possibilities that are presented to us. They are made on the basis of our expectations, and these expectations are actively manipulated. To one degree or another, all media promote their offerings to the public; as with any other product, the promotion indelibly colors our perceptions of the real thing.

In today's era of highly touted book titles and films, the mass audience follows conversation. It goes where the maximum amount of excitement is generated, by promotion and publicity. For an individual to become a star in the entertainment world generally requires a modicum of talent, but that in itself is not enough. To win stardom, talent must be dramatically displayed in a proper role and under skilled direction. Above all it must be effectively publicized.

A recording executive:

Successful groups don't just happen any more; they are made.[14]

The information we get from promotions of media expands our ability to know what is happening on a cultural scene that provides much of the substance for everyday conversational sociability. Even the advertising of media content enters into the current of casual talk. We may not have read the book or even read a review of it, but if we have seen it advertised, we know about it and perhaps feel entitled to express an opinion on its merits. We may not succumb to the temptations to spend our money or our time, but we still have a sense of what other people are doing, and thus we remain in the cultural mainstream.

As with any kind of advertising, the first objective of media promotion is to establish recognition and a sense of familiarity, so that when we encounter the vehicle in the marketplace (the television program listed in the log, the magazine on the rack, the film's name on the marquee) it does not seem like an altogether unknown quantity.

The second objective is to whet the appetite, by identifying the medium with those appeals to which the prospective audience is most likely to be responsive, by promising satisfactions and benefits it cannot resist (vicarious romance or adventure, fulfilling prurient curiosity, mastery of the secrets of the universe).

The third objective (which is more difficult to carry off) is to create an aura of social compulsion, to make it appear that the medium enjoys such enormous popularity that it has become part of the general pool of conversation (at least within a particular population group), so that anyone who has not shared the experience is out of it. Media promoters simply follow long established practices (like the claque in the performing arts or the vernissage in the art galleries) that create an illusion of widespread enthusiasm which one can join respectably without enduring the uncertainties of independent judgment.

To accomplish their objectives, media organizations dedicate substantial budgets to advertising and promotion, which ranges from the sedate mail-order brochures of book publishers to the vivid television commercials for new feature films.

- "Promos"—promotional spot announcements for programs—occupy 7% of air time on the television networks. Promotion represents 10% of the wholesale price for the average book. The promotion budget for a bestselling novel by an established author can reach $750,000.[15] Magazines typically spend sums equal to 8% of their circulation income on mail promotions and general advertising aimed at readers. (They also spend 6% of their advertising revenues on promotion).
- In the popular music business, "payola" to radio disk jockeys occasioned great scandal in the 1950s and was outlawed by legislation in 1960, but the practice was quickly resumed in the face of what were deemed to be compelling sales necessities. Today, promoters typically get about 30% of the pretax profit of a recording. In 1985 as much as $70–80 million was spent by the record companies to get their numbers played on the air. A group of promoters known as "The Network" bribed disk jockeys and kept recordings from being played if its services were not employed.[16] Station program directors have been lured by the record companies with free trips to the

Caribbean (including the services of prostitutes).[17] Typically, $30,000 is spent on a promotional video for a new piece of popular music that might represent a $500,000 investment.

• Hollywood spends nearly half a dollar on promotion and publicity for every dollar spent on the production of a new film. The Walt Disney company spent $46 million to make "Dick Tracy" and $54 million to promote it.

Film exhibitor executive:

> This isn't a rational business. It's a speculative business. And the egos are enormous. Half of the cost of a $13–14 million movie is the advertising budget. After you've got that kind of investment you're not going to worry about spending another million dollars for promotion.[18]

Media promotions sometimes aim at a different sector of the public than the content does. A magazine read mainly by middle-aged businessmen may try to broaden its public through a direct mail campaign aimed at rising young executives, of both sexes—and successfully alter its audience profile.

Publicity thrives on controversy, genuine or contrived. Donald Bain, author of a best-selling book called *Coffee, Tea or Me*, promoted a sequel, *How to Make a Good Airline Stewardess*, by organizing a press-release attack on it from the "Stewardess Anti-Defamation League," a fiction launched by his own literary agent. Within 24 hours, there were forty calls from media requesting interviews.[19]

The shape of commercial culture, or for that matter, of any form of cultural expression, can never be determined entirely by the intentions and proclivities of the audiences it attracts. Tastes are constrained by economics, massaged by hype, and always exercised within the limits of the menu placed before us by the chefs.

Music and Musical Taste

Expression manufactured to meet market demand seems the very opposite of spontaneous welling up of inner spirits, which we associate with music. Both secular and sacred music are important elements of human communication—a vital force for group solidarity, from the mother's lullaby to the priest's funeral incantations. Children's play rhymes, the war chants of savages (if it is still permissible to employ this term), seamen's chanties, drinking songs, church hymns, dance rhythms—all are integral to the shared identity, sentiments, and activities that make us social animals. There is no society without music of some kind, without musical instruments and musical occasions.

Music expresses and evokes emotions, and has therefore always been linked to the spiritual aspects of human life. But music is also a form of play and sharing. Formal composed music was always intended to be listened to—attentively, every composer hopes. The mass media have transformed it into a pervasive background to everyday existence.

The music that we take for granted on radio, television, film, records, cassettes, and discs has only recently been incorporated into common experience. The folk music tradition in the United States has varied origins and regional attributes, but like folk music everywhere it arose from live human contact at work and at play. Its tunes emerged from dance rhythms. Its lyrics articulated perennial themes: romantic longing, anxiety, and bereavement. When the population became sufficiently large and differentiated to support professional musicians and composers, a commercial music industry emerged along lines already well-established in Europe, with managers who booked concert halls and recruited artists, published sheet music, and above all, anticipated popular demand.

The phonograph made music universally accessible, in all its varied instrumental and vocal forms. It brought access to the artistry of famed performers who could formerly have been heard only through considerable expense and travel time. Just as the *New York Times*, in its editorials, denounced brass band music as "a devastating vice" and "a giant evil,"[20] Courtenay Guild, elected president of Boston's Handel and Haydn Society in 1915, warned that "talking machines" would create a "mania for dancing and syncopated time" and create "a taste for a sort of barbarous sequence of sounds that is more worthy of savages than of civilization."[21]

The public had long accepted the idea that a line engraving or a halftone photograph in a book or newspaper was not a literal representation of a face or scene. Similarly, it could easily accommodate itself to the disparity between the tinny sound of early recordings and the reality of the original performance. By the time that radio broadcasting began in 1922, 93 million phonograph records—3.6 for each American household—were being sold each year. Then as now, popular music was dominant and aroused disdain and opposition, perhaps because of its intrusiveness.

The spread of the phonograph stimulated rather than stymied live musical performances. The rise of the silent motion picture industry boosted the sale of sheet music scores prepared for pianists to accompany films, and the commissioned tunes sometimes became popular hits. By the mid-1990s, leading firms in the music industry were owned by the record companies, and most no longer published their own sheet music.

Radio changed the nature of popular music,[22] which was a major component of its content from the start. When television became the principal broadcast medium it took over most of radio's spoken programming. As the soap operas, quiz shows, news documentaries, comedy hours, and variety shows departed, the great radio networks disintegrated and recorded music took over.

With the advent of the transistor, radio became a personal companion, and also an increasingly significant part of the audible environment. The revival of earphones somewhat muffled the din, but coincided with the emergence of audiocassettes—and later of compact discs—as highly mobile substitutes for phonograph records. More than ever, the selection of music became an individual choice rather than merely an acceptance of what was available on the air. The playing of music now also became a proclamation of personal identity, an assertive and often violently aggressive act.[23]

Popular music did not become predominant over classical music in the recording business until after World War II. It is typically written to order to fit an established pattern of demand, unlike classical works composed on commission. As Theodor Adorno puts it, serious music is organic: "every detail derives its musical sense from the concrete totality of the piece, which in turn, consists of the life relationship of the details and never of a mere enforcement of a musical scheme."[24] By contrast, the very appeal of popular music stems from the comfortable sense of familiarity it instills.[25]

On television, music for its own sake has been a negligible factor in programming, except for musical numbers in variety shows and the occasional orchestral appearance on public television. This changed with the introduction of cable and the MTV format of visualized popular recordings. But musical backgrounds and introductions are as common in television drama as in motion pictures, setting mood, building suspense, and bridging visual sequences without speech. Spooky music was even used to accompany interviews with murderers on ABC's "20/20" magazine show. Motion pictures, with their musical soundtracks, account for a large portion of television time. And television commercials, like those on radio, make heavy use of musical jingles and backgrounds to capture attention, disconnect viewers from what went before, support the verbal message, and register the advertiser's identity.

Radio, tape players, television, and other forms of amplified sound have become ubiquitous involuntary presences in public places and not uncommonly intruders into private space. Since we are constantly being bathed in music we have not asked for, we may easily develop the same insensitivity to it that we necessarily develop in response to the overload of visual signals that flood over us. But we are affected by the character as well as the quantity of musical communication that imposes itself upon us. The musical style, format, tone, and delivery that prevails in our daily lives only partly arises out of our own predilections. In substantial degree it reflects the judgments and tastes both of those who control the channels of production and dissemination and of our contemporaries who control the appliances that deliver them to us willy-nilly.

Cynicism and Profit

A distinctive attribute of commercial culture is that those who produce it often prefer not to consume it themselves. They cater to the tastes of others rather than fulfilling their own. The crowning condemnation of the media system is that it is engaged in a cunning and deliberate exploitation of public foibles by people who know better. The radical critic (and former *Fortune* editor) Dwight MacDonald expresses this judgment within a Marxist framework:

> Mass Culture is imposed from above. It is fabricated by technicians hired by businessmen; its audiences are passive consumers, their participation limited to the choice between buying and not buying. The Lords of kitsch, in short, exploit the cultural needs of the masses in order to make a profit and/or to maintain their class rule.[26]

His British counterpart, Raymond Williams, makes the same point this way:

> Much that we judge to be bad is known to be bad by its producers. Ask any journalist, or any copywriter, if he will now accept that famous definition: "written by morons for morons." Will he not reply that in fact it is written by skilled and intelligent people for a public that hasn't the time, or hasn't the education, or hasn't let's face it,

the intelligence, to read anything more complete, anything more careful, anything nearer the known canons of exposition or argument? Had we not better say, for simplicity, anything good?[27]

Williams goes on to an intriguing formulation of the difference between the expression of creative impulse by a "source" and the fulfilment of an assigned task by an "agent" who "cannot thus accept it for himself, but allows himself to be persuaded that it is in a fit form for others—presumably inferiors—and that it is his business merely to see that it reaches them effectively."[28]

The argument is often confirmed by the "agents" themselves. Many talented people who work for mass media express themselves as shocked by what they do to earn a living. Journalists have always offered the most informed and trenchant criticism of newspapers. No one has made more scathing comments on television than those who come out of the industry itself. Don Durgin, former president of NBC-TV:

What you consider normal—honesty and dependability—is so *rare* in this business.[29]

The highly successful television producer Norman Lear refers to "programs that most television executives will tell you privately shame them—or as they put it, are 'not my personal cup of tea.' "[30] Media producers and entrepreneurs have always taken pains to distinguish their own personal preferences from those of the public at large. Appearing on a televised panel discussion, Lear once said he had not seen a new series that his studio had produced, adding, "I do not watch television."[31]

A TV soap opera actor:

I never watch soap operas. Who can watch that shit?[32]

Three out of four station managers agree that there is too much unnecessary violence on television.[33] So do two-thirds of Hollywood's most successful writers, producers, and directors (although three out of four disagree that there is too much sex).[34]

Dick Wolf, producer of "Miami Vice" and "Law and Order," believes that "none of us have a responsibility to do anything more than entertain."[35] But he says,

I have an 8-year-old and a 5-year-old child. They've never seen any of the shows I've ever produced. They shouldn't be watching them. They're not allowed to watch Saturday morning cartoons. . . . When are you going to stop blaming the media and start looking at the home environment, and the fact that parents are supposed to monitor what their children are watching?[36]

Before he became president of NBC, Grant Tinker, then head of MTM Productions, called poor television programming "a national crime" and said "someone should go to jail for it . . . probably network executives."[37]

Former NBC-TV President Fred Silverman:

I'm disappointed at the lack of change and improvement in TV programming. My children aren't all that interested in watching TV. . . . I was responsible for some of the best programs and, unfortunately, some of the worst.[38]

Silverman was booted off the set of "Password" after asking a producer, "Who thinks up this crap anyway?"[39]

TV writer:

> Television is not a creative medium. Creative media are theater or movies. If you're drawn to television, the bottom line is money, not creativity.[40]

Ben Stein, a television writer:

> The business of television is the business of making easy money. . . . The fact that you can get paid a million dollars in TV to do shit inspires you to do shit. There's no such thing as principle, only the deal.[41]

Director Brian De Palma, surveying the crowd in Hollywood's Ivy restaurant:

> Living in this value system makes you think like a deranged king. . . . You get your aesthetic judgment swamped. . . . But that's the nature of movies, which is art and commerce, only the commerce is God. You look at these guys, they get eaten up by the business. One day I'm going to say, "What am I doing this for?" Wrestling with these people, trying to do something unusual and different, and they want something mediocre and stupid![42]

How valid is the proposition that mass media content is created to specifications that its authors consider personally unacceptable? Certainly the motives that inspire a creative vision are not the same as those that produce financial success.

Oliver Goldsmith put into the mouth of a bookseller a remark that resonates in today's era of "instant books":

> I have ten new title-pages now around me which only want books to be added to make them the finest things in nature.[43]

This same spirit prompted Warner Books to commission a sequel to *Gone With The Wind*.[44] Whatever the literary limitations of Margaret Mitchell's original (whose 28 million copies made it the record best-seller after the Bible), it was a work that the author created in all sincerity, not as a hack assignment. Yet its successor, written to order and hyped unstintingly, was also an enormous commercial success. It was one more product in a GWTW industry that included perfumes, dolls, and collectors' plates.[45]

Publishers sometimes publish the posthumous works of successful authors with unfamiliar photographs suggesting that they are still alive. Or, if they own the rights to use the author's name, they may attach it to ghostwritten books that exploit the deceased's popularity.[46]

A publisher considering the book you are reading would ask, "Is there a market for it?" not "Is it any good?" And in the world of low-price publishing, the accepted wisdom continues to be that "the worst books sell best."[47]

The critic Bernard de Voto, commenting on mass market paperbacks:

> Tripe has always been the basis of the publishing business, and in the two bit book it is performing the functions of all popular literature in all ages. At worst it is preventing boredom, assisting digestion and peristalsis, feeding people's appetite for daydreams, giving the imagination something to work on and taking the reader out of a momentarily unsatisfactory life into a momentarily more enjoyable one.[48]

Walter Meade, president of Avon Books:

> If I published only what seemed consistent with what I felt was righteous, I wouldn't be doing very much, because that gets narrower and narrower as I get older and older. . . . I can't ignore the fact that everything has moved down in quality. If I ignore that, then I begin to ignore what my job is. If shoddy workmanship, shoddy clothing, if the impersonalization of life is what it is, then I've got to get in tune with that.[49]

CEO of a multimedia company:

> I separate my professional instincts from my glandular impulses.[50]

But it is the "glandular impulses" that impel the creative process on which mass communication depends.

The Taste-Molders

If much of American mass media content is forgettable junk, does the blame rest on the economic structure that produces it or on human limitations? As the number of media channels and vehicles grows, the demand for talent may outstrip the supply. With 5 million hours of programming broadcast annually, a TV station manager comments: "Hell, there isn't even enough mediocrity to go around."[51]

The incidence of a particular kind of talent in any population seems to reflect a confluence of unique historical circumstances that create the conditions in which genius is recognized and finds a voice. The Greek playwrights, the Italian and Flemish painters of the Renaissance, the Scottish moralists, the American Founding Fathers—all represent extraordinary appearances of talent concentrated in a particular time and place. American mass media, for all the wealth invested in them and all the great financial incentives they provide, have produced no comparable giants.

A limited number of people possess the combination of talent, skill, and energy required for creative success in the media world. In the fields of television, motion pictures, magazines, and books (and to a lesser degree, of musical recordings) they are heavily concentrated in New York and Los Angeles. In Hollywood, a tiny cadre of writers and writer-producers create a high proportion of programming material. Even in the scattered, localized world of daily newspapers, there is a dense network of national and regional associations and meetings that bring executives together. Thus power over commercial culture is centered in a relatively small number of individuals—many of whom know or have access to each other—who are mutually interdependent in spite of all business rivalry and personal competition. How much alike are the people who produce the mass media? Is there, as has been charged, a "media elite," dominated by left-leaning graduates of Ivy League colleges and inspired by a doctrinaire philosophy at odds with that of the American public? Can one indeed speak of an elite that cuts across media boundaries?

In every medium, the outlook and social background of the creative force are unlike those of the executives who manage the finances. Journalists on major newspapers, the news magazines and in network television news departments lean farther left of center than their counterparts in a broad cross-section of the nation's press, for the same reasons that professors at top universities are more "liberal" than their colleagues at lesser institutions. To a greater degree than their colleagues in local news organizations around the country, elite journalists also tend to be unrepresentative and different in their social origins and attributes from the publics they serve.[52]

The people who operate mass media are not necessarily complacent supporters of either the social order or the media system. A sampling finds top television writers and producers to be overwhelmingly liberal, pro-Democrat in their presidential voting record, pro-welfare, sympathetic to the disadvantaged, but also pro-private enterprise. They are generally unhappy with the way society is run. Four out of five disagree that TV is too critical of traditional values. Seven in ten disagree that adultery is wrong. They are a relatively homogeneous group, quite different from the mass audience for which their scripts are fashioned.[53]

It is as unlikely to expect media specialists to be a cross section of the general population, either in origins or beliefs, as to expect this of basketball players or nuclear physicists. In the case of media, today's open market for talent (which did not exist in the recent past) seems to lure individuals with particular combinations of motivations and aptitudes.

Television producers see themselves as conscious crusaders for social improvement. Not surprisingly, the scripts of television and film dramas are infused, often quite irrelevantly, with trendy themes of social uplift.[54] To ascribe higher motives for what one does seems to be a deep-seated requirement of human nature, perhaps especially, of creative human nature. It is possible to retain the creative individual's instinctive stance of rebellion against the powers that be, and at the same time to live comfortably with those powers.

Rationalization

An Eskimo who picks up a piece of ivory and begins to carve finds that the nature of what he is sculpting is imposed upon him by the shape of the raw material.

As the carver holds the unworked ivory in his hand, turning it this way and that, he whispers, "Who are you? Who hides there?" and then, "Ah, Seal." He rarely sets out to cut, say, a seal, but picks up the ivory, examines it to find its hidden form, and if that's not immediately apparent, carves aimlessly until he sees it, humming or chanting as he works. Then he brings it out: Seal, hidden, emerges. It was always there: he did not create it, he released it, he helped set it forth.[55]

Similarly, Jackson Pollock, dripping and flinging paint upon the canvas on his studio floor, must have felt himself to be an agent of forces larger than himself, waiting to be liberated. Samuel Taylor Coleridge, envisioning Xanadu on an opium high, was possessed by a force that dictated the words his fingers merely executed. The art thus spontaneously created was of a very different kind than that which a creative individual produces painfully by design, and still more remote from that produced by a collectively operated media manufacturing establishment.

"I do not compose music," said Gustav Mahler. "Music comes to me." A century earlier, Percy Bysshe Shelley expressed the same sentiments:

> A man cannot say, "I will compose poetry." The greatest poet cannot say it. For the mind in creation is as a fading coal, which some invisible muse, like the inconstant wind, awakens to transitory brightness.[56]

The entire commercial culture rests on the opposite of this premise. Harlequin Books employs a contingent of nearly 1,000 writers to grind out its popular romances. Such practices have a long history in the fine arts. Painters of both the Renaissance and Baroque periods made repeated copies of their own successful works. Antonio Canal (Canaletto) was a commercial artist in a thoroughly modern sense; he painted the same scenes to order, over and over again, catering to the interests of English travelers wanting mementos of their Grand Tours. His talent manifested itself not only in his composition and technique, but also in the individuality which made repeated renderings of the same landscape avoid any exact replication of each other. But his motives appear in retrospect to be no different than those of any later-day hack grinding out a standardized product to suit the predictable taste of a well-defined market.

There is a strong literary image of creative geniuses enchained by the masscult corporation, unable to express their true instincts, chafing as their great gifts are subordinated to serve sordid commercial purposes.[57] Beyond question, many people working in or for media organizations despise their work, hate themselves for "selling out," and yearn for the time when they can retire to pursue, finally, their great destinies.[58] Most, however, feel no such conflicts, and find that their career paths are well-chosen and satisfying. They include not only journalists and those involved in producing entertainment, but also those engaged in advertising—the very embodiment of commercial culture.

Advertising copywriter Paula Green:

> The important thing to me is that I'm proud of it. And I'm proud of it when it suits me. And I'm satisfied with whatever it is.[59]

Former art director Andy Warhol:

> After I did the thing called "art" . . . I went into business art . . . and I want to finish as a business artist. . . . Good business is the best art.[60]"

Advertising creative people of great talent often insist that the criteria of business are the only ones by which their work should be judged.

Agency tycoon Rosser Reeves:

> What do you want from me? Fine writing? Or do you want to see the God-damned
> sales curve stop moving down and start moving up?[61]

It stretches the imagination to lump all of the forces employed to produce mass media content under the heading of "creative talent." People with literary or artistic bents are not the only ones employed in mass communication enterprises; there are jobs for accountants, mechanics, and statisticians. Their work may not be as central to the company's mission as that of the people who craft what appears in print or on the air, but they are a presence.

A pressman at a newspaper, a carpenter on a film lot, a secretary at a magazine— all perform essential functions, and all do their jobs best when they feel good about the organizations they work for. But such indispensable media workers are ancillary to the task of creating communications, which are the heart of the enterprise. There is no sharp line between those who supply the creative expressions and the support troops without whom these would never reach the audience. Writers, reporters, actors, and musicians may think of themselves as just doing a job, in the same way that electricians and ad salespeople do. The difference is that what they say or play is what the public sees or hears.

As in any other kind of business, a major preoccupation of management is to keep all its employees productively occupied. Thus there is a workaday rhythm in all media organizations that resembles that of any other institution in which human beings coordinate their activities to produce a complex assortment of products. The dominant tone is set by social interaction on the job, by aspirations, rivalries, romances and achievements, by the pleasure people take and the small comforts they get in being with each other. The usual web of interpersonal connections in the workplace—rather than the joys or frustrations of the creative process—determines how most professionals in the communications field respond to their work. Journalists routinely work on assignment, covering stories they might never wish to seek out by themselves. Such projects may be accompanied by varying degrees of misgivings or discomfort, or they may be stimulating and enjoyable.

The creative process can itself be a highly challenging one, even when it is applied to such minor tasks as the composition of an obituary notice or the preparation of a radio commercial script for a hardware store.

Comedian Stan Freberg:

> I always create commercials for myself first of all. I am the consumer. I know best. If
> I think it's a great commercial, I figure the rest of the people might think so too.[62]

Some individuals take such mundane assignments with greater ease and pleasure than others, but the rewards inevitably go to those who do their best.

Former TV network president:

> For every witless show you pumped out you had something else you could be proud
> of. If you're talking programming, you want to have quality instead of all that really
> forgettable stuff. And you take pride in the good shows that you can produce.[63]

The demands of the workplace weed out those sensitive spirits who are unable to adapt to them. The rest, who may start as cynics or secret rebels, are inevitably caught in the machinery. They may simply find that they cannot market their skills for more pay or more comfortable working conditions. They may be intrigued by the exercise of crafts they increasingly master. They may be ensnared by the personal loyalties that bind them to a work group, or even to the enterprise itself. But whatever the motives, they are likely to come to accept the notion that what they are doing is good.

It has been customary to think of great talents as "selling out" when they choose to apply themselves to endeavors that do not match their own levels of excellence and integrity. But noble spirits enslaved to ignoble masters can justify their decisions to themselves and can in any case concentrate on technique, if the substance of what they are working on does not accord with their genuine impulses.

Hack work is easily rationalized, and the rationalization can be converted into honest belief in the value and importance of what one is doing. Few creative people in any medium can spend a lifetime despising what they do. They may admit they are making compromises, but on balance they will tell you they are doing more good than ill—dispensing harmless amusement, advancing worthy causes through cryptic references in their copy, helping to preserve fine enterprises that might otherwise succumb to economic pressures.

Nothing about this process of self-justification is unique to the field of communication. Young people enter almost any field of employment with hesitations and misgivings, but come to like it and defend it as their sense of commitment increases. As commonsense tells us and as psychological theory confirms, there is a natural tendency for human beings to defend activities that they may have begun for wholly arbitrary and even irrational reasons. There are individuals who despise what they do and themselves for doing it, but most of us retain our self-esteem by ascribing some genuine meaning or importance to the way we spend our energy and time. Arguments that may at first be adopted out of sheer defensiveness are quickly incorporated into a person's belief system as they are repeated over and over. The copywriter for an analgesic that is just like every other analgesic tells herself that she is keeping the market big and competitive and helping to hold the price of aspirin low. As we saw earlier, the producer of pornographic films knows that he is fighting prudery and bringing much needed pleasure to hundreds of thousands of lonely people. There is no form of communication that cannot be justified—and that is not.

Rationalization may apply not merely to the purposes of the enterprise as a whole, but to specific elements of its content. A newspaper's editorial policies may be dictated by its owner, but editorial writers, once they are assigned to articulate them, quickly accept them as their own. (In practice, management hires writers and editors whose views it has ascertained and found congruent with its own. Moreover, owners and publishers do not have opinions on every subject about which a newspaper is required to write editorials, so the possibility for conflict is minimized.)

Only a fraction of communications content is devoted to controversial opinions, political or otherwise. Most creative assignments are fairly routine tasks that carry no particular emotional overhang. Here the prevailing values set by management are fed by subtle indirection into the flow of activities and judgments. Priorities, prejudices, no-nos, and tastes emerge as generally understood company policies, from the decisions, accolades, and reprimands that are handed down from on high, case by specific case. Newcomers in an organization pick them up one by one from superiors and colleagues, just as they learn the uncodified protocols of office etiquette.

William Randolph Hearst did not command his papers to publish alluring front-page photographs of his friend Marion Davies, as they often did. His editors simply knew that he enjoyed seeing them there. Henry Luce's passionate feelings about China were not expressed in policy memos to the editors of *Time*; they did not have to be. Editors or producers who do not agree with management's ideas become disaffected and move to more congenial havens or find consolation within the company, performing inoffensive tasks. Occasionally, in a well-publicized case, there is an explosion when convictions are put to the test. Owners or managers can bend to soothe the egos of subordinates, but they can never afford to renounce their authority, especially over those areas in which their own egos are involved.

Selling Out

Great artists have created notable works under severe financial pressure and to deadlines imposed by totally nonartistic, practical considerations. Geniuses have always accepted commissions, painted donors in companionship with the holiest martyrs, and written masses for the repose of the dullest souls whose families were willing to pay the price.

Even at a time when creative individuals had patrons with highly cultivated judgment, their style and subject matter was limited by the master's preferences or needs. Painters of the Italian Renaissance were given requirements as to the subjects and dimensions of their works, which were normally designed for specific settings. Even when artists were ostensibly offered freedom to exercise their own wishes, they were aware of barriers they could not transgress.

In the open marketplace, however, artists may defy the prevailing tastes (as the Impressionists did), partly out of the need to express themselves, and partly out of the hope that they will strike the right note with someone who comes along to share their outlook or sensibilities. If integrity is the hallmark of the artist, persistence in defiance of market forces may lead to personal disaster (although alcoholism, depression, or career abandonment are more common fates than starvation) or to the cynical compromise of personal values.

Salvatore Rosa:

> I do not paint to enrich myself but purely for my own satisfaction. I must allow myself to be carried away by the transports of enthusiasm and use my brushes only when I feel myself rapt.[64]

Artists have always felt they had something special and important to communicate that was overcome by triviality when it was set before a mass audience. Implicit in this attitude was the assumption that the mass audience wished only to relax from its routine labors and was unwilling to accept the effort required for the comprehension of art.

Media content manufactured for sale in the market must follow rules different from those that guide works created to express their authors' own impulses. Meaningful communication arouses emotions, and thus creates interest and involvement. The greatest talent is always attracted and applied to highly charged content, because its challenges summon the highest levels of energy. Yet great talent and energy do not assure great success with the public. The most creative communicators may misgauge the audience, or may set the sights above their heads.

Is it necessary to share the tastes of the mass public in order to please it, or is it possible to be disengaged and guileful—planning, writing, composing, or otherwise producing to fit the requirements of the market, against which one's own inner spirit is in rebellion? Commercial hack work requires a high degree of specialized skill that even the most talented individuals may find to be beyond their capacities.

Mediocre talents may be successful because of their affinity for the formulas that correspond to popular taste. Dwight MacDonald relates that the poet and short-story writer Delmore Schwartz

> tried, twice, to sell out, and write a piece of junk that *Liberty* would crown with a $1,000 check [for its weekly 1,000 word short story]; both times he failed. Moral: You have to be sincere to Sell Out; it's like making money—if your heart's not in it, the customer, or editor, sees through the imposture.[65]

Hacks can be deadly serious about their work; most become so to keep their sanity, even if they have tongue in cheek as they start down the slippery slope. Is it excellence of execution or seriousness of intent that distinguishes the valid from the meretricious?

The revulsion against selling out—that is, shaping a creative expression by listening to something other than one's own small inner voice—rests on the ancient notion of the artist as an individual endowed with divine attributes, who instinctively moves in the direction of a higher morality.

Sergei Koussevitzky, to Arturo Toscanini, on July 7, 1933:

> Since last April, when I signed the telegram to Adolf Hitler, with your signature at the top of the list, I have more than once been asked to write to ask you to refuse to direct at Bayreuth this summer. Every time I squarely refused to do so, because a soul like yours, capable of understanding the beauty, truth and depth of music, does not need to be guided or helped in its actions; that soul at the right moment will have to show you the most direct, just and true path.[66]

Creative individuals are commonly regarded as distinct from other people. Ezra Pound:

> The artist is not dependent upon the multitude of his listeners. Humanity is the rich effluvium, it is the waste and the manure and the soil, and from it grows the tree of the arts. . . . This rabble, this multitude—does *not* create the great artist. They are aimless and drifting without him.[67]

As Thomas Mann puts it:

> The artist must be unhuman, extra-human; he must stand in a queer aloof relationship to our humanity; only so is he in a position, I ought to say only so would he be tempted, to represent it, to present it, to portray it to good effect.[68]

Journalism, practiced at the incandescent level of an Emile Zola, is also a morally impelled vocation. Insistence that the creative individual must follow his own star— regardless of whether or not others follow—may be carried one step further, to a demand that his superior judgment must be forced down the throats of an unreceptive and hostile public.

Henry Luce:

> I decided that my ultimate accountability had to be to my Creator.[69]

It is precisely because the moral expectations made of creative individuals are so high that shame is attached to the compromises that reveal them to be ordinary mortals. Yet artistic expression always has some utilitarian motive, even in the most primitive societies. If it seeks to placate or celebrate supernatural forces, is this not always with the end of making life easier and more comfortable here below? Cave paintings, it has been suggested, were executed to capture and dominate the animals that they symbolically depicted. Shamans chanted, danced, and fashioned sacred images to propitiate the supernatural spirits that determined human destiny. The offerings made for their personal use were inseparable from the sacrifices required by the gods. Their exercises were essential to the well-being of the community, supported by their tribes as part of the natural order of things and not as a discretionary expense item.

Wandering minstrels composed their epics in order to cadge a free meal. Virtuosity in technique has always had a payoff of some kind. So it is legitimate to ask whether there is any such thing as pure self-expression apart from its social rewards. The itinerant bard or juggler, the musician, gladiator, or animal trainer could survive only by mastering the tunes or tricks that won the plaudits of the crowd. In the secular world, the success of the entertainer and scholar depends not on the will of the gods or on the mysterious working of fate, but on the ability to please either the patrons or the multitudes.

In the New York City subway train, a blind singer edges his way through the standing crowd, with staff and outstretched cup. What he collects may depend a good deal upon the character and sympathies of those who hear him, and somewhat upon what he chooses to sing and how well he sings it. But more than anything, it depends on the size of the crowd. Performers have always tried to expand their audiences, both to enlarge their incomes and also to increase the pleasure they take from the pleasure and approval they arouse in others.

Like humble artisans who must please their customers, the established author or composer receives a royalty every time a book is sold or a recording is played. At the other end of the spectrum is a Michelangelo designing St. Peter's Basilica, a gigantic public work for which no single worshipper is expected to contribute to the architect directly. There are large grey areas in between. Advertising is a form of patronage, which is always self-serving in one way or another, but which depends on a mass response.

A small audience of the privileged may be able to pay more than a large audience drawn from the mass; moreover, its tastes may accord better with those of the artist. A king, a duke, or an archbishop can offer greater rewards than the general public; his whims may be less fickle, his demands less exigent. While Benvenuto Cellini took the time to execute a single exquisite cup, an artisan in the market place could manufacture thousands to a few popular designs. In both cases, however, the cups had to be sold to someone willing to pay the price. We distinguish the two kinds of cups by their artistry rather than by the motivations of those who create them. With high technology, it is possible to mass-produce kitsch and beautifully designed objects with equal ease.

Howard Kaminsky, publisher of Hearst Trade Books Group:

No one gets a kick out of publishing a book that nobody reads.[70]

Performers thrive on applause and praise but survive on more material compensation. Can one differentiate between the social approval for an artistic achievement and cash payments as a manifestation of that approval? The answer to this question may depend on where approval and compensation come from. Different artists at different times look for acclaim in different quarters—not all from the same publics and commentators. They want to win audiences, to taste approbation, to get a response to what they are saying. But many of them are driven to say things they think are important even if they realize that almost noone wants to listen to them at the moment. They write "for the drawer," like Boris Pasternak, or paint while starving, like Camille Pissaro, in the hope that posterity might recognize the merit of what they wish to express.

Few of the people who produce the content of American mass media prize their artistic integrity as highly as a Pissaro or a Pasternak, or, for that matter, approach that degree of talent. It is a rare artist who has won both critical approval and mass public acclaim from contemporaries. Dickens was recognized by elite critics within his own time as a major literary figure, but millions of people, both in England and in the United States, avidly read the serializations of his novels. The popular 1960s pianist Liberace, responding to critics' sneers, said he cried all the way to the bank. Yet he surely would have been pleased if he could have earned both his fortune and critical plaudits. Anyone who makes a creative effort is anxious to get the regard of those he respects, but respect always rises for those who bestow their approval. Only a few thousand American authors depend on writing for their income, yet tens of thousands dedicate themselves to their craft as best they can. Those who earn their living by it are by no means the purest in heart.[71]

Mae West:

Virtue pays, if you can find a market for it.

A writer:

What this business is about—far and away more than creativity—is money.[72]

A comedy producer:

> I swear to you that artists like to be rewarded for their work at retail, and the freedom comes second.[73]

Screenwriter Dorothy Kingsley:

> I only wrote because I needed the money. I had no desire to express myself or anything like that.[74]

Paul Klein, then late of NBC, explained that he was in broadcasting because "It's kinda fun and they pay big money." His comment on press criticism of him was that "Some guy who makes $18,000 a year says that."

The dilemma of the artist accommodating to the harsh demands of the marketplace was nowhere made more explicit than in the golden era of Hollywood, which attracted such talented writers as William Faulkner, Aldous Huxley, F. Scott Fitzgerald, Dashiell Hammett, Lillian Hellman, Clifford Odets, and Nathaniel West. Long after writing the remark I quoted earlier, Thomas Mann said of this crew, which he observed at close quarters: "Anyone gambling on a career in movies was dependent on Satan's mercies."[75]

George Bernard Shaw (replying by cable to Samuel Goldwyn, who had invited him to Hollywood):

> Deeply regret collaboration impossible. You only interested in creativity. I only interested in money.

Somerset Maugham (in a letter to Edward Knobloch, August 21, 1921):

> I look back on my connection with the cinema world with horror mitigated only by the fifteen thousand dollars.

Not all the creative spirits who have been lured by the material rewards of the commercial culture are as well-known as Mann, Shaw, and Maugham, but many of them share the same ambiguity of feelings. Like journalists and copy editors working anonymously on a daily newspaper, writers in film and television are caught up in a collective enterprise, in which screen credits do not necessarily reflect their actual participation. These writers are not Faulkners or Fitzgeralds, nor do they enjoy the illusion of being in that league. The image-makers of Hollywood are torn between craftsmanship and contempt for their own creations. According to Benjamin Stein, some

> did not consider themselves as visual or literary artists but rather saw themselves as craftsmen or fabricators of a highly salable commodity. This was partly an appealing lack of affectation, but it was also a method of rationalizing the small amount of creative control that any one person ever has over the finished product on a TV show. . . . In Hollywood, almost nothing is explained except on the basis of conspiracies and cabals. . . . It probably has something to do with the unpredictability

and randomness of human life in Hollywood, especially in terms of success and failure.[76]

Stein describes TV writers as extremely productive, successful, and content. The TV image of life, which they have invented, or at least embellished, is that of Los Angeles itself—at least, of West Los Angeles. Yet they rebel against TV fare's "cheerfulness and antisepsis." They are prejudiced against business, the military, small towns, and the rich, though they are rich themselves. "All of them, even those with millions of dollars, believed themselves to be part of a working class distinctly at odds with the exploiting classes."[77]

It seems foolish to belabor creative individuals who adapt their talents to fit marketing requirements or who sell them outright, like scriptwriters in a Hollywood "stable," or advertising copywriters who describe themselves as "hired guns," when artistic geniuses have bowed to the same impulses and have not hesitated to earn their living working for popular media. Walt Whitman reviewed books for the *Brooklyn Eagle* and Henry James wrote miscellaneous magazine pieces to earn money between commercially unsuccessful novels. He once said, on writing a play: "I have been governed by the one sordid and urgent consideration of the possibility of making some money."[78]

The greatest of artists have freely acknowledged their willingness to follow market demands:

Wolfgang Amadeus Mozart:

> Believe me, my sole purpose is to make as much money as possible; for after good health it is the best thing to have.[79]

Igor Stravinsky:

> I do not wish to be buried in the rain, unattended, as Mozart was . . . the very image of Bartok's poverty-stricken demise . . . was enough to fire my ambition to earn every penny that my art would enable me to extract from the *society* that failed in its duty toward Bartok as it had earlier failed with Mozart.[80]

Pablo Picasso:

> In art, the mass of the people no longer seek consolation and exaltation, but those who are refined, rich, unoccupied, who are distillers of quintessences, seek what is new, strange, original, extravagant, scandalous. . . . The less they understood me, the more they admired me. By amusing myself with all these games, with all these absurdities, puzzles, rebuses, arabesques, I became famous and that very quickly. And fame for a painter means sales, gains, fortune, riches. And today, as you know, I am celebrated, I am rich. But when I am alone with myself, I have not the courage to think of myself as an artist in the great and ancient sense of the term. Giotto, Titian, Rembrandt, were great painters. I am only a public entertainer who has understood his times and exploited as best as he could the imbecility, the vanity, the cupidity of his contemporaries. Mine is a bitter confession, more painful than it may appear, but it has the merit of being sincere.[81]

Charlie Chaplin:

I went into the business for money, and the art grew out of it. If people are disillusioned by that remark, I can't help it. It's the truth.

And artists have been willing to modify what they had to say in order to win popular approval for their work. Herman Melville wrote the publisher of *Typee* that "the book is certainly intended for popular reading, or for none at all," and he therefore accepted the elimination of "all passages. . . . which offer violence to the feelings of any large class of readers." The serialization of novels in nineteenth-century newspapers and magazines enabled readers to respond to a work still in progress, and their responses could prompt an author like Charles Dickens to modify his intended plots.[82]

Tricks of the trade are the subject of "how to do it" manuals. Successful experiences are adopted and transmitted spontaneously and by example.

Norman Rockwell:

If a picture wasn't going very well I'd put a puppy dog in it, always a mongrel, you know, never one of the full bred puppies. And then I'd put a bandage on its foot. . . . I liked it when I did it, but now I'm sick of it.

Reminiscent of the blueprint for *USA Today* (evolved through an extensive series of market surveys) was George Gissing's recipe, a century earlier, for a proposed new paper, *Chit-Chat*. It was to be addressed to "the quarter-educated":

the young men and women who can just read, but are incapable of sustained attention. People of this kind want something to occupy them in trains, and, on 'buses and trams . . . bits of stories, bits of description, bits of scandal, bits of jokes, bits of statistics, bits of foolery. . . . No article in the paper is to measure more than two inches in length, and every inch must be broken into at least two paragraphs.[83]

To produce a publication so cunningly to fit a market niche requires a special kind of skill as well as a willingness to make compromises alien to the ideal of the unfettered artistic spirit. In *New Grub Street*, Gissing portrays the triumph of the self-serving, unscrupulous commercial writer over his talented and honest counterpart. His villain, Jasper Milvain, says of the miserable hero:

He is the old type of unpractical artist; I am the literary man of 1882. He won't make concessions, or rather, he can't make them; he can't supply the market. . . . Literature nowadays is a trade. Putting aside men of genius, who may succeed by mere cosmic force, your successful man of letters is your skilful tradesman. He thinks first and foremost of the markets; when one kind of goods begins to go off slackly, he is ready with something new and appetising.[84]

There's no question of the divine afflatus; that belongs to another sphere of life. . . . What on earth is there in typography to make everything it deals with sacred? I don't advocate the propagation of vicious literature; I speak only of good, coarse, marketable stuff for the world's vulgar. . . . If only I had the skill, I would produce novels outtrashing the trashiest that ever sold fifty thousand copies. But it needs skill, mind you; and to deny it is a gross error of the literary pedants. To please the vulgar you must, one way or another, incarnate the genius of vulgarity.[85]

    This chapter has traced the tangled and sometimes ignoble motives of those who produce commercial culture for the market, but it sets forth an essentially optimistic thesis. If popular tastes are not innate, if they are formed by our surroundings and reinforced by the mechanisms of distribution, publicity, and promotion, they do not have to be taken as they are. There is room for change and improvement. If it is the market that rewards "the genius of vulgarity," then presumably another, better standard exists. That standard is familiar to the creators of media content. But what of the more powerful people who manage media enterprises?

10

Managing Commercial Culture

What I want to say to you may or may not be what you want to hear. Reconciling this potential conflict in the realm of opinions is the art of politics. In the domain of culture it is the task of producers, publishers, and other entrepreneurs. As the last chapter has indicated, those who create expressions of one sort or another are engaged in a continuing struggle with those who disseminate what is created, though they are mutually dependent.

The conflict between them exists whether the public pays directly or advertisers pay for the privilege of reaching the public. It is found in elite media as well as in the mainstream of mass culture, and both in successful and financially troubled ones. The tension is present even in public or quasipublic institutions where the profit motive is not involved. In public broadcasting, just as with museums, orchestras, dance and opera companies, managements are engaged in a constant scrabble for funds and must weigh their public responsibilities against the demands of artists and professional staffs. The people who run these organizations spend no less time counting the house than those who run profit-hungry mass media. They need the money from admissions sales or contributions to balance budgets, get matching grants, and satisfy government officials; they also want the satisfaction of being recognized for the value of what they do.

In the last chapter we looked at the relationship between the people who create the content of commercial media and the ones who organize and market it. Now we shall turn to the way that media creators and media entrepreneurs respond to the demands of those who pay them. Here are the key points:

- Media entrepreneurs fill an essential managerial function, in a tradition with long historical antecedents.
- Creative individuals gravitate into managerial roles as their careers progress, and their personal outlook changes accordingly.

- Media tycoons cut a wider swathe in the public imagination than their counterparts in other industries, because the consequences of what they do are highly visible.
- Top media executives are disengaged from the products of their own organizations. Like the creators of commercial culture, they regard themselves as mere instruments of the more powerful forces of the market.

Media Entrepreneurship

Media are engaged in the diffusion of data, sentiments, conceptions, and imagery to large numbers of people, all done second-hand. Diffusion in every case requires a mechanism, a physical plant or facilities, an administrative structure of some kind, and a system of economic support. Assembling these elements demands considerable talent, generally of a different kind than that involved in creating content, which is considerably (though by no means entirely) rooted in artistic temperament. This distinction does not imply that the compiler of basketball scores or of commodity price tables is an artist, and that the builder of a great newspaper chain is not. Those whose career paths are dedicated to examining and explaining human experience, thoughts, and feelings organize their lives toward different goals than do entrepreneurs oriented to the success of their enterprises.

Some management executives are endowed with creative gifts themselves, many empathize strongly with those who possess them. The people who create media content generally share management's hopes for success and may have a high appreciation of the realistic constraints that must be placed on their own work.

Louis-Ferdinand Celine:

> All publishers are pimps and I hate every one of them, but you must accept their usefulness.

There is simply no way, as the history of commercial culture attests, to avoid or eliminate the conflict between those who have something to say and those whose services enable them to get it said. Long before the arrival of modern mass media, creative talents have been both intimate and uneasy with those who sponsor their work. Despite common interests, good will, and mutual understanding, there is an inherent incompatibility between the talent and business roles that sometimes moves into overt conflict when high principles appear to be at stake.

The origins of media entrepreneurship go back to the earliest commercial trade in art objects and experiences. There are parallels in the plastic arts, in publishing, and in the performing arts. Art that enters the market inevitably falls under the control of intermediaries, who buy and sell it like any other craft artifacts, not for their own pleasure, but as commodities whose prices will fluctuate with a demand that they have learned to predict. These intermediaries heighten the communicator's sensitivity to those toward whom the message is being directed, because they bring external criteria and rules to bear on what is produced.

Through most of history, patrons of the arts have dealt directly with artists rather than with the organizers of creative endeavors. With the emergence of mass media, the relationship of artists to patrons steadily became less important than their relationship to the entrepreneurs who could market their works to a larger audience. The art dealer, the book publisher, the producer of operas and concerts—these became the principal figures in encouraging talent, in commissioning works, in directing creative time and energy to produce the greatest return on investment.

The art dealer accumulates objects that can command—later or somewhere else—a better price than the artist can get for it at the moment. But dealers are not merely exploitative and extraneous outsiders; they perform the useful economic function of keeping artists fed and motivated in the intervals between the creation and disposition of their works; they assume the specialized burden of marketing; and, if they are successful, they develop the connoisseurship that enables them to guide the creative process intelligently.

Art dealers in the modern sense began their activities in the late Middle Ages, when paintings left the walls of churches and moved to easels, where they became mobile commodities, easily transferrable from one owner to another.[1] Paintings, originally dedicated to the church or to the private enjoyment of the nobility, thus developed a popular following. Exhibitions of art works, arranged in connection with saints' days and processions, brought painting to the attention of a wide public, made them a subject of discussion and connoisseurship, and encouraged the art dealer's trade.[2] In a market where art collectors seek social position through possessions, dealers use every wile of publicity and every shade of negotiating duplicity to kite artistic reputations. But successful art dealers, no matter how crass and cynical they may be, differ from other kinds of commodities traders in combining aesthetic judgment with an intuition of the potential buyers' response.

Publishers deal in words rather than objects but, like art merchants, they are essential intermediaries in the cultural market. The precedents for publishing entrepreneurship were already set before the invention of movable type. A small market for manuscript copies of literary and instructional works has probably existed since the invention of papyrus. Manuscript production was organized to meet market demands; there were established channels of distribution and sale. Since monastic scriptoria functioned in sloppy fashion, with inconsistent and often distorted texts, it fell to lay "stationers," in the Middle Ages, to produce accurate copies of books for universities and law courts. Fables, romances, and other nonreligious literature also crop up among illuminated manuscripts.[3] (Secular fiction had been disseminated in writing in a tradition that reached from the Greek theater to medieval romances and collections of fables and cautionary tales, but it did not reach a wide public until it took flight in the printed books of the seventeenth century. The wondrous stories in the *Bible* and the lives of the saints were surely experienced as entertainments in print as they had been in manuscript form, and just as morality plays had been for centuries.)

Printing revolutionized the economics of producing information, creating a substantial apparatus of manufacturing and distribution, and producing the first large-scale demand for literary expression. Incunabula, the first printed books, were generally produced in runs of about 200 copies, but their titles did not differ from those of manuscripts already in circulation. Within a relatively short time the preponderance of religious works gave way to instruction in the useful arts and other secular titles with an increasingly popular appeal.

Printers—since they were commonly booksellers, too—moved swiftly from the exercise of their purely mechanical skills to apply judgment over the content of what they wanted to duplicate. Even in their early days, they must have been more sensitive than authors to the public's desires. Since that sensitivity was their main resource, they also had more at stake than the authors, who had their talent to fall back upon. The two parties needed each other, but had their respective interests.

While printers could easily beat the expense of producing manuscripts, they did not necessarily flourish as businessmen. Historian John Feather notes that Gutenberg "was not only the first printer, he was also the first printer to go bankrupt."[4] In spite of financial setbacks, some 20 million copies of 40,000 book editions were printed in the half-century after Gutenberg's *Bible*. (This was an extraordinary flood, considering that Europe had a population of only about 80 million at that time, mostly illiterate.[5]) The sale of almanacs reached 400,000 in 1680. Such a substantial audience represented a market that attracted entrepreneurs and specialized skills. From the eighteenth century on, it was possible for a writer to support himself. By 1722, in London 5,000 people were involved with the production of newspapers alone.[6]

With the growth of subscription publishing in the eighteenth century, writers became "professionals" who had to meet market demand rather than the approval of a few wealthy supporters. They could disengage from direct contact with the reading audience, which was no longer composed of specific and known individuals—patrons and potential patrons; it was an impersonal mass.[7]

Books and other publications required a support structure to be produced, bought, and sold. Dr. Johnson struggled personally to sell subscriptions to his encyclopedia, as John James Audubon did later for *Birds of America*. But more often, as Honoré de Balzac poignantly describes in *Lost Illusions*, the creative individual depended upon a businessman to bring his work before the public. Thus an unpleasant and persistent fissure appeared between the artist's motivation to utter whatever was on his mind and the practical necessity of embodying his works in a form that would win approval and thus satisfy the need to earn a living.

Like publishers and art dealers, impresarios of the performing arts antedate the mass media. They are by definition individuals of taste, or at least persons endowed with exceptional sensitivity to the taste of others. However, taste is insufficient without the managerial and administrative skills required to shape and activate an enterprise.

Impresarios, like publishers (but unlike art dealers coping one-on-one with an exclusive clientele), deal directly with an impersonal consuming public. They hark back to a tradition different from that of publishing—namely, the management of leisure, sport, and play in the era before mass media.[8] The arts have sometimes been identified as a form of play,[9] but they are different. Children can frolic spontaneously in a sand pile; like athletics, the arts demand organization.

In a live performance, the acts of creative presentation and of consumption occur simultaneously in a particular place. Planned arrangements of some kind are required even for a troubadour in a command performance for a lone barbarian king. Artistic presentations commonly involve more than a one-person audience; not uncommonly, a number of artists participate. To ensure that the public and the right combination of performers will assemble in the right place at the right time, protocol may have to be considered and incentives must be offered. (Money represents only one form of compensation, though it presumably distinguishes professionals from amateurs.) Whether the arrangements are handled by a village elder, a witch doctor, a court chamberlain, or an ecclesiastical bureaucrat, someone must be in charge to take care of such practical matters if the show is to go on. Thus entertainment—as opposed to random playful behavior—by its very nature assumes a planning process.

The theater of Periclean Greece, with its linkages to commercialized athletics, had an important place for organizers and impresarios.[10] The dramatists were referred to not as writers, but as producers, "teachers of choruses."[11] The theater was a collective enterprise that required selecting and perhaps commissioning plays, casting and rehearsing actors, getting clearance from the authorities, setting the venue and time, notifying the populace, and handling the expenses.

A continuous line runs from these early efforts to the performing arts of our own time. Even the sacred music of the medieval Church required the handling of a great many practical details. Guilds organized feast days at which plays and other entertainments, often employing elaborately prepared costumes, were part of the proceedings. At one three-day affair in Valenciennes, 562 guests at a banquet in the Wool Hall were serenaded by fifty musicians.[12] In Italy, as early as 1304, Giorgio Vasari mentions the skills required to stage-manage the outdoor performance of sacred plays.[13]

The development of secular orchestral music, both for the court and for the public, steadily increased both the complexity of the activity and the importance of the organizers. At the beginning of the sixteenth century, bands of itinerant musicians were sponsored by aristocrats or by municipal groups.[14] These companies must have had professional managers, possibly drawn from the ranks of the players themselves.

Opera, more than any other art form, requires the recruitment, organization, and coordination of a great variety of talents. When opera left the precincts of the court and entered the realm of the civic theater, it lost its reliance upon noble patronage and became dependent on a paying public. Venetian opera troupes traveled throughout Italy, recruiting local musicians to supplement their own companies, and seeking local patrons. At this point the figure of the impresario emerges.[15]

Similarly, at about this time the English theater became established as a commercial enterprise, though its companies also still received patronage from the Lord Chamberlain, from universities, and from the inns of court. The Renaissance theater had a mass audience, and the professional troupes were run in a businesslike fashion.[16] Staging masques in the days of the Stuarts required the services of 100 artisans just to construct the stage, apart from those needed to operate the scenery. There were a "turning machine" and elaborate stage effects. The Lord Chamberlain handled the seating arrangements for the spectators, who were carefully graded by rank, with no reserved seating.[17]

Andrea Palladio's 1524 Teatro Olimpico in Vicenza was a triumphant adaptation of classical form to contemporary technology and needs. In the ensuing centuries, great theaters were constructed both as emblems of royal majesty and as monuments of civic pride. The substantial investment in the buildings demanded an impressive dedication to the task of keeping them filled. This need strengthened the function of the individuals who could attract the public by mustering creative forces. The organizational structure became steadily more complex.

Eighteenth-century Europe evolved such formalized entertainments as horse racing and the circus. (In Spain, professional bullfighting began at about the same time.) Posters and other forms of advertisements were used to attract the public. As Peter Burke describes it,

> The elements of the circus, performers such as clowns and acrobats, are . . . traditional; what was new was the scale of the organization, the use of a building as a setting for the performance rather than a street or square, and the role of the entrepreneur. Here as elsewhere in the eighteenth century economy, large-scale enterprises were driving out small ones.[18]

This development continued through the next half-century and across the Atlantic. Local permanent stock companies that dominated the American theater were replaced by traveling combination companies. By the close of the nineteenth century, a half-dozen theater owners and booking agents created a centralized national booking monopoly.[19] Even before Hollywood and Radio City, the commercialization of leisure was approaching its present stage of concentrated power.

Switching Careers and Switching Values

In the volatile business of entertainment, as we saw in Chapter 2, many individuals are able to transfer their skills and energies from one media form to another. A common career path carries them from entry-level jobs in agencies or other advertising organizations into television networks and then into the world of the Hollywood studios.[20] In any media organization, the path to advancement leads through added managerial responsibilities: supervising others, coordinating previously unfamiliar activities. When people reach the ceiling of achievement within the creative side of the organization, ambition often propels them over the line, where the financial concerns predominate.

John B. Evans, News Corporation's Executive Vice President for Development.

> I am not a logical person; I think of myself as an artist.[21]

A film producer, commenting on his colleague, Steven Spielberg:

> One part of Steven wants to say, "Hey kids, let's put on a show" and the other part wants to build an empire.[22]

One thread that runs through the vocabulary of successful executives is the theme of business as a game, enjoyed both for the competitive thrill of a possible victory and for the childlike pleasure of manipulation. (NBC's programming "genius," Brandon Tartikoff, before he left for Paramount, called a studio "a big toy to play with.") The producer-director Francis Ford Coppola invested his substantial earnings from the first two "Godfather" films into "Apocalypse Now," which expressed his personal

feelings of revulsion toward the Vietnam War. He persisted in the face of unantici-
pated disasters (a typhoon and the heart attack of a principal actor) that threatened
bankruptcy; ultimately he won both Oscars and huge financial success. It is rare to
find this combination of creative impulse and entrepreneurial spirit in the same
talented individual. In most media enterprises these qualities are embodied in
different people, held together by tact and travail.

Media expressions that begin life as expressions of radicalism or rebellion often
end up by being coopted into the Establishment, as they seek to survive, and
ultimately to flourish, by broadening their constituency and their advertising base.
The alternative press, which began as an expression of the radical "underground" of
the late 1960s, later found a new role as the voice of amusement-minded and upwardly
mobile young singles. Jan Wenner's *Rolling Stone*, an angry voice of the countercul-
ture, became the house organ of the commercial rock music industry, intimately tied
to the giant music recording empires. The *Village Voice* passed through the hands of a
media lord (Rupert Murdoch) into those of a birdseed and real estate king (Leonard
Stern). The *Maine Times* was bought by millionaire Dodge Morgan. Its advertising
department claimed that the average reader had an investment portfolio worth
$90,000, not including real estate.

At a meeting of the Association of Alternative Newsweeklies, according to one
account, the publisher of the Boston *Phoenix* walked around "with a Louis Vuitton-
covered notebook and a gold watch that would knock your socks off," while a
representative of Detroit's *Metro Times* complained that "doing stories on the city's
underclass really hurts distribution in the suburbs. . . . [A] blow-dried management
type . . . didn't see the need for 'messianic zeal' in his papers."[23] This transformation
may be part of an inevitable cycle. Fortunately, a new generation of radicals and
iconoclasts is always ready to emerge.

Media Tycoons

Large media corporations are sometimes run in a fashion that recalls the days of the
nineteenth-century industrial buccaneers, with corporate jets and lavish vacation
homes for key executives.[24] Media tycoons have been objects of public fascination
and gossip since the days of the Victorian press lords. This interest seems to go
beyond the level of curiosity aroused by anyone else of extraordinary wealth and
power. Someone who controls the flow of ideas and emotions to vast numbers of
people is inherently more interesting than someone who merely controls the supply
of their bread and butter. Moreover, the activities of their overlords are of special
concern to all those who work in the media themselves, and this attention produces
secondary waves of titillation in the general public.

In every field of enterprise, tycoons are individuals of exceptional drive, intelligence, and organizing ability. What makes them tycoons is their expansionary
ambitions, their refusal to be satisfied with whatever they already possess, and their
vision of great external forces on which they can ride. Whatever self-doubts they may
harbor, they project an air of great confidence in their own convictions and insights.
Tycoons are decisive; when they make mistakes, they cut their losses. They are rarely

lovable. Sometimes they are charming, even charismatic, but they are also calculating and impersonal. The morals of the new media tycoons, like Ted Turner and Rupert Murdoch, may be no worse than those of such predecessors as Joseph Pulitzer or Robert McCormick, but their power is so much greater that their characters become pertinent public matters. (Robert Maxwell, exposed as a swindler after his suicide, was caught by a declining economy; had he managed to stay the course through an upturn in the business cycle, his character might have remained a matter of gossip rather than of scandal and tragedy.)

In the world of media, some tycoons (like Hearst, Paley, or Murdoch) have started with advantages; others (like Pulitzer, Sarnoff, Turner and Maxwell) have not. Wealthy individuals have inherited media empires and presided over their successful expansion. Self-made managers have ascended to the top of great media companies and run them in effortless style. Tycoons are different from both these breeds. They shun the collegial management and bureaucratic administrative structure of the modern corporation. They want to be omnipresent, but they also know how to make themselves invisible. The publisher of one magazine sought by Murdoch was given 48 hours to respond to a purchase offer. After 1½ hours of conversation, the two men shook hands on the deal. The publisher saw the tycoon only twice in the ensuing two years. "You're left to do your own thing," he says.

Martin Singerman, president of Murdoch's News America Publishing (most of whose properties were sold to liquidate some of its massive debt):

> If we're considering a new magazine [Murdoch] says, "Show me an editor." He's not interested in market surveys.[25]

An associate remarked of one tycoon, "He can't possibly get into the details with all of the properties. But he picks the editors, and he knows what they think." Even though they cannot micromanage every obscure element of their domains, and sometimes give their subordinates the illusion of total autonomy, tycoons maintain a watchful eye over details, offer critiques, render judgments. Like Josef Stalin calling the poet Ossip Mandelstam in the middle of the night, tycoons want subordinates to feel their invisible presence at all time.

Needless to say, all bosses offer criticisms and make demands, but the criticisms and demands made by tycoons are apt to be peculiarly outrageous and imperious. Their behavior becomes legendary, thereby adding to their mystique and fascination, to the perception that they are different from other people. Axel Springer's closest associates referred to him respectfully in public as Herr Springer, befitting the formal traditions of Middle Europe. Maxwell preferred to be known as Bob even among the lower echelons of his troops, but when he acquired control of Macmillan, he summoned his American executives to a 4:00 a.m. meeting at the Waldorf-Astoria hotel to plan the physical occupation of the offices. (That was, after all, already 9 o'clock in London.) According to his former assistant at the *New York Daily News*, Carolyn Hinsey, Maxwell "delighted in throwing faxes in the toilet and then telling the person who had sent them, 'Oh yes, I am reviewing them now.' "[26]

Bob Smith, formerly president of one of Robert Maxwell's subsidiaries:

> He operates as if he is the sun and you are the moon.[27]

Tycoons hire and fire unpredictably, paying fabulous salaries to newcomers whose talents they have spotted, and dismissing, without explanation, faithful retainers who have built important parts of their businesses.

Robert Maxwell:

> When I fire someone it is like a thunderclap. . . . My primary duty is to hire and fire editors. I treat them like a field marshal.

• Stephen Chao, president of News Corporation's Fox Television Stations and Fox News, attacked local censors in a speech before the heads of affiliated stations. (At this time, the Fox network was broadcasting shows like "Studs," which featured sexual banter in which contestants were asked, "Which is the guy who has bounce in his butt?" and "Which one is more likely to find the G-spot?") To emphasize his point, Chao had a young man disrobe for 30 seconds while he was speaking. Rupert Murdoch, who was present, called this "a tremendous misjudgment" and fired him on the spot.[28]

Tycoons generate great enmities from former associates, who, if sufficiently talented, express themselves in memoirs, biographies, and exposes; their currency further enhances the great man's reputation as someone larger than life.[29] Occasionally (as in the case of Allen Neuharth), a tycoon may actually write an autobiography that enhances his own reputation as an S.O.B.[30]

In the past, media tycoons took pleasure in exercising political influence and in giving rein to their personal views. Now they ostentatiously tend to subordinate their private opinions to the financial needs of the enterprise, much as they submerge their personal preferences in media content. Some tycoons prefer to stay out of the limelight; others indulge their egos. Hearst splashed his signed editorials across the front pages of his papers. Maxwell put his own picture on playing cards used in his London *Daily Mirror*'s circulation promotion game. After Murdoch and his wife went to worship in television preacher Robert Schuller's Crystal Cathedral, the minister's "Hour of Power" was given free air time on the satellite Sky Channel.

Why and how then, do tycoons continue to attract to their entourages people of great ability and professional skills, strong will and independent ambition? Tycoons pay well and are skilled in the arts of wooing, but that is only a partial explanation. The main attraction is in the illusion tycoons project of enterprises in perpetual motion and growth, filled with boundless opportunities for adventurers who will play the game. (The game, in Maxwell's case, turned out to be Russian roulette.)

CEO of a large multimedia company, on the subject of motivating executives:

> Every once in a while you have to throw a piece of raw meat into the cage.[31]

Another multimedia CEO:

> I don't think you can't exist small, but I think this is a day of bigness and to attract managers you have to grow; to be healthy you have to grow. Particularly in a moment when our business is topping off, when everything is infringing on everything else, when we're being challenged and our businesses are being challenged.[32]

Tycoons are wreathed in swirls of excitement. Precisely because they can be counted on to do the unexpected, each morning promises a new acquisition, a reorganization, a change in the cast of characters. The uncertainty and anticipation provoke an endless stream of speculation and gossip that enlivens the daily routine of the staff, enhances motivation and morale, and intensifies the dramas that permeate the life of any organization.

Henry Luce, to the *Time* editorial staff, after he decided to back Eisenhower for the presidency in 1952:

> In case some of you don't know me, let me introduce myself. I am your boss. I can hire and I can fire. Any questions?[33]

When S. I. Newhouse Jr. fired Robert Bernstein from Random House (which he had built into a billion dollar company), a flurry of gossip arose in "the publishing community," according to *The New York Times*' Edwin McDowell: One "dismayed senior executive" at Random House commented, "Publishing companies depend on morale. These are not cement companies." McDowell added,

> More than many professions, book publishing is dependent on an atmosphere of collegiality, a feeling of being part of a team. Below the top, salaries are not high, so much of the satisfaction comes from doing work considered important, like publishing books.[34]

Yet staff morale is a secondary concern for tycoons whose eyes are set on financial targets. Whereas media professionals are often motivated by idealism, the need for self-expression, and other nonpecuniary considerations, tycoons have low tolerance for the intrusion of sentiment into what they perceive as straightforward business economics. They may justify their bottom-line concerns with the argument that these make creative expression possible.

S. I. Newhouse Jr.:

> I do not like charity cases. I believe my operations should have the sense of security that comes from knowing their work leads to a profit. Businesses that lose money are insecure and do not take the chances they should to achieve quality.[35]

Tycoons become what they are by making deals, borrowing money, twisting arms, seeking out legal loopholes, using the rented skills of high-priced specialists to put together the imaginative packages that guarantee new expansion. They think in large and daring terms, enjoy money games, and pride themselves on their financial capabilities. Some media tycoons purport to avoid meticulously any interference with the professional or creative people in their own organizations, but most pride themselves on their sensitivity to public taste and consider their strong suit to be their understanding of the mass audience, its predilections, its moods, and the direction of its evolving interests. They do not pretend to share these predilections or interests, but they do pretend to respect them. No tycoon would, even in an unguarded moment, denounce the vulgarity of the tastes to which he caters or the iniquity of the political opinions he helps to promulgate. He tells himself, as he tells others, that his task is to provide large numbers of people with ready access to the kind of information and entertainment they want, and he would insist that this is a necessary task, even a noble one.

Rupert Murdoch:

> When the beaver gnaws down a tree, he isn't thinking of his vital ecological role either. But nevertheless he has one. And I think we have one too. . . . We destroy monopolies because we hope to make money for ourselves, but we enjoy it because it has clear social benefits as well.[35]

Cesare Borgia, Francois I, and the Archbishop of Salzburg knew what they liked, and hired the talent to produce it. Today's media tycoons exercise far greater cultural power, but insist that they are merely instruments of higher forces.

The Media Habits of Media Executives

Unidentified Hollywood mogul:

> This film is better than a masterpiece. It's mediocre![37]

If the rank and file creators of media content are often uncomfortable or ambivalent about their tasks, few such qualms or scruples are evident among their masters. However, both at the top and in the ranks there is a sense that the system operates on its own momentum and by rules that are beyond the power of individuals to alter.

A limited number of powerful individuals run the large multimedia organizations. Some are reclusive or self-important, but a dozen agreed to talk to me in confidence about their own media habits and preferences. Many of them stressed a point we have already heard repeatedly—that they are in business to meet the public's tastes and demands, not to satisfy or impose their own.

There is, as might be expected, no uniformity in their preferences or habits, but there are some recurrent themes. Almost all are diligent students of the businesses they are in, spending vast amounts of office and private time to keep up with the output of their own and rival organizations. They are themselves voracious consumers of media, but little of this consumption is exclusively for their private delectation. Their social and business contacts are interwoven.

A multi-media tycoon:

> Keeping up with the competition comes about through being very active in professional associations. Taking all the time I spend mixing with and cottoning to and charming, I spend 15–20% of my time with competitors. I spend at least half my time looking at media other than our company properties. I start every day reading every newspaper available in the area I'm in. I'm a nomad, a gypsy. But wherever I go, I nearly always call on the local media owners. As CEO I probably devote half my time to eyeballing, or meeting, or otherwise studying other media. Most of my reading and viewing is related to business or professional interests. My reading and viewing would total six or seven hours a day. Newspaper reading in the morning would take a

minimum of two to three hours. I have four TV sets on all the time, to the networks and CNN, trying to find ideas to use. If I go to see a movie that has nothing to do with business, I'll still think of business applications. Even if things are entertainment, I automatically translate it into the business at hand. In the media business, when you're awake you're at work.[38]

This kind of dedication is symbolized by the wall of television monitors that dominates a network president's spacious office, with a paper-covered desk and a magnificent bare marble conference table. A fourway split screen carries CBS, NBC, ABC, and CNN. Another large screen carries the local company-owned station. The sound is on full-blast as I enter the room. Yes, he tells me, the videos are on all day, though he mutes the sound when he has visitors or when he wants quiet. Apparently the noise does not bother him in his routine work. He also gets a feed of new program pilot tapes from Hollywood that he can look at.

> I skim. And I watch at home in the evening. Do I watch for my own pleasure? Yes, I watch the news in various forms, and I'm a great fan of public television and A & E.

(Evidently his personal viewing preferences are different from those that are satisfied by his own organization.) Another network executive, commenting on the monitors:

> They're just humming away there like Muzak, and after a while you just ignore them unless something catches your attention.

Some tycoons arise at five in the morning to examine the fresh day's newspapers; others take home videocassettes of the latest network releases or syndicated programs. Virtually all are regular readers of *The New York Times* and *Wall Street Journal* and compulsive scanners of the trade press.

One reports:

> I read lots and lots of magazines. All of the news weeklies, *Forbes, Business Week, Ad Age, Professional Selling, Cable Week.* I see the *Columbia Journalism Review* and the *Harvard Business Review.* For fun I read *American Heritage, Smithsonian, Runner's World, World War II* magazine. I get *Fortune* at home.

Much of their reading, light and serious, is done on airplanes; one listens to management self-improvement audio tapes in his car on the way to work.

While they are somewhat disposed to disassociate themselves from popular tastes, their remarks reveal few traces of intellectual snobbery; in fact, they occasionally offer a self-deprecatory aside about their own vulgar interests. Apart from business-related subjects, their media exposure tends to conform with the habits of their social class. Not one mentioned reading a book of any heavy intellectual content or seeing a film that might be considered avant-garde or off-beat. One major figure in the media world entertains himself with detective stories. Others are buffs of military history. One has all twenty-one videotapes of "Victory at Sea." Another has 150 on World War II. Still another describes his book reading: "I read great trash. Anything with a swastika on the front, I usually read that." (This is still a different case from that of Time Warner's Steven Ross, who was reported "never" to read any books.)[39]

A number of the executives I interviewed acknowledge that they are under extreme time pressures that restrict their exposure to new ideas, or to any ideas in depth.

Senior television executive:

> Television is a lot less urgent than it used to be. In the course of business I have a certain amount of reading of scripts and treatments, and I have less time than I used to for other kinds of reading. I don't read as easily as I used to.[40]

Some seem to husband their free time, while others expend it in chance and casual fashion, much like the public at large.

Publisher of a large magazine:

> I press the buttons and I stop at anything that looks interesting.

CEO of a station group:

> I'm a big movie guy. I see all the latest films, about two a week, going out to the theater. I like to watch the movies when they first come out. Hollywood picks up all the newest, latest trends. They know what's going on in the world. We turn around and spend a lot of money on movies.

For this reason, some media tycoons find it hard to separate their personal values from their business values.

Senior television executive:

> Personal and professional is one and the same. In the old days everybody sat down and watched the "Ed Sullivan Show." That kind of viewing has gone by the boards. The viewer's attention span is much shorter. There's a lot of grazing and inattentive viewing. They watch less intensely than they used to. I may be in the business, but my viewing isn't all that different. . . . You can watch a relatively little amount and still keep abreast of the programming. I make it a point to see each new show once relatively early in the season.[41]

CEO of a multimedia company:

> I have a set in the office, with a VCR attached, and I watch stuff that our folks are bicycling around the company. At home I'll look at business-related things like Michael Porter's Strategic Planning tapes.

Apart from what they ingest for professional or business reasons, the media preferences of most top media executives are the middlebrow tastes of their counterparts in any business. Most are not bothered by commercialism, vulgarity, violence, or obscenity; it simply does not enter their thinking. They seem incapable of stepping aside from their own work and saying, "Here is where I'm forced to make compromises." They have no particular philosophy that underlies what they do, or at least any that they can easily articulate.

CEO of a station group:

> My taste is different from the average person's, but I respect it. I would never be where I am today if I tried to program a television station to my liking. The first ten years in this business I tried to determine what's black and white; now I live in a sea of gray. By black and white I mean very strong opinions for or against. I don't interject myself into programming decisions. You just have to respect the ideas on the creative side. I just think anyone who feels strongly definitive today becomes argumentative. Things are moving so fast today that people shouldn't get too definitive in their opinions.

Other media tycoons clearly distinguish their personal preferences from those of the mass audiences for which their enterprises produce.
Former TV network president:

> Those people who aren't broadcasters born and raised simply don't have the same sense of responsibility as those with the bottom-line mentality. I don't think you can wrest CBS away from Larry Tisch and give it back to Frank Stanton. The whole thing goes back to the white hot competition in broadcasting today. If you just have three grand old networks plodding along and now you have all those new players doing competitive things, they're going to do what's calculated to get the viewer's attention, and he's going to eschew information and watch something witless and forgettable. Nobody should go to jail for it. The viewer can view whatever he wants. I just deplore it. Now with the new technology you would think you would have a lot of narrowcasting, with a giant menu of choices, but it isn't happening. I'm really bitching about the nature of the viewer. He's going to go for the junk food. Adding all of those other choices doesn't mean adding any new choices at all. . . . The way I feel is negative. All of those opportunities we have to spend our time — as the quantity increases the quality of what we spend our time on decreases.

The CEO of a large multimedia company says he looks at the first 7 minutes of the morning news "to tell me what I should know that's going on", but other than that sees no TV, except the Sunday morning programs, like "Meet the Press."
He explains:

> I have no judgment about programs. I have no interest in them. It bores me. I try to look at the popular shows, but I can't follow them. I can't stand it.

CEO of another major multimedia company:

> TV is a medium of the lowest common denominator. Whoever can generate the greatest numbers wins. Cable has brought in narrowcasting, but it's still a mass medium. I think it's hard with commercial TV to produce anything but passive programming. TV is a passive medium. If you start high-brow stuff that doesn't have broad-based appeal your ratings will be off and you lose your mass audience. I think you're going to continue to see the lowest common denominator approach. It's just the nature of the beast. I think it's more a comment on America than on the media. We're a mirror of society.

CEO of a third multimedia company:

I usually found that when I went to network affiliates' meetings and watched the pilots of the new shows that I never found much that I liked. My tastes are not the same as those of the people who watch them.

Senior film executive:

You can personally like some things and you'll never make them because it doesn't have a commercial potential. Other things you might bend over backwards a little to push them. Is this something that someone would go to see? We're in a business, and you can't run away from that. You have to look at things from the standpoint of whether they'll make a profit.

President of a large multimedia company:

When I was responsible for our broadcasting operations, I went to visit one of our television stations. I had a whole sheaf of questions I had written out on a yellow lined pad, and the station manager had people running in and out of his office to find me the answers, all day long. When I went back to the hotel room before we were meeting for dinner I had our station on and the news show was quite well done. Then came this game show. I couldn't imagine why anyone would watch it. I could hardly believe how bad it was. When I talked to the station manager he said that was the highest-rated show we have. People who are educated and have learned the joy of reading and thinking are going to spend a hell of a lot less time sitting on their ass eating peanuts and drinking beer and watching that crap.

Senior TV executive:

I don't watch a lot of television. I go cherry picking for the newest sporting event or other events. I dip around among the morning shows. I don't watch at all during the day. In the evening, the news, and maybe there'll be something that I'll watch—the beginning of Carson or "Nightline." Series programming—I see almost none of it. I don't think I'm unusual.

In the 1950s and early 1960s, the wealthy publisher John Hay Whitney poured millions of dollars into the New York *Herald Tribune* in an effort to restore its failing readership. In his Fifth Avenue apartment, he discussed reader interests one day with a market researcher, Eric Marder, and spoke of his ceaseless effort to produce a paper that would reflect the highest editorial integrity and quality. Marder said he admired this idealism, but asked, "How many people, Mr. Whitney, own the kind of Impressionist paintings you have on your walls?" Whitney reflected, then replied, "You know, I've never thought of it that way!"

It is possible to acknowledge taste differences while avoiding value judgments. A CEO of a large multimedia company, asked if there was ever any incongruity between his own tastes and his publications, replied

All the time. I keep them separate. . . . I think the unsuccessful publisher or editor is the one who attempts to dictate what people should be reading, what should be of interest to the people rather than developing a product that's relevant to their needs.

Senior Hollywood executive:

> I try to see at least one episode of most new shows. Very rarely would I watch more than one. I look to see what new ideas I can get, or to spot new talent, for things we may cast in the future. I see almost every new film that comes out, three or four a week. [I wouldn't see] the fifth "Rambo," or other sequels. Some of the mindless violence, because I can't stand that stuff. I read. I read script material, and some books that I read for pleasure when I'm traveling. Both fiction and nonfiction. What I read for pleasure and for business overlaps. I read the trades, and seven or eight magazines. You're always looking at material you might be able to use. When I go to the theater in New York or London, I'm also looking to see if it would be a picture.

Intelligent, amiable, and admirable though they may be, the people who run large media enterprises generally appear to regard the output of their own organizations as somewhat beyond their control. They certainly do not regard it as an extension of their personal interests or a reflection of their own values. They are not unmindful of the cultural and political power their companies exercise, but they regard themselves as responsible custodians of a financial trust rather than as keepers of a sacred flame or as crusaders for enlightenment.

The Public Interest

David O. Selznick, to screenwriter:

> Write whatever you want as long as there's a love scene and the girl jumps in the volcano at the end.[43]

For the majority of media executives who defend their output in spite of their personal distaste for it, the rationale is clear; they are in business to give the public what it wants. Marvin Antonowsky, at the time vice-president for programming, NBC:

> The price of failure looms too large for us not to make the pragmatic decisions that are necessary, even though we may not like doing it.[43]

Roger King, syndicator of "Oprah Winfrey," "Wheel of Fortune" and "Jeopardy":

> The people are the boss. We listen to the audience, see what they want and try to accommodate them. I know it sounds simplistic, but that's exactly what it is."[44]

Roone Arledge, then president of ABC News and Sports:

> I don't think it's our responsibility to sit and determine what people must see for their own good. If you don't recognize the forces that play on what people watch and what they don't, then you're a fool and should be in a different business.[45]

Hollywood producer:

We are absolutely a 100% commercially oriented enterprise. . . . Films that don't get the rating points are not going to be made.[46]

Producer:

You have to be a salesperson. We are all salespeople.[47]

Just as media moguls refer to newspapers and magazines as "properties," they refer to television programs as "products," "inventory," "projects," and "brands." Such analogies to manufacturing help to sustain the illusion that impersonal forces are at work, obliterating the need for any value judgments on the part of the participants.

Media producers conscious of the shortcomings of what they produce are quick to point out that they are merely yielding to the pressures imposed upon them; they are only following orders. The blame lies elsewhere, with network or studio heads, with advertisers, with the ratings services. Anthony D. Thomopoulous, then president of ABC's entertainment division, told *The New York Times'* critic John O'Connor that producers would drive the quality of programming down if left to their own devices, adding "the network tells them not what to do but what not to do." Producers, in turn, complain about their powerlessness, their lack of status as "creative artists."[48] Norman Lear (before cable cut into the dominance of the networks):

> It is true that we who produce and write are responsible for physically producing violence, but the men and women in this community who make their living writing and directing television have only three theatres [CBS, ABC, NBC] to sell their wares. So when you go to any of the three theatres, you often find yourself writing what it is they are interesting in buying. And if they are interested in buying a cop show or a private eye show, and within that context they are interested in as much action as they can get, then that's what you, as a craftsman, as a person with something to sell and a family to support, must do because that's what the buyer wants.[49]

The most powerful media tycoons, in turn, can point a finger at the writers and producers when the brutality of content is at issue:

Rupert Murdoch:

> If it involves personal cruelty, sadism—obviously you would never do that. The trouble is, of course, that you run a studio, and how free are you to make these rules? The creative people give you a script and are given last cut on a movie. The next thing, you have a thirty-million-dollar movie in the can which you may disapprove of.[50]

Defenders of the mass media *status quo* have long fallen back on the phrase "cultural democracy" to justify their pursuit of audience numbers and to decry the imposition of other external criteria for judging content.[51] The establishment view in mass media management has always been that the public interest is best defined by the public's interests.

"How do you describe a good book?" Ralph Daigh of Fawcett's Gold Medal Books was asked by a member of the House Select Committee on Current Pornographic Materials in 1952. (The Committee had attacked paperbacks for "the dissemination of artful appeals to sensuality, immorality, filth, perversion and degeneracy.") Daigh replied, "A book is usually a good book if the public buys it in quantity." Pressed on this point, he added, "When the public buys a product in the multimillion lots, that is an endorsement by the public, and it does connote that it is a good book.[52]

Rupert Murdoch:

If William Shakespeare were alive today, he'd probably be the chief scriptwriter for "Dallas."[53] [But this is said cynically, *pour épater les bourgeois*.]

David Sarnoff:

We're in the same position as a plumber laying pipes. We're not responsible for what goes through the pipe.[54]

Frank Stanton, in 1960:

A program in which a large part of the audience is interested is by that very fact a program in the public interest.[56]

This last is a play on words, which confuses desire with well-being. It is like arguing that children with an insatiable craving for chocolate or adults with an incessant yen for cigarettes serve their own interests when they satisfy their wishes. Yet the proposition is central to the workings of commercial culture.

The BBC's Robert Silvey once commented that "giving the public what it wants" is a meaningless phrase that, if replaced by what it means in practice—namely "giving the majority of the public what they seem most disposed to consume"—does not sound so attractive in comparison to "giving various segments of the public what they most need."[56] This still leaves open the question of how the public's "needs" are to be determined.

The repercussions of what is read, seen, or heard affect everyone—not merely the individuals who do the reading, viewing, or listening. It is not merely the interests of its own audience that are engaged when a medium comes up for judgment. Society as a whole has a stake in every form of media expression, inasmuch as it helps to shape values and behavior with which all its members must coexist. The profit-centered rules of the marketplace are not necessarily the only ones, or even the most appropriate ones, that should apply to institutions that shape national values and character.

In the era of private patronage, the aesthetic values of patrons necessarily jibed with those of the creative individuals they supported. When advertisers pay the bills, this congruence of judgment disappears. We saw in the previous chapter that the creators of commercial culture are in many cases uncomfortable with the concoctions they serve up, but they insist that they are simply following the accepted recipes. In this chapter, I have shown that their outlook is shared by at least some of the people on top. Individuals who make the transition from creative work to management generally are transformed in the process. If not, they can hardly handle their new assignments comfortably. Most of the people who run large media organizations approach their work in an impersonal, businesslike spirit, one quite different from the creative individual's impulse to say something that needs saying. Whom will they be trying to please, as advertising's share of the nation's media bill gets smaller?

11

Media Support and Media Substance

Great technological and economic changes are transforming media content. The media system tilts increasingly toward the audiovisual and away from print, altering our perceptions of our surroundings. The blurring of fact and fiction is part of this larger process. It would be a mistake to equate print with information and other media with entertainment. The distinction between information and entertainment is, in any case, obscure and arbitrary, as I pointed out in Chapter 1. Still, the information component in newspapers, magazines, and books is certainly much higher than it is in records, radio, television, or movies. The transformation of the media system has enormous cultural consequences. Key points:

- As the balance of advertising allocations has shifted, media tend to be used more for amusement and less for the more difficult and important task of enlightenment.
- The new technology of video and cable is making media increasingly dependent on direct income from consumers.
- Media that depend on consumers directly are not better than those supported by advertising, but they display a wider range of merit.
- In a world of disagreeable facts, we live steeped in fiction, mostly seen in one or another video form.
- Hollywood, the source of most audiovisual entertainment, is adapting slowly to the changes in its audience. The rules and assumptions set by the advertising system still hold sway.

Advertising's Dwindling Share

We consume media much as we consume other products and services, paying for them not only with money but with our time. There is no hard and fast dividing line between the transactions that occur when we consume media and those that occur when we seek live entertainment or buy sporting equipment, video games, musical instruments, or works of art. Whether they are tangible products (like books) or intangible services (like radio), media are akin to the other objects of our spending, and compete with them in our personal budgets.

Who pays for the upkeep of the media system, and how, determines the nature of the communications it sends out. I have traced many flaws of commercial culture to its dependence on advertisers who are primarily preoccupied with audience size and only incidentally with communication in and of itself. We have already seen that the public's media diet has changed as advertisers shift their support among media—for example, by withdrawing from mass magazines and second newspapers. Since the beginning of commercial radio, broadcasting has, year after year, whittled away print's share of advertising investments. Radio and television, including cable, accounted for 43% of what advertisers spent in 1992 in media not entirely made up of advertising. (These also include daily and weekly newspapers, magazines, and farm and business publications.) These are the carriers of commercial culture; they depend on the voluntary attention and interest of the public. In 1992, advertisers put $79 billion into these media, out of their total expenditures of $131 billion.

But because of cable and the VCR, this huge investment represents a declining share of the upkeep for the nation's mass media system. It will get smaller; and the implications are enormous. Over a sixty-year period the mass media have taken between 2.3% and 3.6% of Americans' personal income.[1] Advertisers' share of total media costs has fallen slightly (from 54% to 52%, but more of their money has been going into media *entirely* dedicated to advertising, like direct mail and outdoor billboards; I also put the yellow page directories under this heading, though their listings *do* include nonadvertisers. The Appendix discusses the problems of measurement and classification and presents some of the statistics.)

Of the total national investment in all media (including those that do not carry advertising), consumer spending in 1992 amounted to $85.5 billion—42%. (This does not include the $60 billion spent to buy, maintain, and power home audio and video equipment.)

Consumers' spending on media that are not exclusively advertising grew more than five times since 1970, slightly faster than advertising expenditures.[2] In 1970, consumers spent about the same amounts for advertising media (newspapers and magazines) as they did for media that carry little or no advertising—movies, records, books, and newsletters. Without cable and home videos, consumer spending on all media would in 1992 have amounted to only $56 billion, while the advertiser investment would have been virtually unchanged (since the money spent on cable would undoubtedly have gone to on-air TV). The new technology, in just the few years it has been around, has added more than 50% to the consumer's entertainment and information budget.

It is difficult for people to anticipate the impact of a new invention or to understand its enormous potential effects on their own living patterns. In 1971, when VCRs were estimated to cost $400–$800, only 3% of the public said they were "very likely" to buy one.[3] But by 1994, three out of four U.S. households had a VCR and 10 million had more than one. (By way of comparison, 96% had color television sets; 35%, telephone answering machines; 28%, cordless telephones; and 25%, personal computers.)

The impact of cable was even more momentous. Remember that *all* cable, basic or premium, entails a substantial direct charge to the subscriber. In 1992, total spending on cable service was nearly $20 billion, more than $2 billion of it in advertising and the remainder from subscribers. Cable penetration had reached 62%;[4] more than two-fifths of the cable subscribers paid extra for premium channels.[5]

The fact that cable television derives eight times as much of its income from the public as from advertisers makes its operating economics profoundly different from those of on-air broadcasting.[6] The creation of what had been hailed in the 1960s as "the wired nation"[7] was to have important consequences for all other media. Cable brought many new choices to subscribers, but left out (the generally lower-income) nonsubscribers in cable areas and a substantial population in areas still without cable access. Thus cable has tended to widen the gap between the "media-rich" and the "media-poor"—a gap also evident in the difference between the large array of print, film, and broadcast choices available in metropolitan centers and the limited assortment available in small towns. (The spread of video stores has somewhat redressed this imbalance.)

Cable and the VCR have sharply reduced print's share of consumer media spending—from 72% to 49% since 1970.[8] (Correspondingly, the percentage of all family expenditures that went for newspapers, magazines, and sheet music dropped by nearly one-half.[9] In 1970, the public spent twice as much money on books ($2.9 billion) as it did at the movies ($1.4 billion). By 1992, more money was spent to rent ($8.2 billion) and buy ($3.7 billion) videocassettes than for trade books ($7.8 billion).

In 1970, advertisers paid 73% of the costs of the nonprint media (broadcast, cable, film, and records). In 1989, they paid only 47%. The escalation of broadcast advertising rates during this period made the shift of economic support for print and audiovisual media even more dramatic. The economic changes brought by cable and the VCR come on top of the longer-term shift of advertising money into broadcasting and away from print. These dull statistics represent dramatic cultural changes.

Advertisers' Choices—and the Public's

Who pays for a creative expression helps to define its character, as we have seen. An individual writer or artist may be driven by inner needs and urges, without any thought of bettering the accomplishments of predecessors or contemporaries. But in the collectively run commercial enterprises of mass media, creative output is governed by a keen awareness of competitive efforts and a desire to take advantage of their weaknesses. This requires identifying those elements of the public whose needs or interests may not yet be completely satisfied. The largest potential is always in the most typical or modal sector of the audience, but the tendency to go after this large middle group is offset by the impetus to seek out opportunities hiding in neglected corners of the market. The influence of advertising often asserts itself as this dilemma is confronted.

It is ingenuous to envision Philistine advertisers purposefully degrading the options that face readers, viewers, or listeners. Advertisers do, however, work by different rules than the ultimate media consumer. Whatever they are after does not automatically correspond directly to the public's own natural preferences. Rather, they try to take advantage of those preferences by supporting media that seem to be generating the kinds of audiences they want at the price *they*, not the public, are willing to pay.

In a direct transaction with the public, book publishers, filmmakers, or record impresarios, left to their own devices, quickly calculate the potential numbers of sales to be made for a particular kind of product at the going market price, and devise their plans accordingly. If production costs are apt to go wildly out of line, they may want to charge a premium, at the risk of reducing total unit sales in order to maximize revenues. This can be done with books, records, and cassettes, though not easily if the distribution channels make it impractical—as in the cases of films and pay cable, where standardized pricing prevails.

If a portion of the public cannot afford to pay what is asked, it is effectively barred from immediate direct access (though in practice the gap is somewhat filled by public libraries, senior citizens' rates at movie matinees, midweek bargain specials on video rentals, and the like). If consumers have a strong enough desire for what is offered, they may sacrifice another purchase in order to buy it. Teenagers in the most impoverished slums manage to buy audiocassettes and CD's and get to see the latest heavy action films.

The public assesses the value of media as *experiences*, while advertisers assess them by the *numbers* exposed. The willingness of the public to pay for a publication or a film reflects the work's meaning in a more direct sense than willingness to stay tuned to a broadcast program that is there for the asking. But advertisers rarely evaluate media with this critical distinction in mind.

Can the character and content of advertising-supported media be sharply distinguished from those of the media that depend directly upon their publics? Media that are funded by advertising differ greatly among themselves, and each exhibits a tremendous variation among its individual offerings and audiences. The same may be said of the consumer-supported media—books, newsletters and "little" literary magazines, films, videocassettes, musical recordings, and pay cable channels. In the aggregate, they cannot be described as manifesting a higher intellectual or taste level than those that depend on advertisers.

The most striking difference lies in the much greater range of choices and tastes that are represented, especially at the extremes, in those media that are consumer-supported. This difference was far more evident before the spread of cable television and the VCR. Books, records, film, and video are dominated by the trivial and the ephemeral, like advertiser-supported broadcasting and periodicals. Large numbers of people are willing to pay for momentary diversion, even if it is utterly senseless. Yet their selections seem to be altered by the fact that they are paying; they are more tolerant of ("free") program content when they want to watch TV than when they are spending money to go out to a movie.

Consumers support more diversity than advertisers do. Readers supply less than one-fourth of the revenues of daily newspapers. When they paid a bigger share, twenty or thirty years ago, they had more competing newspapers to choose among. Magazines get about half their revenue from readers, in a field that supports an enormous array of alternative choices. But advertising's contribution to magazine revenues has dropped substantially—precisely in the era of specialization, which presumably has seen a greater responsiveness to reader interests. To put it another way, advertisers have tended to support a somewhat different assortment of magazines than readers do, in spite of the fact that new magazines, as we saw earlier, are designed with potential advertisers specifically in mind.

Magazines that derive a higher than average percentage of their income from advertisers (like *The New Yorker*) are not necessarily or visibly *less* distinguished by editorial excellence than those (like the *National Enquirer*) that are primarily reader-supported. In the case of newspapers, the same phenomenon holds. Popular tabloids have always relied more on revenues from circulation than their more serious competitors. (*The New York Post* in 1991 was drawing half its income from readers.) In Great Britain, among the national newspapers, the "quality" press (The *Times, Telegraph, Guardian,* and *Independent*) got two-thirds of its revenues from advertisers; the tabloids (*Sun, Mirror, Express,* and *Daily Mail*) got two-thirds from readers. Advertisers' support for the serious over the simple-minded in this instance reflects their pursuit of spending power, not of excellence. The crucial point is that they followed their own purposes, not simply the public's choices.

What If There Were No Advertising Support?

The dependence of media upon advertising is so deeply entrenched and widely approved that it seems highly fanciful to envision a market-supported alternative. Still, if such an alternative, smaller in scale, were to be constructed, how different would it be from the advertising-based media system we know?

To answer this hypothetical question, we have to look at the media one by one. Television, for example, lends itself to direct comparisons: the programming formulas of advertiser-supported channels against those of viewer-supported pay cable channels, or even against those of feature films and videocassettes. Such comparisons are really spurious, because all media operate with a strong awareness of each other, borrow from each other's innovations and successes, feed on common fashions, and seek to find opportunities that others have missed or by their very nature cannot fill.

Advertising of some kinds and in some media represents desirable, even necessary, information that consumers want and expect. The success of specialized publications devoted to classified advertising for cars and homes has shown that people will actually pay for the privilege of having advertisements to read, and the growth of telephone recorded voice (audiotex) services indicates that there is a substantial market for straight commercial information.

Specialized newsletters operate successfully without advertising income, but there are few examples of general publications that have managed to do so. New York's short-lived newspaper *PM*, in the 1940s, was a notable example of the perils of this kind of publishing. *Ms.* magazine, renouncing advertising and raising its cover price to $4.95, has managed to survive on a circulation of 150,000. *Mad* has a circulation of 2 million. These exceptions seem to prove the rule.[10]

The question of how the media world would look without advertising would have to be reframed if we wanted to consider alternative forms of economic support, like direct state subsidization or the use of taxes on radio and television sets, funneled through an independent broadcasting authority like the BBC. Each of these possibilities raises a different set of questions and issues than those involved in the free play of supply and demand in a consumer-driven media marketplace. Taking all the many ways that media are organized around the globe, there are simply no examples of a media system that is funded entirely by the public's voluntary payments and that has neither advertising nor government support.

Eliminating advertising would greatly reduce the number of vehicles in those media that now depend on it entirely or substantially. The same number of readers would not be willing to pay $4 for a magazine that cost $1.95 in 1994, or $2 for a newspaper that cost 35 cents. If television came only at a price, as it does on cable now, but at a price considerably higher than it commands on cable, some viewers would opt to view fewer channels, to view fewer hours, or even to do without it altogether. (If every family had to pay for the four networks, PBS, and an independent channel at the same rate now charged for HBO, the average TV bill in a wired household would amount to almost $100 per month.)

To be sure, consumers are already paying the price of the advertising-supported media. We pay the electric bills and the maintenance costs for our radios and television sets. We also pay for most periodicals, and give less attention to free publications than to those we have paid for. Even though most people probably have no idea what proportion of the production costs they bear, there is a tacit public understanding that advertisers are carrying much of the load, and that therefore the editorial matter is a bargain.

People generally understand, somewhere in the backs of their minds, that the operating expenses of the "free" media are buried in the cost of the advertised goods they buy. (In 1993, these expenses worked out to $540 per capita for all advertising in all media.) But the connection is sufficiently attenuated that it seems abstract and meaningless. The benefits are immediate and tangible; the payments remote and atomized, out of awareness.

Consumption of free or public goods takes place outside the market system. This is true of the air we breathe and the public services we use. It is also true of the entertainment and information that come to us "free" as incidental byproducts of marketing forces, but not as the direct result of our own individual market behavior.

It is perfectly clear to most people, once they reflect on the matter, that the support of advertising-financed media is ultimately a social cost, tacked on to the price of advertised goods and services. Certain goods can be bought at a premium price for optional extra features, but advertising is not one of these dispensable extras. Since we never associate the price of deodorant or brake repair with the quality or character of the television or radio programs we watch or hear, we think of these media as "free." We do not think that way of daily newspapers, even though as readers we bear only a minor part of the cost of producing and distributing them.

Listeners and viewers of radio and television regard advertisements as intrusions and do not particularly welcome them. (The advertisers themselves want to be intrusive, with messages of a kind that readers would rarely seek out on their own initiative, to inform themselves.) At the same time, the public understands that the broadcast system is dependent on advertising. Faced with the alternative of supporting the system through taxes or accepting the present system of absorbing advertising through the cost of goods, it always says it prefers the latter option even though ultimately, of course, it must pay in one way or another.

Opinion surveys always show a majority saying that the presence of commercials is a price worth paying for "free" television. This finding indicates the difference between monosyllabic responses to prepackaged questions and reasoned discussion of an issue in all its complexity. But it also indicates that when costs are as highly diffused as they are in commercial broadcasting, audiences lose a sense of any direct involvement in the economic transactions to which they are actually a crucial party. After all, the system would continue functioning in the same way even if they were not contributing their mite. This disengagement has considerable consequences, since advertising affects the character of even those media that do not carry it.

Ad-Supported Media and Others

The audiences for consumer-supported media are drawn from narrower bands of the public than the audiences for television, radio, newspapers, and magazines. The cost of a movie ticket, a cassette rental, a phonograph record or a book is, to utter a tautology, most easily borne by people who can afford to spend the money and who have the youthful energy to go out and shop for it. Unlike these media (except for book clubs, newsletters, and pay TV—once the decision to subscribe is made), those that are consumer-supported do not come automatically into the home.

As a generalization, those media that are wholly or substantially supported by advertising tend to be less demanding and absorbing than those that are supported directly by the public. This statement needs to be qualified. A newspaper article or a magazine short story can arouse great interest and emotion. Television coverage of a football game can evoke many of the same passionate feelings that capture the live spectators. A musical recording issues the same sounds on a home tape deck as it does when played on the radio. Reading a chapter of a whodunit at bedtime is no more intellectually strenuous than the same few moments spent with a late-night talk show. These exceptions do not invalidate the proposition that our most intense media experiences are likely to be those that stand by themselves, that we approach purposefully, that are sustained and essentially uninterrupted, and that we pay for directly and entirely.

Almost any periodical contains more than a given reader will want to read or find it possible to read, in part because of the presence of advertising. The very quantity and variety of the contents encourage browsing and selectivity, which by their nature make the reading process a series of disjointed activities rather than a single commanding one. (Browsing appears to arouse just as much intellectual energy, however, as reading.[11]) In reading a newspaper, we are buffeted by a series of stimuli that activate memory traces already set by what we have read or heard or seen about the same subjects on previous occasions. We are generally left not with an impression of that day's issue of that specific paper, but rather with a series of minor, sometimes barely detectable impressions of all the things we have looked at. Much the same is true of magazines, although these characteristically have fewer elements and less heterogeneity in any single issue.

It is difficult to compare the merits of the books that the public pays for with the magazines to which advertisers contribute half the cost. There are probably worse books than anything distributed in the format of a regularly published magazine, and the best books are much better than what most magazines commonly publish. It would be hard to sustain the argument that today's magazines, which carry only minor dollops of fiction, are on the whole any more taxing to the intellect than the content of most nonacademic nonfiction books.

I noted earlier that musical recordings played "free" on the radio represent a slightly different mix of styles from those sold in the shops. Classical music represents ten times as many purchased recordings as station formats. In either case it is a tiny fraction of all the music played, though its emotional and cultural impact cannot be judged by its share either of consumer spending or of listening time.

Broadcast programming on radio and television flows continuously. A population that for the most part has never known a world without commercial television might find it inconceivable to pass a normal evening at home without the periodic intrusion of advertising messages. Viewers' connections to the plot erode because dramatic tension cannot be sustained. On the stage, dramatic performances are also interrupted by intermissions, but authors intentionally divide plays into acts and scenes to serve their own purposes, not extraneous commercial ends, the way "timeouts" at football games are placed to accommodate advertisements.

The experience of watching a film on TV is quite different from the experience of seeing it in the darkness of the theater, even with neighbors who eat popcorn and laugh at the wrong moments. Watching the same film on videocassette or on a pay or noncommercial channel eliminates the interruptions, but still falls short of the theater experience. The sheer size of the screen in relation to the viewer, reinforced by a magnified sound level, gives the images an extraordinary power that diminishes when they are reduced to the dimensions of a cathode ray tube. Seeing the same images on the small television tube amidst commercial interruptions and the distractions of domestic life, a viewer would rarely become so engrossed as to be oblivious to the alternatives available with a flip of the zapper.

The difference in length between the feature film and the typical television program also creates a different level of emotional response, a different expectation of closure (given the serial nature of much television programming), a different level of realism (reflecting television's more limited production budgets), and a different kind of involvement between viewers and protagonists. Television drama is an experience of very low intensity, remote indeed from Aristotle's notion of arousal and catharsis. It is subject to continual interruption and many distractions. The intensity of theatrical film leaves a strong after-image that evokes replay in the imagination. Only a rare television drama manages to break through the limitations of its format.

Television programs are expected to get much or even most of their audience at one showing, even in the era of syndication and reruns. Only a relatively small number of popular series are broadcast repeatedly. By contrast, a motion picture's distribution takes place over a period of months. Driven by competitive anxieties to avoid repeating itself, commercial television is prodigious in its consumption of raw material to fill its vast amount of air time. Each network alone feeds about 3,000 hours of programming a year to its affiliates. By comparison, Hollywood's annual feature film output fills about 1,000 hours.[12] Television devours over 100 hours of original drama each week, on the networks alone. About seventy series are aired by all four networks at any one time, a third of them new; of these, only half last the whole season. In contrast, only 414 feature films were released by the Hollywood studios in 1992, making each one a considerable effort.

All this would seem to imply that films (taken as a whole) convey substantially more meaning than television drama; they represent more compelling experiences for the audience; their characterizations are more apt to be complex ("rounded" as opposed to "flat," in E.M. Forster's memorable apposition), the actions that make up their plot lines are more understandably motivated. Drama in both media covers an enormous range of subtypes and wide variations in merit and seriousness of intent. But television is much more ephemeral, and is both conceived and taken more lightly.

These inherent distinctions complicate the tasks of comparing the output of commercial television with that of the feature film industry and attributing any differences to the market forces at play. Coarse inspection does not lead to a fast conclusion that higher standards of taste prevail in the public's choice of theatrical films it will pay for than in the television programs (many of them created in the same studios) to which its response, embodied in the ratings, translates into advertising support.

A much higher level of technical excellence prevails in every aspect of film, reflecting the much greater financial investment made in each of a much smaller number of vehicles. Everything is better on the surface—writing, acting, direction, sets—even when the themes are no more profound, the conceptual integrity no deeper. But this impressionistic judgment is made on the averages when what is important is precisely at the extremes.

With an almost predictable frequency that is never matched on television, some films made for the theater have the stirring quality of great art. These may be films that can win vast audiences and commercial success; sometimes they are *succès d'estime* and commercial disasters. Like book publishers, film producers are gamblers. They are not locked to the middle of the road and do not have to conform to the homogeneous standards of a relatively small group of advertising media decision-makers.

What conclusion can we take from these comparisons? A media system resting directly on market demand would not be markedly different in its general character from the advertising-supported system we know, though it would probably have a different range and assortment of elements. The control and content of free and paid media are interwoven, as we have seen. Most important, consumer-supported media have tended to follow the practices of the media in which advertisers define the ground rules.

Fiction as Part of Everyday Life

Thus far I have pointed out that audiovisual media have become preeminent both as a result of advertisers' spending decisions and because consumers have also been spending much more themselves. Film and video—in whatever format—are overwhelmingly media of fiction, and packaged fantasy fills most of the time we devote to media.

In past times, fiction in any form must have acquired added intensity from the very singularity of its appearance. Even the theater of Aeschylus and Euripides would have lost its compelling power if its audiences had been subjected to it as a matter of daily routine. Today we take for granted the overwhelming presence of packaged imagination in our lives. The average person spends about 200 hours a year with newspapers and magazines (in which fiction barely occurs) and less than a third as much with books. By comparison, 60 hours a year are spent with videocassettes and 12 hours with film in the theater. But at least 1,200 hours are spent with television. Interlarded with live (mostly sports) events, news, quiz and game shows, over 90% of network prime-time programming is devoted to one variety of fiction or another.[13]

What does it mean to devote so much of our attention to vicarious experience, seen through the prism of imaginary relationships among unconvincing characters? Inevitably, it alters our perception of the dramas of public life, as journalism depicts them for us. As more of our time is spent on fiction, less is used to assimilate the information we need to cope with with what is going on around us. How did this happen?

In the nineteenth-century heyday of vaudeville and theater, imaginary presences were still a minor element in American daily life. Periodicals, circulating in vastly greater quantities than books, represented the principal sources of fictional experience in an era when theater-going was for most people only an occasional activity, even a rare one. Most of them featured a mixture of fiction and nonfiction.

Short stories and serialized novels were a staple element of newspapers. Comic strips introduced children to the world of reading matter through colorful cartoon drawings whose distorted, simplified representations of reality evoked imaginary experiences. But grownups, not children, were and are comic strips' main readers.[14]

Unlike the subjects of political cartoons, comic strip characters—villains as well as heroes—are patently unreal and nonthreatening. Their adventures parody the vicissitudes of everyday existence. As daily newspaper readership became less regular, the running narrative—which fostered adventure, action, or romance, and which brought readers back from day to day— gave way to the free-standing single episode strip. A space of thirteen square inches does not lend itself to much complexity of plot or character of the kind that a continuity strip requires. Thus the last vestige of narrative fiction in the daily press appears to be headed for oblivion.

The ubiquitous presence of fiction on television and video has virtually eliminated it from both newspapers and magazines. Books remain the preeminent medium of printed fiction, and they command a large and growing audience in spite of the insistent encroachment of electronic media. On any given day, about one person in five reads a book other than the *Bible*.[15] Two-thirds of the 760 million trade books bought each year are fiction, most of them of a dubious order of merit—tawdry romances, thrillers, and other potboilers. Perhaps a tenth of the public, strongly defined by education and social class, ever reads serious contemporary literature. The book publishing industry promotes reading as a sign of intellectual accomplishment, but most of what is read in the way of fiction is as intellectually shabby as its counterparts in television and film.[16]

Radio, and especially serial drama, made fiction a routine part of daily life, in contrast to fleeting contact with fiction in print. In the 1930s, fiction was easily available at almost all hours of the day and evening in forms that ranged from comedy skits to domestic dramas, science fiction, and murder mysteries. In its day-in day-out accessibility, radio represented a different kind of media exposure than the much more powerful medium of film. Going out to the movies was a special event in the typical individual's weekly schedule, although more people did it than ever went out to the theater; it was not, except perhaps in the case of the eccentric or very rich (Hearst at San Simeon), incorporated into the daily routine.

Motion pictures reduced the expense of dramatic entertainment. In 1915, Walter Prichard Eaton commented that, in the theater, ticket prices consigned the worker to the gallery. With the advent of the movies, he could mingle with "the 'shirt-front' contingent below stairs, the class which employs him by day."[17] The first feature film shown in the United States ("Queen Elizabeth," with Sarah Bernhardt), imported by Adolf Zukor in 1911, could not be shown in nickelodeons because of its four reel length, nor shown at a price that the working-class audience for nickelodeon shorts could afford. The advent of feature films prompted the construction of movie theaters in city centers and shifted the audience base back upward in the social scale.[18] Film broadened the public for drama, but also changed the response. The quiet restraint of the film audience contrasted with the raucous behavior of nineteenth-century theater-goers. The relationship of spectators and actors was no longer direct, intimate, and bilateral, as it was on the stage.

Fiction, experienced in many forms, has always fed the imagination, but never like the movies. The author of a book can stand aside from the narrative to comment, play God, or provide a change of perspective. In film and its video offspring, the audience sees only what is in the camera's eye. No other mass medium requires the total immersion of the senses that film does, viewed in the theater.

The opulence of the sets and the good looks of the stars gave films a glamor that powerfully stimulated the subconscious. Movies have shaped the fantasy life of twentieth-century America. They have provided some of its most notable heroes, enriched the content of innumerable conversations, and induced a sense of familiarity with people and places remote in time and geography.

The personalities of the "silver screen" were perceived as larger than life, their passions of supranormal force, the settings more opulent or exotic than everyday reality. The magnificent downtown film palaces of the Golden Era enshrined these heroic images and made going out to the movies a special experience—even a compelling one. The vivid imagery of gigantic figures, watched in the dark, worked its way into the unconscious, like any other intense life experience. In dreams, the sleeper reorganizes daytime experiences, anxieties and desires. In daydreams, we normally indulge our desires alone. Motion pictures, more than any other form of communication, bridge the gap between real and dream worlds.

Political psychologists Martha Wolfenstein and Nathan Leites defined them as shared daydreams.[19] Social worker Jane Addams called the movie theater a Dream Palace. Anthropologist Hortense Powdermaker described Hollywood as "The Dream Factory."[20] The social science notion that film provided the stuff of fantasy for millions of people, whom it lifted out of their humdrum, unglamorous lives, was incorporated into the thinking of Hollywood moguls themselves. "A picture," said film mogul Harry Warner, "all it is is an expensive dream."[21]

As in other forms of popular culture, film used familiar, conservative, accepted themes of great simplicity, with stereotyped depictions of personality and a high element of suspense to pull the audience along. Movie plot lines harbored no intellectual threat or ambiguity. Hollywood, with its glittering stars and flashy producers, simply extended on a more opulent national scale the show business traditions of the nineteenth-century popular theater.

The public's fascination with the stars of the performing arts stems partly from their mere celebrity and partly from the special intimacy that members of an audience feel for the face and voice and words of someone (like the TV newscasters) who repeatedly enters their lives. Unlike other personal intimacies, the relationship is one-sided and narrow in scope. Even at the crudest level of popular entertainment, it evokes a desire to penetrate into other, deeper aspects of the celebrity's personal affairs. This voyeurism is an attempt at fantasied reciprocity, since it removes celebrities from their two-dimensional roles and, by making them multifaceted, reduces them to humble human proportions. A promo for the Entertainment Channel, a cable network, promises enticingly, "Now you can watch your favorite celebrities 24 hours a day."

The great film impresarios were in the tradition of P.T. Barnum—showmen whose stock in trade was their ability to assemble talent to meet the insatiable desire for entertainment. Was this desire always there? The reduction of work hours and the rise in the standard of living were necessary conditions for the growth of the entertainment market, but they do not appear sufficient to explain the enormous increase in film attendance and film production from the early years of the twentieth century to the advent of television. The pace and the stresses of contemporary life may have heightened the demand for diversion and prepackaged fantasy, and the vastly greater flow of available film offerings may have created its own audience.[22] Double features, which began in 1931, were a response to the collapse of the economy in the Great Depression; they gave the customers more for their fifteen-cents admissions, and filled more of the dreary time many had on their hands. The better A film was tied to the booking of the B film, produced on the cheap.

For over half a century, theaters were the channel through which Hollywood made its impact on American culture. For several generations, moviegoing was a family activity that brought people to city centers on expeditions that included eating and shopping. The presence of crowds attracted crowds. Downtown film palaces closed when pedestrian traffic dwindled after business hours, but the very fact that fewer theaters were open reduced pedestrian traffic and discouraged attendance. The process fed on itself. Television pulled away audiences at the same time that cities changed character and disintegrated. Theater owners followed their customers and moved into suburban shopping centers. They sought to cut costs and increase their revenues by establishing multiscreen complexes, operated by a small staff of employees. Expanded food and drink concessions became ever more important to their profits. The finances of the business changed. Theatrical attendance continued to drift downward as aggressive admissions pricing made moviegoing ever more of a luxury.

In most cases, people go out to the movies not merely to be amused or aroused by the actual plot of the film they are about to see but as an occasion for conversation, shared emotions, and diversions from normal daily routine. Theater-going represents a very different form of entertainment from watching movies on TV.

A senior Hollywood executive:

> Going to the movies is a social event. Kids want to get laid, get out of the house, away from their folks. The movies are a place to go.[23]

The allure of dating in the darkness of the theater remained a principal motivation for moviegoing throughout the years of television's ascendancy. Not surprisingly, therefore, the theatrical movie audience became progressively more youthful. Teenagers spend 27% less time watching television than does the average American adult.[24] They spend more time out of the house, and their moviegoing is at twice the average adult level. Young people aged eighteen to twenty-four, who are 18% of all adults, account for double that proportion of frequent moviegoers.[25] (By contrast, among those over fifty, 72% do not go out to the movies from one year to the next.)

When television captured the family audience, it took Hollywood some time to adjust to the fact that its theatrical public was made up of young people in their teens and twenties. For years afterwards, its preoccupation with the youthful filmgoers altered its themes, production style, and star selection. The tastes of young people differ from those of older ones. They particularly like comedies, horror, sex, and scenes of gore, killing, maiming, fires, explosions, and crashes. The film industry has not neglected these interests.[26]

As the theatrical filmgoing experience changed, its audience changed and dwindled too. Movies were still being watched more than ever, but not in the theater. On television they have continued to be a universal medium of entertainment for every age group.[27]

Films seen in the theater are generally approached as experiences that are fresh and new, whereas those seen on television have, until quite recently, been relics of another era, culled from those ancient archives that the studios have been willing to release.

A substantial chunk of the growing sums spent on cable goes for movies. Films have been so popular, and the need to fill air time so insistent that television networks and stations have been willing to pay substantial sums for permission to show them. As independent stations and cable channels captured more of the television audience, the demand for films grew steadily, increasing the value of the studios' film libraries and thus prompting takeovers by media conglomerates.[28] (Independent stations gave nearly a fourth of their time to movies and over half to syndicated shows in the 1987–88 season. By contrast, a typical network affiliate station devoted 2% of its 18-hour broadcast day to movies, two-thirds of it to network programs, and a fifth to syndicated programs.[29])

This situation changed dramatically with the rapid growth of cable. The original lure of the premium cable networks was their presentation of recent Hollywood movies that had just completed their theatrical runs. Limits were set by the relatively small number of blockbuster films produced each year—about twenty. But the time demands of television created a need for additional new productions, which by 1993 occupied a third of HBO's program budget and time.[30]

While the pay cable audience is somewhat better off than the average and more inclined to heavy viewing, its age distribution, like that of television itself, resembles that of society. It is not the young audience of the movie theater. Neither is the audience for videocassettes, which represent a major new component of fictional experience. Four out of five films seen by the public are viewed on a VCR. About half of all viewing on the VCR is of rented movie tapes, and a good chunk of the remainder is undoubtedly made up of movies taped when they are broadcast.[31]

As the videocassette market expanded, Hollywood became increasingly dependent on this new source of income. (The studio gets about 55% of a videocassette's retail price.) In 1980, only 3% of major film studios' revenues from feature films came from videocassette sales and rentals. By 1993, home video sales and rentals amounted to $12 billion, while U.S. domestic box office receipts were $5 billion.[32] A family of four could rent nine cassettes for little more than the cost of a single night out at the movies.[33] The average family spent $114 a year renting home videos, about twice as much as it spent on theater tickets.[34] Two out of five American VCR homes rented cassettes during a typical week, and spent two to three hours watching them.

A senior Hollywood executive:

Whether a film is sold in one form or another the studios are going to benefit.[35]

Hollywood—the production center of audiovisual entertainment—still focuses on the theatrical film audience as the primary target of its creative energy. It has continued to produce for that youthful audience long after the adult public has returned to the movies in one or another video form. As the film industry began to earn more revenues from cassettes and cable than from theatrical showings, producers should have been led to think again of the broad mass public they had before television, rather than of the teenagers and dating-age young adults who had sustained them during the 1970s. The country's age pyramid was changing shape as the baby boom faded. The theatrical film audience changed rapidly too. Movies on the home television set, however they arrived there, were more likely to be the shared family experience they once were. In 1985, people of thirty or over accounted for only 32% of theatrical movie attendance. Only three years later, they represented 42%.

Long after the handwriting was on the wall, Leonard Goldberg, president of Twentieth Century Fox, asserted cautiously: "If there is a shift and we don't have to rely on teenagers as much, it will allow us to make a wider range of movies."[36] But the powers in the film industry were slow to abandon their formulas of the television era and adapt to the dramatic changes in the audience.

Hollywood was not, of course, oblivious to the repercussions of the switch from theatrical to video viewing. Since the dimensions of the video tube are different from those of the theater's wide screen, the very art of cinematography had to be adapted to the dual circumstances of showing in the theater and at home. Not only the composition of the audience, but its circumstances, attentiveness, and response were different.

A totally new form of distribution system arose, with a set of players very different from the old movie house proprietors. Although there were more video stores and other types of retailers offering video rentals, the consumer was still typically faced with a very limited number of selections. Video distribution followed the pattern already made familiar in book publishing, with concentration on a limited number of bestselling titles. Most VCR owners had already had an opportunity to sample the classics. Video stores had to expand and stock a great number of slow-moving titles that affected their profits,[37] but their inventories were aging, and there were not enough new films to meet the potential demand. Rentals therefore no longer enjoyed the strong annual growth they had shown in the period of steadily expanding VCR penetration.[38]

The range of offerings would be immeasurably broadened if it could include all the tens of thousands of motion pictures produced throughout the world since the early days of the century. (By 1993, 15,000 were already catalogued as video-cassettes, though not all were easily available.) Was the public about to be over-whelmed by the sheer number of choices before it? The question became more pertinent as it became likely that access to the archives would not be through the video store, but in a digitized format accessible through a telephone line or cable.

The Changed Economics of Television

Cassettes have given a second life to many films that perhaps should have been permitted to find their own peaceful path to oblivion. Even though consumer choices on cable are substantially greater than on over-the-air television, they remain limited, and do not compare with the vast repertory available on videocassette. Pay cable faces competition from Pay-per-View, direct broadcasting to the home by satellite, and telephone-transmitted "video on demand" – all potentially linked to a centralized cinematheque accessible through interactive directory listings.

The programming selections offered on cable to a very substantial degree parallel the programming attributes long ago established in commercial broadcasting: drama, sports, games, and talk shows, with a heavy reliance on film. A substantial new element in the flow of popular culture became represented by the feature-length movies produced especially for pay cable. Compared with regular theatrical films, they generally lacked both the known quantity of outstanding star actors and the element of unpredictability in their story lines and production styles. Their production budgets were not insubstantial. Showtime spent $5 million and up for a movie; HBO between $5 and $8 million.[39] (HBO spent $9 million to produce a single 2½ hour movie, "Josephine Baker.") These specially made feature films cost considerably more than a typical network made-for-TV film, but still a fraction of the cost of most Hollywood films made for theatrical release.

The presence of relatively new films on pay cable affected mainline broadcasting. It spurred the major television networks to offer higher prices to the studios for broadcast rights and eventually to commission their own made-for-TV movies. Partly as cause and partly as effect, prime-time network television program schedules increasingly departed from the predictable regular half-hour weekly format.

The infusion of large additional revenues through pay cable has probably raised its quality level somewhat above the standards that had prevailed in commercial TV. This assumes that uninterrupted feature films, spun out at full length and made on much bigger budgets, are likely to be artistically superior and more satisfyingly entertaining than run of the mill network or syndicated television productions—a contention that I think is sound (for the reasons I have just reviewed), but that could still be disputed.

Because there is no need to worry about advertising pressures, pay cable permits more complex subjects than network television:

A producer:

> They don't have to worry about offending people. . . . It has a different kind of audience, although it's the same audience. . . . It's the same people but the technology is different. People are having to pay for something, and their expectations are different than for network programs.[40]

However, most of the made-for-cable productions closely resemble those of the on-air networks in content and character, except that their script structure does not have to take account of commercial breaks. Premium or basic, cable networks make heavy use of reruns, repeating some programs three times a week or more often. TNT ran its made-for-TV films (which cost $3–4 million each) six times in 24 hours and repeated them later in the same week. Most of TNT programming actually consisted of MGM movies, to which the parent Turner Broadcasting Company owned the rights.

As producers derive their income from a mixture of media, they are less dependent on audience size in any one of them and more concerned with their earnings from the total package. A smaller audience, motivated to pay a higher price, may be more profitable than a larger one that is less eager. It may be less costly and more rewarding to fish in smaller pools if the larger ones become too crowded. If this were not so, all media entrepreneurs (rather than just most of them) would be rushing after the same mass audience with the same prescriptions.

In the 1950s, when the networks were fighting the first, unsuccessful attempt to launch pay TV, CBS's Frank Stanton paraphrased Lincoln: "Television cannot exist half fee and half free." Premium cable demonstrated that these two forms of television could indeed coexist. About half the viewing time in pay cable households was spent with cable-originated programming. But the logic of the argument introduced over thirty years ago still holds up. A program of unusual appeal, like a major sporting event or acclaimed film, can earn as much from a paying audience as it could from advertising sold to reach a "free" audience many times the size.

At the start of the 1970s, Gillette offered Teleprompter $400,000 for exclusive broadcast rights to a heavyweight championship fight. Irving Kahn, the company's president, turned them down and put the fight on closed-circuit TV, where it grossed $2.5 million. He proclaimed, "Advertising money is nice. But box-office money is best."[41] A single wrestling match in 1991 took in $35 million. In the same year a Metropolitan Opera broadcast, at $34.95, was seen in 34,000 households, while the heavyweight match between Evander Holyfield and George Foreman, brought in 1,450,000 homes at the same price.[42] Pay-per-View can charge this much for a championship prize fight and take in more money from thousands than from a mass showing to millions. It cannot do it for every boxing match, every day.

Nonetheless, this added a new dimension to the competition that kept ratcheting up the cost of sports and entertainment talent and production. Effectively, pay television could often outbid the networks in the endless battle for programming. As a result, access to sporting events of wide public interest was sometimes confined to pay channel subscribers and denied to millions of other fans. (In 1987, New York Yankees baseball games that had formerly appeared free on WPIX-TV were put on a pay channel, Sportschannel.)

Inevitably, changes in the economic structure of media have secondary repercussions on the creative process. An investment banker points to the effects of falling network ratings resulting from cable competition:

> Since the relative value of the [network] slots has declined, the revenue stream that you can get from winning a slot isn't enough to pay for high-class software. So logically you've got to get garbage.[43]

A network president:

> Audience fractionation increases the demand for blockbuster programs. It get's down to "the show's the thing."[44]

The broadcast networks were caught in a bind; as their advertising revenues flattened, they dreamt of charging cable system operators for the privilege of disseminating their shows, just as the cable networks did. The viewers the networks sold to advertisers increasingly received their programs via cable. If cable systems were required to pay for rights to carry broadcast network programs, subscriber rates would have to go up accordingly (and undoubtedly, with the usual markup), further accelerating the shift of support from the advertiser to the consumer. The major cable companies (Time Warner, TCI, Turner) all had an interest in programming, as did the studios. "If we give it away free, who will buy it?" asked MCA's Sidney Sheinberg.[45]

Different cable offerings obviously have different values for the public at large. A survey that asked, "How much would CNN be worth to you?" got an average answer of $2.40; otherwise the range was from $1.78 for ESPN to $1.28 for the Weather Channel.[46] However in the real world of cable, as in the realm of printed matter, the options are not reduced to a matter of either–or. The Weather Channel might be worth as much as $10 to enough people to make it a profitable venture if it were out on its own rather than a "free" offering of the cable system.

The multiplication of viewing choices has eroded the networks' share of the audience. But a parallel development, with far greater consequences, is that a growing share of society's expenditures on entertainment media is now accounted for by the public's *individual* decisions rather than by advertisers' decisions. Ultimately the consumer foots the bill in any case.

The emergence of cable television brought to the fore the question of whether and how the conduits of communication might be disengaged from the content itself. Even though cable operators are required to carry all local on-air television channels, they still have discretion over their selection of other programming sources. The ultimate consumer is not a totally free agent.

Only if and when cable becomes a public utility and viewers pay for their individual program choices, will their selections truly conform to market values. Program choices are bound to be different—and more considered—when the audience pays than when they are "free." Even then, they will be largely determined by long-established viewing habits that date from an earlier era of technology. Right now, cable viewers are paying for the privilege of receiving advertising that they have repeatedly said they regard as a necessary evil, as well as an array of programs essentially designed to meet advertisers' perceptions of what they ought to like.

Spectrum Scarcity and the Problem of Choice

The most significant and unarguable consequence of the public's growing financial stake in cable—pay and basic—has been the massive expansion of video channels. The frequency spectrum imposes limits on the number of choices that can be provided through broadcast communications, though engineering advances have made it increasingly possible to crowd additional channels into the same limited range of frequencies.

An increase in choices would have come about even without cable. Between 1975 and 1993 (and this may be attributed to deregulation), commercial TV stations grew from 706 to 1,118, up 58%.[47] In the same period, the number of cable systems grew by 214%, from 3,500 to 11,000, adding even more options to the on-air menu. Basic cable networks grew from seventeen to more than forty.

From the outset, cable promised a world of specialization that conformed to the advertisers' increasing demand for target marketing. In 1994, one channel offered courtroom coverage, another was devoted to food, and others proposed to deal with cowboys, science fiction, and senior citizens' interests. The average number of channels available to cable subscribers had grown to thirty-six in the top 125 markets. Using data-compression technology, systems offering 500 cable channels were in the works. (Any given program can be aired at different hours on different channels.)

In any medium, the number of voices raised is not in itself a reliable index of the number of tunes being sung—or listened to, because exposure tends to be concentrated in only a part of the spectrum. The biggest 10% of daily newspapers in the country account for 60% of the total daily circulation. The biggest 15% of all consumer magazines have two-thirds of all magazine circulation.

Needless to say, not all the choices available are put to use. A household with thirty cable channels tunes in to only about ten of them in the course of a month. Individual cable networks get a high proportion of their total viewing time from a small segment of viewers. (People who watch music video, sports and news channels spend twelve to fifteen times more time with them than does the general cable audience.[48]) Specialization reduces the potential size of audiences and therefore restricts cable's income. David Waterman, a media economist, concludes that

> television viewers simply have too little interest in having programs narrowly targeted to them for cable to overcome the huge economies of scale achieved by spreading the costs of popular stars and high production values over a broad-based audience.[49]

The vast new array of choices masks a subservience to established programming formulas. Media analyst Ben H. Bagdikian points to two basic flaws in the asserted vitality of the media marketplace:

> One is the equating of the quantity of media outlets, the volume of their output, and their impressive revenues with diversity and richness of content. . . . The other common flaw is to ignore . . . who and what can become part of the media message.[50]

Increasing the number of channels does not mean a commensurate increase in the variety of tastes and interests that are being satisfied, since media entrepreneurs gravitate to the mode where the largest numbers are clustered.

The economist Harold Hotelling has posed the problem of merchants selecting their sites. "Suppose that A's location has been fixed but that B is free to choose his place of business. Where will he set up shop?. . . . He will come just as close to A as other conditions permit," because he will find more customers there even though he will face keener competition. A third seller, C, will also gravitate close to that same location, since

> his desire for as large a market as possible will prompt him likewise to take up a position close to A or B, but not between them. . . . As more and more sellers of the same commodity arise, the tendency is not to become distributed in the socially optimum manner but to cluster unduly. . . . Distance as we have used it for illustration, is only a figurative term for a great congeries of qualities.

Hotelling attributes the "excessive sameness" in consumer goods mainly to "the tendency to make only slight deviations in order to have for the new commodity as many of the buyers of the old as possible, to get, so to speak, *between* one's competitors and a mass of customers."[51] This explains why the increased number of television channels has not meant greater variety of content.

TV programming diversity actually declined between 1953 and 1974,[52] and there is no reason to assume that this trend has been arrested. (More recently, a similar process appears to have taken place in European countries as additional television channels were added).[53] The persistent movement toward the middle ground of tried and true programming formulas is impelled by the commercial culture's compulsive need: to accumulate audiences.

The movement to place more of the direct cost burden of media on the consumer seems inexorable; so does the parallel shift away from print to visual imagery, from information to entertainment. The economics of the advertising-supported television industry and of the mainly consumer-supported film and cable industries are inextricably interwoven. However, even as the consumer pays a greater and greater share of the upkeep, the media system is still mainly propelled by the advertiser's avid pursuit of mass numbers. Is there a better way to run things?

V

IS THERE A BETTER WAY?

12

Reform, Restructure, or Leave It Be?

Media create popular tastes at the same time that, as commercial enterprises, they respond to them. Can the cycle be broken? Even if everyone could agree on the criteria of cultural or intellectual merit, how can merit be made acceptable to those whose instinct is to reject it? We must seek answers to these questions by looking in two directions: at the pride of media practitioners, sustained by their critics, and at the actions that government takes, or might take, to foster merit and diverse expression while preserving freedom of opinion and taste.

Enriching media choices has two aspects: providing the largest possible number and variety of channels and improving quality. Few readers of this book would dispute the value of enlarging opportunities to pursue different interests, aesthetic appetites, and political viewpoints. But there is never a consensus about quality.

Can standards be set to ensure that the media attract and utilize the highest possible levels of talent and creativity? If so, how can they be imposed anywhere except within the media organizations themselves? Budgets undoubtedly impose some constraint on excellence, but there is no indication that a more expensive media production is inevitably better—either by critical criteria or by those of the cash register—than one that costs less. The annals of Hollywood are filled with the stories of outrageously costly films that flopped at the box office and of "sleepers" made on shoestring budgets that turned into enormous successes. The chief inhibitor of media quality is less likely to be the greed of owners thinking only of the current quarter's bottom line than limitations of the human resources necessary to produce the best under all circumstances.

In this chapter, we shall consider the role of government in relation to media, the professionalism of media practitioners, and the need for constant criticism of commercial culture. American tradition rejects government interference with the press. Does this rule out the idea of a national media policy? I contend that we already have one — full of holes and inconsistencies — and that it needs continual overhauling. Here are the main points:

- Judgments about media are best left to those who create their content. But *journalists* have no consensus on what constitutes professional responsibility, and the very idea of professionalism cannot be applied to the field of *entertainment*, which makes up most of media content.
- Media lack the kind of continuing intelligent public criticism that maintains the practitioners' sense of responsibility.
- Audiences would not get smaller if all media raised their sights, but there is no practical possibility that their managements would be responsible enough to do so.
- If the market cannot move media to a higher level, government must play a part, as it does in public broadcasting. But the political hazards make public subsidy a dubious cure for the ailments of the media system.
- The media system is too important to be left to chance. It should be in the spotlight of public attention. Serious efforts should be made to coordinate policies that are now made separately by different branches of government.

Professionalism and Media Practice

Can the improvement of the media system be consigned to those who operate it, to their own awareness of their talent, their instinctive sense of excellence, their pride of craftsmanship? A great chasm separates those who work at the business of entertainment from those who define themselves as providers of information. We have recurrently come to the edge of this chasm throughout this book; to understand it fully we must examine the conscience of those who regard their occupation as a calling rather than as a trade. Can the variegated assortment of people who produce media content be described as professionals?

Every emerging profession struggles to establish proper standards of practice and to formulate a public service rationale for its activities. The sociologist Bernard Barber points out that while such activities may be dismissed as "mere public relations," they have the value of making the members of the craft face up to the questions of what their social goals and practices should be.[1] Leaders of emerging professions are apt to be in conflict both with those members of their own organizations who fail to adhere to the newly developing standards and also with outsiders who might be labeled charlatans.

For centuries, the professions have been strongly rooted in the academy, where pursuit of knowledge is an objective of greater social scope than the specific tasks performed each day. Practitioners of the arts are surely not professionals in this tradition. In old and established professions, like medicine and the law, practitioner and client are engaged in face to face contact, and the fate or well-being of the client is in the practitioner's hands. This direct responsibility toward other individuals implies that standards of training and competence must be set and met, and sanctions provided against infringements of the rules. The nature of the relationship also offers a rationale for state authority to intervene directly in the form of accreditation or licensing, of the sort that is taken for granted in most countries. In journalism, which often claims professional status, the contacts between practitioner and public are impersonal and attenuated; there is no commonly accepted set of qualifications for practice and no universally agreed upon curriculum of studies that leads directly to professional status.

Can one trust the professional pride of individuals who lack any common training and meet no official requirements in order to practice their craft? Accepting the primacy of the public interest is the essence of professionalism, and represents a reasonably simple basis for the pursuit of integrity in interpretative journalism. There are no comparable agreed upon standards of acceptability in other realms of commercial culture.

Established professions are characterized by strong associations that guard their members' vested interests, while they preserve the myth of public service. In the field of journalism, organizations like the American Society of Newspaper Editors and the Radio and Television News Directors Association represent small elites rather than the whole corps of those engaged in practice.

Sociologist Emile Durkheim once asked (rhetorically, one suspects), "There are professional ethics for the priest, the lawyer, the magistrate; why should there not be one for trade and industry?" Why not, indeed, for journalists? American newspaper editors in fact have such a code. The ASNE's "Statement of Principles," adopted in 1975 reiterates the point made in the "Code of Ethics or Canons of Journalism" a year after the society was founded in 1922. That Code proclaimed "freedom from all obligations except that of fidelity to the public interest." It stood for "independence," "sincerity," "truthfulness," "accuracy," "impartiality," and "fair play" (headings reminiscent of the Boy Scout oath that had been adopted a few years earlier). Finally, it called for "decency." Having stated the canons of good practice, the Code concluded on a somewhat wistful note:

> Lacking authority to enforce its canons, the journalism here represented can but express the hope that deliberate pandering to vicious instincts will encounter effective public disapproval or yield to the influence of a preponderant professional condemnation.

Only a year after the Code was adopted, the revelations of the Teapot Dome scandal involved a copublisher of the *Denver Post*, Frederick Gilmer Bonfils (described by Gene Fowler as "a former lottery operator, swindler and confidence man") who had accepted a million dollars from the oil promoter Harry Sinclair to keep the story out of his paper. Although the ASNE's board and committee on ethical standards investigated the case, Bonfils was never censured and never expelled from the society, though he eventually resigned.[2] In fact, no one has ever been expelled from ASNE—except for not paying dues or losing a job—though the Society's Constitution was amended in 1931 to set up an involved procedure for suspending or expelling members. The impotence of the "Canons of Journalism" subscribed to by so elite a group as newspaper editors must raise grave doubts about the possibility of achieving a sense of professional identity among the lesser breeds of journalists, particularly among those whose specialties are narrow and only incidentally manifested in the final product.

At the behest of journalists' trade unions, some countries in Latin America have actually tried to impose formal rules for admittance to work, with disastrous consequences. To deny newspaper reporters or television news producers the right to work because they had not completed some specified examination would be like denying the right to write novels to anyone who did not have a university degree in literature or denying the right to paint to anyone who had not attended the Academy.

Can the news media be called to heel when they transgress the rules of accuracy or fair play? One attempt to do so through a voluntary mechanism was the Markle-Foundation-supported National News Council, which investigated complaints and issued judgments during the period 1973–84. The Council was opposed by some of the most responsible organs of the press, on the grounds that it threatened their total independence, including the right to make mistakes in fact and judgment. During its brief life, it not only managed to embarrass some powerful media organizations, but to sensitize the press generally to pay attention to its own principles. The need for such a mechanism is all the greater today, when the vigilance of local competition has been virtually eliminated.

If it has proven impossible to set up or enforce rules of competence or proper conduct in journalism, it is surely preposterous to conceive that a professional ethos could be postulated or established among those who work in other media-related occupations. There is no lack of trade unions and guilds, in a tradition that harks back to the theater crafts, but these are exclusively concerned with the bargaining position of the members *vis à vis* their employers; they have never been concerned with the standards of work performance or of public responsibility. In the entertainment business there is no counterpart to the peer group pressures and professional traditions in fields like history and journalism that are self-consciously dedicated to the pursuit of truth.

The thought of setting up formal prerequisites to the practice of any artistic endeavor is ludicrous, but so is the notion I already disputed in Chapter 6 — that there are *no* standards in this domain. Not only in the fine arts, but in mass culture, there are disagreements on aesthetic philosophy and endless disputations over the merits of specific works, but there tends to be a main body of agreement as to what should be taken seriously and what is unworthy. If the practitioners of mass culture ever felt that they shared professional goals, they would inevitably be led closer to the standards of high culture.

In the mass media, professionalism requires procedures and an organizational structure that give practitioners a high measure of autonomy and enhance their sense of importance, worth, and pride in the work. Such feelings may be especially hard to preserve when the role of so many media practitioners is defined as strictly auxiliary to the advertising of commodities. But the frustrations media professionals face in a commercial culture may seem less irritating when they consider the alternative, which is to let politicians or bureaucrats decide what is worthy and what is not.

The Need for Media Criticism

If the standards of media practice are to be raised through a greater sense of craftsmanship, such standards can hardly be left to the practitioners alone. The effort requires a continuous infusion of external judgments and constant debate over the merits of what is being produced.

There is no quarreling about taste, goes the Latin proverb. Ideologues insist that there be only one accepted standard of taste—their own. Josef Goebbels, November 27, 1936:

> I forbid once and for all the continuance of art criticism in its present form, effective as of today. From now on, the reporting of art will take the place of an art criticism which has set itself up as a judge of art—a complete perversion of the concept of "criticism" which dates from the time of the Jewish domination of art. The critic is to be superseded by the art editor. The reporting of art should not be concerned with values, but should confine itself to description.[3]

To hold the members of a profession to a sense of public responsibility, what they produce must constantly be commented upon in the light of ideal standards of performance, and the standards themselves must continually be questioned. Indeed, it is essential that critics disagree, in evaluating media as well as the fine arts. Criticism includes immediate responses to specific works as well as more reflective and comparative writings in a historical perspective. The worlds of letters, music, dance, and the plastic arts are dependent on it to provide the web of discussion and common intellectual concerns that bind their practitioners together.

Performers before live audiences are in immediate and intimate touch with their publics, but most producers of creative works must wait for a reaction; they must also learn to distinguish between the informed judgments they respect and those that emanate from circles that they do not consider to be part of their potential public.

Intelligent criticism is essential to the fulfillment and discipline of creative effort, and its valuable functions are generally understood and accepted in principle, unwelcome as they may be in the execution. From the standpoint of writers, artists, performers, and all those connected with arts and letters, critics are powerful figures who control the fate of their creations. They look very different and considerably less important when seen in the context of media content overall.

Given the enormous importance of the media in the daily time budget of most Americans, there is an astonishing paucity of criticism, evaluation, and interpretation through which those who operate media might be forced to contemplate the merits and effects of what they do. Intelligent commentary is absent or minimal in much of the press, which should logically be its appropriate vehicle. Much of what passes for reviews is rewritten from publicity handouts.

The increasing concentration of ownership seems to reduce the willingness of media to attack and criticize each other, although mutual criticism is obviously a way to keep practitioners on their toes. Movies are an exception to this. Film-makers are constantly goaded, exhorted, commented upon in publications that reach the general public and therefore affect the immediate success of works in current release. More significantly, perhaps, comment on their accomplishments and failures appears in specialized publications directed to their colleagues and peers in the film business. Such a mirror image is almost totally lacking for those who produce newspapers, magazines, and broadcasting programs.

A handful of critics on the television networks, and a few handsful on local television and radio stations, offer intelligent comments on popular films and an occasional bestselling book. There is, however, no lack of uncritical promotion. Book authors and film stars are favorite interview subjects on broadcast talk shows, which are now regarded as prime vehicles for unpaid publicity tours.

Commercial television by and large avoids critical comment on the media. Networks and stations are not given to public evaluations of their competitors' programs, let alone of their own. The scarcity of criticism on television can be attributed both to the presumably low audience appeal of such commentary and to the very limited amount of air time that is allocated to current events, including news. In Europe, extensive time is devoted to quoting and commenting on the newspapers of the day; American broadcasters tend to quote without using quotation marks.

Media devoted to other media must inevitably be supportive rather than critical, since their very existence is dependent on the devotion of the audience. Movie "fanzines" can reveal the hidden foibles and scandals of the stars, but must never question their talents or the merits of the institutions they work for. Early in the history of *TV Guide*,[4] its editor, Merrill Pannitt, said, "We can't take TV apart, because the people who buy the magazine like it, and so do we." Nearly forty years later, *TV Guide* was part of Rupert Murdoch's News Corporation empire, which included the Fox TV network and a number of important television stations. Its coeditor, David Sendler, said, before he was fired, "The philosophy is that we're in the business to sell magazines, and the philosophy is that shorter stories and more personalities will help us sell more magazines and make us livelier."

Trade and professional publications do extensive reviewing of books in their own specialties. However, among general interest magazines, from the *Reader's Digest* to *Modern Maturity*, only some dozens employ reviewers of books, films, or television programs. Of these, few review more than one or two of each in any given issue. Of the 100 top magazines (the smallest of which had a circulation of about 800,000 in 1993), no more than half a dozen review books on a regular basis, and most of them review no more than a single book per issue.

Daily newspapers are the principal avenue for criticism.[5] Most of their critics are working journalists without any particular background in the arts or media field on which they were presently writing.[6] Reviewing is a part-time assignment for most, except on large metropolitan dailies.[7] Newspapers deal overwhelmingly with popular rather than elite culture,[8] and they deal with the cultural scene primarily for its amusement value rather than as a form of serious expression. Unfortunately, cultural news (including news of pop culture) is not high on the public's "most read" list.[9] Of the 43,000 new book titles published in the United States each year, only a small handful are ever reviewed in the general press. This handful is heavily concentrated among bestsellers and books deemed likely to be bestsellers because of the heavy advance orders placed by the buyers of the two leading chains.

Most press coverage of both the popular and elite arts deals with their personalities, not with their substance. The personality of performing artists is inseparable from the characterizations they project and from the technique they employ, and to this extent it is appropriate for critics to comment on it. Such comment is quite distinct from the treatment of performers as newsworthy, or rather, gossipworthy subjects, whose private lives are endlessly fascinating to at least some sectors of the public.

• There is a long tradition behind this practice. Daniel Defoe's *Weekly Review*, which he started in 1704,[10] included a section entitled "the Scandalous Club, being a weekly history of nonsense, impertinence, vice and debauchery." This kind of gossip continues to characterize most media reportage on the arts. Joseph Addison wrote in *The Spectator* of March 1, 1711,

> I have observed, that a Reader seldom peruses a Book with Pleasure 'till he knows whether the Writer of it be a black or a fair Man, of a mild or cholerick Disposition, Married or a Batchelor, with other Particulars of the like nature, that conduce very much to the right Understanding of an Author.

The same preoccupation with personalities is reflected in the way books are marketed today.[11] A "tour book," whose author is off on the interview circuit, will have copies sent to television stations, not for on-air reviews, but to stimulate talkshow appearances. In fact, the size of an author's advance may depend on personal attractiveness as much as on literary talent.

Do the reviews just follow the ads? The book industry accounts for only 0.16% of all newspaper advertising—hardly enough to get most publishers' attention. Newspapers run bridge columns even though playing cards are not heavily promoted. They get $1 billion a year in motion picture advertising. Hollywood moguls complain loudly to publishers both that there is not enough film criticism and that what there is is too critical. They seem to regard free publicity on the entertainment pages as their natural right.

Criticism that makes sense needs more than a single critic, which is all that remains in most American cities. The vitality of criticism is menaced today by the decline of newspaper competition, especially in the larger markets that have not only the bulk of the population but most of the nation's cultural institutions. City magazines and alternative weeklies have flourished because of their coverage of the arts and entertainment scene, but they reach only a fraction of the mass audiences that second and third newspapers once covered every day.

The absence of another daily newspaper voice means that the public at large gets only a single (and often highly fallible) judgment on any work that gets reviewed—thus enormously, and unjustifiably, raising the power of critics on the surviving newspapers to an unconscionable degree. Their biases and predilections are known to those who plan cultural events. The critics themselves are relieved of the competitive pressures that test their mettle, arouse them to better performance, and create the kind of controversy that generates public interest. Even more significantly, cultural reporting is reduced to purveying succulent tidbits about the transient and irrelevant minutiae of show business. It is driven farther away from debate and discussion of the artistic expressions and intellectual concepts that change human sensibilities, values, and history. And, for the most part, it fails to fulfill what should be one of its most important functions, which is to remind media producers that they can be rated by noncommercial yardsticks.

Should Choice Be Restricted?

The first essential of a media operation that truly serves the public interest must be independence of action for its professional personnel. This means freedom from direct political supervision and also from the false criterion of audience size as the only measure of achievement.

Popularity is not an index of cultural merit, nor is there any alternative arbiter of the good, the true, and the beautiful. No individual or group, however well-qualified by sensibility or training, can claim to have perfect judgment over what deserves a hearing and what does not, over what should and what should not be prominently displayed. In a free society, the self-restraint of media practitioners is the best form of control over pornographic and violent content. Offensive subject matter presents fewer dangers than puritanical censorship.

Media audiences tend to congregate where the effort is least, and they prefer formulas to innovation. If the choice is between excellence and garbage, the prevailing assumption is that garbage will win out every time. If viewers must choose among varieties of junk, they will, of necessity, consume junk. In a competitive media environment, any vehicle would lose share of audience if it raised its standards while the others did not. In broadcasting, high-level cultural programming has always been a financial disaster. At those rare times when the networks have all broadcast programs of quality or in the public interest, independent stations have inevitably increased their share.

Media must always strike a balance between the existing level of public taste and the level to which their own producers might wish to raise it. Media choices are made from the available options. The better these are, the higher the public's level of taste. Local publications and broadcast channels show a variety that arises from two idiosyncratic sources: the nature of the community and the motivations of the management.

• To illustrate the point: in Boston, the public television channel, WGBH, has long held the best channel allocation (2, whose signals go out farthest), and its share of the prime-time audience is 25% higher than that of the typical public television station.[12] Boston is, needless to say, a city of great intellectual traditions and numerous universities, but WGBH has also had unusually strong leadership and civic support. Is it the programming practices and personalities of the station that win it an unusually high level of interest, or are those practices merely a response to market demand? The answer must be, a little of both.

Similarly, New York, Washington, and Los Angeles have dominant newspapers that manage at the same time to be extraordinary engines of the local economies and also to act as sparkling catalysts of intellectual enrichment in public life. Great cities like San Francisco and Cleveland simply have nothing comparable. *The New York Times*, in its coverage of ideas, of social and political forces, of the arts, has made itself into an indispensable ingredient in the shaping of daily conversation and thought. Undoubtedly it reflects the city's character (or at least the character of the city's upper and middle classes, for the *Times* is out of touch with large elements of the population who prefer the tabloids or else read no paper at all). But the *Times* is also a powerful shaper of that character, and its cultural role is not predestined by the mere fact of its preeminence in the market for advertising.

Audiences would not get smaller if media content improved across the board. We have seen that, while people distribute their attention to accord with their tastes, they will not usually change the total time they devote to a particular form of entertainment or information. In broadcasting, if the choice is limited to programs of merit, viewers will opt for quality in one form or another, and the total size of the audience will remain about the same. However, if the audience must choose among closely similar offerings, there may be an unfortunate redundancy of effort and talent.

It has long been suggested that children's programming be arranged so that viewers are faced with similar options, all equally excellent. Ken Mason, then president of Quaker Oats, once proposed that three consecutive hours of "quality" programming be broadcast on all three networks simultaneously on Saturday morning.[13] Each hour would be produced by a different network but carried on all of them. This was one of those rare instances where an advertiser has spoken out imaginatively on an issue of responsible broadcasting policy. Nothing came of the idea, although Quaker was a big advertiser on children's programming.

When an organization called Viewers for Quality Television urged the networks to set aside a "ratings-free" hour a week for quality programming, NBC Entertainment president Brandon Tartikoff said "the problem with the concept is that it suggests we're not trying to do it anywhere else. . . . All we might accomplish is to vastly increase the ratings on independent stations." Tartikoff, who called himself a "ratings-monger," insisted that the networks had demonstrated their commitment to quality by planning to run programs for a two-year period—an avowal that was rapidly ignored in practice.[14]

In today's world of expanding cable choices, it is beside the point to argue for uniform programming practices of any kind, for any audience, at any time. But this does not mean that there is no room for policies that intrude the needs of society (however vaguely defined or diversely interpreted they may be) into the programming practices of producing organizations for which they are presently irrelevant. Broadcasters are no longer required—as they once were—to acknowledge that they have any public responsibilities. If they were again held to pay lip service to such a principle, the subject might at least move higher up on their own agendas for discussion.

Government and Culture

In no country does the free exercise of aesthetic tastes in an open market provide sufficient support for cultural activities at the level its advocates deem appropriate. There is no demand (as yet) for government funding to preserve and encourage comic strips, girlie magazines, or TV soap operas, because these genres still hold the audiences they were created to amuse. Museums, orchestras, opera ensembles, and dramatic repertory groups almost inevitably lose money and can only be sustained through government subsidy or by raising private funds to supplement income from the sale of admissions.

Public sponsorship of the arts descends in an unbroken line from Myceneas and reflects an understanding that art enhances the quality of life. Its premise is that society has a collective need to nurture creative spirits, even when its individual members have no disposition to support them. American cities recognized in the nineteenth century that the arts were engines of municipal progress and therefore served a commercial purpose.[15] More recently, at times of budgetary crisis, when cultural institutions have been threatened, their defenders argue that they foster tourism and are therefore good for business.

Government subsidies make high culture available to a broader spectrum of the population than would willingly support it at the price required to pay for its cost directly. Subsidies build an audience for the display of established talents and foster the discovery and nourishment of new talents. The more sources of subsidy there are and the greater the autonomy on the part of the functionaries who decide what and whom to subsidize, the less is the danger of a rigid official academicism in which certain cultural styles are encouraged and others throttled at birth.

State-supported broadcast media extend the traditions of government patronage of the performing arts. Elite standards are applied, rather than those of popular demand. The operating premise is that an additional channel, even with a very small share of the audience, keeps alive a type of programming that would not survive on its own in a free competitive commercial market and prominently displays it as an alternative.

Long before the Public Broadcasting System was established in 1969, municipal governments and state-supported universities operated radio and television stations whose programming was designed to serve social purposes rather than to maximize audience size. If improving media quality is a desirable social objective, does this automatically suggest a role for government in establishing and maintaining cultural standards? The First Amendment bars such interference in principle.

In mass communications as in the arts, cultural policy is indistinguishable from cultural politics that involve the conflict of personalities, cliques, and cabals and the clash of larger political doctrines. In a democracy, cultural politics are inseparable from the broader spectrum of politics in which culture may from time to time become an issue of public debate.

Controls over the technical means of diffusion cannot be separated from controls over content, in spite of efforts to keep the two areas distinct. And controls over content in the domain of taste and creative expression are in no way clearly distinguishable from controls over content in the domain of information and political expression. To conclude that the fatherly hand of the state should guide the people onward and upward in the cultural sphere is inevitably linked to the doctrine that the same kindly guidance should also determine what information is important and unimportant and how that information should be interpreted to the public at large. This is a compelling argument. To be sure, political guidance—along with cultural guidance—occurs in any case as a result of decisions made by media operators, not necessarily with the public's best interests uppermost in mind. But this is not a convincing rebuttal.

Twentieth-century history affords ample evidence of the horrors that follow state intervention into the flow of ideas. Dictatorships have always sought to impose their superior taste upon the ignoble instincts of the masses.[16] Communist doctrine affirmed the didactic function of the media and considered entertainment acceptable only to the degree that it ensured attention to the message when it arrived. In any society, said the doctrine, media serve the class interests of those who rule. There could, therefore, be no such thing as nonpolitical media content; even the most trivial entertainment symbolically embodied a world view that either enhanced or detracted from the cause of socialism. A proletarian society also required affirmation of its glories and of its hopes for ever greater glories. The free play of ideas and tastes, even in what was ostensibly outside the political realm, would lead inevitably to a weakening of the proper Communist outlook and to indulgence in degenerate forms of cultural expression: violence, licentiousness, bourgeois romanticism, sentimentality, deviationist satire, and other corruptions of socialist morality.

The Nazi Ministry of Propaganda and Public Enlightenment similarly combined political and cultural tasks in its manipulation of the media into a monolithic form. A transcript of one of Josef Goebbels' morning conferences showed directives like the following:

> Despite the dramatic report [from United Press] the Plymouth raid is to be reported on page 2.
>
> Nothing is to be reported in the German press about an ostensible peace feeler by the Pope. . . .
>
> For the time being, even big raids on England must be carried on page 2 and less noise made about them.

Goebbels' daily preoccupations, David Schoenbrunn observed, included not only the news from the war front, but

> strippers (he was for them), dirty jokes (he was against them), the Mozart–Schubert ratio in the radio concert schedule (Goebbels wanted less Mozart, more Schubert), performances of Shaw on German stages (he was Irish, Goebbels emphasized), the predictions of Nostradamus (the French were showered with them), the practicability of radio recipes.[17].

No such system of control can be airtight. Market demands must be met, even when the state exercises tight supervision of all mass media. Books, periodicals, and film admissions have to be bought one at a time and thus reflect public preferences, even though the choices are confined within a narrower range than in a free society.

Even under the most authoritarian regimes there are still some constraints on the way official ideology is imposed, since the diffusion of righteous messages is purposeless if no one is listening to them. Therefore, a certain number of broadcast hours must be devoted to popular music, sports broadcasts, and other frivolities, if only to sustain audiences that would disappear if programming time were devoted exclusively to the on-air reading of political tracts.

In most countries of the world, broadcasting is state-controlled, and the listening and viewing options are highly limited. Many governments operate newspapers and broadcasting systems directly or through closely connected surrogates. The perils of thought control surface even under democratic regimes with state-supported broadcasting systems that ban advertising. The prevailing philosophy is often didactic, though it is not carried to the same censorious extremes as it was in the Communist East or is in China.

In France, under Charles De Gaulle, news commentators on the government-run broadcasting services were given policy directives each day. Only a limited amount of opposition to the government line was allowed to appear on television, even during national election campaigns. Documentary programs dealing with controversial issues interviewed "average citizens" who all expressed a pro-government point of view. The government defended these practices as a necessary corrective to the mainly anti-Gaullist opinions of the French press.[18]

Even at this time, the Radio-Diffusion Française and its counterparts in Western Europe were highly sensitive to the shifts in audience demand and employed a substantial and highly sophisticated research apparatus to study them. In no sense, however, could the programming decisions of these organizations be considered to reflect market forces, because the sense of public mission remained paramount. The entertainment formulas of the commercial culture still dominate most government-run broadcasting systems. Even before the changes of regime in Eastern Europe there was a substantial infusion of American television fare, which was inevitably the most popular programming on the air. The home-grown entertainment was also often highly imitative of American patterns.

The BBC exemplifies the principle that an organization that is quasigovernmental in its financial support and managerial appointments can still preserve a high measure of independence in its operations. Its long-time director-general, John Reith, expressed the credo of public broadcasting in a democracy, years ago:

> It is occasionally indicated to us that we are apparently setting out to give the public what we think they need—and not what they want, but few know what they want and very few what they need. . . . In any case it is better to overestimate the mentality of the public than to underestimate it.

It was easier for the BBC to operate by this philosophy before it was faced with commercial competition that sharply reduced its share of audience and forced it to popularize its programming. The BBC has learned how difficult it is to balance high standards with the mass appeal that can justify its tax on viewers. Despite its excellence, it has been forced to follow the lead of its commercial competitors, and its future appears to hold a greatly restricted role.

Government control over content—political or cultural—is harder to exercise when publications, cable channels, and radio stations exist in enormous variety and when they focus on minor sectors of the public. That is the case in the United States, but American media are not immune to political pressures.

Political Power and Media Power

American media institutions have a curious reciprocal relationship with those who hold the reins of government; each exerts great power over the other. The influence of commercial culture is strongly expressed throughout our political system. Politics is the stuff of news; we saw in Chapter 7 that the way the news is presented follows the rules imposed by the pursuit of the mass audiences that advertisers want.

Antagonism between politicians and the press has been evident throughout American history, but television has added new dimensions to the relationship. Only pale shadows remain of the American press's strongly partisan political cast in the first two-thirds of the nineteenth century. The attrition of local competition has forced many papers into a centrist political stance, with columns expressing a diversity of viewpoints. Although newspapers' editorial support still counts for a great deal in local contests, their influence is generally discounted in presidential politics, in part because their partisanship—reflecting their overwhelmingly small-town character— is so predictably and overwhelmingly Republican. Even great papers like the *Miami Herald* no longer make presidential endorsements. Some papers have eliminated *all* editorials, on the theory that readers can make up their own minds by reading the columnists.

However close the personal bonds between government officials and politically ambitious newspaper publishers, they have rarely had, even in the days of Horace Greeley and later of Warren Gamaliel Harding and James Cox, the same kind of intimate and tangled connections as those that have arisen in the twentieth century between politicians and broadcasters. Television advertising costs now represent the main expense of running for national or statewide public office. They amounted to half of the half billion dollars spent in the 1992 presidential race. TV debates and talk shows are powerful factors in political campaigning, and television is the principal means by which presidents communicate with the electorate.

There are grave implications in the precarious balance between the power of the media—whose news functions provide an essential constraint upon government—and the power of government to set the ground rules to which media dependent upon public franchises must conform or die. The relationship has made Congress more than properly solicitous of the broadcast industry's business interests. At the same time it seems to temper the sharpness with which broadcast news treats members of Congress. Under the sainted Dwight D. Eisenhower, Senator Joseph McCarthy was instrumental in designating several appointments to the FCC.

• By playing the power game, Congressman Lyndon B. Johnson (in his wife's name) acquired a radio station license and a network affiliation in Austin, which he parlayed into a television franchise that remained a monopoly for many years and made him very wealthy.[19] A substantial number of senators and members of Congress have held shares in broadcasting properties, and broadcasters have been generous contributors to reelection campaigns.

Huge financial interests are at stake in both government legislation and administrative rulings that affect broadcasting operations, and media institutions respond predictably. Both the National Association of Broadcasters and the cable industry, through their Political Action Committees, donate money to the campaigns of congressional representatives who support their interests.[20] NBC's president, Robert Wright, tried—unsuccessfully, because of opposition from the news division—to start a political action committee in the model of General Electric (the parent company), warning that "employees who elect not to participate in a giving program of this type should question their own dedication to the company and their expectations."

Hollywood made substantial political donations in its fight to maintain the FCC's financial and syndication rules, which kept the networks out of the lucrative syndication market and thus limited their ability to compete for the top talent.[21]

An unnamed network official, describing the FCC's modification of the rules:

> It is basically a story about the use of regulation to change power relationships in the industry and, in a sense, who's got control over what goes on the air.[22]

President Reagan's FCC abandoned the fairness doctrine (which required balanced expressions on controversial subjects) and equal time rule (which governed political debate). But because broadcasters depend upon government sufferance, and do not enjoy the First Amendment privileges accorded to the press—they are reluctant to tangle with any arm of the federal government.[23]

Journalism and government are antagonists by nature. The best reporters are the most intelligent, knowledgeable, analytical, and irreverent. Unlike their editors at home or headquarters, many of them lean more to the left than to the right in their personal politics. (Among working journalists, Democrats outnumber Republicans three to one.) Conservative politicians think of the Washington press corps as prejudiced against them. Richard Nixon to Robert Haldeman, May 9, 1971:

> As we approach the election we are in a fight to the death for the big prize. Ninety-five percent of the members of the Washington press corps are unalterably opposed to us because of their intellectual and philosophical background. Some of them will smirk and pander to us for the purpose of getting a story but we must remember that they are just waiting for the chance to stick the knife in deep and to twist it.[24]

In spite of the prevailing assumptions, television news has been demonstrated, at least in the past, to favor the party in power.[25] But for the Nixon administration, any hint of opposition was intolerable, as was demonstrated in the desperate attempts to halt publication of the Pentagon Papers. Nixon objected to "offensive left-wing commentators" and forced the Corporation for Public Broadcasting to redistribute funds to smaller stations across the country at the expense of the more sophisticated voices in the big cities.

The public condemnation of the "news media" by that exemplar of civic virtue, Vice-President Spiro T. Agnew, reflected the administration's anger at the television commentaries that followed an earlier address by Nixon outlining his Vietnam policy. Agnew's first speech, on November 13, 1969 (written, incidentally, by the future presidential candidate Patrick Buchanan[26]), preempted regularly scheduled programming, as in a public emergency, although its contents were known in advance by the networks, and although no vice-presidential utterances had ever before been granted such preeminence. Agnew accused the commentators and producers, living in Washington and New York City, of

> their own provincialism, their own parochialism. We can deduce that these men read the same newspapers. They draw their political and social views from the same

sources. Worse, they talk constantly to one another, thereby providing artificial reinforcement to their shared viewpoints.

At the same time that Agnew attacked "a tiny enclosed fraternity of privileged men elected by no one and enjoying a monopoly sanctioned and licensed by Government," Nixon moved secretly to muffle independent reporting by applying pressure on the television networks, even pressing to get newscaster Dan Rather reassigned. The White House also threatened the Washington Post Company's valuable broadcast licenses in retaliation for the newspaper's reporting. In an unprecedented and sinister move, Nixon's newly appointed FCC chairman, Dean Burch, asked the networks for transcripts of their commentaries on Nixon's speech. A few months later, the Justice Department tried to subpoena unused television film footage, unpublished magazine photographs, and newspaper reporters' notes—all dealing with radical organizations.

To their great credit, at least some of the network heads refused to buckle under the intimidation of their news departments. CBS News head Richard Salant did not find out until the Watergate hearings that network Chairman William Paley and President Frank Stanton were under pressure from the White House. Thus in the last analysis, the personal character of the individuals who run its powerful institutions continues to make a difference, even in the workings of a media system that has become essentially a cold-blooded financial enterprise.

Pressures on Public Broadcasting

Public broadcasting—independently financed and autonomously managed to advance social, cultural, and civic goals—is subject to many of the same pressures that confront its commercial counterparts. Long-term, its funding depends on public approval, or at the very least, on public acquiescence. This means that its managers, conscious of their program ratings, avoid the didactic and the difficult and know the perils of potentially controversial content.

Programming is only one element of the budget for which public broadcasters must fight. They must worry about transmitting equipment, payroll, and other operating costs. If they operate at a deficit, as is generally true in the United States, they must devote both money and a considerable amount of effort to seek out donors. The irritation of fund-raising appeals on public TV stations matches the irritation of unwanted advertising on the commercial channels. Especially choice program offerings are husbanded for the weeks of fund-raising drives and also for the weeks of the ratings sweeps, exactly as they are by commercial broadcasters. David Othmer, general manager of public TV station WHYY, Philadelphia:

> We've grown beyond the point of doing things because they're good for people—castor oil television—and saying, "You've got to watch this." We have got to make television that people want to watch. . . . In the early days, all we were concerned with was producing quality programming, and then we began to want people to watch. . . . We will not survive unless we get people to support us.[27]

Caught between a desire to serve social need and the wish to uplift the general level of taste, public TV stations have joined the pursuit of audiences and ratings to justify their budgets to the public bodies that support them. To attract more viewers they have bought rerun rights to series like "Lassie" and "Leave it to Beaver." Jennifer Lawson, chief programming executive of the Public Broadcasting Service (PBS), has said she was willing to introduce game shows to raise audience levels and that she favored "more culturally diverse programming," suggesting that ethnic criteria might replace professional judgments of inherent merit. (PBS has been largely unsuccessful in its effort to win minority viewers.) Announcing that "our public is everyone with a TV set,"[28] Lawson killed a carefully crafted proposal for a "Voter's Channel," sponsored by the Markle Foundation, that would have supplanted the networks' diminished coverage of the 1992 election campaign.

In 1994, PBS controlled more than $250 million in federal funding for the 351 local public television stations. Half that amount went directly to local stations. The federal contribution represented only 16% of public television's total income; larger amounts came from viewers, state governments, and business. Growing financial dependence on corporate institutional sponsors (euphemistically termed "underwriters") has made public broadcasters highly cautious in their assessment of potentially controversial programs. (The president of the National Association of Broadcasters sneeringly suggested that PBS stood for "Petroleum Broadcasting Service.")

From its inception, public television has been embroiled in politics at the federal, state, and local levels. (Federal funding for the Corporation for Public Broadcasting was delayed in 1992 by Senate Republicans who attacked public broadcasting for being "liberal.[29]) Because of their limited funding sources, public broadcasters are also vulnerable to vigilante pressure. Their judgments are perennially under attack from one or another ethnic group or political faction, even when scrupulous attempts are made to preserve neutrality.

• To cite one instance: In 1989, New York's Channel Thirteen was strongly criticized for accepting a documentary on the Palestinians, after other stations had refused to air it. The criticisms came from pro-Israelis who objected to the program's viewpoint and its distortions of some historical facts, and also from others who felt that its sponsorship by a lobbying group should have barred it from presentation. The station management honorably held its ground, after first changing the time of broadcast. But it preceded the program with disclaimers and followed it with a panel discussion that presumably brought matters back into balance. In this particular instance the fuss was short-lived, since the program was not interesting or provocative enough to prompt any sustained indignation. But the episode illuminates the anxieties that beset public broadcasters who venture afield from content that is politically bland or culturally inoffensive.

Like their commercial counterparts, public broadcasters—even when they stand firm in an individual case—must necessarily think twice the next time a parallel appears to be emerging on the horizon. Not only does their personal experience affect their standards of self-censorship, but so also does the collective experience of their peers. No matter how intense their moral convictions—or perhaps their self-righteousness—they must still weigh their principles in the balance against the practical need to sustain their income.

The controversies that arise from time to time over politically contentious public television programs are akin to those that have raged about publicly sponsored art. These involve, ultimately, the question of whether the criteria to be applied should be those of the creative professionals in the field or those of the general public and its elected or appointed representatives. In the arts as in all other domains, it is difficult to obtain consensus from a political system designed to balance divergent special interests.[30]

In public art, as in public television, the fear of controversy is induced by a mixture of psychological and economic reasons, especially where publicly funded support is confounded with freedom of artistic expression. Two cases, both involving serious, talented, and established artists, demonstrate this confusion.

• Richard Serra's giant sculpture, "Tilted Arc," aroused indignation not because of its abstract design, but because, with its shape and dimensions specific to its location in the courtyard of a large public building in lower Manhattan, it changed the character and utility of the site for the people who worked there and for passersby. The artistic statement was intentionally aggressive; its meaning would have changed if it had been moved to another location, as was originally suggested and as the sculptor refused to permit. The argument that ensued was essentially over turf, over the imposition of someone else's taste and will upon the daily life patterns of thousands of people who had to walk tens of thousands of extra steps each day to get to and from their place of work. The courtyard, shunned by the public while the sculpture was in place, became a popular gathering place when it was removed and benches were installed. Yet "Tilted Arc" had been commissioned and wrought as a creative expression, conceived in the public's aesthetic interest.

• Quite a different set of debating points were involved in the aftermath of the Corcoran Gallery's cancellation of a scheduled 1989 exhibition of the photography of Robert Mapplethorpe. It included several homoerotic photos; one showed a man urinating into another's mouth. In another federally funded Corcoran show, "Piss Christ," a photograph by Andres Serrano, depicted a crucifix in a vial of urine. The National Endowment for the Arts had spent $45,000 in support of the exhibits that included the offending Mapplethorpe and Serrano works. The irresistible combination of sacrilege and pornography prompted legislation that forbade the Endowment from funding "obscenity" and, in effect, placed it on probation.

The debate centered on the propriety of using public money to display works that would undoubtedly offend most of the public if they were exposed to them, but that most would never be exposed to in the normal course of events. If the purpose of government support for the arts is to stimulate expression that would not be viable in the commercial marketplace, clearly a price has to be paid in occasional transgressions of prevailing tastes and proprieties by serious artists. (The rub is in defining who is serious—as in the case of three conceptual artists who handed out $10 bills to illegal immigrants as part of a project in small part funded by the NEA.[31]) Creative innovation has always flown in the face of prevailing taste and sometimes in the face of conventional mores.

• John E. Frohnmayer, president of the Endowment in the Bush administration, withdrew a $10,000 grant from an exhibition at a respected New York gallery, Artists'

Space,[32] and rejected grant applications from several performance artists, including one who dramatized the degradation of women by smearing her body in chocolate, to simulate excrement. Frohnmayer was eventually forced out of his job.[33] His replacement swiftly vetoed two grants strongly recommended by the Endowment's Advisory Council.

The entire budget of the National Endowment for the Arts is less than the Defense Department's allocation for military bands. The Endowment's travails are worth mentioning here only because they marvelously exemplify the perils of politicizing the controls over mass media content as a possible alternative to the chaos of its present commercially driven management. (The chair of the Corporation for Public Broadcasting was awarded to Sheila Tate, former press secretary to Nancy Reagan.) It is frightening to imagine the consequences of entrusting media to any public body that might be vulnerable to political activism, often exercised by groups and individuals whose behavior may be not merely malevolent but irrational.

Even without advertising to lose, public broadcasting has already felt this kind of heat. It suffers from utterly inadequate funding as well as occasional political difficulties; it is susceptible to the temptation to accept audience size rather than merit as its main operating principle. Yet for all of that, public broadcasting serves essential cultural functions for which no commercial alternatives exist. It deserves a multiplication of its financial resources and a liberation from dependence on handouts by viewers and corporate donors (which can only be achieved by making commercial broadcasters pay what it takes).

The nation's $1.2 billion annual investment in public broadcasting works out to less than $5 a head[34] and represents only 2% of the annual spending on television and cable. A distinguished commission appointed by the Carnegie Foundation concluded years ago that PBS's budget should be five times as large as it is.[35] This seems like a conservative judgment, though there is no reason to assume that public broadcasters are capable of increasing their production of good programs to such a degree.

The real lesson to be drawn from the controversies over publicly funded art is that public broadcasting, to fulfill its social function, requires a governance system that gives it ironclad autonomy from political demands. Such a system can exist only if society—and government—have confidence in the good intentions, good judgment, and competence of the professionals who run it—or who might be attracted to run it if the terms were right.

Toward a National Media Policy

Media can be improved by a heightened sense of mission among those who produce them and by a broadened public discussion of their accomplishments and failures. But a regeneration of the media system requires more than that. The future of media, like their past, depends on the actions of government, in all its forms. To suggest the need for a national media policy, in a society that cherishes free expression, conjures up disturbing images of potential thought control. Actually, the United States already has a national media policy, made up of the many regulations that affect the operations of media, existing and potential. That web of unrelated and sometimes inconsistent rules arises out of the separate histories and circumstances through which the individual media have evolved. It is constantly being adjusted and revised, by legislation, administrative actions, and judicial rulings. Both the rules and the chances for inconsistency among them have multiplied as communication technology has grown more complex, the once well-defined boundary lines between individual media have crumbled, and individual and mass communication increasingly share common delivery methods.

Government determines the ground rules under which different media operate, and thus indirectly shapes the essential nature of the system itself. Present American media policy is replete with anomalies and unresolved issues. Given the rapid rate of change both in the media business and in the rules, it would be foolish to offer a comprehensive policy blueprint on subjects that are complex, enveloped in specialized technicalities, and, in some instances, intensely controversial.

Other democratic countries pursue media policies in a conscious way, seeking to limit commercialism in broadcasting (as most European and many Asian countries did for many years by making television a state monopoly), or (as in Germany) by limiting the amount of broadcast advertising, in order to keep the press economically healthy. In Sweden, state newsprint subsidies permit the survival of a minority press that is commercially unable to sustain itself. This has been done to preserve freedom of expression rather than to inhibit it. But although democracy prevails in Scandinavia, similar practices in fascist Spain and in Africa demonstrate how the same policy may be used for antidemocratic ends.

Media are affected by government actions in spheres that at first glance seem to have nothing to do with communications at all; at the same time, the regulation of media often has repercussions in other areas of society. Media are largely governed by rules that apply to all businesses; but they are also distinctive, and applying general rules to them may have unusual or unintended consequences.

For example, when state and local governments impose sales taxes on periodicals, their costs are raised and they are less able to compete for revenues with nontaxed advertising media like broadcasting, direct mail, and telephone yellow pages. Local taxes on advertising and federal tax rules that treat advertising as an expense rather than as a depreciable investment affect the balance sheets of advertising media and thus alter their market positions relative to other media.

It is commonly supposed that the First Amendment protects print media from government intervention. But since the beginnings of the American republic, national policy on postal rates has actively fostered a vigorous and competitive press and has helped to assure the economic well-being of magazines and newspapers. Early in its history, the U.S. Post Office introduced a reduced second-class postal rate for paid periodicals in a deliberate effort to encourage their circulation, and thus the flow of ideas that the Founding Fathers considered essential to democracy. Other forms of mail delivery, or government subsidy, have had to make up the difference between the revenues from periodicals and the true delivery costs.

Magazines' pricing to readers, and thus their ability to achieve high audience levels attractive to advertisers, depend in most cases on their second-class subscription mailing costs. Maintaining a readership base also demands constantly soliciting new subscribers, through mass third-class promotional mailings. (Computer technology makes it possible to print different versions of a magazine while maintaining the proper zip code delivery sequence; postal rates geared to this technology favor the big operators, and thus unintentionally abet the concentration of media power.)

Newspapers—other than small weeklies and such national giants as *The Wall Street Journal*—are far less concerned with second-class postal rates than they are with the issue of third-class mailings and their use. But in the case of advertising-related third-class mail, postal policy has worked against the press as well as for it. Rates are set by an autonomous Postal Rate Commission, which is subject to intensive lobbying pressures—from mailing houses, periodical publishers, and the postal unions—whenever a review occurs, which is fairly often.

When the Post Office became the Postal Service in 1970, it received two contradictory charges: to maintain the existing level of service to every community in the nation, six days a week, but at the same time to operate within budget, without a profit but also without additional federal support. The agency is constrained by its impossible dual mandate to act like a business but to act like a government service, too. As independent private carriers began to deliver packages in competition with parcel post and then with the mail itself, the Postal Service undertook to become competitive and marketing-minded, like the business executives who were appointed to head it. It saw third-class advertising mail as an opportunity to expand its volume; operating costs were regarded as marginal additions to the basic expense of carrying out the primary mission of delivering first-class letter mail. This basis of calculation permitted low rates that attracted a vast amount of new business. (Third-class mail volume soared from 23 billion pieces in 1977 to 63 billion in 1992.)

Facilitated by the growth of computerized lists that targeted potential customers, direct mail has been the fastest-growing advertising medium, attracting large categories of advertising that formerly appeared in magazines and (especially) newspapers. Newspapers have responded by developing substantial mailing programs of their own, to send circulars to nonsubscribers. Newspapers have also been affected indirectly but significantly, as mail order catalogue houses (using third-class privileges) have expanded their share of the retail market at the expense of the traditional retail merchants who had used the press as their main promotional vehicle. The economics of telemarketing would be changed by proposed legislation requiring local sales taxes to be paid on merchandise ordered by mail or phone; since such a law would benefit local merchants—and newspapers—it would constitute national media policy.

Faced with a dwindling share of advertising, newspapers have sought economies in a distribution process that, to a large degree, has rested on another element of government media policy—the exemption of juvenile carriers from the child labor laws. Changes in living styles and in job opportunities for youth reduced the available pool of "little merchants." As adult moonlighters and retirees filled the gap, and as computerized subscriber information systems grew, it was possible to consider profit-making possibilities, using the industry's equipment and manpower to deliver magazines and other products. This in turn raised new policy questions—about how far the press's First Amendment privileges could legitimately be extended to cover its activities in other areas. It also suggested ambiguities in the status of distributors who were classified as "independent contractors," but in effect functioned as employees. Newspapers also benefit, like all other private companies in the mass distribution business, from an aspect of national transportation policy that is never identified as part of media policy, but is—their use of the government-subsidized highway system.

This last issue immediately suggests another social expense not yet reflected in the price of any publication—the cost of recycling or otherwise disposing of it. This expense is equivalent to about 5% of the cost of the newsprint used and perhaps as much as 10% of what the reader pays for the paper. Related to this subject is a longstanding element of government media policy: the tariff exemption (since 1911) for imported newsprint (54% of U.S. consumption). The cost of paper has been rising along with the cost of energy, a major factor in producing and transporting it. In this instance, national energy policy becomes national media policy.

While the rising cost of paper restricts the competitive position of print media in the advertising marketplace, the cost of transmitting information electronically has steadily fallen. (The cost of retrieving a name and address from a remote database dropped from over more than $7 to less than a dime in ten years.) As this process continues, there is a shift in the competitive economic balance of electronic and print communication.

Will "newspapers" of the future be available in a format other than print on paper? The evolution of such electronic devices as liquid crystal displays will make it possible to present text and illustrations over a large surface equivalent to a newspaper page. Accelerated computer speed makes it faster and easier to browse and move along through a lengthy document the size of a present-day newspaper. By the same token, it should be easier to produce a customized or "tailored" product for electronic display than by inkjet printing techniques, thus hastening the transformation of mass media into individual communications.

Independent market forces do not in themselves account for this process of change. Commitment—or a lack of it—to the development of such new communications technology has purposeful government support in Japan and France, and, to a degree, has been a byproduct of military spending in the United States. National policy in science, and in research and development, is thus transformed into national media policy.

The greatest obstacle for someone who wants to start a newspaper is to get copies to the readers in a timely and inexpensive way. Automation has drastically reduced the cost of manufacturing. A news story can now be written, copyedited, and set in type for final production without the intervention of more than a single copyeditor working from a computer terminal. Computerized makeup and pagination complete the process, and platemaking is automated, too. By contrast, setting up and managing a carrier force is extremely costly; so is the physical movement of papers into the field. In an era of irregular reading habits, fewer papers are home-delivered, more sold individually. On a national scale, *USA Today* has shown the way by creating a massive system for distributing copies to its own vending racks. Even in very difficult markets like New York City, it has been possible for new business publications (like *Crain's New York*) to set up and service racks in a variety of locations at manageable expense.

A step that might encourage newcomers to enter the business would be to develop a low-cost technology for distributing newspapers—not the facsimile newspapers of fantasy (no one has yet figured out how to solve the paper-storage problem) or the electronic news services of the future, but the familiar, convenient, and efficient newspapers of today. Will the development of such technology emerge from the newspaper industry itself? Not likely from a business that has been investing 0.2% of its revenues in research and development. Would a modest investment along these lines serve the public interest? Indeed it would. Where should the funding come from, if not from the public purse? Such an expenditure would imply a commitment by government to certain national goals in the governance of media. But if government intrudes into the picture, does this not inevitably raise the prospect of a threat to liberty?

Media and the Sherman Act

Government has been inconsistent in its posture toward the concentration of media power. We have seen throughout this book that the ownership structure of the media profoundly affects the diversity of their content. The Sherman Act (or the principles behind it) has been invoked by the courts and by the Federal Communications Commission (the primary agency in creating policy for electronic media), to keep media companies from owning newspapers and broadcasting stations in the same market, to restrict the number of stations a broadcasting network can own, and to keep the telephone companies out of the television business. But these principles are not applied uniformly.

On a national scale, as we saw in Chapter 2, major media industries are each dominated by a handful of corporations, and multimedia conglomerates continue to grow without intervention. There is no limit to the number of newspapers that can be owned by a given group, but the ownership of broadcast properties has long been restricted.

The FCC's longstanding rules on station ownership were set up to encourage stability and dedication to the public interest. No station could be sold in less than three years, to discourage trading in the precious public franchises. In 1984, the FCC changed its rules in the name of deregulation, encouraging the kind of speculation and takeover that were rampant in the era of junk bonds and corporate acquisitions. Under new rules enacted by the FCC in 1992, a broadcasting company could own up to sixty radio stations (and up to six in a given market) it can also own twelve television stations reaching 25 percent of the population.

In the same year, the perpetual tension between highly profitable television station owners and the less profitable and sometimes money-losing networks was heightened when the networks demanded that the stations compensate them for carrying programs, rather than the other way around. None of the ensuing negotiation among private parties, in which the networks ultimately gave in, was regarded as being within the purview of possible intervention by any public body, in spite of the enormous consequences for programming quality.

Newspapers have been exempted from the antitrust laws under the Newspaper Preservation Act of 1970. As we saw in Chapter 4, the number of daily newspapers actually competing head to head has steadily gone down, and there has been a steady amalgamation of morning and evening papers published by the same ownership. There were still twenty-nine of these combinations left in 1994. Their future might be assured if ownership and responsibilities for news operations could be exchanged. Business management, including control of advertising and circulation, could be left in the hands of the existing owner in each city, but it would swap its editorial management of the unprofitable (usually evening) paper with that of another comparable paper in another market. In effect, such a new arrangement would create joint operating agreements where there are monopolies now. The proposal would be resisted by any publisher who now puts out an evening paper with only a marginal editorial staff and could envision no return from an investment in a new editorial venture in another city. This resistance would be shortsighted, because the future of the press depends on the strength of the reading habit, which withers in the absence of competition. Whatever publishers wanted to do, they would not able to do it without the government's approval.

- The potential for mischief in this area is illustrated by Senator Edward Kennedy's successful effort to prevent Rupert Murdoch from obtaining a waiver to continue publishing the money-losing *New York Post*, after his News Corporation bought a New York television channel as part of its acquisition of MetroMedia. (The *Boston Herald*, then owned by Murdoch, had been a vigorous critic of the Senator.) The *Post* went through a series of owners and into a steady slide. When the paper was about to close down in 1993, Kennedy and the FCC relented and Murdoch was permitted to recover and save it. But if the rules can be waived in this case, why should not any owner of a profitable television station be free to start up a *new* newspaper in the same market?

It is illogical for the government to allow competitors to collaborate to keep failing newspapers alive and yet be concerned about local cross-ownership of newspaper and broadcasting properties, especially in the cable era, with its explosion in the number of channels. Such inconsistency is rampant in the crazy quilt of rules that make up our national media policy.

In most branches of American industry, the companies that manufacture goods are different from those that distribute them, and the two parties live in an uneasy symbiosis. In the magazine field, it has been considered tolerable for two major publishing companies—Time Warner and News Corporation—to control the channels of distribution to retail outlets for about two-thirds of the single-copy circulation. Yet in other areas of mass communication, vertical integration has run afoul of federal regulators, as in the 1949 consent decree that divorced the film studios from the theater organizations that originally started them.

By similar reasoning, the FCC's financial and syndication rules[36] already mentioned, were revised in 1991 to permit a limited expansion of the networks into the production of syndicated programming, which fills a growing amount of nonnetwork broadcast and cable network time. In 1993, in the face of strong lobbying from the Motion Picture Association, the ban on in-house production was lifted and the networks were allowed to invest in producing shows made for their own use.

The creation of the market for syndicated programs itself illustrates how government regulations directly affect media content, though not always in the intended way. The FCC's 1970 "prime-time access" rule limited the networks' evening feed to the three hours between 8 and 11 p.m. (with an extra half hour for news, if the local news was broadcast before 7 p.m.). There was a sharp increase in the number of commercials shown in the "access time" between 7:30 and 8 p.m. While the intention was to foster original, locally produced shows, stations opted instead for cheap game shows and reruns of old network programs. By changing the economics of the broadcast business, syndication enlarged the power of the Hollywood studios.

The 11,000 cable system operators claim a First Amendment right to control the content that they transmit, but under the Cable Act of 1992, they cannot carry a signal without the consent of the broadcaster.[37] (This provision led to bitter and protracted bargaining, in which networks and station owners demanded fees for "retransmission rights" on cable, analogous to those the systems pay to the cable networks. When the huge cable system operators held firm, the broadcasters—faced with the prospect of unacceptable audience losses—capitulated.[38])

Giant organizations have become powerful presences in every part of the media business, but the rules that allow them to become players in some arenas capriciously restrict them from entering others. Between 1970 and 1992, broadcast networks were not allowed to own cable systems (although they did and do own cable networks.) Under the new rules a network could not own systems that accounted for over half the households in any television market or 10% of the national total. Although many cable system operators supported the change, almost all of them vigorously opposed telephone company efforts to provide video signals. As the way was opened for the phone companies to launch a vast array of new entertainment and information services (which they had been barred from doing under the 1984 Cable Television Act), the structure of the media system would be shaken to its foundations. The rules were being changed almost from day to day, with no particular plan, and with no one clearly in charge.

The Politics of Telecommunications Policy

Both Congress and every administration in power regard telecommunications policy as politically important. (Although the president nominates its members, the FCC is a creature of Congress, not of the executive branch.) In the domain of electronic media, the FCC wields powers that would be considered highly dangerous if they had counterparts in print. Broadcasting frequencies must be allocated to avoid chaos on the airwaves, but the FCC's rulings have consequences for aspects of national life that have little to do with the management of the spectrum. The members of this politically appointed body, overwhelmingly drawn from the legal profession, have generally manifested less interest than they should in the long-term social and cultural consequences of their actions.

A recent exception has been the Commission's preferential award of franchises to members of certain minority groups, establishing affirmative action as an instrument of national media policy. (A 1992 court decision decreed that this principle did not apply to women.) The practice has made some individuals wealthy, but there is no indication that it has served the general interest of the designated groups. Similarly arbitrary benefits have been mandated by Congress on behalf of the hard of hearing, adding about $5 to the production cost of a television set, and $15–20 to its consumer price.[39]

Nationalism is another element that has entered existing national media policy. Foreign companies can and do own newspapers, magazines, book publishing houses, musical recording companies, cable systems, television and film production studios. The nation's second wire service, UPI, was bought in 1992 by a brother-in-law of King Fahd of Saudi Arabia. Yet only U.S. citizens are permitted to own more than 20% of any over-the-air broadcast property. With the imminent changes in media technology, it is not at all clear why there should be such an exclusion.

Media have been extraordinarily profitable enterprises, even though some individual publications and stations lose money. Broadcasting's enormous profit margins have set yardsticks for business goals and advertising rates in print media as well. High broadcast profits (up to 50% annual return on investment in some instances) have been justified on the grounds that licensees assume a risk and are required to make substantial capital investments in setting up station facilities. But when a television station is sold for nearly half a billion dollars, it is obviously not for its transmitting equipment, its studios, or its office furniture. The value lies in the franchise—a public property and trust. The same point applies to cable operations as well as to on-air broadcasting. Three-fifths of a cable system's equity represents intangibles, and only two-fifths is in the replacement value of equipment and plant. (By 1992 the price per subscriber of a typical system was about $2,000.)

The FCC only awards franchises for over-the-air terrestrial TV. Cable franchises are awarded by local governments. From the earliest days of the medium, they have been embroiled in local politics, and sometimes enveloped by the smell of corruption. (A cable pioneer, Teleprompter's Irving Kahn, went to jail for bribing civic officials; Warner Cable, negotiating for a franchise in Queens, New York, had a relationship with Borough President Donald Manes, who committed suicide.) Six firms competed for the East San Fernando Valley cable franchise in Los Angeles. They not only contributed more than $300,000 to political campaigns but assigned several lobbyists to each member of the city council, offered stock at low rates to community leaders (known as "rent-a-citizens"), lavishly entertained council members at restaurants, receptions, the theater, and racetracks, and offered money and television equipment to citizens' groups to get their endorsements.[40]

Joe Cerrell, consultant to Westinghouse's Group W:

> We have to do these things, to make these contributions. . . . It's just part of the process.[41]

Local governments handle cable franchises by widely varying criteria and procedures. The lack of uniformity in standards makes little sense in an era when mass communications are inextricably linked on a national scale.

Since early radio days, it has periodically been proposed that broadcast channels be auctioned off to the highest bidder, with the proceeds going into the public treasury and some substantial part allotted to strengthen public broadcasting. This reasonable idea was never seriously discussed either in Congress or in the press until the early days of the Clinton administration. An auction of cellular radio frequencies arouses less consternation than the prospect of making broadcast franchise-holders pay for the use of the airwaves. The companies that own *The New York Times, Washington Post, Chicago Tribune* and *Los Angeles Times* all own television stations—as do Knight-Ridder, Hearst, and Gannett. All would be hit directly if such an outrageous scheme were to be taken seriously. The suggestion (by former FCC Chairman William Sikes, later an executive of the Hearst Corporation) that licensees pay an annual fee may be interpreted either as the first step toward an auction of franchises or as an effort to forestall it.

As communications technology grows and changes, the boundary lines that separated media in the past become increasingly difficult to sustain, and the need for new rules becomes more apparent. The need for a meaningful, consistent, and coherent public policy becomes all the greater as the technological lines between electronic and print forms of communication continue to blur. The dissemination of text, audio, and video communications will inevitably move through common channels requiring government allocation and supervision in ways that have thus far not been clearly defined. The reduction of information to the binary digital code, says media scholar Anthony Smith, means that

> the stream never concludes. There is no last edition, but an endless series of opportunities for changing meaning and text, for alteration and revision. The stream can be stored in many places, and its very ownership is increasingly open to question. The distinction between manuscript and revision, between manuscript and publisher's copy is hard to determine. In the blurred choices that offer themselves to a text once it has entered a word processor—between becoming a personal letter, a personalized circular, an institutional document or a freely available file in a database—much of the Gutenbergian fixity of mode, meaning and possession is dissolved.[42]

Paradoxically, a communications system that is easier and simpler for users to operate requires a more complex and costly technology. A new set of policy issues has been raised regarding the relationship between the telephone companies—public utilities highly regulated at the local level—and mass media protected by constitutional guarantees. Broad-band communications through fiber optic networks were destined to lower the artificial barrier between data processing and communication, both mass and private. They would make obsolete the distinction that regulators had drawn among the various types of communications companies, in or out of the mass media field.

The $95 billion telephone business demands cautious respect from competitors in any field it enters. At a meeting with newspaper executives, shortly before the judicial consent decree that split up AT&T, its chairman, Charles Brown, had been asked by an editor whether he felt that his managerial prerogatives would be threatened if his company were enjoined from entering the ice cream business, which, with its enormous resources, it could easily dominate. Brown's reply was unhesitating: "If we want to enter the ice cream business there's absolutely no legal reason why we shouldn't." The telephone industry has continued to insist on its freedom to enter any business it likes, as well as on its freedom to communicate through any channel, just like any private individual.

In allowing the phone companies to move into video programming, a federal court referred, significantly, to the companies' First Amendment right to communicate, as though it were to be equated with an ordinary individual's freedom of expression.[43] The phone companies were already scrambling to enter the entertainment field by acquiring cable systems outside their telephone franchise territories. Fiber optic cables could expand the capacity of the "video dial tone." Digitizing and compressing signals could bring new potential to the existing copper wire telephone network.

Cable franchises have, in practice, been geographically exclusive. With the telephone companies poised to enter the business, it remained unclear whether or not local monopolies would be preserved through bilateral deals, or whether true competition would emerge, perhaps even with other operators—like the electric utilities—in the picture.[44] The argument for exclusivity is, of course, that it entails no wasteful duplication. The presence of a directly competing system reduces cable's costs to the consumer by 27%[44]. And the prospect for competition through "over-building" or "redundancy" was increased by the entry of the telephone companies into the video arena.

The companies had also been given the right, by a 1991 court decision, to offer telephone-accessible voice information services. Daily newspapers were understandably concerned over the prospect that the telephone companies might take over a significant part of their classified advertising (and perhaps even some of their news functions). The phone companies retorted that newspapers were simply trying to maintain their position as local news monopolies and were resistant to competition in any form. Seeking to overrule the court, the publishers pressed for Congress to take legislative action. They argued that, as a public utility, the phone companies could use their monopoly position to subsidize the cost of providing information, and that it would be improper to have them control both the channel and the content in the states where they have the local telephone franchises. Newspapers also invoked the issue of personal privacy, citing the phone companies' access to vast amounts of information on credit card purchases and other transactions that might be analyzed and applied to telemarketing purposes. The publishers' lobbying campaign faltered as chains and individual papers made pacts with the Devil and became electronic information-providers.[45] Other papers made alliances with computer-based data networks.[46]

The courts, the FCC, and Congress were separately dealing with aspects of the same fundamental policy issues, with remarkably little attention to the broader social consequences of opening up new competition in the distinctive spheres of information and entertainment. A similar lack of integration has prevailed in other areas where new communication techniques will inevitably require government policy decisions.

Different countries have employed different technical systems of television diffusion (the U.S. with 60 cycles/second, Europe with 50), but the productions themselves have been compatible. Newer developments suggest that this may not continue to be the case. The move to worldwide technical standards is inevitable but more difficult to implement as the capacities of broadcasting become more versatile and complex.

Broadcasting policy-makers have periodically faced the question of how to introduce advanced technology without depriving the public, locked into an existing system, of its stake in the equipment it already owns. This issue, which came up when rival systems of color television vied for FCC approval in the 1950s, arose anew in the 1990s, with the impending advent of High Definition Television. (HDTV would improve upon the 900 TV lines/second resolution of a movie seen in the best possible conditions. For thirty years, television programs have been shot in 35-mm film, for which there has long been a worldwide standard.) In this case, more than the interests of rival networks were involved; there were national rivalries as well, with Japanese, European, and American manufacturers scrambling for preeminence.[47] (Incredibly, the Commission was importuned to base its decision on the number of domestic manufacturing jobs that would be created by the choice of one engineering approach rather than another, rather than on the quality of service to be provided to viewers.) Under pressure from the FCC, an agreement was reached in 1993 among three groups of manufacturers and research institutes.[48]

The new HDTV system was to use digital compression, which also has the capacity to make television interactive, putting viewers not only in control of channel choices but of alternate feeds on a given channel—for example, selecting among different camera angles from which to watch a football match. Interactivity brings a new dimension to the relationship between the consumer and the medium and exemplifies the conversion of mass to individual communication.

- The program "Saturday Night Live" asked people to call in if they wanted to save a large lobster from being cooked and eaten. Half a million people called a 900 number at 50 cents each. A majority wanted to save him, but he was dropped into the pot anyway. CNN applied the same principle in a late night experiment in which they suggested that viewers call in to determine which news items should be aired from a menu presented at the start of a program. (The precedent may have been the Broadway adaptation of Dickens' unfinished novel, *The Mystery of Edwin Drood,* for which each night's audience picked its own ending.)

The agreed-upon system allowed each television station to transmit in different formats, thus permitting a gradual transition. Momentous consequences would follow the FCC's actions. As in a similar case involving the transformation of radio to a digital technology, the decision was being made on a bureaucratic level rather than through a national policy debate. Media attention and public discussion failed to match the enormous effect the action would ultimately have on consumers' pocketbooks and media habits. Under one solution proposed by the broadcast industry and supported within the FCC, existing television-station-owners would each be awarded an additional channel, ostensibly for HDTV, but readily convertible to other programming purposes. (In principle, these channels would be relinquished after a transitional period; in practice this proposal could well lead to a case of "finders-keepers.")

We have seen that the balance of economic support for the media has increasingly shifted from advertisers to the public. Cable operators have provided premium services at an extra price that typically adds 56% to the basic subscription fee. The rise of the VCR (and the potential advent of direct broadcasting by satellite to the home) raised serious questions about the future of premium cable. Why, except for inertia and convenience, should viewers be willing to pay extra simply to see, a few months earlier, films that will shortly be available on cassette in the video store? If the answer is that they want what is new, will they want it badly enough to sit through the kind of commercial interruptions they accept as the price of getting their entertainment "free"?

Advertisers generally believe that with the passage of time, the pay cable channels will take on advertising in order to reduce the cost to subscribers. If this were to happen, it would change the economics of television, increasing competition and probably accelerating a shift to programming on low production budgets.

But the matter of what is basic and what is pay is in many cases defined by regulators rather than by the cable system operators. The Cable Act of 1984 defined basic cable service to include local broadcast stations and exempted premium channels from local government price controls. Cable systems thereupon moved to shift cable network channels like CNN, Discovery and ESPN—long offered as part of the basic service—into the premium category.

Cable operators pay nothing for the most popular shows, which come from the networks. In 1985, a federal court decision voided the FCC's "must carry" rule that required cable operators to carry all broadcast station signals transmitted within their areas. Thus a cable system no longer had to offer local broadcast channels that, for whatever reason, it preferred to ignore. This decision was bound to reduce the chance of exposure to public television and independent stations. The very notion of "public access" programming through cable represented a policy of maximizing the number of voices heard on controversial local issues.[49] One small cable system had spent a third of its revenue to provide the required public access channels, which had virtually no viewers at all. Should the public pay for what it does not want? If the answer was to be no, awesome implications would follow for all programming with serious intellectual content, for which audiences—however dedicated or passionate— were inevitably small. With the multiplication of cable channels, it seems quite likely that the present system of charging subscribers by tiers of channels might give way to a rate structure in which they pay for what they consume. The odds are that they will be paying more.

Since cable systems have generally operated as monopolies, it is difficult to see why their prices should not be regulated, like those of public utilities. Congress established controls over rates in 1993, since these had escalated much faster than the Consumer Price Index. However, it failed to provide the FCC with an adequate budget to police the incredibly intricate pricing formulas that were instituted. The net effect was that many subscribers ended up with higher bills.

A major issue still to be resolved was whether local cable systems should be common carriers or should also control access to the substance of the programming they carry. (Since giant multisystem operators like TCI are also major stockholders in cable networks like Turner Broadcasting, this issue is actually one more aspect of a fundamental policy question I have already raised: whether the vertical integration of content production and dissemination should be discouraged.) As channel capacity grows, it becomes less urgent to question a cable operator's decisions about what programs to carry, since fewer options are excluded. If the cable system is a public utility (and it certainly is), should it have any more incentive to promote premium channels than the electric company has to promote washing machines or air conditioners? With the impending convergence of television, the telephone and the computer, the problems of regulating content become even more acute.

Media Content and Media Policy

No tenet of American democracy is more fundamental or more jealously guarded than freedom of expression in the media, enshrined in the First Amendment. Newspapers have published a diagram showing how to get a plastic bomb through airport security systems, and *The Progressive* magazine ran instructions for the manufacture of an atom bomb. In such much-debated cases, the right of the free press and the public's right to unrestricted access to information face off against another important right—the ability of the state to maintain deadly secrets. A host of comparable issues arise when free expression appears to be in conflict with an individual's right to privacy or to preserve a reputation from calumny or a child's right to remain uncorrupted by adult vices.

A public official's occasional attempt to manage the news must be considered in the light of the self-censorship commonly exercised by the media to withhold news whose release might not be in the public interest. *The Chicago Tribune*'s revelation that the U.S. Navy had broken the Japanese code was denounced by President Roosevelt as an act of treason, but it is uncertain whether the editors were motivated more by a misguided notion of the public's right to the information, by an irrepressible and vain desire to score a scoop, or by an eagerness to sell papers. *The New York Times* suppressed the full story of the planned invasion of Cuba's Bay of Pigs, and some of its editors blamed their own self-control for the subsequent fiasco. But actually, the first news of the CIA's invasion plans appeared in *The Nation* even before the Kennedy administration had taken office, and other stories about the Cuban exile training camps in Guatemala appeared in *The New Republic*, the *Times*, and on CBS.[50] The facts were certainly known to Fidel Castro.

In spite of such historical testimony to American press freedom and the principle of nonintervention, media content is not immune from government policy regulation. It is readily understandable why government should become involved in one way or another with the technical and business aspects of electronic media. The content of programming is an altogether different matter and represents a potential quagmire. Yet this is an area that government cannot and does not avoid altogether. (For instance, there is the constraining influence of libel laws—though their application varies from state to state. The FCC, however half-heartedly, imposes its own rules on obscenity and bias.)

Government involvement with media content is periodically expressed in an explosion of concern over media violence and pornography, and occasionally on the effect of advertising on children. (Discussion of this last subject has very often concentrated its attention on the advertised products—for example, the sugar content of cereal or the dangerous properties of toys—rather than on the advertisements as such.)

A 1954 Senate investigation of the baleful influence of comic books concluded that it was up to publishers and distributors to regulate their own industry. Hearings and investigations on media topics by Congressional committees and by administrative agencies have come and gone over the years, leaving very little sense of continuity or coordination with any prior or related effort.

The First Amendment, happily, has discouraged efforts for government to intervene directly in news content, no matter how offensive it is considered to be, though—as I have just described—it did not stop President Nixon. He set up the Office of Telecommunications Policy in 1970, with the mission of formulating policy recommendations in a domain that closely overlapped that of the FCC. With a budget of $3 million and a staff of 65, OTP was the instrument of his efforts to intimidate television news. (OTP atrophied after Nixon resigned; it was replaced by the National Telecommunications and Information Administration in the Commerce Department in 1977.)

No requirements of ideological balance or objectivity have ever been set for American publications, nor has it ever been suggested that their content should be monitored to ensure that the public interest was not being abused. Yet broadcast programming has been a continuing subject of Congressional concern; in the past, there were safeguards to ensure against one-sidedness in treating controversial subjects. From 1929 until 1984, the "fairness doctrine," embodied in FCC decisions and formally stated in the Commission's 1949 "Report on Editorializing by Broadcast Licensees," obliged broadcasters to present both sides of controversial issues. It also required them to notify the target of an attack on the "honesty, character, integrity, or like personal qualities of an identified person or group," and give the "victim" (or culprit) a "reasonable opportunity" to respond to it over the air. (The rarity of complaints or requests for rebuttal indicates how bland most local newscasts are.) Clay Whitehead, then director of the Office of Telecommunications Policy, said of the fairness doctrine in 1971: "Whoever thought up the name was a genius—it's even harder to be against fairness than it is to be against motherhood."[51]

In the same year, the U.S. Court of Appeals held that "the public's First Amendment interests constrain broadcasters not only to provide the full spectrum of viewpoints, but also to present them in an uninhibited, wide-open fashion and to provide opportunity for individual self-expression."[52] A broadcaster cannot refuse to sell air time to anyone wishing to present a controversial issue, even though this sale may lead to demands for free rebuttal time, with consequent expense to the broadcaster.

Section 315 of the Federal Communications Act of 1959 required a broadcasting station to give equal time, outside regularly scheduled newscasts, to candidates for national office. For a while, this obligation was interpreted to mean that candidates of minor fringe parties should receive equal time with the Republican and Democratic contenders; it discouraged debates. No similar requirements for political balance have been imposed on newspapers and magazines—and with good reason.

The latitude of free expression that print enjoys under the First Amendment extends to cable transmissions, but over-the-air broadcasting is subject to regulation by the FCC. (In 1992, it levied large fines against radio stations carrying the particularly scatological broadcasts of a $3 million-a-year talk show host, Howard Stern, but it stepped back from a threat to prevent his employer, Infinity Broadcasting, from acquiring three more radio stations.) Broadcast journalists have insisted that they should be permitted to operate by the same ground rules as their press colleagues. Their case becomes stronger as news increasingly finds its way to the public through electronic means.

Should media that make use of public air time be held accountable to some meaningful standard of public service, or should they be given free rein in the commercial market for entertainment and information? Under the 1934 Federal Communications Act, broadcast stations were required to operate in "the public interest, convenience and necessity." In applying for renewal of their franchises every three years, they were asked to report on the extent of their news and public affairs programming, past and intended. The Act made it explicit that the FCC should not engage in censorship. In practice the Commission was reluctant to police closely the extent to which stations complied with the public service provisions of the Act or to evaluate the merits of the programming they reported under the category of public affairs. (One station included "Amos 'n' Andy" under this heading.) No station license was ever revoked because of low programming quality, although charges were filed in a few obscenity cases. The public interest requirement was effectively abandoned as part of the Reagan administration's deregulation moves of 1984–85. The "good character" required of prospective licensees was redefined and limited to actual felonies or broadcast-related misconduct.

The Children's Television Act of 1990 limited the number of commercials in programs directed at children and required franchise-holders to serve "the educational and informational needs of children through the licensee's overall programming, including programming specifically designed to serve such needs"—language sufficiently vague to be effectively ignored. Under the law, broadcasters are required to broadcast "educational and informational" programs. Stations quickly redefined the purpose of their existing children's shows (like "The Jetsons," "G.I. Joe" and "Leave It to Beaver") to fit this rubric. When the hero of "Yo Yogi!" captured "a bank-robbing cockroach," he showed the virtue of "using his head rather than his muscles," according to one station's report.[53] In 1993, the FCC announced that such reasoning would no longer be acceptable, prompting broadcasters to complain that their audiences would flee to the unregulated drivel on cable channels.

When government agencies like the FCC, the Justice Department, or the courts become the guardians of media diversity, it must be evident that the rules of free expression have changed. These rules are no longer simply guaranteed by law and maintained by open competition in the marketplace if they require the constant vigilance and intervention of higher authority.

Putting Media Issues on the National Agenda

Edmund Spenser:

> Be bold, be bold and everywhere be bold. But be not too bold.

Throughout this book, I have described the ways in which large media organizations shape and channel the commercial culture. Should the great multimedia conglomerates be broken up or limited in size? The argument in favor of such a policy is not only the standard argument against monopolistic tendencies in any line of business. It represents a recognition that the realm of ideas, values, and tastes is qualitatively different from air travel or the manufacture of biscuits or electric turbines.

The case against interference involves not merely the standard argument against government interference with business. It rests on the principle that ideas, values, and tastes must be left free to follow the laws of supply and demand, that the intrusion of the state into the exercise of market power inevitably leads to the control of ideas. And it makes the powerful and undeniable point that it is no longer possible to think in terms of a communications system made up of individual media, when in fact these are interlocked in a way that calls for large-scale organizations to manage them.

Unless one falls back on outmoded ideological clichés, there is no easy, comprehensive alternative to substitute for the present order of things. Institutions, large or small, do not change their ways except under pressure – which can come from outside or from within. Organizations that wield enormous power should have to be held publicly accountable by criteria that are rarely brought up in share-holders' meetings. Written statements of social objectives should be required as well as periodic reports of how those objectives are being met. The performance of media should be made a matter of continuing discussion in the chambers of government, in the educational system, and, most of all, within the media themselves, by their own practitioners and by their critical contemporaries.

Do we need a comprehensive national media law? The mere prospect of attempting one is unsettling. The legal system continually weighs the often inherently contradictory contentions of justice and equity, and reinterprets received doctrine to meet the needs of changing times. It better serves the causes of free expression and of technological innovation to have the rules governing mass communication arise out of different components of government, dealing with individual cases, as in the common law, and with a variety of precedents to choose among, rather than to have them all assembled and written down in one place, like a Napoleonic Code. Still, the lack of clarity and consistency in the rules should not be supinely accepted.

As we move toward the extraordinary communications challenges of the twenty-first century, it seems appropriate to consider the possibilities of instituting a process that might mesh, coordinate, and smooth out the contradictions in our present anarchic national media policy. The device might be a presidential commission working together with a joint standing committee of both houses of Congress. Its purpose would be to examine and review periodically inconsistencies and problems in the working of the present rules and to recommend remedial legislation.

A useful point of departure may be to attempt to articulate national goals for mass communication. These are inherent in the national media policy that already exists: (1) to encourage a variety of channels for expression; (2) to discourage concentration of control over the channels of expression; (3) to ensure that the necessity of awarding franchises to use scarce public goods (like the frequency spectrum) does not result in financial exploitation of the public; (4) to facilitate an extensive and fair exchange of ideas, and to protect society, and especially children – its most vulnerable members – from abuse; (5) to subsidize forms of expression that enrich the national culture and its collective intellectual resources, but that are not necessarily viable in the commercial marketplace.

It is not likely that there is universal agreement on all these points. There would be even less agreement on the more specific measures I would propose:

• Reaffirm the doctrine of public responsibility as the price of any franchise that gives away public goods and establish criteria of acceptable performance. Reinvigorate the requirement of the 1934 Federal Communications Act for broadcast stations to operate in "the public interest, convenience and necessity" and extend this principle to cable system operators and program providers. If broadcasters were once again required to acknowledge that they have a social duty, the subject might at least move higher up on their own agendas.

• Make broadcasters pay for their franchises. Putting the whole broadcasting system up for grabs would create unacceptable upheavals, and is almost inconceivable. Still, any rational media policy would have to accept the principle that no one has an inalienable right to use public goods for private gain without paying a price and being held accountable.

• Reexamine the media cross-ownership rule, so that it works to discourage media monopoly rather than to bring it about.

• Encourage competition for existing cable franchises, from other cable operators, from telephone companies, and from any other possible sources. Discourage the type of deal-making between telephone companies and cable system operators that preserves monopoly instead of undercutting it.

• Recognize communications channels as public utilities, and separate their ownership and control from their content. By strict logic, this rule would apply to print and over-the-air broadcasting and force newspaper owners to divest themselves of their printing plants and radio stations of their transmitting towers—not a politically likely or feasible possibility. As a practical matter, the principle of separation should apply to all wire-transmitted programming and information, by cable, telephone, or even (as has been suggested) over the electric power grid, and it should apply to microwave direct broadcasting by satellite, too. Why is such separation desirable? Because it would weaken the combination of two awesome powers—the financial clout of a monopoly utility and the power to determine what ideas and images are fed into the cultural mainstream.

• Develop a modest fund to stimulate research into aspects of mass communications technology that are not responsive to market forces. An example might be the development of new low-budget ways to distribute newspapers, to match the much lowered cost of producing them. Such technology would make it easier for new papers to start up in the face of constricted advertising revenues, and could restore competitive energy to local journalism.

• Increase funding for public broadcasting, and safeguard its governance system to ensure ironclad autonomy from political demands. The public accepts huge (though probably still insufficient) expenditures on the schools as a necessary social obligation. (What would happen if parents had to pay for their children's education directly on the open market?) Television is no less mighty a formative influence and deserves to be taken more seriously as an educational resource.

- Discourage the intrusion of commercial ventures (like that of Time Warner affiliate Whittle Communications' Channel One) into the public schools.
- Eliminate complacency about media violence—not through labeling or censorship, but by continually spotlighting its crass origins and harmful effects. The glare of relentless publicity has worn down smoking habits; it might induce some changes in Hollywood, too.
- Accept media policy as social policy, not as the legal administration of technical complexities. The FCC wields powers in the domain of electronic media that would be considered highly dangerous if it had a counterpart in print. Broadcasting frequencies must be allocated to avoid chaos on the airwaves, but the FCC's rulings go well beyond management of the spectrum; they have consequences for every aspect of national life. Educational policy is properly made by educators, not left to attorneys. Why should the FCC be a lawyers' preserve?

The recommendations I have just listed are framed in the light of a passing moment in mass communications history. Any reader might choose to amend the list or add to it. I have not included a proposal that might seem like a logical extension of some of the things this book has said: limit the concentration of control over media by a small number of large corporations, some of them rooted outside mass communications. Historical precedents suggest that such limitations are made arbitrarily and not always reasonably. If one company owned two-thirds of the circulation of the press (as News Corporation does in New Zealand), corrective action would certainly be desirable, but the United States is a long way from this kind of situation. It is socially unhealthy for a Time Warner to have the power it does in so many media fields, but by what precise criteria can one single out Time Warner and exempt TCI or Capital Cities/ABC, or include all three and exempt the owners of a small station group or newspaper chain? Should the entry of the powerful phone companies into the information and entertainment business be resisted, when its effect will be to introduce vigorous new competitive forces? What *is* needed is not so much an immediate limitation on size and power as the constant threat of such limitation. This requires vigilance and surveillance by other media rather than direct government action.

Many readers will disagree with this last conclusion. Opinions differ on how to reach our national media goals, and even as to the goals themselves. Vigorous discussion, and not just by experts, is precisely what media policy needs as it deals with ever more complex matters and has ever greater social repercussions.

There is much to praise in the American media system, much to be thankful for, and much that the rest of the world has envied and emulated. The media system has achieved its size, variety, and skill as a result of the steady expansion of its advertising base. Advertising, which contributes less each year to the nation's total investment in mass communication, is an integral part of a dynamic, competitive market economy rooted in the excitation of consumer demand—an economy that has been historically linked to the exercise of diverse opinions and political freedom.

Taken altogether, the media system, embedded as it is in a well-established economic and political framework, enjoys widespread public approval. It is staffed and run by decent and highly talented people. Demands for its radical overhaul would be extremely unpopular. But the advertising on which the system depends saturates it to excess. Some of it is so meretricious in its style of argument that it desensitizes us to the absence of integrity in human discourse—most blatantly in our political lives, and perhaps even in our personal lives.

The system has obvious flaws that cannot be corrected in the marketplace. It is increasingly controlled by a handful of people who wield enormous power, but whose interests and energies are spread too thin to permit them to take much interest or pride in any noncommercial aspect of their endeavors. Media content has been driven primarily by the need to maximimize audiences for sale, rather than by the desire to communicate the truth about our world or to express deep thoughts and feelings. To this end, broadcasting and film have vied with each other in pursuit of violence and vulgarity. Left to its own devices, the public persistently drifts toward amusement rather than enlightenment, avoiding confrontation with the pressing, perhaps overwhelming problems that confront the nation and the world. The daily press, traditionally the forum for contention and iconoclasm, has undergone a steady attrition of competition and a general retreat to the safety of the middle ground. As a result, newspapers have lost power and influence, and American cities have lost irreplaceable sources of civic pride and energy.

Can the laws of supply and demand be relied upon to correct the imbalances between individual media choices and what is in the collective interest? The exercise of choice among today's assortment of media vehicles is commonly defended as a response to the laws of the free market. The right to pick a periodical or a television program is usually described as a fundamental personal right, in which democratic societies are distinguished from totalitarian regimes that try to dictate opinion and taste. But choices are always made from available options, and a selection from limited alternatives is something less than free. We cannot ignore the processes and powers that provide those alternatives or the possibility of finding ways to supplement, enrich, or even replace them.

The exercise of individual choice, it must also be remembered, can lead to consequences that society can only confront through collective action; such action can infringe on what individuals usually consider to be their rights and freedoms. Individually, we may prefer playing hookey to sitting in class, or dumping our garbage wherever it is most convenient, but society coerces us into doing what is in our own long-run best interest, and most people accept this necessity. Is culture any less of a collective good than the quality of education or of the environment? Society has a stake in maintaining standards, in upholding traditions, and in raising the level of taste. Moreover, society has a right to make exemplars of high standards, noble traditions, and good taste accessible and familiar to everyone.

The acceptance of social responsibility is an index of personal morale. A high level of civility prevails in communities where individuals pay the consequences of antisocial acts—in ostracism if in no other way. In a village society of intimate proportions and shared activities, the distinction between personal and collective property may be imperceptible. It is understood that a threat or cost to the group is a threat or a cost to each individual member. But in our complex and impersonal world, responsibilities are so widely diffused that they can be ignored. In this crowded, technologically intricate society, we face ever more costly collective consequences for individual actions. Personal acts of consumption are "paid for" in the eyes of the consumer. Social consumption (pollution, destruction of public amenities, disintegration of the physical infrastructure of transportation and public places—all the anxiety and wasted time that represent the diffused consequences of individual acts of social pathology) is not perceived as an expense for which the individual bears responsibility.

We use water differently as a freely dispensed public good than we do when it is metered. But most of the services we pay for as a part of the body public can easily be regarded as someone else's worry and expense. We are easily tempted to become bystanders to destruction, vandalism, and waste, because there is no authority standing by to assess and claim our share of the damage we see around us. Society's costs can only be met by taxation, which is generally regarded as the unfair exaction of tribute by an external force rather than as a necessary fulfillment of individual consumption needs.

To the argument that many citizens do not want their tax money used to pay for what they regard as objectionable, the rejoinder is that there are countless other government expenditures that some people find objectionable and from which they derive no direct benefit but which they tolerate as part of their membership in society.

Since social costs are rarely calculated into the balance of profit and loss, the market mechanism operates to push economic activity into channels that may be efficient and productive for the individual firm, yet harmful to the society and the economy at large. The social expenses of highway deaths and air pollution are not calculated into the price the consumer pays for a new car or for gasoline, but are distributed and paid for in other, not necessarily equitable, ways.

Something of the same process may be at work in the case of advertising and the mass media. Advertising costs are borne by consumers as part of the prices they pay for advertised products. Media costs are borne by advertisers as the principal part of the price they pay for the opportunity to advertise. The allocation of advertising expenditures to media, while it follows the advertiser's sense of immediate economic yield or productivity relative to the sales of the product and the profit of the firm, acts as a support to some media and a handicap to others, in a way that does not serve the broader interests of the firm, of advertisers in general, or of the public. Decisions made in individual advertisers' short-run self-interest add up to large-scale collective controls that profoundly affect the whole American cultural and political experience. Those controls are still dominant, as cable subscription fees account for a growing share of the television industry's aggregate expense and as the overall cost of maintaining the media system is increasingly borne directly by the ultimate consumer.

A generation ago, farsighted people were beginning to be concerned about the environment and what the free play of market forces was doing to it. Today this subject is given high priority on the public agenda, though we are still very far short of taking the measures required to arrest the disastrous process of deterioration. Few people would now deny that we have a problem, or suggest that it should not be taken seriously, or agree that things will take care of themselves if they are just left alone. We stand in the same position with respect to our precious communications environment as we did not so long ago on the physical environment.

No *deus ex machina* is about to descend onto the proscenium to put this all to right. The political might of media organizations is too great to permit any thorough-going government investigation of the kind that Harry Truman launched in Congress before World War II to look at the concentration of industrial power. The media would strongly and properly resist any suggestion that their content or management be placed under the surveillance of official bureaucrats. The public would support them. Yet in one form or another, sooner or later, the content and control of mass media is likely to become an issue of political debate.

Can we preserve freedom of expression and democracy of taste and at the same time make a national commitment to upgrade the integrity and quality of expression and taste? There is no simple answer to that tough question, any more than there is to the question of how we can raise standards of living without polluting the atmosphere. Changing the present system requires imagination and flexibility, with due regard for the established tastes and vested interests that discourage change.

The first step is to recognize that a problem exists, and that market forces cannot solve it.

The second step requires us to look at mass communications policy as an integrated whole, rather than to continue to resort to occasional piecemeal gestures that deal with one form of communication or another. We have passed the point where the shortcomings of individual media can be addressed one by one. For better or worse, they are now part of a single system. That system cannot be legislated or administered into excellence. It needs to be constantly scrutinized, nudged, and needled into painful self-consciousness.

Appendix

A Note on the Measurement of Expenditures on Media

Advertising expenditures have been estimated for some sixty years by McCann-Erickson, which has used a combination of government and industry sources, adjusted by its own formulas. Data have been compiled by Leading National Advertisers (owned by the Dutch media conglomerate VNU, which acquired such services as the Publishers Information Bureau, Media Records, and Broadcast Advertisers' Reports). The measurement of print advertising is done directly, with a ruler, with published rates applied to the number of lines or pages. The abandonment of the rate card by magazines during the 1980s and the increasing flexibility of newspaper rates made both these procedures increasingly difficult to take literally. Television advertising is sampled by recording commercials and identifying them by the advertisers. Dollar estimates can be generated by applying assumptions about the applicable costs, even though the market for broadcast advertising is, as the text points out, an auction. The advent of barter and syndication has made the problem of measurement even more difficult. Radio expenditures are estimated by the Radio Advertising Bureau from surveys conducted among its member stations, which yield a limited response that must be projected to the universe of stations.

While the measurement of advertising expenditures is essential marketing information used by advertisers to plan their competitive marketing strategies, there is no parallel need to measure spending by consumers. The Commerce Department lumps media together in assembling the data it releases from its annual survey of consumer expenditures. Individual trade associations have varying degrees of interest in estimating industry totals. For this reasons, any attempt to estimate what the public spends on the media must start almost from scratch, examining directories and reconciling conflicting estimates.

A variety of organizations track consumer expenditures on specific media: Paul Kagan Associates for cable, the Motion Picture Association of America, the Recorded Music Industry Association, and the Book Industry Study Group. An economic research firm, Wilkofsky Gruen Associates, produces an authoritative compilation annually for Veronis, Suhler and Associates, a media business investment, brokerage, and consulting firm.

In deciding what to include under the heading of mass media, I have made some judgments that might be debated. For example, I have included under books all texts and professional books, even though they are not directed at the general consumer. My reasoning is that virtually all book audiences are specialized to some degree and it is hard to know where to draw the line. I have included shoppers as part of the weekly newspaper medium, even though they are distributed free; the rationale is that few of them are totally dedicated to advertising, without any other editorial lure for the reader. The cost of technical publications is not, strictly, speaking, a consumer expense, since it is commonly borne as a business cost, but it is very difficult to segregate them from other publications that appeal to specialized groups of readers. Many of these publications are distributed free through controlled circulation; others are sold like consumer magazines; for my purposes, since they are impossible to distinguish, I have lumped them together.

Particularly in the area of business information, there has been a striking increase in the expenditures for services that I would not classify as mass media, i.e., those produced with uniform content provided by someone who takes a chance on satisfying consumer demand. A recorded weather report or time signal accessible on the telephone might come under this heading, while a call to an operator-staffed 800 number would not. An edition of *Time* magazine that contains special pages of medical interest and is distributed only to physicians still represents a mass medium by my definition. A teletext database accessible by home computer produces only individualized communication and is not a mass medium. There seems to be a general assumption that new technology will facilitate the growth of interactive media. To the degree that the user will be able to select "personalized" content from prepackaged modules, it will still be a mass media experience. This would not be true if someone has to go to work to generate information or entertainment in a command performance just for that individual. I have not included business reference services, which consist largely of compilations of statistical and technical data.

I have excluded some categories that are customarily (by McCann-Erickson, for instance) incorporated into aggregate estimates of advertising expenditures—for example, the substantial corporate expense of administering advertising budgets and functions. Miscellaneous forms of promotion, like in-store point-of-sale placards and streamers, are left out. (As I observe in the text, it is hard to tell where advertising ends and sales promotion begins.)

My definition of media, in this book, eliminate those that carry *only* advertising content. If these were included, the trends I have described would look somewhat different, since direct mail and yellow pages (both print media) grew at a faster than average pace during the period I have described.

I have pointed out in the text that advertising matter is not without its interest for readers, so that an argument might be made for including advertising-only media within the grand total. However, including them would not significantly change the broad picture I have been describing.

Specifically, if we add outdoor and transit, direct mail and yellow page advertising into the mix, and consider them part of print, the total print share of advertising went from 64% in 1970 to 68% in 1992, while print's share of the combined expenditure by advertisers and consumers fell from 69% to 60%.

The inclusion of these media naturally reduces sharply the consumer's share of the nation's total media budget, to 39% in 1970 and 42% in 1992. But when we look at the grand total from this perspective, the polarization described in the text becomes even more apparent, between print media increasingly dominated by advertising and audiovisual media relying more and more on consumer support.

The Nation's Media Budget, 1992
(In $ billions)

Media Supported Only by Consumers

Books	21.1*
Audio Recordings	9.0
Theatrical Film	4.9
Video Recordings	12.0
Newsletters	9.0

Media Supported by Both Consumers and Advertisers

	Consumers	Advertisers
Daily Newspapers	9.9	30.7
Weekly Newspapers	.3	3.3
Consumer Magazines	6.4	7.0
Business, Farm Magazines	2.4	5.0
Cable Television	17.5	2.2

Media Supported Only by Advertisers

Television	27.2
Radio	8.6
Direct Mail**	25.5
Telephone Directories**	9.3
Outdoor, Transit**	1.2

Sources: McCann-Erickson, Paul Kagan Associates, Motion Picture Association of America, Recorded Music Industry Association, Wilkofsky Gruen Associates.

*Includes $7.7 billion in sales of educational and professional books.

**These advertising media are not included under my definition of the media system.

Notes

Introduction

1. *New York Times*, 2/21/93 (hereafter *NYT*).
2. Cf. Leo Bogart, *The Age of Television*. New York: Frederick Ungar, 1972.
3. The sociologist Pierre Bourdieu uses the term "cultural capital" to describe the intellectual resources that give individuals a start in life that may be more valuable than any material wealth they inherit. (*Distinction: A Social Critique of the Judgment of Taste*. Cambridge, Mass: Harvard U. Press, 1984.)
4. Harris poll.

Chapter 1

1. William Smith, *Advertise: How? When? Where?* London: Routledge, Warne and Routledge, 1862.
2. Marshall McLuhan, *Understanding Media*. New York: McGraw Hill, 1964.
3. Eric A. Havelock, *The Literate Revolution in Greece and Its Cultural Consequences*. Princeton, N.J.: Princeton University Press, 1982, pp. 264–65.
4. Havelock observes that "The alphabet converted the Greek spoken tongue into an artifact, thereby separating it from the speaker and making it into a 'language,' that is, an object available for inspection, reflection, analysis." (Ibid., p. 8.)
5. Havelock notes, though, that the preliterate period, 900–650 BC, saw some of Greece's greatest achievements, in technology, politics, and the arts.
6. By expanding knowledge, literacy stimulated the differentiation of skills and the growth of specialization. The arts of music, poetry, dance, and embellishment, whether sacred and ritual or commonplace and secular, are embodied in collective life and inseparable from shared activity. The intimacy between performers and spectators has since been attenuated by the changing architecture of the theater, which began with the open stage of the classical age. The proscenium arch, separating the public from the players, became common in the mid-seventeenth century to suit the conventions of the Italian opera, which required the singers to see the conductor, who stood in the orchestra with the pit between them, and between

performers and audience. Footlights, a fire hazard, interposed yet another barrier, reinforcing the social gulf between the courtly spectators and the socially inferior players. As the director Tyrone Guthrie points out, stylized utterances were delivered against artificial backdrops. At the same time, "an immense emphasis was thrown onto artifice. . . . acting, writing and production were all aiming to be a closer imitation of real life." (Tyrone Guthrie, "Do We Go to the Theater for Illusion?" *NYT*, 1/16/66).

7. Draft preamble to the Virginia bill for establishing religious freedom. Quoted by Hannah Arendt, *On Revolution*. New York: Viking, 1965, p. 493.

8. Both of these quotations are cited by David Paul Nord, "A Republican Literature: A Study of Magazine Reading and Readers in Late Eighteenth Century New York," in *American Quarterly*, Vol. 40 (March 1988), pp. 42–64.

9. Ibid., p. 53.

10. Members of political, business, and cultural elites, gravitating to Washington or New York, come to rely more on national media than on the local press of their places of origin. Cf. Bernard C. Cohen, *The Press and Foreign Policy*. Princeton N.J.: Princeton University Press, 1963.

11. Exhortations in radio commercials, critical cues in the plots of film and television dramas—all depend on the supposition that the public can easily convert letters to speech and vice versa. Is this assumption correct? Concerns have been raised in recent years, as surveys and educational achievement tests produce a succession of well-publicized horror stories about "functional illiteracy." The attractions of television, the resumption of large-scale immigration, and the weakening of family structure have all put pressure on scholastic reading scores. Fortunately, there is no indication of a reversal in the long-term upward trend in educational attainment.

12. In a preliterate society, culture is transmitted through interpersonal relations within the family or the tribe. The design and fashioning of implements, the crafts of hunting or agriculture, the lore of everyday life, the traditions of the past, the mythology and religious beliefs that ascribe meaning to the inexplicable—all of these are passed along through a network of direct human contacts. Individuals' feelings for those who surround them and the mutual expectations they share with them are inseparable from the information they acquire in the course of their attachments. Traditional preliterate culture still exists in many parts of the world. Until quite recently it has coexisted with the culture of literacy in most Western societies. The literate elites of ancient Egypt, Assyria, Greece, and Rome lived in the midst of nonliterate masses. This type of symbiosis continued in the Western world until the nineteenth century, in Russia and Japan until the twentieth, and in much of Latin America to the present day.

13. Contemporary estimates of its incidence varied greatly. Early in the sixteenth century, Sir Thomas More thought that half the English population could read, while his contemporary, the Bishop of Winchester, estimated the proportion at 1%. Cf. Kenneth Levine, *The Social Context of Literacy*. London: Routledge and Kegan Paul, 1986, p. 68. In 1641, only 22% of London men could not sign their names, compared to about seven out of ten in most counties of England. (David Cressy, *Literacy and the Social Order: Reading and Writing in Tudor and Stuart England*. Cambridge: Cambridge University Press, 1980. p. 121). By way of comparison, in France, around 1690, 27% of men and 14% of women signed their names on wedding contracts. (Robert Muchembled, *Popular Culture and Elite Culture in France 1400–1750*. Baton Rouge: Louisiana State University Press, 1985, p. 11). By 1797, about 47% of the men and 27% of the women were literate. (ibid., p. 283). In 1700, three out of five men and three out of four women in England were illiterate; by 1800 this proportion had fallen to two out of five men and three in five women; in 1850 it was three men in ten and less than half the women. By 1910, less than 5% of both sexes were illiterate. (Levine, op. cit., p. 177).

14. The rise of the book encouraged privacy, because it permitted individuals to be occupied with learning, fantasy, and reflection. Cf. Philippe Aries, Introduction, to Roger Chartier, ed., *A History of Private Life*, Vol. III: *Passions of the Renaissance*. Cambridge, Mass.: Belknap Press of Harvard University Press, 1989, p. 129.

15. Lee Soltow and Edward Stevens, *The Rise of Literacy and the Common School in the United States: A Socioeconomic Analysis to 1870*. Chicago: University of Chicago Press, 1981.

16. The average soldier in the Union Army during the Civil War had 4.4 years of schooling (ibid., p. 118), compared to 12.9 for the average man of 20–29 in 1990. (U.S. Census.)

17. Leo Lowenthal, *Literature and Mass Culture*. New Brunswick, N.J.: Transaction Books, 1984, p. 126.

18. In the preface to the second edition of *Lyrical Ballads*, quoted by Lowenthal, op. cit., p. 40.

19. Letters of Aug. 9, 1797 and Jan. 3, 1798, quoted by Lowenthal, op. cit., p. 29.

20. *Democracy in America*, New York: Knopf, 1945, Vol. 2, p. 59.

21. *The Leisure Hour*, July 6, 1872, cited by John M. Golby and A. W. Purdue, *The Civilization of the Crowd: Popular Culture in England, 1750–1900*. New York: Schocken, 1984, p. 144.

22. In England, by the 1850s, it had fallen from six days to five and a half. (Ibid., 110.)

23. Thorstein Veblen, *The Theory of the Leisure Class: An Economic Study of Institutions*. New York: New American Library, 1899, 1953. There is a commonality of outlook between the aristocrats of prerevolutionary France and the criminal underclass of today's urban American slums. "You can't live off the breeze, man," is how a drug dealer explains why selling crack is a better option than a dead-end minimum wage job. In this milieu, where traditional family structure has been shattered, men who hustle for their living on the street actually have more flexible and disposable time than women who face the demands of children and the welfare system. A century ago, in Sicily, "Their life is threaded through by poverty, sickness, and despair, but rarely do they lack time for leisure." (A report cited by Mary Douglas and Baron Isherwood, *The World of Goods*. New York: Basic, 1979, p. 196.)

24. This may be more perception than reality. Leisure time studies conducted by John Robinson indicate that between 1965 and 1985, total leisure time activity increased from 34.4 hours a week to 41.1 hours for men and from 34.4 to 39.6 for women.

25. Twenty-eight percent of all radio listening is outside of the home, most of it in the workplace. About the same proportion is in cars. (Radio Advertising Bureau.)

26. There is some other activity during 64% of the time TV is viewed. Robert Kubey and Mihaly Csikszentmihalyi, *Television and the Quality of Life: How Viewing Shapes Everyday Experience*. Hillsdale, N.J.: Lawrence Erlbaum Associates, 1990.

27. Cf. Elizabeth Eisenstein, *The Printing Press as an Agent of Change*, New York: Cambridge University Press, 1979.

28. A $40-million investment in the film "At Heaven's Gate" represented almost a dead loss, though it was an ego trip for the producer–director. Cf. Steven Bach, *Final Cut: Dreams and Disaster in the Making of Heaven's Gate*. New York: Morrow, 1985.

Chapter 2

1. *The Economist*, 10/12/91.

2. Personal interview.

3. *NYT*, 7/14/85.

4. Peanuts' creator, Charles Schulz, was the country's fourth best-compensated entertainer in 1986, after Bill Cosby, Sylvester Stallone, and Bruce Springsteen. There are theatrical

precedents for this: "Buster Brown" became the hero of a Broadway musical in 1905, and "Little Nemo" followed a few years later. Little Orphan Annie lost her appeal to newspaper readers, but found new life in the musical theater.

5. *NYT*, 4/23/89.

6. Time Warner's *Entertainment Weekly* produced a four-minute promotional feature for broadcast on the same company's Home Box Office. (*NYT*, 11/4/91.)

7. Another 18% are trade paperbacks and 19% hardcover. Book Industry Study Group survey, 1990–91.

8. In 1961, Fawcett extended its full trade discount of 40% to all its retail customers. After other publishers followed suit, paperback sales in the following years went into the millions. By 1987, paperbacks accounted for 30% of the new titles and editions published. (According to an estimate by Chandler B. Grannis for *Publishers Weekly*.) Sales of mass market paperbacks stayed at about 500 million copies a year from the mid 70s to the mid 80s, while total book sales went from 1.5 to 2 billion.

9. This seems to represent a change. A film exhibitor executive: "Twenty years ago anyone successful on TV would never be successful in the movies. I don't know why. Actors couldn't cross over. It may be the over-exposure factor on television. Today they cross over back and forth. They want to make the movies. That's where they make the money—someone who makes 30 sitcoms a year."

10. G. Serge Denisoff, *Inside MTV*. New Brunswick, N.J.: Transaction Books, 1990, p. 255.

11. *NYT*, 3/21/91.

12. *NYT*, 4/20/92.

13. *NYT*, 9/26/90.

14. Tom Engelhardt, "The Shortcake Strategy," in Todd Gitlin, ed., *Watching Television*, New York: Pantheon, 1987.

15. *Business Week*, 3/25/85.

16. *Marketing News*, Feb. 1989.

17. Axel Madsen, *The New Hollywood: American Movies in the '70s*. New York: Thomas Y. Crowell, 1975, p. 69.

18. Dan Lacy, "From Family Enterprise to Global Conglomerate," *Journal of Media Studies*, Summer 1992, pp. 1–13.

19. Personal interview.

20. He also acquired Delphi Internet Services, a large online computer information company.

21. *Wall Street Journal*, 5/4/90. (Hereafter, *WSJ*.)

22. *NYT*, 6/25/90.

23. *Electronic Media*, 6/12/89. TCI had at one point requested financing from the criminal Bank of Credit and Commerce International. Two of its top executives were investors in a BCCI subsidiary.

24. *Inside Media*, 1/20/93.

25. Ken Auletta, "Late Night Gamble," *The New Yorker*, 2/1/93.

26. From an analysis of nineteen years of box-office receipts, by *Variety*, Jan. 18, 1989. In 1988, Disney had 20%, Paramount 16%, Warner and Fox tied at 11%, Universal and MGM at 10% each. But in 1985, Disney had only 3%, Warner was up at 18%. Universal went from 5% in 1971 to 25% in 1975 and 30% in 1982, but dropped to 8% two years later.

27. *NYT*, 9/30/90.

28. Personal interview.

29. Personal interview.

30. Personal interview.

31. As an example, Microsoft acquired a British publisher in 1991 to use its picture library in multimedia applications.

32. *NYT*, 4/15/90. Since the syndication market offers a dependable income for a greater number of shows than does network television, there is a longer lead time in production, and hence, more relaxed working conditions for all concerned.

33. My estimate, projected from 1990 data. In that year, Simon & Schuster's volume rose to $2.0 billion when it acquired Macmillan in 1993; Time Warner Trade Publishing was just short of the billion-dollar level. Bantam, owned by Bertelsmann, did $550 million volume annually. The Newhouses' Random House published a thousand books a year through its various subsidiaries and did a business of $800 million.

34. Of this total, $9 billion is in the United States.

35. They were Visnews (owned 50% by Reuters—of which News Corporation was a major share-holder, 38% by NBC, and 12% by the BBC) and Worldwide Television News Corporation (80% owned by Capital Cities/ABC).

36. Hearst, the runner-up, had revenues of $631 million in 1990, and Newhouse's Conde Nast had $549 million. Parade Publications, also owned by Newhouse, had another $355 million.

37. According to Barry Umanski, deputy general counsel of the National Association of Broadcasters. (*NYT*, 8/3/93.)

38. G. Serge Denisoff, *Tarnished Gold: The Record Industry Revisited*. New Brunswick, N.J.: Transaction Books, 1986, p. 99.

39. Eric W. Rothenbuler and John W. Dimmick, "Popular Music: Concentration and Diversity in the Industry," *Journal of Communication*, Vol. 32 (Winter 1982), pp. 143–49.

40. Cf. Anthony Smith, *The Age of the Behemoths: The Globalization of Mass Media*. New York: Priority Press, 1991. For an earlier discussion of the American influence, cf. Jeremy Tunstall, *The Media Are American: Anglo-American Media in the World*. London: Constable, 1977.

41. *NYT*, 12/16/91.

42. Connie Bruck, "Leap of Faith," *The New Yorker*, 9/9/91, pp. 38–74.

43. *The Economist*, 9/2/91.

44. *WSJ*, 9/26/90.

45. By David E. Sanger in *NYT*, 11/28/90.

46. Personal interview.

47. Personal interview.

48. Personal interview.

49. Personal interview.

50. Cf. comment by Dave Cuzzolina, managing editor of the Altoona *Mirror*, in the *ASNE Bulletin*, Nov. 1988. In spite of his gaffe, Topping was subsequently elected president of the ASNE.

51. David Bordwell, *The Classical Hollywood Cinema: Film Style and Mode of Production*. New York: Columbia University Press, 1985, p. 368.

52. Personal interview.

53. Address before the Overseas Press Club in 1989.

54. Cited by Richard Clurman, *To the End of Time: The Seduction and Conquest of a Media Empire*. New York: Simon and Schuster, 1992, p. 309.

55. Cf. his letter to the *NYT Book Review*, 3/29/92, in response to the review of Clurman's book.

56. Clurman, op. cit., p. 209.

57. Personal interview.

58. Personal interview.

59. Quoted by Richard M. Clurman, *Beyond Malice*. New Brunswick, N.J.: Transaction Books, 1988, p. 264.

60. Ian Charles Jarvie, *Movies and Society*. New York: Basic Books, 1970.

61. Michael Ermarth, ed., *Kurt Wolff: A Portrait in Essays and Letters*. Chicago: University of Chicago Press, 1991.

62. *Economist*, 12/26/87.

63. Walter W. Powell, "From Craft to Corporation: The Impact of Outside Ownership on Book Publishing," in James S. Ettema and D. Charles Whitney, eds., *Individuals in Mass Organizations: Creativity and Constraint*. Beverly Hills, Cal.: Sage, 1982, p. 48.

64. Ibid., p. 47.

65. *Library Quarterly, June 1954*.

66. *NYT*, 12/29/83.

67. It was bought by Barnes and Noble's Leonard Riggio in 1986, and 50% of it was sold to Vendex, a Dutch conglomerate, in 1992. Barnes and Noble had 938 stores, including 110 superstores (plus 37 more planned for 1994), each stocking between 60,000 and 120,000 titles. It owned Doubleday and Scribner's as well as B. Dalton.

68. The pressure to do so increased when, in 1980, the IRS ruled that profit-making publishers could no longer take tax writeoffs on their overstocks.

69. Scholar–publisher Irving Louis Horowitz suggests that computers have shifted publishers' interests from knowledge to information, with a consequent "internalization of intellectualism." Cf. Irving Louis Horowitz, *Communicating Ideas: The Crisis of Publishing in a Post-Industrial Society*. New York: Oxford University Press, 1986, p. 89.

70. Technical, reference, and professional books were capturing a growing part of the total market. Adult trade book sales were 28% of the total dollar volume in 1992, of which educational texts and professional books made up 37%. Since profit margins in educational publishing run half again as much as those in trade publishing, major houses have switched their emphasis. (Cf. William F. Lofquist, "Book Publishing," in U.S. Industrial Outlook—1988. U. S. Department of Commerce, Washington, D.C.: GPO, 1988.)

71. Over 300 presses—many of them at universities—now publish books in the natural and social sciences, with a high degree of specialization accomplished by building lists of titles over time. Noncommercial publishing plays an intellectual role out of all proportion to its sales volume. University presses represent 1% of sales, 10% of annual new titles, and 20% of book awards since 1950.

72. Eric Boehlert, "Nightmare in Elm City," *Inside Media*, 11/21/90.

73. Benjamin M. Compaine, *Who Owns the Media? Concentration of Ownership in the Mass Communication Industry*. New York: Harmony Books, 1979. Cf. also Ben Bagdikian, *The Media Monopoly*. Boston: Beacon, 1990.

74. Cf. John C. Busterna, "National Advertising Pricing Conduct: Chain versus Independent Newspapers," *Journalism Quarterly*, Vol. 65 (1988), p. 305.

75. John C. Busterna, "Daily Newspaper Chains and the Anti-Trust Laws," *Journalism Monographs*, No. 110, (March 1989), p. 9.

76. Cf. Stephen Koss, *The Rise and Fall of the Political Press in Britain* (2 vols.), Chapel Hill: University of North Carolina Press, 1981–84.

77. The president of News World is Bo Hi Pak, who is also president of the World Media Association, an affiliate of Moon's Unification Church that "studies journalistic ethics." (*NYT*, 10/16/89.)

78. Loren Ghiglione, ed., *The Buying and Selling of American Newspapers*. Indianapolis: R.J. Berg, 1984.

79. *Editor and Publisher*, 11/4/89.

80. For a recent example of the conspiracy theory of media, cf. Noam Chomsky and Edward S. Heerman, *Manufacturing Consent: The Political Economy of the Mass Media*. New York: Pantheon, 1993.

81. For a brief review of Gramsci's extensive writings, cf. Bennett Berger, "Disenchanting the Concept of Community," *Society*, Vol. 25, No. 6 (Sep./Oct. 1988), pp. 50–2.

82. Cf. Martin Jay, *The Sociological Imagination*. Boston: Little Brown, 1973.

83. Cited by Leo Lowenthal, *Literature and Mass Culture*. New Brunswick, N.J.: Transaction Books, 1984, p. 187.

84. Ibid., 254–55.

85. "The situations into which the product of mechanical reproduction can be brought may not touch the actual work of art, yet the quality of its presence is always depreciated. . . . That which withers in the age of mechanical reproduction is the aura [that is, the uniqueness] of the work of art." (Benjamin, quoted by Lowenthal, op. cit., pp. 220–21.)

86. In 1986, Americans spent $3.4 billion to attend cultural events and $3.1 billion to attend sports events. (Twenty years earlier, more had been spent for sports than for culture.) John P. Robinson, "The Arts in America," *American Demographics*, Sep., 1987, pp. 42–50. In 1970, spending for admission to cultural events was less than half that for sports events. In 1986, it was 10% higher.

Chapter 3

1. "Culture" may be defined as the whole body of beliefs, practices, and material artifacts that a society uses and passes on from one generation to the next. The term "culture," applied in this anthropological sense, is of fairly recent vintage. Its application to the arts is even more recent. "With the decline of religious emphasis, in the eighteenth century, 'culture', or more specifically 'art' and 'literature' (themselves newly generalized and abstracted) were seen as the deepest record, the deepest impulse, and the deepest resource of the 'human spirit.' " (Raymond Williams, *Marxism and Literature*, Oxford University Press, 1977, 1985, p. 13. Cf. also Williams, *Culture and Society 1780–1950*, New York: Columbia University Press, 1958, 1983.)

2. Max Weber in *The Protestant Ethic and the Spirit of Capitalism* (in Hans H. Gerth and C. Wright Mills, eds., *From Max Weber*, New York: Oxford University Press, 1946) linked the ascetic spirit to the accumulation of material goods. Weber's prototypical capitalist Protestants, as Chandra Mukerji describes them, "were supposed to live modestly, save their money, and make wise investment of profits . . . precisely the opposite of the hedonist consumers associated with industrial capitalism, people looking for happiness in a second car and a Cuisinart. . . . [Actually] Capitalist Man was not transformed overnight with the industrial revolution, suddenly losing self-control and developing a voracious appetite for goods, but rather has always displayed some mixture of asceticism and hedonism." (Chandra Mukerji, *From Graven Images: Patterns of Modern Materialism*. New York: Columbia University Press, 1983.)

3. Cited by Neil McKendrick, John Brewer, and J. H. Plumb, *The Birth of a Consumer Society: The Commercialization of Eighteenth-Century England*. London: Europa Publications, 1982, p. 19.

4. Mukerji, op. cit., pp. 254–55.

5. The cultural historian Rosalind Williams suggests that "the pleasure of the illusion of wealth disappears into the distance as the mass market keeps encroaching, transforming the rare into the commonplace." (Rosalind H. Williams, *Dream Worlds: Mass Consumption in Late Nineteenth Century France*. Berkeley: University of California Press, 1982, p. 102.) As described by Georges d'Avenel in *Le Mécanisme de la Vie Moderne*, "The character of the new luxury is to be banal. Let us not complain too much, if you please: before, there was nothing banal but misery." (Quoted by Williams, p. 98.)

6. Richard Wightman Fox and T.J. Jackson Lears refer to "therapeutic consumption" – "the promise of health and worldly contentment." (Richard Wightman Fox and T.J. Jackson Lears, ed., *The Culture of Consumption: Critical Essays in American History 1880–1980*. New York: Pantheon, 1983.)

7. Colin Campbell links fashion in "modern consumerism" to romantic aspirations. "Self-illusory hedonism is characterized by a longing to experience in reality those pleasures created and enjoyed in imagination, a longing which results in the ceaseless consumption of novelty." (Colin Campbell, *The Romantic Ethic and the Spirit of Modernism*. Oxford, England: Basil Blackwell, p. 205.) Rosalind Williams traces the rise of fashion to Louis the Fourteenth, "The Consumer King." At Versailles, "furnishings were continually being changed. Upholstery and curtains in all rooms were altered according to the season – red and green velvet in the winter, silks of all colors and brocades trimmed with gold and silver in the summer – and the building itself was always being remodeled." (Op. cit., p. 26.) More than a century later – in 1852, the first department store, Bon Marché, opened in Paris. With its successors, it became the prime vehicle for mass merchandising the evanescences of fashion. With standardized prices, shopping became a kind of walking dream, an exciting new form of entertainment quite different from haggling with individual merchants. Department store architecture was characterized by exotic decoration that heightened the mood of fantasy. "In exchange for the freedom to browse, meaning the liberty to indulge in dreams without being obligated to buy in fact, the buyer gave up the freedom to participate actively in establishing prices and instead had to accept the price set by the seller." (Rosalind Williams, op. cit., p. 67.)

8. Slaves may be resigned to a fate that assigns their masters' fineries to a realm beyond their reach, though surely not beyond their imaginations. But that is because they and their masters are part of the same society.

9. Quoted by Lillian B. Miller, *Patriots and Patriotism. The Encouragement of the Fine Arts in the United States, 1790–1860*. Chicago: University of Chicago Press, 1966, p. 11.

10. Fyodor Dostoyevsky, *The Possessed*. New York: Modern Library, 1936, p. 268.

11. For a review of the relevant literature, see Leo Bogart, *Strategy in Advertising*, Lincolnwood, Ill., NTC Books, 1990.

12. 1985 Roper poll.

13. A Hart poll for the *WSJ* (9/19/89) shows that 72% are "extremely" or "pretty" satisfied with their lives, and only 6% are dissatisfied.

14. This includes the public service messages that are run when there are not enough paid advertisements to fill all the allotted slots. Ads fill about 60% of newspaper space and 52% of magazine pages. (The average person spends about seven hours or so with newspapers and magazines in a week.) In 1992, nonprogramming material on the networks averaged 18.6% of prime time, 27.8% of daytime, 23% in early morning, 26.8% of late night, and 12% of news shows. But this time refers only to the commercials on the national hookups. There were also six minutes of spot commercials an hour on a typical television station, including network affiliates as well as independents. (American Association of Advertising Agencies/Association of National Advertisers study.) Altogether, advertising accounted for 23% of network television prime-time and Saturday morning children's time (including the occasional public service commercials and promotional commercials for programs), 27% of network programming other than prime-time, and an additional 10% of all broadcast time on local television stations – network affiliates and independents – over and above the network feed. Syndicated programs carried 14 minutes and 34 seconds per hour – nearly one-quarter of their total time. There were slightly more than twenty commercials per hour in prime time on the networks, thirty-seven in daytime. The cable networks carried two minutes more commercial time per hour than the major networks. Advertising filled 18% of radio time, too. The typical AM radio station had ten minutes an hour in commercials. On FM, which is more music and less talk,

commercials ran 9 minutes and 18 seconds. (Noncommercial radio and television account for an insignificant proportion of total broadcast hours).

15. In 1972, according to studies made for the U.S. Postal Service, the average household received 7.4 pieces of first class mail a week, 2.3 magazines or newspapers, and 3.0 pieces of third-class or advertising mail. By 1987, the number of first-class letters had grown slightly, to 8.6 pieces; second-class publications had fallen substantially, to 1.7 per household; and third-class pieces had grown over three times, to 9.8 pieces. Cf. Jean Li Rogers, "Consumer Response to Advertising Mail," *Journal of Advertising Research*, Dec. 1989/Jan. 1990.

16. Of people who had rented videocassettes 28% had encountered ads on at least one in the last three months; 36% found them "very annoying" and 31% "somewhat annoying," but only 42% fast-forwarded past them. 1990 Gallup poll, *Advertising Age*, 5/28/90.

17. *NYT*, 6/1/91.

18. I adapted these figures from a study of the four (including Fox) network-owned and -operated stations in Chicago by a team from Northwestern University, conducted over a 24-hour period in April 1993. (*Advertising Age*, 1/12/93.)

19. *WSJ*, 2/19/91.

20. *NYT* 2/11/83.

21. Bruce Barton, *The Man Nobody Knows: A Discovery of the Real Jesus*. Indianapolis: Bobbs Merrill, 1924.

22. Donald W. Hendon and William F. Muhs, "Outdoor Advertising and Other Media in the Tribal Man and Gutenberg Man Eras," *Journal of Advertising History*, No. 8, (March 1984), pp. 12–24.

23. Mark Girouard, *The English Town: A History of Urban Life*, New Haven, Ct.: Yale University Press, 1990, 224–26.

24. "By the 1840's the streets of London were clogged with the effigies of things. . . . Though intended to show how important commodities were, these gigantic commodities were actually only a carnivalesque inversion of the low regard in which everyday articles were commonly held." (Thomas Richards, *The Commodity Culture of Victorian England: Advertising and Spectacle, 1851–1914*. Stanford, Cal.: Stanford University Press, 1990, p. 48.)

25. James L. Crouthamil, *Bennett's New York Herald and the Rise of the Popular Press*. Syracuse, N.Y.: Syracuse University Press, 1989.

26. N. W. Ayers' national brand campaign for the newly formed National Biscuit Company in 1899 was one of the first for packaged foodstuffs. (Daniel Boorstin, "Welcome to the Consumption Community," Fortune, 9/1/67.)

27. Cited by Robert Atwan, "Newspapers and the Foundations of Modern Advertising," in John W. Wright, ed., *The Commercial Connection: Advertising and the American Mass Media*, New York: Delta, 1979, p. 18.

28. From a series of studies by the Newspaper Advertising Bureau.

29. Video Storyboard Tests.

30. American Association of Advertising Agencies (AAAA).

31. J. Walter Thompson Company, *Flippers: Changes in the Way Americans Watch TV*, New York, 1986.

32. *WSJ*, 2/12/91.

33. Ernest Dichter, *The Strategy of Desire*. Garden City, N.Y,: Doubleday, 1960.

34. Quoted by T. R. Nevett, *Advertising in Britain: A History*, London: Heinemann, 1982.

35. Ibid., p. 12.

36. Anthony Trollope, *The Struggles of Brown, Jones and Robinson: By One of the Firm*. New York: Harper, 1862.

37. 1988 Gallup poll.

38. Reported by Philip H. Dougherty in *NYT*, 10/1/85.

39. Kenneth Roman, "The Neo-Prohibitionists," address to the International Radio and Television Society, 2/8/89.

40. Diane E. Liebert, Joyce N. Sprafkin, Robert M. Liebert, and Eli A. Rubinstein, "Effects of TV Commercial Disclaimers on the Product Expectations of Children," *Journal of Communication*, Vol. 27, No. 1 (Winter 1977), pp. 118–27.

41. Cited by William Leiss, Stephen Kline, and Sut Jhally, *Social Communication in Advertising: Persons, Products and Images of Well-Being*. New York: Methuen, 1986, pp. 218–31.

42. A Calvin Klein supplement in *Vanity Fair*, as described by Stuart Elliott, showed "two men lying near each other on a bed, one with his hand on his knee, the other with his hand inside his pants." (*NYT*, 12/15/91.)

43. When we eliminate these elements, concentrating on the goods and services for which advertising is customary, a number of important categories are out of line. Transportation (mostly automotive and airlines) accounts for 22% of the buying but for only 16% of the advertising; furniture and household articles are 13% of the spending and 17% of the advertising; apparel and accessories are 11% of the spending and 15% of the advertising.

44. Food represents 16% of consumer spending, 24% of the national ads, and only 10% of local ads. Personal care (including health and beauty aids) is only 2% of the spending, less than 1% of the local ads, but 10% of the national and 5% (or 2-1/2 times its expected weight) in the total. Apparel and home furnishings and recreation show up largely in the local advertising column; transportation, mainly as national.

45. Toiletries, health and beauty aids, and toilet goods account for about 8% of television advertising, 8% of magazine advertising, and a fraction of a percent of both outdoor and newspapers. Automotive represents 19% of national newspapers, 12% of magazines, 15% of television, and 8% of outdoor.

46. Only 15% of newspaper display ads show photographs of the human figure or face; another 8% use drawings of people. The remainder divide evenly into those with and without illustrations. In two out of five newspaper ads, the advertiser considers that the text is sufficient to convey the necessary information about the product. By contrast, only 1% of magazine ads carry copy with no illustration. (Leo Bogart, "The Multiple Meanings of Television Advertising," *Society*, Vol. 25, No. 4 (May 1988), pp. 76–80.)

47. Frank Brady, *Citizen Welles: A Biography of Orson Welles*. New York: Scribner's, 1989.

48. A White House speechwriter, Peggy Noonan, coined two of George Bush's: "a thousand points of light," and "a kinder, gentler nation."

49. Address to New York's City Club, 1/8/88.

50. By John Lister, in *Advertising Age*, 11/28/88.

51. Quoted by Joe McGinniss, *The Selling of the President*, New York: Trident, 1969.

52. *NYT*, 10/25/87.

53. Bruce Oudes, ed., "Richard Nixon: By the Press Obsessed," *Columbia Journalism Review*, May/June 1989, pp. 48–51.

54. *The New Yorker*, 1/6/88. Illustrating the interpenetration of politics and the media was the appointment of Ailes to head General Electric's CNBC cable network in 1993.

55. *Advertising Age*, 10/31/88.

56. *Advertising Age*, 1/14/92.

57. *NYT*, 10/21/90.

58. *Persilgepflegt musst Waesche sein!*

59. At the end of the 1980s the private savings rate in Japan was three times as high as in the United States. The American savings rate had fallen to 2% of GNP, while it had been

about 8% of GNP in the 1960s and 1970s, a period in which the economy's expenditures on advertising had been proportionately greater.

Chapter 4

1. Address to the International Association for Cultural Freedom, 12/3/68.

2. John Fischer, "The Perils of Publishing: How to Tell When You Are Being Corrupted," *Harper's*, May 1968, p. 13.

3. Response Analysis Survey, 1982.

4. David R. Bowers, "A Report on Activity by Publishers in Directing Newsroom Decisions," *Journalism Quarterly*, Vol. 44 (Spring 1967), pp. 43-52.

5. J.B. Bishop, "An Inside View of Commercial Journalism," *The Nation*, 6/12/90.

6. *NYT*, 4/30/90.

7. Edwin Diamond, "Behind the Peacock Throne," *New York*, 2/13/89.

8. Calvin Trillin, "U.S. Journal: Nampa, Idaho," *The New Yorker*, 10/31/1970.

9. However, only about one in six said, "our newspaper seldom runs stories which our advertisers would find critical or harmful." Cf. Lawrence C. Soley and Robert L. Craig, "Advertising Pressures on Newspapers: A Survey." *Journal of Advertising*, Vol. 21, No. 4 (Dec. 1992), pp. 1-10.

10. Quoted by Ronald K. L. Collins, *Dictating Content: How Advertising Pressures Can Corrupt a Free Press*, Washington, D.C.: Center for the Study of Commercialism, 1992, p. 21.

11. Marvin Barrett, ed., *Survey of Broadcast Journalism*, 1970-1971). New York: Grosset and Dunlap, 1971.

12. A.Q. Mowbray, "Free Press and Fancy Packages," *The Nation*, 12/11/67.

13. *Editor and Publisher*, 11/18/92.

14. Les Brown, *Television: The Business Behind the Box*, New York: Harcourt Brace Jovanovich, 1971. Cf. also Reuven Frank, *Out of Thin Air: The Brief Wonderful Life of Network News*. New York: Simon and Schuster, 1991, pp. 320-21.

15. Cited by Collins, op. cit., p. 40.

16. According to Reginald Brack, president of the Time Inc. Magazine Company.

17. *NYT*, 11/11/88.

18. Steve Pasternack and Sandra H. Utt, "Newspapers' Policies on Rejection of Ads for Products and Services," *Journalism Quarterly*, Vol . 65, No. 3 (Fall 1988), pp. 695-701.

19. *WSJ*, 10/15/90.

20. Alexander Kendrick, *Prime Time: The Life of Edward R. Murrow*, Boston: Little Brown & Co., 1969, p. 51.

21. R.C. Smith, "The Magazines' Smoking Habit," *Columbia Journalism Review*, Jan./Feb. 1978, pp. 29-31. A more recent analysis found that only 5% of women's magazines that carry cigarette advertising also carried articles on the health hazards of smoking in a typical year, compared to 12% of those without cigarette ads. (Kenneth Warner, "Cigarette Advertising and Magazine Coverage of the Hazards of Smoking—A Statistical Analysis," *New England Journal of Medicine*, Vol. 326, No. 5 (1/30/92), pp. 305-9.)

22. *WSJ*, 2/21/91.

23. *NYT*, 1/30/92.

24. *WSJ*, 1/30/92.

25. Foote Cone and Belding survey, reported in *NYT*, 2/20/91. Four out of five agreed that news program sponsors were "performing a public service by keeping the public informed" and only 11% felt less favorable about commercials in local news shows. (Frank Magid survey.)

26. *NYT*, 2/7/91.

27. Bob Shanks, *The Cool Fire: How to Make It in Television*. New York: W. W. Norton, 1976.

28. Quoted in Hal Himmelstein, *Television Myth and the American Mind*. New York: Praeger, 1984, p. 21.

29. Survey by J. Walter Thompson.

30. *Advertising Age*, 11/18/91.

31. Quoted by Erik Barnouw, *The Sponsor: Notes on a Modern Potentate*. New York: Oxford University Press, 1978, p. 54.

32. Bryce Rucker, *The First Freedom*, Carbondale, Ill.: University of Southern Illinois Press, 1968, p. 105.

33. Newton N. Minow, *Equal Time: The Private Broadcaster and the Public Interest*, New York: Atheneum, 1964, p. 15. On a more serious level, Bryce Rucker accused Chrysler, a major supplier to the military, of killing a proposed program that it deemed too antimilitary. Cf. Rucker, op. cit., pp. 105–6.

34. Reuven Frank, op. cit., p. 42.

35. Minow, op. cit.

36. *Advertising Age*, 8/31/81.

37. *NYT*, 4/23/88.

38. *NYT*, 4/23/88.

39. Frank Mankiewicz and Joel Swerdlow, *Remote Control: Television and the Manipulation of American Life*. New York: Times Books, 1978, p. 232.

40. *Madison Avenue*, Sep. 1981, p. 56.

41. According to Arnie Semsky, a senior vice-president of the BBDO advertising agency. (*NYT*, 6/17/81.)

42. *Inside Media*, 2/21/90.

43. No more than 3% of the viewers were in favor of removing any of sixteen criticized shows from the air, and only 9% of the public claimed to have refused to buy an advertised product because they objected to a program. Two percent supported a proposed boycott, which ultimately fizzled completely.) Wildmon's Christian Leadership for Responsible Television ("Clear") boycotted Clorox and Mennen in 1989. Only 1.8% of adults claimed to have boycotted Clorox products, 0.8% Mennen; these were probably gross overstatements. (From studies by ABC, NBC, and the Lintas agency.)

44. *Television Radio Age*, 10/2/89, p. 45.

45. For the Texaco executives who bring their wives and friends to the company box at the Metropolitan Opera House for the long-standing Saturday afternoon broadcast, the fun and thrill of participation and "ownership" may be more compelling emotions than the quiet knowledge that millions of radio listeners are identifying their employer with the strains of Verdi or Wagner.

46. Barnouw, op. cit., p. 33.

47. In that case by McCann-Erickson's Dorothy McCann.

48. *Channels*, October 1988, p. 44.

49. Robert C. Allen, *Speaking of Soap Operas*. Chapel Hill: University of North Carolina Press, 1985, p. 11.

50. Ibid., p. 176.

51. *NYT*, 4/27/89.

52. Inintoli, op. cit.

53. "Illnesses, accidents, violence and death appear to take up a major part of the story line of the daytime television serial." (Horace Newcomb, "A Humanist's View of Daytime

Serial Drama," in Mary B. Cassata and Thomas Skill, *Life on Daytime Television: Tuning in American Serial Drama*. Norwood, N.J.: Ablex, 1983.)

54. Larry Gross and S. Jeffries Fox, "What Do You Want to Be When You Grow Up, Little Girl?" in Gaye Tuchman, Arlene Kaplan Daniels, and James Benet, eds., *Hearth and Home: Images of Women in the Mass Media*. N.Y.: Oxford University Press, 1978.

55. According to Meredith Berlin of *Soap Opera Digest*, on one of the rare occasions when a "good girl" had an abortion, "she had a total breakdown and went to an insane asylum. That was her punishment." (*NYT*, 5/31/92.)

56. Gillette began sponsoring radio sportscasts in 1935, with the Baer-Braddock heavyweight title fight. The company has been a major factor in sports broadcasting ever since. Red Barber, the celebrated sportscaster, was directly on Gillette's payroll. The close involvement of advertisers later brought sports to television, over the initial resistance of network programmers. The first Olympics broadcast, by CBS in 1960, got a very small audience. It was ABC's "Wide World of Sports" that brought track and field to the mass audience and created a huge viewership for the Olympics in more recent years, with the aid of tremendous promotion.

57. Cf. Ron Powers, *Supertube: The Rise of Television Sports*. New York: Coward McCann, 1984.

58. The psychologist Herbert Krugman suggests that the growth in familiarity with previously obscure sports has raised the level of sports connoisseurship. He points to the example of rodeo, which is generally considered to be a spectacle, not a competitive sport, and therefore receives virtually no press coverage. However, rodeos use a subtle form of scoring well-understood by their participants and aficionados. As televised coverage of rodeos grows (which seems likely, given the inexhaustible appetite for programming), the rules of the game will become more widely understood and its status will also change.

59. The 1992 Olympics carried 17 minutes of commercials per hour, compared to 14.5 in the average NBC prime-time show. But stadium signs, logos, blimps, and other incidental messages added considerably to the commercial impact. ABC paid $309 million for broadcast rights to the 1988 Olympic games, while Western European television systems paid a total of only $5.7 million. The networks lost over $200 million during the first two years of their contracts with the National Football League. CBS's $1.06 billion bid for the four-year major league baseball contract was 30% higher than its rivals, thus raising the ante in subsequent negotiations with the National Collegiate Athletics Association, the National Basketball Association, and the National Football League. The network lost an estimated $500 million; when it decided not to renew, its two rivals negotiated a profit-sharing package that would limit nationally televised baseball games after the season, with a new round of playoffs appearing simultaneously in different regions of the country. (*NYT*, 5/13/93.) CBS also lost between $150 and $200 million on its football broadcasts. In 1993, Fox outbid CBS (at $395 million for each of four years) to win broadcast rights to the National Football Conference games, ending a relationship of nearly forty years. CBS also lost its bid to replace NBC in broadcasting the American Football Conference games, which have smaller audiences than the NFC.

60. In 1991, the average major league baseball player earned $891,000. There were nine teams in which the average player's salary exceeded $1 million (For Oakland, the average was $1.35 million). That year, the New York Mets signed a player, Bobby Bonilla, to a $29 million five-year contract. New franchises awarded for 1993 in Miami and Denver paid fees of $95 million each. (When teams were last added, in 1977, the franchise went for $7 million.)

61. Quoted by Ken Auletta, *Three Blind Mice: How The TV Networks Lost Their Way*, New York: Random House, 1991, p. 301.

62. Quoted by Joseph C. Goulden, *The Curtis Caper*, New York: G.P. Putnam's Sons, 1965, p. 26.

63. *Inside Media*, 10/23/91.

64. Ibid.

65. Fred Pfaff, "Special Effort," *Inside Media*, 4/17/91, p. 33.

66. Some tastes cut across the standard lines. For example, people's *motivations* for viewing different kinds of television programs do not vary among demographic groups. (Russell W. Neuman, *The Future of the Mass Audience*: Cambridge, U.K.: Cambridge University Press, 1991.)

67. By Barbara Bank, vice-president of Lord Geller Federico Einstein, reported in *Inside Media*, 1/10/90.

68. *NYT*, 10/30/89.

69. *NYT* 11/19/90.

70. A survey by Action for Children's Television (ACT) in 1985.

71. Personal interview.

72. Anthony Gottlieb, "The Music Business," *The Economist*, 12/21/91.

73. G. Serge Denisoff, *Tarnished Gold: The Record Industry Revisited*. New Brunswick, N.J.; Transaction Books, 1986, p. 133.

74. Murray Levin writes, "Talk show is the only medium that often provides an audience for working-class sentiment. . . . The host. . . . is a pitchman, and a poseur, always sensitive to the show's ratings and commercial appeal. He must prod and promote, excite and involve his listeners. He often does this by creating a political melodrama, replete with heroes, knaves, fools and conspirators." (Murray B. Levin, *Talk Radio and the American Dream*. Lexington, Mass.: Lexington Books, 1987, p. 16.)

75. *Inside Media*, 4/29/92.

76. However, most of the approximately 12,000 commercial radio stations are outside the major markets. Only 6% specialized in classic or soft rock in 1993; 22% were devoted to country music, 19% to "adult contemporary." Half of one percent of the stations concentrated on classical music, 8% on news or a combination of news and talk. (*Broadcasting and Cable Yearbook*, 1993.)

77. In 1992, the shares were 17% for country music, 14% for black urban, another 14% for pop and easy listening, and 6% for jazz.

78. Denisoff, op. cit., p. 128.

79. Robert P. Snow, *Creating Media Culture*. Beverly Hills, Cal.: Sage, 1983, p. 104.

80. *NYT*, 6/13/82.

81. Among 100 top executives of *Fortune* 500 companies, only 46% watch TV "just about every day" and 21% "at least several times a week"; 32% watch "only once or twice a week" and 1% "never." (J. Walter Thompson survey, 1987.)

82. Speech accepting the Pulse Man of the Year Award for 1968.

83. At a meeting of the Deadline Club, 1/16/69.

84. Eyewitness report.

85. *Adweek*, 8/31/81, p. 18.

86. The case of national advertising is different, because it represents such an enormous potential volume. Over half of national advertising now goes into television, and many smaller papers have given up on it, though it represents a $3.8 billion investment in newspapers. The problem of getting national advertisers to listen to sales proposals has not become any easier as marketing decisions have become more concentrated in the hands of fewer organizations and individuals.

87. These included the Campeau Corporation's Federated and Allied Stores, R.H. Macy, and Carter Hawley Hale.

88. However, these faced vigorous opposition from other local media owners, from employee unions and from others who argued that the newspaper's owners (Knight-Ridder) had kept its advertising and circulation rates artificially low in order to make a case for the Joint Operating Agreement. This seemed unlikely, given the fierce competitive realities of the Detroit market. Heath J. Meriwether, executive editor of the *Detroit Free Press*, said after the JOA was approved, "This is as close to hand-to-hand combat as you get in American journalism. This is a real blood feud here, and it's not going to stop. We don't like those people, and we don't want any part of them." (*Washington Post*, 11/24/89.)

Chapter 5

1. It is not always possible to determine with accuracy what company or agency billings actually are. Agencies generally exaggerate the size of the billings on an account when they first acquire it, and minimize its size when they lose it.

2. In England, Charles Mitchell's 474-page *Newspaper Press Directory*, published in 1846, noted that "the advertising agent is a principal in his own independent line of business."

3. *The Saturday Evening Post*'s research department—the first in a mass medium—was established in 1910. Advertising agencies established research departments at the time of the First World War. The use of sample surveys became widespread only in the 1930s.

4. *Advertising Age*, 10/2/89, p. 3.

5. Jason Rogers, *Building Newspaper Advertising*. New York: Harper, 1919.

6. A number of research firms acquired by conglomerates have since reestablished their private identities: Burke Marketing Research from Control Data, Opinion Research Corp. from Arthur D. Little, NFO from (then Robert Maxwell's) AGB, National Analysts from Booz Allen Hamilton. The world's twenty-five largest research organizations (of which twelve are based in the U.S.) had 1992 revenues of $3.7 billion, or 55% of the total.

7. According to Jack Honomichl, a specialist in these estimates. (*Marketing News*, 6/7/93.)

8. It acquired the largest research firm, A.C. Nielsen, in 1984, and the second largest research firm, I.M.S., in 1988. D & B was rebuffed by the Federal Trade Commission when it tried to go for another giant, Information Resources. Marketing information services accounted for $1.7 billion of Dun and Bradstreet's $4.3 billion annual billings. These also included a diverse array of nonresearch activities, among them Reuben H. Donnelley, the largest publisher of classified telephone directories, and data-management and collection services, including credit information on virtually every individual in the United States. The ominous potential existed, for many hundreds of thousands of people, to combine data on their financial status with comprehensive information on their television viewing and consumption habits (from the company's A.C. Nielsen subsidiary). Nielsen's 1992 revenues were estimated at $1.3 billion, of which 61% were from outside the United States.

9. Both Nielsen (with Home Scan) and Arbitron (with ScanAmerica) introduced single-source services, but were unable to make them commercially viable.

10. *NYT*, 6/22/91.

11. *NYT*, 10/3/75.

12. In May 1990, Nielsen showed TV viewing levels down 8% from a year earlier in daytime, down 2% in prime time, and down 14% for nightly newscasts for the three networks. The proportion of usable data varied with the composition of the household. Differences in research methodology produce other discrepancies in results. The level of Homes Using Television (HUT) is lower in people meter samples than in household meter samples. In 1994, the networks launched a major research effort to introduce an alternative to the Nielsen

service. A few years earlier they had failed to support AGB, which lost nearly $70 million in its attempt to compete with Nielsen.

13. Electronic Industries Association estimate.

14. Walker research reported in *Advertising Age*, 6/10/91.

15. A 1978 Marketing Science Institute study of 182 telephone surveys by thirty-two research organizations, involving a million dialings, showed that 40% of the designated respondents were not contacted. Among those contacted, the median refusal rate was 28%. A Walker Research survey in 1984 had a 46% refusal rate, and found that of those interviewed in the preceding year, 18% had been interviewed four or more times.

16. Of the original sample, 45% refuse to cooperate; another 10% cannot be included on any given day, when contacted by phone, because of problems with the metered data. Another 5-8% have not completed the recruiting process, making the overall response rate 35-39%. Half of the Nielsen audience composition national diary sample (which used a meter to record total tuning time) dropped out within a year.

17. CBS analysis.

18. Paul L. Klein, "TV Program Creation and Broadcast Research: Conflict or Harmony?" *Marketing Review*, Vol. 36, No. 8 (May 1981), p. 13.

19. *NYT*, 2/27/89.

20. *NYT*, 4/24/76.

21. The sweeps of November 1989 for the first time were met by the networks with a changed philosophy. They left their regular series on the air and avoided the specials and miniseries they had traditionally used to swell their ratings.

22. Lawrence Friedman, "How Good is the Seven-Day Television Diary Now?" *Journal of Advertising Research*, Vol. 29, No. 4 (Aug./Sep. 1990).

23. Jay G. Blumler and Carolyn Martin Spicer, "Creative Prospects and Threats in the New Television Marketplace: The Voice of the Program Maker," paper presented to a forum of the American Film Institute, at the Annenberg School, USC, 11/14/89, p. 2.

Chapter 6

1. One should not have the illusion that these tabloids operate on a shoestring. *The National Enquirer*'s newsroom budget was $16 million at one point.

2. *NYT*, 12/8/87.

3. Compiled by National Coalition on Television Violence.

4. Cited in *The New Yorker*, 12/6/82.

5. Cited in Louis James, *English Popular Literature, 1819-1851*, New York: Columbia University Press, 1976, pp. 63–64.

6. John Golby and A. W. Purdue, *The Civilization of the Crowd: Popular Culture in England, 1750-1900*, London: Batsford, 1984, pp. 191–92.

7. "Masses was a new word for mob," says Raymond Williams, "and the traditional characteristics of the mob were retained in its significance: gullibility, fickleness, herd-prejudice, lowness of taste and habit." (*Culture and Society*, New York: Columbia University Press, 1958, p. 298.) Williams protests, "I do not think of my relatives, friends, neighbors, colleagues, acquaintances, as masses; we none of us can or do. The masses are always the others, whom we don't know, and can't know." In a similar vein, John Golby writes, "The sensational and violent nature of much of popular culture and the ubiquity of drinking and gambling were nothing new but were more noticeable and threatening in a more urban, crowded and complex society." (Golby and Purdue, op. cit., p. 84.)

8. Cited in ibid., p. 159.

9. John Cowper Powys, *The Meaning of Culture*. New York: W. W. Norton, 266–67.

10. Cited in *Commentary*, Aug. 1981, p. 51.

11. Editorial in *The Dial*, 6/14/19, reprinted in *Essays in our Changing Order*. New York: Viking, 1934, 450–53.

12. "The Doctrine of Fascism" (1932) in Adrian Lyttelton, ed., *Italian Fascisms: From Pareto to Gentile*. New York: Harper and Row, 1973, p. 56, cited by Patrick Brantlinger, *Bread and Circuses: Theories of Mass Culture as Social Decay*. Ithaca: Cornell University Press, 1983, p. 28.

13. In *Theories of Surplus Value*, quoted by Brantlinger, op. cit., p. 117.

14. Ibid., p. 147.

15. Maggie Mahar, "What Price Art?", *Barron's* 6/29/87, pp. 6–32.

16. Auctions obliterated the distinction between wholesale and retail prices and heightened the social competition that made collectors less interested in an artist's works than in who else owned them.

17. Quoted in a 1940 *Harper's* article by Mortimer J. Adler. Cf. James Sloane Allen, *The Romance of Commerce and Culture: Capitalism, Modernism, and the Chicago-Aspen Crusade for Cultural Reform*. Chicago: University of Chicago Press, 1983, pp. 94–95.

18. Theodor Geiger, "A Radio Test of Musical Taste," *Public Opinion Quarterly*, Vol. 14 (1950), pp. 36–48.

19. Richard Posner points out that Marcel Duchamp's toilet seat "achieved a secure niche in art history, along with Goya's disgusting painting *Saturn Eating His Children*. . . . Nowadays there is no objective method of determining what is art or what is offensive. . . . If this is right, it implies that offensive art should get a lot, or a little—or even no—protection from governmental interference, however that interference should be defined. . . . You don't take apart a Maserati and announce, 'This is the carburetor and that is the speed.' " (Richard A. Posner, "Art for Law's Sake," *The American Scholar*, Vol. 58, No. 4 (Autumn 1989), pp. 513–20.)

20. Quoted by Joseph Berger, "U.S. Literature: Canon Under Siege," *NYT*, 1/6/88.

21. The critic Harold Schonberg writes: "The arts have always been an elitist manifestation. Great art always has been the product of a mind working alone, thinking as no previous mind has done, arriving at concepts that through the centuries still amaze and startle. . . . Elitism of the intellect should be a term of praise rather than disparagement."(*NYT*, 2/5/78).

22. "Looking for Poetry in America," *New York Review of Books*, 11/7/85.

23. In Leo Lowenthal's description, "Its products are nothing more than the phenomena and symptoms of the process of the individual's self-resignation in a wholly administered society." (Leo Lowenthal, *Literature and Mass Culture*. New Brunswick, N.J.: Transaction Books, 1984, p. 168.)

24. Cf. Peter Burke, *Popular Culture in Early Modern Europe*, New York: Harper & Row, 1978.

25. Fifty six percent of the public report reading a novel, poem or play in the course of a year. Twenty percent say they listen to classical music on the radio; 24% watch it performed on TV. Cf. John P. Robinson, *Americans' Participation in the Arts: A 1983–84 Arts-Related Trend Study*. College Park, Md. University of Maryland Survey Research Center, 1986.

26. The ancient public art—temples, monuments, plazas, and palaces—that has endured to this day was constructed to different standards than prevailed in the private art market, as seen in the wall decorations of Pompeiian villas or the beads worn by plebeian Egyptians. Since these mundane constructions survived less often than the tombs of kings, we are left with a somewhat exaggerated notion of the aesthetic excellence that generally prevailed in antiquity.

27. Two out of three people call it a positive influence in life, with younger people more positive than older ones. (Channels Magazine, *How Americans Watch TV: A Nation of Grazers*. New York: CC Publishing, 1989.)

28. Most of the public agrees that television "presents a permissive and immoral set of values which are bad for the country." (*Time*, 6/1/81.)

29. *NYT*, 5/23/93.

30. Robert Sklar, *Prime Time America: Life On and Behind the Television Screen*. New York: Oxford, 1980, p. 7.

31. *Inside Media*, 2/17/93.

31. *Inside Media*, 2/18/91.

33 Richard Richter, "The Network Documentary—Never More." paper presented at the Wilson Center Conference on the Future of News, 1989.

34. Admissions totaled 964 million in 1992, compared to 1.2 billion in 1984. (Motion Picture Association of America.)

35. Study by Robert Cain of over 1,000 films, cited by Michael Medved, *Hollywood vs. America: Popular Culture and the War on Traditional Values*. New York: HarperCollins, 1992. p. 287.

36. Address to the Dutch Treat Club, 2/22/93.

37. Edward K. Palmer, *Children in the Cradle of Television*. Lexington, Mass.: Lexington Books, 1987, p. 35.

38. Stephen Farber, "The Bloody Movies: Why Film Violence Sells, *New York*, 11/29/76, pp. 39–45.

39. James B. Twitchell, *Carnival Culture: The Trashing of Taste in America*. New York: Columbia University Press, 1992.

40. As Robert and Linda Lichter and Stanley Rothman put it, "television manages to enforce the law without glorifying the law-enforcement establishment. . . . More and more often on prime time, the insiders break the law and the outsiders enforce it." (S. Robert Lichter, Linda S. Lichter, and Stanley Rothman, *Watching America*. New York: Simon and Schuster, 1991, p. 230.)

41. As Thomas Morgan describes it, "dealers and pushers are often depicted as enjoying the good life. They generally live in luxurious mansions, hold extravagant parties aboard yachts or on sprawling well-groomed lawns; they wear the finest designer clothes and drive the most expensive sports cars." (*NYT*, 9/3/86).

42. A cover photo of Donna Rice, girlfriend of presidential candidate Gary Hart, boosted *People's* newsstand sales by 26%. When Rice appeared on ABC's "20/20," ratings jumped by 53%. Notoriety rather than prurience seems to have been the main motivation. "Nightline's" rating jumped by 128% when the felonous TV preacher Jim Bakker and his wife Tammy made a guest appearance.

43. Alexander Cockburn, "Violence has Become the Pornography of the '80s," *WSJ*, 6/19/86.

44. Three out of five Americans disagree with the right of newsstands to sell "any kind of magazine even if it is what many people call pornography." (1986 survey by ABC News/*Washington Post*.) Two out of three would totally ban sexually violent films and videocassettes, which appear to be in a distinct category of offensiveness. (1985 Gallup Poll.)

45. *NYT*, 4/5/79.

46. *WSJ*, 4/21/86.

47. *San Francisco Chronicle*, 2/6/85.

48. In 1985, 9% of the public bought or rented an "adult" video (according to the Gallup poll), and the market for X-rated films was estimated to exceed a half-billion dollars annually, with women or couples accounting for two thirds of all the rentals. (*NYT*, 10/6/86.)

49. *WSJ*, 10/14/88.

50. Kenneth C. David, *Two Bit Culture: The Paperbacking of America*. Boston: Houghton Mifflin, 1984, p. 135.

51. *NYT*, 1/9/84.

52. "The average R-rated movie contain[ed] 22 F-words, 14 S-words, and 5 A-words." Of PG-13 films, presumably geared for the juvenile audience, 39% used the "F-word," 66% the "A-word," and 73% the "S-word." Bob De Moss, analyzing "2Live Crew's" 60-minute album, *As Nasty as They Wanna Be* counted 226 uses of "fuck," 81 of "shit," and 117 references to genitalia. (Michael Medved, op. cit., p. 100.)

53. Medved cites lyrics like these, from a best-selling album by a rap group known as "Niggers with Attitude": "Because the dumb bitch licks out their asshole. . . . And if ya got a gang of niggers the bitch'll let ya rape her."

54. Louis Harris study of 129 shows in the 1987–88 season cited in Jane D. Brown, Kim Walsh Childers, and Cynthia S. Waszak, *Television and Adolescent Sexuality.* New York: Gannett Center for Media Studies, 1990.

55. Nancy Signorielli, after an extensive content analysis, observes that "references to program themes (for example, the mention of nature, science, education, politics, drugs, etc.) health and illnesses, sexual behavior, eating and drinking, and the time-place-setting of a story tend to occur with the same frequency and with the same degree of emphasis no matter what type of program is seen. . . . Life is portrayed across genres in a remarkably similar way. . . . Whether characters are good or bad, are successful or fail, use drugs, are physically or mentally ill, or drink alcoholic beverages does not differ much from program type to program type. Moreover, characters tend to exhibit similar personality traits: they are attractive, fair, sociable, smart, etc." (Nancy Signorielli, "Selective Television Viewing: A Limited Possibility." *Journal of Communication*, Vol.36 No. 3 [Summer 1986], pp. 64–76.)

56. "Television characters and their doings may be more exciting than people in their everyday lives, but in another respect televised fantasy is tamer than the real world. While reality can be uneven and full of surprises, our nightly entertainment is highly regular and patterned." (Jib Fowles, *Television Viewers Vs. Media Snobs: What TV Does for People.* New York: Stein and Day, 1982, p. 45.)

57. They account for 12% of the characters in identifiable jobs, but for 32% of all the crimes (generally motivated by naked greed) and 40% of the murders. Their portrayal, more positive in television's earlier period, became sharply negative in the Vietnam War era. Moreover, programs that raised the theme of business ethics presented a progressively worse picture of corruption over the three decades analyzed. By contrast, professionals are overwhelmingly portrayed in a positive light, and their preoccupations have increasingly moved to broader social concerns. (Ibid., pp. 132, 179.) Nine out of ten private detectives are heroes, but only a little over half of the police officers. (Linda and Robert Lichter, "Prime Time Crime: Who and Why," *WSJ*, 1/6/84.)

58. George Gerbner posits the notion of a "cultivation effect": Viewers perceive the real world in terms of what they see on TV and acquire feelings related to these perceptions. To illustrate this point, heavy viewers among blacks are more likely to believe that racial integration is prevalent, that blacks and whites are similar, and that most blacks belong to the middle class. (Paula W. Matabane, "Television and the Black Audience: Cultivating Moderate Perspectives of Racial Integration," *Journal of Communication*, Vol. 38, No. 4, [Autumn 1988], pp. 21–31.)

59. Jennings Bryant and Dolf Zillmann, "Pornography, Sexual Callousness, and the Trivialization of Rape," *Journal of Communication*, Vol. 82, No. 4 (Autumn 1982), pp. 10–21.

60. Survey by the Radio and Television News Directors Association.

61. Charles Atkin, "Effects of Realistic TV Violence vs. Fictional Violence on Aggression," *Journalism Quarterly*, Vol. 60, No. 4 (Winter 1983), pp. 615–21.

62. Times-Mirror survey, 1993.

63. Quoted in Edward Donnerstein, Daniel Linz, and Steven Penrod, *The Question of Pornography: Research Findings and Policy Implications*. New York: Free Press, p. 113.

64. Violent crimes grew 355% between 1960 and 1990. Murder rates doubled, and reported rapes increased fourfold. The death rate for persons 15–24 was 19% higher in 1973–74 than in 1960–61, because of the increase in violent deaths. (These figures are assembled by the Federal Bureau of Investigations from local statistics; as Christopher Jencks points out, surveys of victimization show a far less alarming rate of change.)

65. Lichter, Lichter, and Rothman, op. cit., p. 185. In 180 hours of prime-time programming on April 2, 1992, there were 1846 acts of violence, of which 175 resulted in death. (MTV videos were just as violent as the networks. Cf. study conducted by the Center for Media and Public Affairs and reported in *TV Guide*, 8/22/92.)

66. Violent crimes shown on television have actually decreased somewhat in recent years, but the overall depicted crime rate is up. In a reappraisal of television, Newton Minow called "the most troubling change . . . the rise in the quantity and quality of violence." By the time a child reaches the age of eighteen, Minow estimated, he had seen 25,000 televised murders. (Newton N. Minow, "How Vast the Wasteland Now," address to the Gannett Foundation Media Center, 5/9/91.)

67. Lichter, Lichter, and Rothman, op. cit., p. 204.

68. Deadly weapons appeared nine times in each hour of prime-time action programs in 1977 (though 84% of the shots they fired were misses). (Maria Wilson and Patricia Beaulieu Higgins, "Television's Action Arsenal: Weapon Use in Prime Time," U.S. Conference of Mayors, 1977.)

69. Robert H. Knight, "Hollywood, You Slay Me," *WSJ*, 10/5/89.

70. Joseph W. Slade, "Violence in the Hard-Core Pornographic Film: A Historical Survey," *Journal of Communication*, Vol. 34, No. 3, (Summer 1984), pp. 148–51.

71. David Levy, "Guns, Sex and Network Secrets," *Washington Post*, 8/1/93.

72. 3/2/77.

73. Personal interview.

74. Cf. Cedric Cullingford, *Children and Television*, New York: St. Martin's Press, 1984.

75. Opinion Research Corporation survey reported in *Marketing News*, 9/2/83.

76. In a 1977 Trendex survey.

77. 1982 Gallup poll.

78. Times-Mirror survey, 1993.

79. These figures are reported by A. C. Nielsen. Other estimates of viewing time, based on academic studies, run well below the figures projected by the commercial ratings services, which indicate that there is, on average, about one viewer for every set turned on. In a pioneer use of the "people meter," a device that measures individual viewing, AGB found that the proportion of people viewing was 56% of the household rating.

80. Newton N. Minow, "TV's Still a Vast Wasteland—But Improving," *TV Guide*, 5/17/86, pp. 2–3.

81. George Gerbner, "Miracles of Communication Technology: Powerful Audience, Diverse Choices and Other Fairy Tales," in Janet Wasko, ed., *Illuminating the Blind Spots*. New York: Ablex, 1993.

82. "It is possible," write Dorothy and Jerome Singer, "that the immediacy of television precludes our more active integration of images and words. We need time to replay mentally material just witnessed and also to link pictures and sounds to word labels that make for the most efficient kind of storage and retrieval. So rapidly does television material come at us that it defies the capacities of our brain to store much of it unless we actively turn our attention from the set and engage in some kind of mental rehearsal." (Dorothy G. Singer and Jerome L.

Singer, "Is Human Imagination Going Down the Tube?" *Chronicle of Higher Education*, 4/23/79, p. 56.)

83. Fred Emery and Merrelyn Emery, *A Choice of Futures*, Leiden, Martinus Neihoff, 1976. pp. 38, 67.

84. Robert Kubey and Mihaly Csikszentmihalyi, *Television and the Quality of Life: How Viewing Shapes Everyday Experience*. Hillsdale, N.J.: Lawrence Erlbaum Associates, 1990.

85. Men who watch television for three or more hours a day are twice as likely to be obese as those who watch for less than an hour. (Study by Larry Tucker, in *Adolescence*, Vol. 21 [1987], pp. 797–806, reported in *Psychology Today*, Sep. 1989, p. 8.) High-school boys who watch more than four hours of television a day do significantly less well on tests of physical exertion than infrequent viewers.

86. Analysis by William Deitz of data from the National Center for Health Statistics. *Psychology Today*, Nov. 1988, p. 12.

87. Heavy viewing correlates with low school achievement. Cf. Gary D. Gaddy, "Television's Impact on High School Achievement," *Public Opinion Quarterly*, Vol. 50, No. 3 (fall 1986) pp. 340–59. The students most adversely affected are both those who watch television most attentively and those who are most studious. Socially advantaged children are most harmed academically by heavy television watching.

88. A report prepared by Daniel Anderson and Patricia Collins for the Department of Education reviewed more than 200 studies and did not find significant proof that television viewing affected homework performance. (*APA Monitor*, March 1989.) Jerome L. Singer points out, however, that this conclusion merely reflects the need for more research.

89. The National Assessment of Educational Progress studied 13-year-old children in Ireland, Korea, Spain, the UK, and four Canadian provinces. In every country, the more time a child spent with TV, the lower the performance in math and science. When sixth- and seventh-grade children were asked to provide ideas for solving social problems presented in video, audiotape, or print form, those exposed to video consistently gave fewer and less original solutions, and also more hackneyed ones. (Caroline W. Meline, "Does the Medium Matter?" *Journal of Communication*, Vol. 26, No. 3 [Summer 1976], pp. 81–89). Television increases aggressive behavior both for children who are highly aggressive to begin with and for those who initially exhibit low aggressiveness. (Tannis MacBeth Williams, ed., *The Impact of Television: A Natural Experiment in Three Communities*. Orlando, Fla.: Academic, 1986.)

90. The substance still affects the common currency of known personalities and symbols. When there were fewer choices on TV, a single program could be familiar to proportionately far more viewers than today. "I Love Lucy" had a 46 rating in 1956. In 1992, the top show, "Roseanne," had a 20.

91. Study by Gervasia Schreckenberg and Harvey Bird in the *Bulletin of the New Jersey Academy of Sciences*, Vol. 32, pp. 77–86, reported in *Psychology Today*, Nov. 1988, p. 29.

92. *NYT*, 6/12/91.

93. Quoted by Thomas Richards, *The Commodity Culture of Victorian England: Advertising and Spectacle*, 1851–1914. Stanford, Cal.: Stanford University Press, 1990, p. 87.

94. To stave off further restrictions on tobacco and beer advertising, the tobacco companies and their allies in the advertising business launched a campaign on behalf of "freedom of commercial speech" in 1989. Philip Morris spent a reported $60 million for institutional advertisements celebrating the Bill of Rights and entered into an arrangement with the National Archives to facilitate this promotion. (The Archives were made an independent agency, authorized to accept gifts, in 1984, after Nixon henchmen removed tapes and records from its files.) The ongoing debate over whether any restrictions should be placed on the advertising of a product that is legally available for sale echoes questions we shall be confronting later regarding the inconsistencies in American public policy on the media.

95. One recent example came from a 1988 campaign to heighten awareness of colon cancer, created for the Advertising Council. It was exposed in test markets at a level equivalent to 565 ads (the equivalent of a campaign that would cost $21 million on a national scale), and raised awareness of the ailment from 15% to 45% among women and from 6% to 35% among men. But even in this case there was no indication of how awareness was translated into changes in diet or daily routine.

96. Joseph Klapper, *The Effects of Mass Media*. New York: Free Press, 1960.

97. Planned Parenthood Federation of America.

98. *Report of the U.S. Commission on Pornography, Washington, DC: GPO, 1970*. Quoted by Donnerstein, Linz, and Penrod, op. cit., p. 32.

99. An analysis of state by state statistics (by Larry Baron and Murray Straus) finds that rape is high in the same places where there is high readership of outdoor magazines.

100. Edward Donnerstein and Charles G. Hallam, "Excitation Transfer in Communication-Mediated Aggressive Behavior," *Journal of Experimental Social Psychology*, Vol. 7, (1971), pp. 419–34.

101. "Normal" men shown a series of commercially available "slasher" films were desensitized; they were less depressed, saw less violence against women, were more likely to enjoy the film, and less likely to sympathize with the victim in a simulated rape trial. Cf. Dolf Zillmann and Jennings Bryant, "Effects of Massive Exposure to Pornography," in Neil M. Malamuth and Edward Donnerstein, eds., *Pornography and Sexual Aggression*. New York: Academic, 1984. Cf. also Dolf Zillmann, "Effects of Prolonged Consumption of Pornography," in Dolf Zillmann and Jennings Bryant, eds., *Pornography: Research Advances and Policy Considerations*. Hillsdale, N.J., Lawrence Erlbaum Associates, 1989, pp. 127–58. Film scenes of extremely brutal violence against women make men less sympathetic to female victims in more realistic settings. In one experiment, men were shown five movies depicting violence against women. They had fewer negative reactions after this heavy dosage and perceived the movies as less violent and degrading to women. (Edward Donnerstein and Daniel Linz, "Sexual Violence in the Media: A Warning," *Psychology Today*, Jan. 1984, pp. 14–15.) (Neil M. Malamuth and Donnerstein, eds., *Pornography and Sexual Aggression*, Orlando, Fla.: Academic, 1984.) (Daniel Linz, Edward Donnerstein, and Steven Penrod, "The Effects of Multiple Exposures to Filmed Violence Against Women," *Journal of Communication*, Vol. 34, No. 3 [Summer 1984], pp. 130–47.) Sexual fantasizing increases arousal and also increases sexual satisfaction in general. But exposure to massive doses of erotica for six weeks makes experimental subjects less aggressive. Men who watched such films as "Texas Chain Saw Massacre" were depressed and anxious at first, but repeated viewing on subsequent days brought them back to normal levels. They found the scenes less offensive the more they were exposed to them, and found violence to women less offensive, more humorous, and more enjoyable.

102. Robert W. Kubey, "Television Use in Everyday Life: Coping with Unstructured Time," *Journal of Communication*, Vol. 36, No. 3 (Summer 1986), pp. 108–23.

103. Cited by John Weisman, "Public Interest and Private Greed," *Columbia Journalism Review*, May/June 1990, p. 47.

104. Cedric Cullingford, *Children and Television*, New York: St. Martin's, 1984, pp. 136–37.

105. Nielsen reports they watch TV 29 hours a week; those between 2-1/2 and 5-1/2 are said to watch over 35 hours, and those 6 to 11 average 27 hours a week.

106. Marianne P. Winick and Charles Winick, *The Television Experience: What Children See*. Beverly Hills, Cal.: Sage, 1979.

107. J. Ronald Milavsky, Horst H. Stipp, Ronald C. Kessler, and William S. Rubens, *Television and Aggression: A Panel Study*. New York: Academic, 1983.

108. Jean Piaget, *The Child's Conception of the World*. New York: Harcourt Brace, 1929, p. 140.

109. Children aged 9–11 were less frightened by a scene from "The Wizard of Oz" when told to remember it wasn't real than when asked to imagine themselves in the heroine's place. But with 3–5 year olds, there was no difference in the reaction. Cf. Joanne Cantor, "Fright Responses to Mass Media Production," in Jennings Bryant and Dolf Zillmann, eds., *Responding to Television*. Hillsdale, N.J., Lawrence Erlbaum Associates, 1991.

110. Cf. Timothy P. Meyer, "Children's Perceptions of Justified/Unjustified and Fictional/Real Film Violence," *Journal of Broadcasting*, Vol. 17, No.3 (Summer 1973), pp. 321–32. Cf. also Jonathan L. Freedman, "Effect of Television Violence on Aggressiveness," *Psychological Bulletin*, Vol. 96, No. 2 (Sep. 1984), pp. 227–46. Children's antisocial behavior diminishes and their prosocial behavior increases when they perceive television programs to be realistic. (Byron Reeves, "Children's Perceived Reality of Television and the Effects of Pro- and Anti-Social TV Content on Social Behavior," paper delivered to the Association for Education in Journalism, 1977.) Personal experience with the subject matter of TV programming does not appear to change the child's perceptions of whether or not it is real.

111. The most influential analyses of this subject, directed by George Gerbner, have classified violence in cartoons (characters beating or otherwise assailing each other) just like violence in other forms. A former CBS public relations executive, Gene Mater, scoffed, "Do you look upon that as violence? I sure in hell don't." (*WSJ*, 10/19/76.) Another observer, in the same vein, comments: "Much of what children see on television passes them by. The more they see, the less likely it is that they will pay attention." (Cullingford, op. cit., p. 32). But the more they see, the more profound the effects may be. Indeed, children who watch a lot of television are less aroused (as measured by their skin conductance and blood volume pulse amplitude) by a violent film than light viewers, suggesting a "definite and measurable desensitization," comparable to what has been found among adults. (Victor B. Cline, Robert G. Croft, and Steven Courrier, "Desensitization of Children to Television Violence," *Journal of Personality and Social Psychology*, Vol. 27, No. 3 [September 1973], pp. 360–65.) Affirmation of the damage done by television violence is found in: The Committee on Social Issues, Group for the Advancement of Psychiatry, *The Child and Television Drama: The Psychosocial Impact of Cumulative Viewing*, New York: Mental Health Materials Center, 1982.

112. The question of media responsibility for individual acts of violence has been intensely debated for many years. It was a major focus of attention by the Presidential Commission on the Causes and Prevention of Violence. Cf. R.K. Baker and S.J. Ball, eds., *Violence and the Media*, Washington, D.C.: GPO, 1969. For a major series of studies on the effects of televised violence on children, cf. *Television and Growing Up: The Impact of Televised Violence*, Report to the Surgeon General from the Scientific Advisory Committee on Television and Social Behavior. Washington, D.C.: GPO, 1972.

113. David P. Phillips and John E. Hensley, "When Violence is Rewarded or Punished: The Impact of Mass Media Stories on Homicide," *Journal of Communication*, Vol. 34, No. 3 (Summer 1984), pp. 101–16. An attack on the statistical validity of the findings was met by a convincing rejoinder: James N. Baron and Peter C. Reiss, "Same Time, Next Year: Aggregate Analyses of the Mass Media and Violent Behavior," *American Sociological Review*, Vol. 50, No. 3 (June 1985), pp. 347–63. David P. Phillips and Kenneth A. Bollen, "Same Time, Last Year: Selective Data Dredging for Negative Findings," ibid., pp. 364–71. Cf. also David P. Phillips, "The Influence of Suggestion on Suicide: Substantive and Theoretical Implications of the Werther Effect," *American Sociological Review*, Vol. 39, No. 3 (June 1974), p. 340. This kind of epidemiological evidence has not been replicated in the psychological laboratory.

114. Barrie Gunter, "The Cathartic Potential of Television Drama," *Bulletin of the British Psychological Society*, Vol. 33 No. 48 (1980) pp. 448–50.

115. A more cautious look at the same body of research found "a consistent small positive correlation between viewing television violence and aggressiveness" but "little convincing evidence that in natural settings viewing television violence causes people to be more aggressive." (Lynette Friedrich-Cofer and Aletha C. Huston, "Television Violence and Aggression: The Debate Continues," *Psychological Bulletin*, Vol. 100, No. 3, (April 1983), pp. 364–71. Jonathan L. Freedman, "Television Violence and Aggression: A Rejoinder," ibid., pp. 372–38.)

116. Alan Wurtzel and Guy Lometi, "Researching Television Violence," in Arthur Asa Berger, ed., *Television in Society*. New Brunswick, N.J.: Transaction Books, 1987, pp. 117–132.

117. Steven H. Chaffee, George Gerbner, Beatrix A. Hamburg, Chester M. Pierce, Eli A. Rubinstein, Alberta E. Siegel, and Jerome L. Singer, "Defending the Indefensible," in Arthur Asa Berger, ed., ibid., pp. 133–142.

118. The association reaffirmed this position in 1992 through its Task Force on Television and Society. Leonard Eron, a task force member, reported to a congressional hearing on 200 studies of television violence conducted between 1970 and 1990 and reckoned that an elementary school graduate had seen 8,000 televised murders and over 100,000 other violent acts. The task force report is: Aletha C. Huston *et al.*, *Big World, Small Screen: The Role of Television in American Society*. Lincoln: University of Nebraska Press, 1992.

119. Congressman Edward Markey of Massachusetts suggested a blocking device that parents could use to cut automatically a child's access to appropriately labeled shows.

120. *NYT*, 7/7/93.

121. Cf. Dolf Zillmann, "Anatomy of Suspense," in Percy H. Tannenbaum, ed., *The Entertainment Functions of Television*. Hillsdale, N.J.: Lawrence Erlbaum Associates, 1980.

Chapter 7

1. In a 1978 Gallup poll, only 19% of Americans expressed disbelief in the Devil, while 8% had no opinion. In 1990, another Gallup poll showed that 72% believed in Heaven, but only 60% in Hell. Of those who believed in Heaven, 78% thought their chances of getting there were good or excellent.

2. NORC poll, reported in the *Columbia Journalism Review*, Sep./Oct. 1987.

3. In 1990, less than 20% of those old enough to vote in the primary elections did so. Among voters in the main election that year, 16% were under 30; they were 39% of the nonvoters.

4. At the height of the 1988 campaign, only two-thirds of the voters knew the name of the Democratic vice-presidential candidate (Senator Lloyd Bentsen). Three years after the 1984 election, 52% could not identify Geraldine Ferraro, the Democratic vice-presidential candidate. (1987 survey by Research and Forecasts.)

5. W. Russell Neuman, *The Paradox of Mass Politics*. Cambridge, Mass.: Harvard University Press, 1986.

6. When Edwin Meese's battle for confirmation as attorney general was a top news story, only 36% of the public knew why he had been in the news. (Michael Robinson and Maura Clancey, "Teflon Politics," *Public Opinion*, Vol. 7, No. 2 [Apr.-May 1984] pp. 14–18.)

7. In 1986, the National Assessment of Educational Progress found that more than two-thirds of 17 year olds could not identify the Reformation or Magna Carta or place the Civil War within the correct half-century. In 1983, 13% of the public knew that the United States was backing the insurgents in Nicaragua, while 7% thought it backed the Sandinista government, and the remainder acknowledged that they did not know. Four years later, 32% of the public correctly placed Nicaragua in Central or "Latin America"; 21% put it in South America, 15%

in other parts of the world; 32% did not know. (*New York Times*/CBS Poll, 7/18/87.) In May 1989, 21% of the public had not heard of NATO, and 40% of the remainder thought the Soviet Union was a member of NATO or weren't sure whether it was. (CBS/NYT poll.)

8. Six percent recall the average story without aid, 23% when aided. Twenty-two percent claim to recall it, but can give no substantiating details. (Study among 232 newscast viewers in the San Francisco Bay Area, in 1971.) W. Russell Neuman, "Patterns of Recall Among Television News Viewers," *Public Opinion Quarterly*, Vol. 40, No. 1 (Spring 1976), pp. 115–23.

9. In January 1990, approximately equal minorities (of between 12 and 16% each) selected as the story "followed most closely": "the political changes taking place in Czechoslovakia, Hungary and East Germany," "the crash of the Colombian airliner near Kennedy airport", "the suicide in Boston of Charles Stuart, who murdered his pregnant wife and blamed it on a black man," "the acquittal of the owners of [a] day care center who were charged with sexually abusing children," and "the legalization of banned black opposition groups in South Africa. (National poll by Times-Mirror.)

10. Cf. D. Charles Whitney and Ellen Wartella, "The Public As Dummies: Comments on American Ignorance," paper presented to the American Association for Public Opinion Research, 1987.

11. Cf. Leo Bogart, *Press and Public: Who Reads What When Where and Why in American Newspapers*. Hillsdale, N.J.: Lawrence Erlbaum Associates, 1989.

12. 11/21/85.

13. Quoted by Edward Jay Epstein, "The Selection of Reality," *The New Yorker*, 3/3/73, p. 41. Cf. also his *News from Nowhere*. New York: Random House, 1973.

14. *NYT*, 11/28/69.

15. Personal conversations.

16. *NYT*, 3/22/88.

17. The three network stations had a combined audience share of 52%, while movies on two other channels had a 28% share. These are average ratings. Many of the movie-watchers undoubtedly flipped over to catch up on the voting results during commercial breaks.

18. Martin Schram, *The Great American Video Game: Presidential Politics in the Television Age*. New York: William Morrow, 1987, 107.

19. *NYT* 10/20/88.

20. 1989 study by the Center for Media and Public Affairs.

21. *Broadcasting*, 5/15/77.

22. The length was the same for election news items and for all others in the same newscasts analyzed. Daniel Hallin, *Sound Bite News: Television Coverage of Elections, 1968–1988*. Washington, D.C.: Woodrow Wilson Center, 1991, p. 11.

23. Households headed by older people spend more time with television (2-1/2 times as much for those 65 and over as for young people 18–24), and they watch more news and issue-oriented programs. Households headed by college graduates watch less TV in general, but news represents a higher proportion of the programming they watch. There is no strong relationship between the educational level of the household head and the aggregate pattern of home viewing for news and other types of programs. (Arbitron analysis reported in *Television/Radio Age*, 3/3/86.)

24. That is, the ratio of the audience in the average minute to that of the cumulative total audience for a program is about the same for entertainment and news.

25. John R. Robinson and Mark R. Levy, *The Main Source: Learning from Television News*, Beverly Hills, Cal.: Sage, 1986.

26. According to Vincent Young, chairman of Young Broadcasting. Not surprisingly, 81% of the public would turn to the networks for coverage of a major story. And while 44% want

more network news, only 20% want more local news. (NBC survey in 1986.) Eighty-four percent prefer separate network and local newscasts. Naturally! That is the format with which they are familiar. A network affiliate typically spends half of its operating budget on news programs, which generate 12% of its revenues. (Between 35 and 40% of a station's revenue is earned between 4 and 8 p.m.) In New York, each of the three network-owned stations produces over $100 million in revenues per year. (Each rating point is worth between a $1 million and $1-1/2 million.) Only a third of independent stations make money on their own local news programs, while four out of five network affiliates do. (1986 survey of TV station news directors by Vernon Stone, reported in the *RTNDA Communicator*, May 1986.)

27. From an analysis of fifty-seven early evening local newscasts. (Raymond L. Carroll, "Market Size and TV News Values," *Journalism Quarterly*, Vol. 66, No. 1 [Spring 1989], p. 51.

28. *NYT*, 4/22/74.

29. Conrad Smith and Lee B. Becker, "Comparison of Journalistic Values of Television Reporters and Producers," *Journalism Quarterly*, Vol. 66, No. 4 (Winter 1989), pp. 793–800. Turnover is also higher than in print news organizations. The average TV station news director stays on the job for two and a half years. Among network-affiliate station managers in the top fifty markets, 44% feel that network news is of little or no importance to their stations. Among all the 101 station managers contacted in markets of all sizes, 26% gave this answer. (*Media Week*, 9/2/91.)

30. At their conventions, broadcast news directors could look at "remote-controlled cameras and fancy transmitters, cameras, relays, recorders, etc., etc., etc. It looked like a TV (and radio) newsman's idea of F.A.O. Schwarz on a Saturday afternoon." (Mark Monsky, "News vs. Entertainment—Do Local Directors Care," *Television Quarterly*, Vol. 16, No. 4 (Winter 1979–80), pp. 27–32.)

31. WVLA, the NBC affiliate in Baton Rouge, replaced its 11 p.m. newscast, which had a rating of 3, with a sitcom that got a 10. Larry Dietz, the station's operation director, commented, "With 'Mama's Family,' all we do is plug it into a tape machine. News involves much more." (*WSJ*, 5/22/91.) To put this all in perspective, the average independent station's net profit is 30% for VHF, 25% for UHF. News is 2% of an independent UHF station's budget, 9% of a VHF's.

32. *NYT*, 11/13/86.

33. *NYT*, 12/5/85.

34. Remarks at the Gannett Center for Media Studies, 4/28/87.

35. *NYT*, 2/20/89.

36. Cited by Jay Blumler in "The Future of Civic Information," (unpublished paper).

38. *Inside Media*, 6/23/93.

39. *Columbia Journalism Review*, Fall, 1964, p. 7.

40. Robert Stein, *Media Power: Who is shaping your picture of the World?* Boston: Houghton Mifflin, 1972.

41. Cf. Seymour Spilerman, "Structural Characteristics of Cities and the Severity of Racial Disorders," *American Sociological Review*, Vol. 41, No. 5 (Oct. 1976), p. 790. Word about disorders travels rapidly. In spite of a self-imposed media blackout on news of the Detroit riots on July 23, 1967, 58% of the whites and 69% of the blacks claimed to have heard about them that same day. (S. R. Levy, "Communications During the Detroit Riot," *Journalism Quarterly*, Vol. 48 [Summer 1971], pp. 339–343.)

42. Television coverage of the Iranian hostage crisis, David Altheide concluded, reflected "criteria of production formats involving resolutions of practical concerns like accessibility, visual quality, drama and action, audience relevance and encapsulation and thematic unity." ("Impact of Format and Ideology on TV News Coverage of Iran," *Journalism Quarterly*, Vol. 62, No. 2 (Summer 1985), pp. 346–51.

43. *Electronic Media*, 10/21/85.

44. Michael J. Arlen, "Politics from the Rectangle," *The New Yorker*, 10/25/76.

45. A 1977 Trendex survey found that 82% of the public agreed that "I enjoy seeing the people who give the news, sports and weather on local newscasts."

46. Daniel Schorr, " 'Network' News," *Rolling Stone*, 12/16/76.

47. Robinson and Levy, op. cit.

48. *Washington Post*, 7/27/78.

49. *NYT*, 8/4/83 and 8/6/83.

50. *NYT* 8/11/83.

51. Cited by Norman Solomon in an op-ed piece in the *NYT*, 5/14/91.

52. Caryl Rivers, "It's Tough to Tell a Hawk From 'Lonesome Dove' ", *WSJ*, 2/10/91.

53. *NYT*, 1/19/91.

54. The networks proposed a change in the format of the presidential debates, with direct confrontation of the candidates for 90 minutes, rather than questions and answers by the press. After intense negotiation with both parties, and with H. Ross Perot's candidacy complicating matters, several different debating formats were adopted.

55. Thomas E. Patterson, *Out of Order*. New York: Knopf, 1993.

56. *NYT*, 7/16/85.

57. Schram, op. cit., p. 59.

58. Richard West, "Royal Family Thais," *New York Review of Books*, 1/30/92.

59. Robert Thompson, *No Exit from Vietnam*, New York: David McKay, 1969, p. 9.

60. Lee M. Mandell and Donald L. Shaw, "Judging People in the News—Unconsciously: Effect of Camera Angle and Bodily Activity," *Journal of Broadcasting*, Vol. 17, No. 3 (Summer 1973), pp. 353–62.

61. Kurt and Gladys Engel Lang, "The Unique Perspective of Television and its Effects: A Pilot Study," *American Sociological Review*, Vol. 18 (1953), pp. 3–12.

62. Allan Rachlin, *News as Hegemonic Reality: American Political Culture and the Framing of News Accounts*. New York: Praeger, 1988, p. 68.

63. The officer was Colonel Gaines Hawkins. (David Zucchino, "Outtakes for the Defense," *Washington Journalism Review*, Jan. 1985, pp. 41–44.)

64. In the Little Rock disturbances of September 1957, CBS News crews got anti-integration demonstrators to stage actions that had actually taken place earlier when no cameras were present. (Sig Mickelson, *The Electric Mirror: Politics in an Age of Television*, New York: Dodd Mead, 1972, p. 41.) In 1966, CBS helped finance an armed invasion of Haiti (eventually aborted by U.S. Customs) in exchange for exclusive news coverage rights. Testimony before a subcommittee of the House Commerce Committee in the early 1970s cited a number of episodes of faking by TV correspondents. A young man was hired to buy dynamite to show how easily it could be done. A police cruiser was sent on an "emergency run." Actors were posed as gamblers at Las Vegas. Preserved specimens were placed on a California beach to illustrate "dead sea life" for a feature on water pollution. (*NYT*, 10/6/72).

65. In a panel discussion, 1990, at the Radio-Television Executives Society.

66. *NYT*, 2/10/82.

67. *NYT*, 11/26/89.

68. *NYT*, 12/17/89.

69. The film merely reenforced existing public suspicions. Months before its release, a survey showed that a majority of the public thought there had been a conspiracy to murder President Kennedy, and only 19% believed the Warren Commission report.

70. *NYT*, 2/4/85.

71. *NYT*, 11/21/89.

72. *NYT*, 7/27/89.

73. After Gartner's departure, NBC shifted responsibility for its "I Witness Video," which specialized in lurid footage, from its news to its entertainment division. (*NYT*, 3/4/93.)

74. Columbia Journalism School gathering in Nov. 1989.

75. *NYT*, 2/4/85.

76. *NYT*, 11/25/80.

77. More (18%) called it news than entertainment (14%). (Gallup poll for Times-Mirror in 1989.)

78. *New York*, 10/30/1989.

79. Peter Conrad, *Television: The Medium and Its Manners*. Boston: Routledge and Kegan Paul, 1982, p. 42.

80. *NYT*, 5/6/89.

81. Isaac Clark Pray, *Memoirs of James Gordon Bennett and His Times*, New York: Stringer and Townsend 1855, 363–64.

82. Cited by Jason Rogers, *Building Newspaper Advertising*. New York: Harper, 1919, 24.

83. Sunday, when people have more time, remains a strong day for newspapers; it accounts for a growing percentage of advertising, and readership has now passed the daily level. Even so, Sunday circulation has not grown as fast as the number of people or households.

84. In 1992, there were 994 evening papers and 596 morning papers (compared, respectively, with 1,459 and 312 in 1960.) Evening circulation in 1992 was 17.7 million; morning, 42.3 million.

85. Examples: the *Orange County Register*, the *Contra Costa Times*, Long Island *Newsday*, and the Bergen *Record*.

86. John Busterna, "National Advertising Pricing Conduct: Chain versus Independent Newspapers," *Journalism Quarterly*, Vol. 65 (1988), p. 305.

87. Cited in Irving Louis Horowitz, *Communicating Ideas: The Crisis of Publishing in a Post-Industrial Society*. New York: Oxford University Press, 1986, p. 50.

88. John Hohenberg, *The News Media: A Journalist Looks at His Profession*, New York: Holt, Rinehart and Winston, 1969, p. 92.

89. Cf. Warren Breed, "Social Control in the Newsroom: A Functional Analysis," *Social Forces*, Vol. 23 (May 1955), pp. 326–35.

90. Maxwell E. McCombs, "Effects of Monopoly in Cleveland on Diversity of Newspaper Content," *Journalism Quarterly*, Vol. 64 (Winter 1987), pp. 740–92.

91. Richard K. Schwarzlose, "The Future of News: The Wire Services", paper presented to the Woodrow Wilson Center Conference on The Future of News, 1989.

92. Cf. Jerome Barron, *Freedom of the Press for Whom?: The Right of Access to Mass Media*. Bloomington, Ind., Indiana University Press, 1973.

Chapter 8

1. George Orwell, *Nineteen Eighty Four*. New York: New American Library, 1981, p. 36.

2. Cited by Voice of America correspondent Alan Pessin, in the *Gannett Center Journal*, Fall 1989.

3. A. R. Butz, *The Hoax of the Twentieth Century*. Torrance, Cal.: Institute for Historical Review, 1976.

4. Robert Muchembled describes how spoken words can blend fantasy, history, and current events, in his account of an evening gathering in a seventeenth-century French village: "A story teller, more often than not a woman, would make spines tingle as she retold terrifying legends or stories revolving around werewolves, witches, monsters, and so forth. . . . Such evenings undoubtedly rekindled everyone's memory (even the young men's) of identical tales told by their own mothers when they were small. The company probably returned to these

themes before and after the taletelling, repeating the proverbs and advice of popular lore, commenting on events, propitious or disastrous, in the village and elsewhere, and exchanging family news and reviewing the local chronicle of gossip and scandal." (Robert Muchembled, *Popular Culture and Elite Culture in France, 1400–1750*. Baton Rouge La.: Louisiana State University Press, 1985, pp. 69–70.)

5. Bruno Bettelheim, *The Uses of Enchantment: The Meaning and Importance of Fairy Tales*. New York: Vintage, 1977, p. 60.

6. "After the age of approximately five—the age when fairy tales become truly meaningful—no normal child takes these stories as true to external reality. . . . Stories which stay closer to reality by starting in a child's living room or backyard, instead of in a poor woodcutter's hut hard by a great forest; and which have people in them very much like the child's parents, not starving woodcutters or kings and queens; but which mix these realistic elements with wish fulfilling and fantastic devices, are apt to confuse the child as to what is real and what is not." (Bettelheim, op. cit. p. 64.)

7. Women who watched a highly emotional film of a therapy session for abused women responded similarly whether they thought the session was real or staged, while men responded much more strongly when they thought the scene was real. (Study by David Ross and John Condry, *APA Monitor*, Nov. 1985, p. 35.)

8. Tyrone Guthrie, "Do We Go to the Theater for Illusion?" *NYT*, 1/16/66.

9. Eric A. Havelock, "The Alphabetization of Homer," in Eric A. Havelock and Jackson B. Hershbell, eds., *Communication Arts in the Ancient World*. New York: Hastings House, 1978, p. 16. Eric A. Havelock, *The Literate Revolution in Greece and its Cultural Consequences*. Princeton, N.J.: Princeton University Press, 1982, pp. 264–65.

10. In 1989.

11. Hayden White, *Tropics of Discourse: Essays in Cultural Criticism*. Baltimore: Johns Hopkins University Press, 1978, p. 125.

12. Thucydides, *The Peloponnesian War*. New York: Penguin, 1954, p. 48. "It is better evidence than that of the poets, who exaggerate the importance of their themes, or of the prose chroniclers, who are less interested in telling the truth than in catching the attention of the public, whose authorities cannot be checked, and whose subject matter, owing to the passage of time, is mostly lost in the unreliable streams of mythology." (Ibid., p. 47.)

13. Quoted by Joseph Kraft in "The Imperial Media," *Commentary*, May 1981, pp. 36–47. Journalism was a plebeian occupation, Kraft observes.

14. Feb. 1993.

15. *NYT*, 7/3/89.

16. Harold C. Schonberg: "Most recordings, ever since the introduction of magnetic tape are dishonest in that the majority are collages rather than interpretations. All recordings, except those made from live performances, are the results of many takes. Wrong notes are corrected and spliced in. Voices are boosted to the point where a pipsqueak soprano can sound like Nilsson. Pianists can repeat a passage until their fingerwork on the disk is as impeccable as Rachmaninoff's. . . . The artificial recordings of today, made under artificial conditions, are conditioning music lovers to a set of unreal conditions. The medium itself becomes the real thing. The real thing becomes an imitation." (*NYT*, 9/22/68.)

17. In his Preface to William Wordsworth and Samuel Taylor Coleridge, *Lyrical Ballads*. Oxford, N.Y.: Woodstock Books, 1990.

Chapter 9

1. Robert F. Bornstein, "Exposure and Affect: Overview and Meta-Analysis of Research, 1968–1987," *Psychological Bulletin*, Vol. 106, No. 2 (March 1989), p. 267.

2. In a 1980 experiment by William Kunst-Wilson, in collaboration with Robert Zajonc at the University of Michigan Institute for Social Research.

3. Vernon R. Padgett and Timothy C. Brock, "Do Advertising Messages Require Intelligible Content? A Cognitive Response Analysis of Unintelligble Persuasive Messages," in Sidney Hecker and David W. Stewart, eds., *Non-Verbal Communication in Advertising.* Lexington, Mass.: Lexington Books, 1988, pp. 185–203.

4. Lawrence Levine argues that he was. (*Highbrow/Lowbrow: The Emergence of Cultural Hierarchy in America.* Cambridge Mass.: Harvard University Press, 1988.)

5. Quoted by Lawrence Levine, ibid., p. 230. Levine reports that "highbrow" was first used in the 1880s, lowbrow in 1900. (p. 221). The notion of a cultural hierarchy, he argues, developed in the nineteenth century, and replaced a public culture that was widely shared by all classes of society, and was "less hierarchically organized, less fragmented into relatively rigid adjectival boxes than their descendants were to experience a century later." (p. 9). Levine points out that "a film like D.W. Griffith's *Birth of a Nation,* which was popular or lowbrow culture when it was released in 1915, is transformed into high culture when time renders its 'language' – its acting styles, technology, kinetics – archaic and thus less familiar and accessible to the masses." (p. 234.) (Of course, innumerable films produced by contemporaries of Griffith have moved into oblivion, although their styles are just as archaic and inaccessible.) Similarly, and more recently, such vernacular expressions as comic strips have been transformed (with the help of Roy Lichtenstein and other pop artists) into what is, for the moment at least, accepted as high art.

6. I.C. Jarvie. *Movies and Society.* New York: Basic Books, 1970, p. 184.

7. *Inside Media,* 8/6/91.

8. 1988 survey by Frank Magid Associates for *Channels* Magazine.

9. Television Audience Assessment survey. A fourth of viewers report that they switch to another show within a half-hour of viewing, and only 10% of this group return to the original program. (Frank Magid Survey, 1988.) Those who change channels indicate that they are looking for something more enjoyable rather than trying to avoid commercials. Altogether, 58% want a different program; only 22% are fleeing commercials.

10. The Lichters and Rothman, who analyzed a sample of 620 prime-time network shows aired between 1955 and 1986, note that "there have been so-called seasons of rebellion, seasons of the younger generation, seasons of rekindled warmth, etc. . . . [Actually,] the television family has been a fairly stable institution. Its cast of characters and their familial relationships may change, but the basic distribution of power and wisdom remains unaffected." (S. Robert Lichter, Linda S. Lichter, and Stanley Rothman, *Watching America.* New York: Simon and Schuster, 1991, p. 103.)

11. Another 18% were created to exploit the appeal of an established star; 10% were adapted from films, and another 6% were inspired by films. Although only 3% were "spinoffs" from existing shows, these had by far the greatest rate of success; programs derived from films, cartoons, books, plays, and radio programs had the lowest. (*Media Matters,* 2/88.)

12. *NYT,* 9/22/91.

13. *NYT,* 2/26/89.

14. *NYT,* 6/11/73.

15. *WSJ,* 6/19/91.

16. Fredric Dannen, *Hit Men: Power Brokers and Fast Money Inside the Music Business.* New York: Random House, 1990.

17. *NYT,* 7/26/91.

18. Personal interview.

19. *Advertising Age,* 2/13/89.

20. Lawrence Levine, op. cit., p. 165.

21. Ibid., p. 217.

22. Ethan Mordden points out that "before radio, performers had theatres to fill; naturally, the gestures were large. Radio was intimate. The audience sat not across an orchestra pit and up in balconies but, in effect, a few feet away from the microphone. Radio mellowed the American singing voice. Men who would have been inaudible beyond Row F could be heard from coast to coast. . . . So pervasive was radio's euphony that even show tunes became just that: *tunes*, songs without a story." (Ethan Mordden, " 'Show Boat' Crosses Over," *The New Yorker*, 7/3/89, pp. 79–94)

23. In director Spike Lee's "Do the Right Thing", a film introduced at a time of racial turbulence in 1989, a character named Radio Raheem meets his death because he insists on playing his boom box at maximum volume in a restaurant whose proprietor, understandably, objects.

24. T.W. Adorno, "On Popular Music", *Studies in Philosophy and Social Science*, Vol. 9 (1941), p. 74.

25. "The customers of musical entertainment are themselves objects, or indeed, products of the same mechanisms which determine the production of popular music. Their spare time serves only to reproduce their working capacity. It is a means instead of an end." (Ibid., p. 79.) "Not even the most gullible individuals believe that eventually everybody will win the sweepstakes. The actual function of sentimental music lies rather in the temporary release given to the awareness that one has missed fulfillment." (Ibid., p. 80.)

26. "A Theory of Popular Culture," in Bernard Rosenberg and David Manning White, eds., *Mass Culture: The Popular Arts in America*. Glencoe, Ill.: Free Press, 1957, p. 60.

27. Raymond Williams, *Culture and Society, 1780–1950*, New York: Columbia University Press, 1958, p. 305.

28. Ibid., pp. 303–4.

29. *Videa 1000*.

30. Norman Lear, "Does Television Have the Courage to Pioneer a New Commercial Ethic?" *Television Quarterly*, Vol. 21, No. 4 (1985), pp. 7–14.

31. *NYT*, 4/15/79.

32. Overheard locker-room conversation.

33. *Electronic Media* 8/2/93.

34. Stanley Rothman and Robert Lichter, "What Are Movie Makers Made Of?" *Public Opinion*, Dec./Jan. 1984, pp. 14–18.

35. *Inside Media*, 2/17/93.

36. *TV Guide*, 8/22/92.

37. Mark Christensen and Cameron Stauth, *The Sweeps: Behind the Scenes in Network TV*, New York: William Morrow, 1984, p. 49.

38. On ABC's "Good Morning America," 11/14/83.

39. Christensen and Stauth, op. cit., p. 41.

40. Quoted by Jay G. Blumler and Carolyn Martin Spicer, "Creative Prospects and Threats in the New Television Marketplace: The Voice of the Program Maker," paper presented to the American Film Institute, 1989.

41. Ben Stein, *The View from Sunset Boulevard: America as Brought to You by the People who Make Television*. New York: Basic Books, 1979, pp. 274–5.

42. Julie Salamon, *The Devil's Candy: The Bonfire of the Vanities Goes to Hollywood*. Boston: Houghton Mifflin, 1991, p. 312.

43. Quoted by Stein, Ibid., 93.

44. Alexandra Ripley, *Scarlett*, New York: Warner Books, 1991.

45. Patricia Storace, "Look Away, Dixie Land," *New York Review of Books*, 12/19/91.

46. *NYT*, 3/4/91.

47. Kenneth C. David, *Two Bit Culture: The Paperbacking of America*. Boston: Houghton Mifflin, 1984, p. 86.

48. Cited by David, p. 129.

49. *NYT*, 12/29/83.

50. Personal interview.

51. Robert C. Allen, *Speaking of Soap Operas*. Chapel Hill: University of North Carolina Press, 1985, p. 45.

52. David H. Weaver and G. Cleveland Wilhoit, *The American Journalist: A Portrait of U.S. News People and Their Work*. Bloomington, Ind.: Indiana University Press, 1991.

53. Lichter, Lichter, and Rothman, op. cit.

54. Still, the public disagrees overwhelmingly (67%–16%) with the statement that "the people who run commercial television have my best interests at heart." (The answers are almost identical when they are asked about public television.)

55. Edmund Snow Carpenter, *Eskimo Realities*, New York: Holt Rinehart and Winston, 1973, p. 59.

56. In *The Defense of Poetry*, 1821.

57. Cf. Richard Hofstadter, *Anti-Intellectualism in American Life*. New York: Knopf, 1963, p. 234: "The values of business and intellect" have long been "seen as eternally and inevitably at odds: on the one side, there is the money-centered or power-centered man, who cares only about bigness and the dollar, about boosting and hollow optimism; on the other side, there are the men of critical intellect, who distrust American civilization and concern themselves with quality and moral values."

58. Cf. George Orwell, *Keep the Aspidistra Flying*. London: Secker and Warburg, 1987.

59. Larry Dobrow, *When Advertising Works Harder*. New York: Friendly Press, 1964, p. 92.

60. Andy Warhol, *The Philosophy of Andy Warhol (From A to B and Back Again)*. New York: Harcourt Brace Jovanovich, 1975, p. 4.

61. Cited by Bruce Bendinger, *The Copy Workshop Workbook*. Chicago: The Copy Workshop, 1988, p. 27.

62. *It Only Hurts When I Laugh*. New York: Times Books, 1988, p. 175.

63. Personal interview.

64. Ibid., p. 21.

65. Dwight MacDonald, "Notes on Selling Out," *Grand Street*, Vol. 2, No. 1 (Autumn 1982), p. 167.

66. My translation of manuscript in New York Public Library.

67. In *Poetry*, 1914.

68. In *Tonio Kroeger*, quoted by Janet Wolff, *The Social Production of Art*. New York: St. Martins Press, 1981.

69. Quoted by Richard M. Clurman, *Beyond Malice*. New Brunswick N.J.: Transaction Books, 1988), p. 87.

70. *NYT*, 2/2/88.

71. Lewis A. Coser, Charles Kadushin, and Walter W. Powell, *Books: The Culture and Commerce of Publishing*, New York: Basic Books, 1982.

72. Cited by Blumler and Spicer, op. cit.

73. Ibid.

74. Pat McGilligan, ed., *Backstory 2: Interviews with Screenwriters of the 1940s and 1950s*. Berkeley, Cal.: University of California Press, 1991.

75. *NYT*, 10/4/89.

76. Stein, op. cit., p. 13.

77. Ibid., 26.

78. Lyall H. Powers, ed. *Henry James and Edith Wharton: Letters 1900–1915*. New York: Scribner's, 1990.

79. 4/15/83. Quoted in the *Economist*, 5/2/92.

80. Igor Stravinsky, with Robert Craft, *Themes and Episodes*. New York: Alfred A. Knopf, 1966, p. 91. According to the economist William Baumol, Stravinsky was in error. Mozart had a conventional funeral and earned a decent living throughout his short life.

81. Cited in a letter by Walter Berns to *Commentary*, Feb. 1990, p. 13.

82. John Updike, "The Artist and His Audience," *New York Review of Books*, 7/18/85, pp. 14–18.

83. George Gissing, *New Grub Street*. New York: Modern Library, 1985, pp. 379–80.

84. Ibid., p. 8.

84. Ibid., p. 12.

Chapter 10

1. Raymonde Moulin, *The French Art Market: A Sociological View*. New Brunswick, N.J.: Rutgers University Press, 1987, p. 1.

2. At first, dealing in works of art was regarded as a debasement of the works: The Accademia di San Luca complained that "It is serious, lamentable, indeed intolerable to everybody to see works destined for the decoration of Sacred Temples or the splendour of noble palaces, exhibited in shops or in the streets like cheap goods for sale." (Quoted in Francis Haskell, *Patrons and Painters: Art and Society in Baroque Italy*. New York: Harper and Row, 1971, p. 121.)

3. Though the cost of a manuscript book was high, those who produced them were not too well-compensated when one considers the amount of labor required to produce a typical volume. In 1480 a manuscript scribe got 46 ducats for a book, an illuminator 27; by way of comparison, a horse cost 12 ducats. (The labor required to produce a book obviously depended upon its nature. Thomas a Kempis took twelve years to copy a multivolume folio *Bible* for his monastery, at the rate of fourteen or fifteen two-sided leaves a month, while a less eminent and dedicated scribe might knock out sixteen sides of a minor manuscript in a day. Roger Wick of the Morgan Library provides this estimate, and comments that a Book of Hours cost the same as the repair of a roof.)

4. John P. Feather and David McKitterick, *The History of Books and Libraries: Two Views*. Washington, D.C.: Library of Congress, 1986, p. 6.

5. Peter Burke, *Popular Culture in Early Modern Europe*. New York: Harper and Row, 1978, p. 250.

6. Leo Lowenthal, *Literature and Mass Culture*. New Brunswick, N.J.: Transaction Books, 1984, p. 101.

7. Raymond Williams explains that, under the system of patronage, writers had personal relationships with patrons and their friends, even though they were dependent and subject to "patronal caprice." The market may have improved their social position, but it still left them open to fluctuating tastes, which were now impersonal. (Raymond Williams *Culture and Society*, New York: Columbia University Press, 1958, pp. 32–33).

8. Eric A. Havelock, *The Literate Revolution in Greece and Its Cultural Consequences*. Princeton, N.J.: Princeton University Press, 1982, p. 265

9. By the critic I.A. Richards, for one.

10. There was boxing on Crete in 1,160 BC. At Olympia, besides athletic competition, there was poetry and music, contests in flute playing and singing to the accompaniment of a stringed instrument. Plato called musicians "athletes"—contestants for a prize—and "Greek

athletics had prizes at their heart." The classicist John Humphrey writes that "Ball games were 'play' to the Greeks, what we originally meant by 'sport'—diversion and recreation." (John Humphrey, "Roman Games," in Michael Grant and Rachel Kitzinger, eds., *Civilization of the Ancient Mediterranean: Greece and Rome*. New York: Scribner's, 1988, 1133, 1140.) At Athens victors could win large jars of olive oil, which were valuable in the export market. Musicians' prizes were even more valuable. (David C. Young, "Athletics," in ibid., pp. 1131–42.)

11. Havelock, op. cit., p. 266.

12. Robert Muchembled, *Popular Culture and Elite Culture in France 1400–1750*. Baton Rouge: Louisiana State University Press, 1985, pp. 150–51.

13. W.J. Henderson, *Some Forerunners of Italian Opera*. New York: Henry Holt & Co., 1911, p. 19.

14. John Stevens, *Music and Poetry in the Early Tudor Court*. Cambridge, U.K.: Cambridge University Press, 1961. p. 299.

15. Stanley Sadie, *History of Opera*. Houndmills, England: MacMillan, 1989, p. 553.

16. "Michael D. Bristol, *Carnival and Theater: Plebeian Culture and the Structure of Authority in Renaissance England*. New York: Methuen, 1985 p. 112.

17. Allardyce Nicoll, *Stuart Masques and the Renaissance Stage*. New York: Harcourt Brace, 1938.

18. Burke, *op. cit., p. 249.*

19. Lawrence Levine, Highbrow/Lowbrow: The Emergence of Cultural Hierarchy in America. Cambridge, Mass.: Harvard University Press, 1988, p. 79.

20. For example: Lee Rich, Marvin Antonowsky, Harvey Shepherd, Steve Sohmer, Grant Tinker.

21. Quoted by Roger Cohen, "Rupert Murdoch's Biggest Gamble," *NYT Magazine*, 10/21/90, p. 31.

22. *NYT*, 1/26/92.

23. Mary Ellen Schoonmaker, "Has the Alternative Press Gone Yuppie?" *Columbia Journalism Review*, Nov./Dec. 1987, p. 60.

24. Time Warner's chairman, Steven Ross, routinely used a company helicopter to fly to his weekend home. Ross's compensation in 1990 — not a very good year in the media business — was $78.3 million, considerably more than the combined salaries of those dismissed by his company in a single cost-cutting move the following year. (*NYT*, 7/15/91.) When Graef Crystal, a specialist in executive compensation, evaluated Ross's take at $39 million, the editors at *Fortune* were under such pressure that Crystal reported a "major reaction" and resigned from the roster of contributors. (*WSJ*, 6/26/91.)

25. *NYT Magazine*, 10/21/90, p. 31.

26. Carolyn Hinsey, "Eight Months Before the Masthead," *New York*, 2/10/92, p. 33.

27. *WSJ*, 9/13/91.

28. *NYT*, 6/23/92.

29. As an example, cf. Harold Evans, *Good Times, Bad Times*. London: Weidenfeld and Nicolson, 1983.

30. Allen H. Neuharth, *Confessions of an S.O.B.*, New York: Doubleday, 1989.

31. Personal conversation.

32. Personal interview.

33. Norman Podhoretz, *Making It*, New York: Random House, 1968.

34. *NYT*, 11/6/89. The Newhouse brothers (whose newspaper empire was built by their father) bought Random House from RCA for $70 million in 1980. Random House already encompassed such formerly independent imprints as Alfred A. Knopf, Pantheon, Times Books, Villard, Vintage, Clarkson N. Potter, Harmony, Del Rey, and Ivy. Ten years later the company was worth over a billion, having acquired Crown, Times Books, Fodor travel

guides, Fawcett, Schocken, and British publishers Chatto and Windus, Bodley Head, Century
Hutchinson, and Jonathan Cape. (Random House already owned Knopf, Vintage, Ballantine,
and Ballard.)

35. *NYT*, 3/19/90.

36. Address to the Manhattan Institute, 11/8/89.

37. *The Economist*, 9/26/87.

38. Personal interview.

39. According to several informants of Richard Clurman, *To the End of Time: The
Seduction and Conquest of a Media Empire*. New York: Simon and Schuster, 1992.

40. Personal interview.

41. Personal interview.

42. Ian Hamilton, *Writers in Hollywood, 1915–51*. London: Heinemann, 1990.

43. *NYT*, 10/12/75

44. Tom Dunkel, "Big Bucks, Tough Tactics," *NYT Magazine*, 9/17/89, p. 80.

45. *NYT*, 4/20/78.

46. Quoted by Jay G. Blumler and Carolyn Martin, Spicer, "Creative Prospects and
Threats in the New Television Marketplace: The Voice of the Program-Maker," paper
presented to a forum of the American Film Institute, at the Annenberg School, USC, 11/14/89,
p. 1.

47. Ibid., p. 2.

48. Ibid., p. 35.

49. Horace Newcomb and Robert S. Alley, *The Producer's Medium: Conversations with
Creators of American TV*. New York: Oxford University Press, 1983, p. 189.

50. Quoted by Ken Auletta, "What Won't They Do?" *The New Yorker* 5/17/93.

51. Cf. Bernard Berelson, "The Great Debate Over Cultural Democracy," *Public Opinion
Quarterly*, in Donald N. Barrett, ed., *Values in America*. Notre Dame, Ind., University of
Notre Dame Press, 1961.

52. Quoted by Kenneth C. David, *Two-Bit Culture: The Paperbacking of America*, Boston:
Houghton Mifflin, 1984, p. 224.

53. Quoted in *World Press Review*, Sep. 1984, p. 34.

54. Quoted in a 1958 *Fortune* article cited by Clurman, op. cit.

55. Erik Barnouw, *The Sponsor: Notes on a Modern Potentate*. New York: Oxford
University Press, 1978, p. 123.

56. R. E. Silvey, "Giving the Public What It Wants," *Contemporary Review*, May 1961.

Chapter 11

1. Curiously, this variation of nearly 50% has been characterized as "remarkably stable."
Cf. William C. Wood and Sharon L. O'Hare, "Paying for the Video Revolution: Consumer
Spending on the Mass Media." *Journal of Communication*, Vol. 41, No. 1 (Winter 1991), pp.
24–30.

2. Consumer spending went from $10.8 billion to $83.7 billion; advertising in these media
grew by 512%, from $12.7 to $84 billion.

3. Nine percent said "fairly likely." (Gallup poll.)

4. It varied by location; it was 71% in New England and 47% in metropolitan Chicago. Of
the 82 million homes passed by cable 50 million actually subscribed, and the first to subscribe
were the heavy viewers: Cable households viewed 55.8 hours a week; noncable households,
42.1 hours.

5. Time Warner's HBO had 17.6 million subscribers, Cinemax (also owned by Time
Warner) had another 6.3 million. Because pay cable subscriptions were not growing, Time

Warner planned to add two additional channels to each system, giving subscribers added choices. (*NYT*, 5/9/91.)

6. In 1990, the cable networks spent about $700 million on original programming production, over half of their total $1.28 billion programming expense. By contrast, the three major television networks spent $5.6 billion for programming of all kinds, including film rights, while local stations spent $2 billion for syndicated programming, making a $7-1/2 billion market. (The cable market for syndicated programs now equals that of on-air stations.) Barter was a billion dollar business in 1990, with the top twenty-five syndicated programs averaging a 7 rating.

7. Carnegie Commission on Educational Television, *Public Television: A Program for Action*. New York: Harper and Row, 1967.

8. In 1970, print media, including books, represented 52% of the advertising allocations in media that consumers support at least in part. (Remember, this category excludes the advertising-only media.) By 1992, print's share of the advertising increased only slightly, from 52% to 55%.

9. They went from went from 0.9% in 1967 to 0.54% in 1989. The census compilation does not itemize books.

10. The economics of publishing are much different for a daily publication than for a bimonthly.

11. Cf. Leo Bogart, *Press and Public: Who Reads What Where When and Why in American Newspapers*. Hillsdale, N.J.: Lawrence Erlbaum Associates, 1989.

12. All of the 15,000 feature films produced in the U.S. between 1915 and 1960 represent approximately 22,500 viewing hours. (David Bordwell, Janet Staiger, and Kristin Thompson, *The Classical Hollywood Cinema: Film Style and Mode of Production to 1960*. New York: Columbia University Press, 1985, p. 10). This figure has probably more than doubled in the past thirty-four years.

13. My estimates. The remainder goes to sports, game shows, and informational programming. Feature-length movies were 9% of the total 41 hours of TV tuning per household in 1960, 13% of the 54 hours in 1986. Between 6 and 11 p.m. for one week in 1990, feature films represented 16% of on-air programming time on New York stations and 36% of cable time. In all other day parts they were 8% and 31%. With more films competing for the same viewers, their individual average audience shares declined at the same time that their aggregate audience increased.

14. Cartoons emerged from the ancient practice of political caricature, extended to constitute pungent commentary on familiar social types as well as on well-known public figures. Comic strips shifted the technique into a regular Sunday version of the children's illustrated chapbook, which had flourished earlier in the nineteenth century.

15. Twenty-one percent of the adult public in 1987, compared with 14% in 1955. (Gallup polls.) Eighty six percent read a book or magazine in the course of a year. Nicholas Zill and Marianne Zinglee, "Literature Reading in the United States: Data from National Surveys and Their Policy Implications," *Book Research Quarterly*, Vol. 5., No. 1 (Spring 1989), p. 24.

16. It is also apparently highly forgettable. Of the 40% of the public who said they had read one or more novels in the last year, nearly a fourth could not name a work or author. Thirty percent named light popular fiction; 10% a classic work; 17% a contemporary work of some literary merit. (Altogether, 11% of the total adult population had read a good book, and 7% a contemporary good book.) Romance novels, a $750 million market with 1,500 titles a year, account for 46% of mass paperback sales. (*NYT*, 8/23/93.) A study of arts participation in 1983–84 found that the 17% of novel-readers who had read a contemporary work of literary merit worked out to 7% of the public; another 1% had read contemporary poetry. Twenty percent had read a short story and could describe it in some way, 6% had read poems of literary

merit. (John P. Robinson, *Americans' Participation in the Arts: A 1983–84 Arts-Related Trend Study*. College Park, Md.: University of Maryland Survey Research Center, 1986.)

17. Quoted by Lawrence Levine, *Highbrow/Lowbrow: The Emergence of Cultural Hierarchy in America*. Cambridge, Mass.: Harvard University Press, 1988, p. 103.

18. John Izod, *Hollywood and the Box Office, 1895–1986*. London: MacMillan, 1988.

19. *Movies: A Psychological Study*. Glencoe, Ill.: Free Press, 1950.

20. *Hollywood: The Dream Factory: An Anthropologist Looks at the Movies*. Boston: Little, Brown, 1950.

21. Neal Gabler, *An Empire of Their Own: How the Jews Invented Hollywood*. New York: Crown, 1988, p. 189.

22. This exemplifies the economist Jean-Baptiste Say's theorem that supply creates its own demand.

23. Personal interview.

24. A. C. Nielsen data.

25. Opinion Research Corporation survey, 1985.

26. Newspaper Advertising Bureau survey, 1981. Cf. Leo Bogart, "The Return of Hollywood's Mass Audience" in Hubert O'Gorman, ed., *Surveying Social Life*, Middletown, Ct.: Wesleyan University Press, 1988.

27. Film buffs watch movies on TV more often too, but they prefer to go out to see a new movie rather than to watch it on TV.

28. In 1985, under complicated financing arrangements, Rupert Murdoch purchased 20th Century-Fox, and Ted Turner bought MGM.

29. *Media Matters*, 2/88.

30. The remainder goes to regular movies. In 1993, Time Warner's HBO was a $1.5 billion business with 17 million subscriber homes at an average monthly fee of $10.

31. In 1993, videocassettes of a film were generally available about six months after its theatrical release; release on pay-per-view television followed shortly. Ordinary showings on pay TV channels like HBO came a year after theatrical release, and release on broadcast television another year later.

32. Data from MPAA and Video Software Dealers Association. A film that earned $30 million from worldwide theatrical showings earned another $20 million from television and cable and $30 million from video, according to David Londoner, of Wertheim Schroder.

33. The videocassette release of "E.T.: The Extraterrestrial" sold 14.5 million units at a list price of $24.95. Sales prices were steadily lowered in a successful effort to make ownership attractive, relative to rentals.

34. Wilkofsky Gruen Associates and Paul Kagan Associates estimates.

35. Personal interview.

36. *NYT*, 3/7/88.

37. According to Paul Lindstrom, a Nielsen executive, "In the old days, everything was always new. Now there is saturation, and there are fewer new customers. That means the inventory gets older faster. If all you have is the hits, then the activity will decline."(*NYT*, 5/6/90.)

38. Through the 1980s, cassette sales expanded as retailers enlarged the shelf space devoted to them, and budgets for advertising and promotion also increased. Although more and more homes had a VCR, VCR owners were renting only two tapes a month on the average, according to Nielsen data. (In 1986, the figure was 3.26.)

39. *WSJ*, 12/17/90.

40. Quoted by Jay G. Blumler and Carolyn Martin Spicer, "Creative Prospects and Threats in the New Television Marketplace: The Voice of the Program Maker," paper presented to the American Film Institute, 198? p. 12.

41. Marvin Barrett, ed., *Survey of Broadcast Journalism, 1970–1971*. New York: Grosset and Dunlap, 1971.

42. *NYT*, 11/12/92.

43. Blumler and Spicer, op. cit., p. 18.

44. Personal interview.

45. R. Serge Denisoff, *Inside MTV*. New Brunswick, N.J.: Transaction Books, 1988, p. 21

46. Discovery got $1.61; Headline News $1.57; WTBS $1.51.

47. Nonnetwork independent TV stations grew from 77 to 321, up 317%. Commercial AM radio stations grew from 7,230 to 9,070, up 25%. Commercial FM stations grew from 2,767 to 4,155, up 50%.

48. James G. Webster, "Audience Behavior in the New Media Environment," *Journal of Communication*, Vol. 36, No. 3 (Summer 1986), pp. 77–91.

49. David Waterman, "The Failure of Cultural Programming on Cable TV: An Economic Interpretation," *Journal of Communication*, Vol. 36, No. 3 (Summer 1986), pp. 92–107.

50. Ben Bagdikian, "The U.S. Media: Supermarket or Assembly Line," *Journal of Communication*, Vol. 35, No. 3 (Summer 1985), pp. 97–109.

51. Harold Hotelling, "Stability in Competition," *Economic Journal*, March 1929, Vol. 34, pp. 41–57 (reprinted in Adrian C. Darnell, ed., *The Collected Economics Articles of Harold Hotelling*. New York: Springer Verlag, 1990, pp. 50–63). This theory was applied to the subject of television audiences by Patrick Barwise and Andrew Ehrenberg, *Television and Its Audience*. London: Sage, 1988.

52. Joseph R. Dominick and Millard C. Pearce, "Trends in Prime-Time Programming," *Journal of Communication*, Vol. 26, No. 1 (Winter 1976), p. 77.

53. In Sweden, Olof Hulten noted that adding a second channel did not change the overall composition of programming. Viewers' choices shifted more toward fiction. (Similar gravitation occurred with the addition of channels in Holland and Belgium). The British experience, says Elihu Katz, demonstrates that competition creates similarity rather than dissimilarity.

Chapter 12

1. Bernard Barber, "Professions," *International Encyclopedia of the Social Sciences*, New York: MacMillan, 1968.

2. The rationale for inaction was provided by Casper Yost, one of the ASNE's founders: "Enforcement is not feasible, neither. . . . is it desirable. . . . Differences of opinion over causes, means, and methods would inevitably split us into warring factions, creating disharmony, disunity and disorder, destroying rather than strengthening the influence the Society should wield for the betterment of journalism. . . . We condemn censorship in any form. How then can we consistently endeavor to set up a censorship of our own?"

3. Quoted in Joseph Kosuth, *The Play of the Unmentionable*, New York: Thames and Hudson, 1992, p. 125.

4. May 1953.

5. In 1987, 6% of newspaper pages were dominated by editorial matter that dealt with entertainment, the movies, and show business celebrities. Reviews and coverage of the arts and cultural events consistently represented only about 2-1/2% of all items in daily newspapers, as shown by Newspaper Advertising Bureau studies made in 1971, 1977, and 1982.

6. This was at least true in 1970, when a Harris survey was made for the United Church of Christ

7. Progressively fewer newspapers seem to be employing full-time critics. Of the 230 members of the Music Critics Association (80–90% of whom write for newspapers), only

about half are employed full-time by their publications, and many of these cover dance and other assignments.

8. From a 1983 analysis of fifty dailies, prepared by the National Endowment for the Arts. Of the total space devoted to the arts—including program listings and ads as well as feature articles and reviews—television and radio got 36%; film had 24%. A third of the text dealing with films is syndicated. Over 80% of the coverage dealt with commercial as opposed to not-for-profit arts.

9. Even movie reviews rank twenty-second of thirty types of items "usually read" and twenty-sixth by the criterion of "most like to read." (From a national Newspaper Advertising Bureau survey in 1987.) Book reviews rank next to last (ahead of crossword puzzles) for usual reading (even among college graduates they were third from the bottom), and last of all for "most like to read." Similarly, cultural events and reviews rank next to last in interest among thirty-seven types of content.

10. Needless to say, eighteenth-century English fiction was not all on the level of *Robinson Crusoe*; it included far more titles like *Adultery Atomized* and *Female Falsehood*, which have not quite stood up to the test of time.

11. Coverage is not the same as criticism. Press clipping files are commonly kept confidential, but Doubleday let me look at the notices for *Confessions of an S.O.B.*, by former Gannett chairman Allen Neuharth. This bestseller was heavily promoted with advertisements and television appearances by the author. It promised to reveal "how you can outfox your enemies, outcharm your friends, outdo yourself. . . . and have a helluva lot of fun!" The elaborate four-color press kit that accompanied review copies included several releases and a glossy photograph. Although Neuharth is a notable and controversial press tycoon, only forty-two daily newspapers (almost all large ones) printed something about the book. A look at the clippings shows that only two of them ran *bona fide* reviews. One ran a press release almost verbatim, and twelve others ran feature articles based on a release. (Incidentally, these did not include any of the four Gannett papers in the group). In several cases, the articles were picked up by one paper from another. The other papers carried feature stories or brief notices that dealt with Neuharth as a personality or with his creation, *USA Today*, rather than with the book itself.

12. In absolute terms, the share figures are 5% versus 4%, and the ratings are 3.0 versus 2.3.

13. Edward K. Palmer, *Children in the Cradle of Television*. Lexington, Mass.: Lexington Books, 1987, p. 139.

14. *Broadcasting*, 10/2/89, p. 49.

15. Lillian B. Miller, *Patriots and Patriotism. The Encouragement of the Fine Arts in the United States, 1790–1860*. Chicago: University of Chicago Press, 1966.

16. On Chinese television, "a typical evening's highlights include calculus, calligraphy, economic achievements, a hoary drama of the Chinese Revolution, and perhaps a special feature on plowing." (*NYT*, 2/1/91.)

17. David Schoenbrunn, review of Willi Boeleke, ed., *Kriegspropaganda, 1939–41*, Stuttgart: Deutsche Verlagsanstalt, 1966, in *Journalism Quarterly*, Vol. 46, No. 4 (Winter 1969), 849–50.

18. De Gaulle's resignation came about as the result of a referendum preceded by a campaign in which the president's speeches were exempted from the television time otherwise equitably allocated among the various political parties. The interim president who succeeded De Gaulle, Alain Poher, made a special point of reminding the head of the state broadcasting service of the law, which called for "objectivity and accuracy" and access to "broad currents of opinion." (The establishment of a second television channel, with its own autonomous news operation, facilitated the reestablishment of responsible and professional television news reporting.)

19. Robert A. Caro, *The Years of Lyndon Johnson*. New York: Knopf, 1982.

20. *NYT*, 12/9/86.

21. The rules were adopted in 1982. In 1991, they were altered to permit the networks to syndicate up to 40% of their prime time programming for domestic use. (This effectively still left them out of the first-run syndication business.) They also were allowed to acquire foreign syndication rights, but only after a thirty day waiting period that effectively hamstrung them. In 1993, the FCC, concerned about the weakened financial position of the networks, allowed them to reenter the syndication market, but the studios challenged this ruling in the courts.

22. *WSJ*, 4/10/91.

23. NBC News former president, Reuven Frank, inferred that his former company's decision to join the other two networks in broadcasting the first Bush-Dukakis debate and to eliminate 90 minutes of Olympics coverage, was because "the network thought it wiser to give up some or all of $8 million in expected revenue than face the possibility that a Democratic House and a Democratic Senate would be sworn in next January, convinced in its hearts that if only NBC had carried the debate it would also have won the White House." (*NYT*, 9/23/88.)

24. Bruce Oudes, ed., "Richard Nixon: By the Press Obsessed," *Columbia Journalism Review*, May/June 1989.

25. Irving Fang analyzed 103 hours and 44 minutes of ABC newscasts in 1969 and found 14 hours and 35 minutes of news that supported the administration viewpoint, 9 hours and 35 minutes tending "not to support the administration." One of the network anchormen (Peter Jennings) exhibited pro-Reagan body language during the 1984 election campaign, in the judgement of student observers, and his newscasts actually drew more pro-Reagan voters than did NBC and CBS (whose newscasters were rated unbiased). (Study by Brian Mullen, reported in the *Columbia Journalism Review*, May/June 1987.)

26. Robert J. Donovan and Ray Scherer, *Silent Revolution: Television News and American Public Life*. Washington, D.C.: Woodrow Wilson Center, 1992, p. 116.

27. *NYT*, 10/27/87.

28. *NYT*, 3/3/91.

29. Senate Minority Leader Robert Dole particularly objected to the airing of radical films like "Citizen Dhoruba," which dealt sympathetically with a former Black Panther activist who had shot two New York City police officers. (Senator Jesse Helms acknowledged that "Sesame Street's" Big Bird was politically impeccable.) The *Wall Street Journal* editorialized: "The best option for the people who think 'Citizen Dhoruba is what America needs to watch is to start their own cable TV network." (*WSJ*, 2/7/92.) Under pressure from Senate Republicans, the Corporation for Public Broadcasting allocated nearly $800,000 in 1993 to monitor "balance and objectivity" in the programs it funds. (*NYT*, 5/7/93.)

30. Just as evaluations of scholarly attainment are now increasingly determined by ethnicity or gender in academic settings, independent criteria of cultural merit appear to be giving way to politically imposed standards. In Chicago, a jury selected ninety works of art from among 1,400 submitted for a bank-sponsored exhibit designed to demonstrate the city's ethnic diversity. Fewer than 100 of the submissions came from minority group members, and six were selected on their own merits for "The Chicago Show." There was an uproar, with charges of "racism." Finally an additional twenty works by minority painters were hung in the show, interspersed with the others, and with no indication that they were *hors de concours*. (*NYT*, 4/20/90.)

31. The grant was withdrawn after the project was publicized.

32. The catalogue of the exhibition, which concerned art about AIDS, was a diatribe against Helms, John Cardinal O'Connor, and other public figures.

33. Cf. John E. Frohnmayer, *Leaving Town Alive: Confessions of an Arts Warrior*. Boston: Houghton Mifflin, 1993.

34. By comparison, per capita spending in the United Kingdom on the BBC (supported by a $120 annual license fee) was about ten times as large; Canada spends over six times as much per head on the CBC. Japan's spending on the state broadcasting service, NHK, was about seven times as large. *Quality Time: The Report of the Twentieth Century Task Force on Public Television* (New York: Twentieth Century Fund Press, 1993) reckons U.S. per capita spending at $1 per person, based only on the federal contribution.

35. Carnegie Commission on the Future of Public Broadcasting, *A Public Trust*. New York: Bantam Books, 1979. Cf. also the earlier report of the Carnegie Commission on Educational Television, *Public Television: A Program for Action*. New York: Harper and Row, 1967.

36. Under the finsyn rules (imposed by the FCC in 1970 and reaffirmed ten years later in an antitrust decree imposed by the Justice Department), each network was only allowed to produce up to 3 (after 1988, 5) hours of weekly entertainment and paid $1 billion a year in program license fees to the studios.

37. Cable systems have paid fees ranging from $.10 to $.40 a month to the cable networks whose programs they carry. (The Weather Channel is at the low end of the scale; CNN, at the high end). Under the Cable Television Consumer Protection and Competition Act of 1992, broadcast stations had the option of demanding that cable systems in their area (defined as a zone within 50 miles of their transmitters) retransmit their signals under the "must-carry" rule or of negotiating with them for a retransmission fee. Cable systems "must carry" local on-air channels, but what is local is based on the ADI (the Area of Dominant Influence, a market definition by the now-defunct Arbitron television ratings service). In 1993, a three-member FCC gave home-shopping channels the same right as other broadcasters to demand that cable systems carry their programs without charge—in some instances crowding out more popular channels. (John Malone's Liberty Media, which he spun off from TCI in 1992, owned 42% of Home Shopping Network and 22.3% of QVC, the two principal networks in this field.)

38. As part of the deal, the cable companies agreed to pay for new special-interest cable channels established by the individual networks (except of CBS). The networks were thus able to move into cable with almost automatic clearances.

39. In the Television Decoder Circuitry Act of 1990 closed-caption circuitry is mandated for all sets sold after 1993.

40. Thomas W. Hazlett, "Private Monopoly and the Public Interest: An Economic Analysis of the Cable Television Franchise," *University of Pennsylvania Law Review*, Vol. 134, No. 6 (July 1986), pp. 1, 360.

41. Cited by Hazlett, ibid.

42. "Books to Bytes: The Computer and the Library". Gannett Center for Media Studies, Occasional Paper No. 7, 1988.

43. The decision, by a U.S. district court in Virginia, held that the ban on cross-ownership of local telephone and video services was unconstitutional, because it "burdens substantially more speech than is necessary." (*NYT*, 8/25/93.)

44. Stephen R. Rivkin and Jeremy D. Rosner, "Shortcut to the Information Superhighway: A Progressive Plan to Speed the Telecommunications Revolution." Washington, D.C.: Progressive Policy Institute, Policy Report No. 15, 1992.

45. This is based on FCC data (*NYT*, 4/2/93). However, rates in twelve open-entry cable systems, in low-density communities, did not differ from the national averages. Hazlett, op. cit., p. 371.

46. "Duopolistic Competition in CATV: Implications for Public Policy, *Yale Journal on Regulation*, Jan. 1990.

47. While the Japanese had developed a system of heightened visual fidelity, it was based on an analog method, while American and European systems used digital techniques compati-

ble with computers and easily adaptable to a variety of additional communication and information-processing services.

48. One was a team representing General Instrument and M.I.T. The second was made up of Zenith and AT&T. The third was the Dutch Philips Electronics, the French government-owned Thomson, the Sarnoff laboratories and NBC. A fundamental technical problem remained to be resolved between two competing types of technology that illuminate the computer and television screens in different fashions through different scanning methods.

49. Under a 1984 law, public access channels must supply time on a first-come first-served basis, without censorship. Only one local resident is required as a sponsor. Appearing on public access television in suburban Westchester, a "high priest" of the "Black Israelites" threatened viewers: "We're going to take your little children and dash them against the stones" and "We're going to rape and ravish your white women." In Manhattan (where some 800 public access programs are broadcast on four channels) a Nazi called for blacks to be deported to Africa. (*NYT*, 5/22/93.)

50. John Hohenberg, *The New Media: A Journalist Looks at His Profession*, New York: Holt, Rinehart and Winston, 1969, p. 121.

51. Speech at the University of Montana, 5/21/71.

52. Business Executives Move for Vietnam Peace vs. F.C.C., 40 U.S. L.W. 2082 D.C. Cir., Aug. 3, 1971.

53. Study of fifty-eight stations by the Center for Media Education, reported in the *NYT*, 9/30/92.

Index